Optimise

Teacher's Book Premium Pack

B1

macmillan education

Welcome

ABOUT *OPTIMISE*

- *Optimise* is a fantastic new secondary-level exam-preparation course for 21st century learners. The course is designed to prepare teenagers for international exams (Preliminary (PET) for Schools, etc.) or local state exams.
- *Optimise*'s highly respected team, including authors Malcolm Mann and Steve Taylore-Knowles, and Course Consultant, Karen Ludlow share their exam expertise and many years of experience of official exams to ensure that your students achieve exam success.
- *Optimise* offers attractive images, stimulating, age-appropriate topics and carefully guided skills development, which prepare students for everyday life as well as exams.
- *Optimise*'s print and digital package gives you the flexibility to choose the approach that works best for your teaching situation: from print to blended to a fully interactive digital approach.

For students

Student's Book or Digital Student's Book

See pages 4–13 for details of the Student's Book content.

See page 14 for more on the Digital Student's Book.

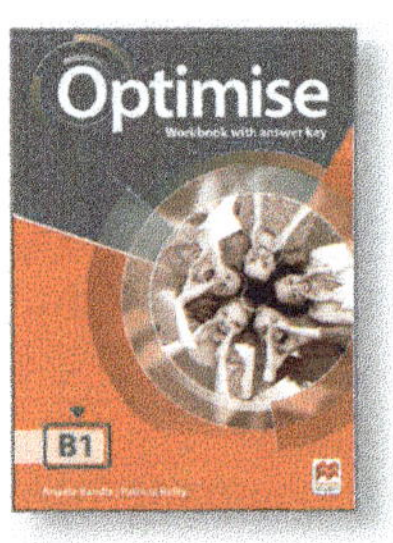

Workbook with/without answer key or Online Workbook

See pages 17–20 for details of the Workbook content.

See page 21 for more on the Online Workbook.

Student's Resource Centre

See page 22 for a full list of resources available on the Student's Resource Centre.

Student's eBook

An eBook version of the Student's Book is included.

For teachers

Teacher's Book

Your Teacher's Book Premium Pack includes:

- Presentation Kit
- Digital Student's Book
- Student's eBook
- Online Workbook
- Test Generator
- Teacher's Resource Centre
- *Talk2Me* videos
- Speaking test videos
- Class and Workbook audio

See pages 22–23 for details of the worksheets and tests available.

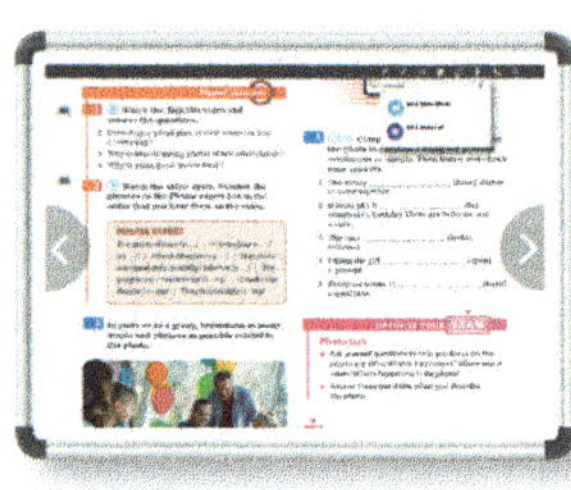

Presentation Kit

See page 15 for more information about the Presentation Kit.

Teacher's Resource Centre
Digital Student's Book
Online Workbook
Test Generator
Student's eBook

See page 22 for a full list of resources available on the Teacher's Resource Centre.

Class Audio CDs

Class audio on CDs. Also available on the Resource Centres.

ABOUT THE *OPTIMISE* AUTHORS

Malcolm Mann and Steve Taylore-Knowles have written a number of exam courses for teenagers, including the highly successful *Laser* series. They are also the series editors of Macmillan's *Improve your Skills for First (FCE)* and *Improve your Skills for Advanced (CAE)* series.

Malcolm

Malcolm lives and works in Athens, Greece. He's responsible for the production of the LAAS exam suite, and is a former Chairperson of TESOL Greece.

Steve

Steve lives and works in the UK. He is a former Cambridge oral examiner and also provides government-endorsed teacher training in many countries throughout Europe, Asia and South America.

A MESSAGE FROM THE *OPTIMISE* AUTHORS

Thank you for choosing to use *Optimise*.

Optimise is an exam course with a difference.

In *Optimise*, we effectively combine exam training, language development and 21st century skills to prepare students not only for language exams, but also for life beyond the classroom.

Below we have listed our principles and the key features which we believe make *Optimise* an outstanding exam-preparation course.

We very much hope you and your students enjoy using *Optimise B1* and benefit from its motivating content, syllabus and structure.

All the very best for the school year!

Malcolm and Steve

Principles

The following principles are at the heart of the *Optimise* series:

- **Motivation:** The more that 21st century teens can be motivated by engaging and interesting content (texts, topics, tasks, etc.), the more likely they are to improve their skills, and develop their linguistic competence.
- **Practice:** Exam practice is essential. In order for students to feel confident and perform at their optimum, they need to be familiar with exam tasks. Language and exam skills tested in the exam have to be practised and developed.
- **Guidance:** The most effective way to help students develop their language and exam skills is to deal with them in a systematic and guided way, through a carefully-planned course syllabus.
- **Coverage:** Vocabulary does not only consist of individual words; it also includes collocations, phrasal verbs, idioms, word formation and word patterns, as well as topic vocabulary, which all need to be covered comprehensively.
- **Support:** Students require expert guidance and support in order to produce exam-level pieces of writing. The process of writing involves different drafts, proofreading and feedback, and is essential in helping students develop their skills.
- **Consolidation:** Regular consolidation makes a vital contribution towards ensuring students understand and retain the information they need in order to prepare for exams.
- **Personalisation:** Personalisation is key in enabling students to relate the material in their Student's Book to their own lives, opinions and culture.

Key features

- An extensive range of print and digital materials, providing you with a variety of flexible options for your students.
- Strong focus on exam-skills development, with each lesson focusing on a specific skill and offering detailed advice on how to complete the task effectively.
- Resource Centres for both students and teachers, with a wide variety of worksheets including CLIL and Culture, Grammar and Vocabulary.
- Unit tests, Progress tests, End-of-year test, all set at two levels – Standard and Higher – are available as PDFs and also adaptable to suit your own requirements on the Test Generator.
- A Placement test to check your students' level and a Diagnostic test to highlight students' strengths and weaknesses.
- Preliminary (PET) for Schools Practice tests: one at the back of the Workbook and another complete Practice test available on the Teacher's Resource Centre as a printable PDF.
- Systematic language and exam-preparation development throughout every lesson.
- Personalisation tasks to foster 21st century skills, such as critical analysis, collaboration and learning strategies, presented through the Think, Research, Culture, Learn and Me features.
- *Talk2Me* videos in every Speaking lesson feature teenagers using everyday functional language in a variety of situations that students will relate to. The Flipped classroom approach is suggested as an alternative approach for this video to encourage learner autonomy and create more time to focus on activating the target language.
- A Speaking test video with an examiner shows a pair of students completing all four parts of a speaking test. This video is exploited in the *Optimise your speaking* section of the Student's Book *Optimise your exams* pages, along with an additional worksheet on the Resource Centre.
- Systematic Writing lessons which include a writing model, a paragraph planner and a writing exam task, along with a post-writing Checklist for students to refer to.
- A Progress check, after every two units, reviews the grammar and vocabulary of the preceding two units and includes a self-assessment tool for students to chart their learning.

Course components

STUDENT'S BOOK | Reading lesson

Every unit starts with a two-page Reading lesson.

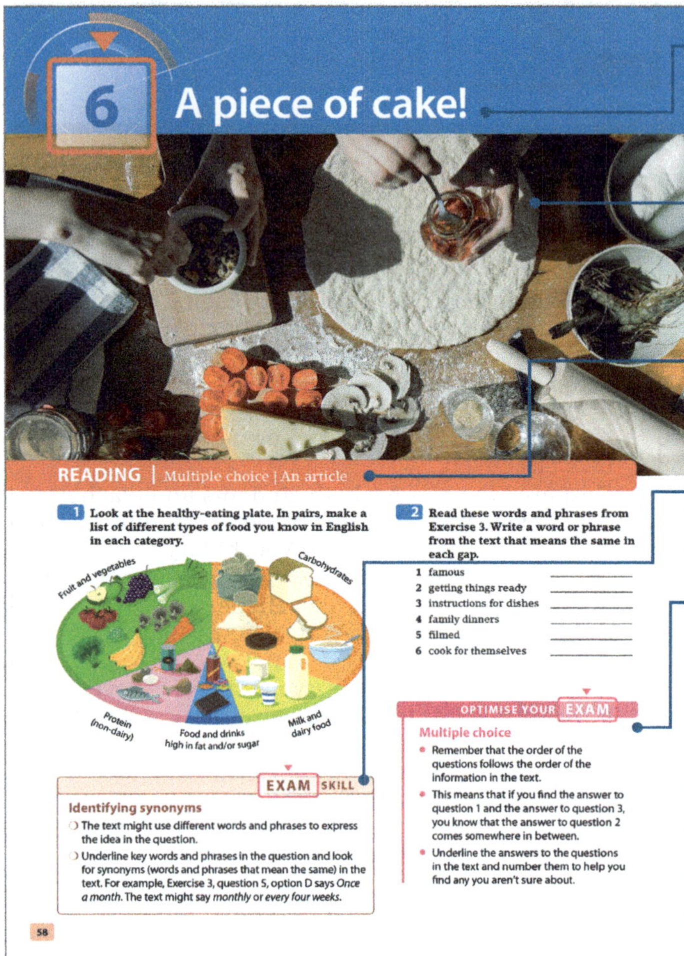

6 A piece of cake!

READING | Multiple choice | An article

1 Look at the healthy-eating plate. In pairs, make a list of different types of food you know in English in each category.

2 Read these words and phrases from Exercise 3. Write a word or phrase from the text that means the same in each gap.

1 famous ______
2 getting things ready ______
3 instructions for dishes ______
4 family dinners ______
5 filmed ______
6 cook for themselves ______

OPTIMISE YOUR EXAM

Multiple choice

- Remember that the order of the questions follows the order of the information in the text.
- This means that if you find the answer to question 1 and the answer to question 3, you know that the answer to question 2 comes somewhere in between.
- Underline the answers to the questions in the text and number them to help you find any you aren't sure about.

EXAM SKILL

Identifying synonyms

- The text might use different words and phrases to express the idea in the question.
- Underline key words and phrases in the question and look for synonyms (words and phrases that mean the same) in the text. For example, Exercise 3, question 5, option D says *Once a month*. The text might say *monthly* or *every four weeks*.

58

Unit topics and themes chosen to be interesting and engaging for teenage students.

The opening spread of each unit has colourful and impactful images connected to the unit topic, which can be used at the start of the lesson to stimulate on-topic discussion.

Clear labelling of the exam task and text type in the lesson will help you and your learners.

All Reading lessons feature an Exam skill box, with targeted advice on how to approach different exam tasks and the specific sub-skills required.

All Reading lessons include an *Optimise your exam* feature, which gives students tips and strategies to help them prepare for the lesson exam task.

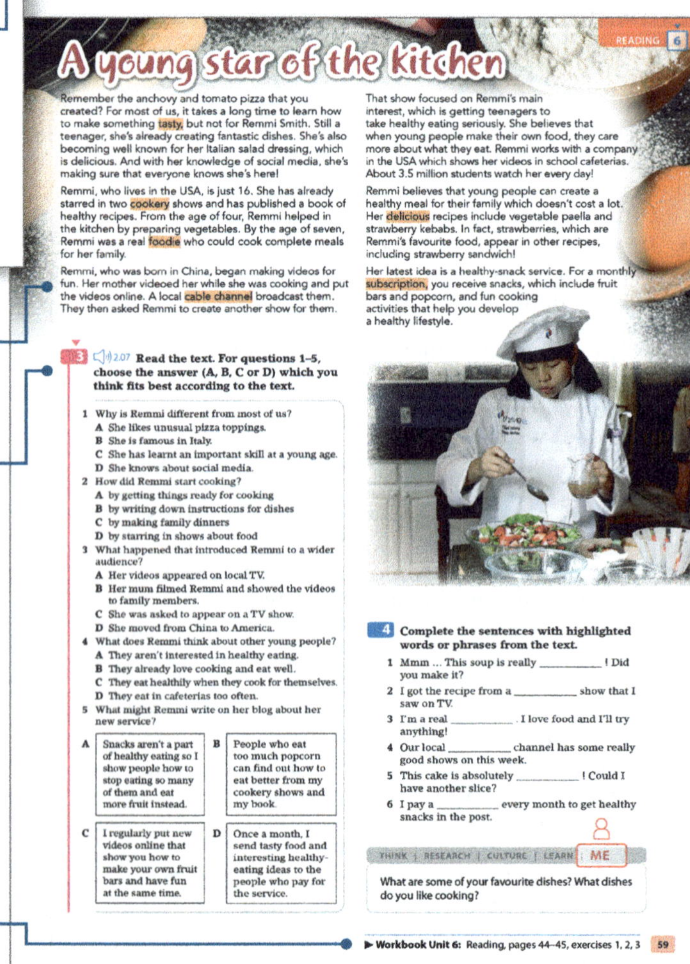

READING 6

A young star of the kitchen

Remember the anchovy and tomato pizza that you created? For most of us, it takes a long time to learn how to make something tasty, but not for Remmi Smith. Still a teenager, she's already creating fantastic dishes. She's also becoming well known for her Italian salad dressing, which is delicious. And with her knowledge of social media, she's making sure that everyone knows she's here!

Remmi, who lives in the USA, is just 16. She has already starred in two cookery shows and has published a book of healthy recipes. From the age of four, Remmi helped in the kitchen by preparing vegetables. By the age of seven, Remmi was a real foodie who could cook complete meals for her family.

Remmi, who was born in China, began making videos for fun. Her mother videoed her while she was cooking and put the videos online. A local cable channel broadcast them. They then asked Remmi to create another show for them.

That show focused on Remmi's main interest, which is getting teenagers to take healthy eating seriously. She believes that when young people make their own food, they care more about what they eat. Remmi works with a company in the USA which shows her videos in school cafeterias. About 3.5 million students watch her every day!

Remmi believes that young people can create a healthy meal for their family which doesn't cost a lot. Her delicious recipes include vegetable paella and strawberry kebabs. In fact, strawberries, which are Remmi's favourite food, appear in other recipes, including strawberry sandwich!

Her latest idea is a healthy-snack service. For a monthly subscription, you receive snacks, which include fruit bars and popcorn, and fun cooking activities that help you develop a healthy lifestyle.

3 2.07 Read the text. For questions 1–5, choose the answer (A, B, C or D) which you think fits best according to the text.

1 Why is Remmi different from most of us?
A She likes unusual pizza toppings.
B She is famous in Italy.
C She has learnt an important skill at a young age.
D She knows about social media.

2 How did Remmi start cooking?
A by getting things ready for cooking
B by writing down instructions for dishes
C by making family dinners
D by starring in shows about food

3 What happened that introduced Remmi to a wider audience?
A Her videos appeared on local TV.
B Her mum filmed Remmi and showed the videos to family members.
C She was asked to appear on a TV show.
D She moved from China to America.

4 What does Remmi think about other young people?
A They aren't interested in healthy eating.
B They already love cooking and eat well.
C They eat healthily when they cook for themselves.
D They eat in cafeterias too often.

5 What might Remmi write on her blog about her new service?

A	Snacks aren't a part of healthy eating so I show people how to stop eating so many of them and eat more fruit instead.	B	People who eat too much popcorn can find out how to eat better from my cookery shows and my book.
C	I regularly put new videos online that show you how to make your own fruit bars and have fun at the same time.	D	Once a month, I send tasty food and interesting healthy-eating ideas to the people who pay for the service.

4 Complete the sentences with highlighted words or phrases from the text.

1 Mmm ... This soup is really ______ ! Did you make it?
2 I got the recipe from a ______ show that I saw on TV.
3 I'm a real ______ . I love food and I'll try anything!
4 Our local ______ channel has some really good shows on this week.
5 This cake is absolutely ______ ! Could I have another slice?
6 I pay a ______ every month to get healthy snacks in the post.

THINK | RESEARCH | CULTURE | LEARN | ME

What are some of your favourite dishes? What dishes do you like cooking?

▶ Workbook Unit 6: Reading, pages 44–45, exercises 1, 2, 3

59

Reading texts focus on stimulating, out-of-the-ordinary topics, which will be of interest to teenage students.

Every Reading lesson has an exam task. These tasks are level-appropriate and reflect the tasks students are likely to encounter in most official exams.

All lessons include references to the Workbook, and other relevant reference material.

STUDENT'S BOOK | Grammar lessons

Every unit has two separate Grammar lessons.

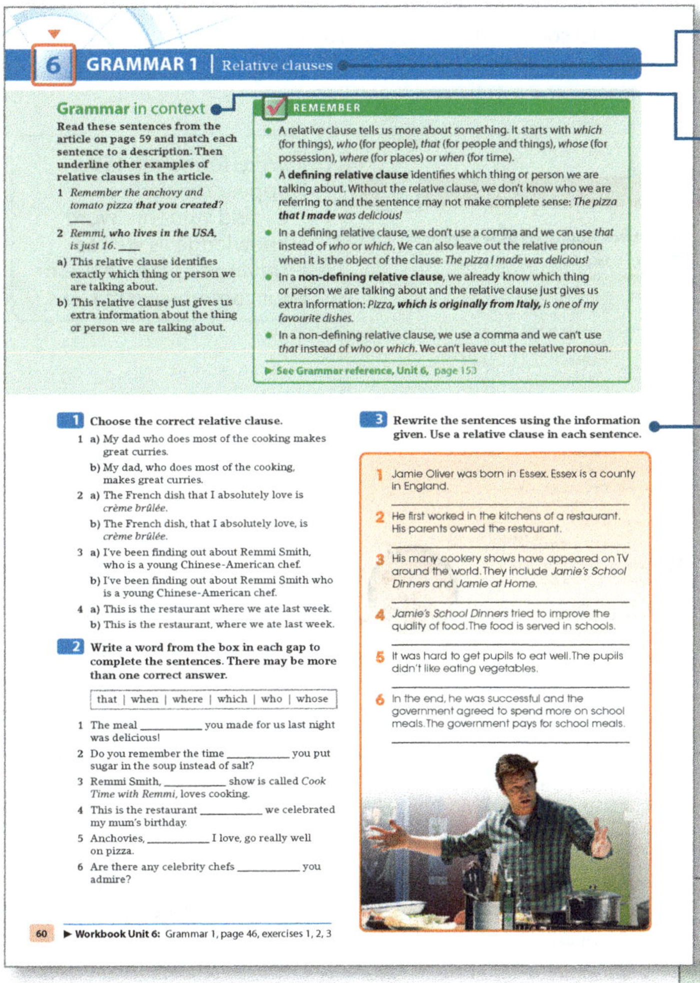

6 GRAMMAR 1 | Relative clauses

Grammar in context

Read these sentences from the article on page 59 and match each sentence to a description. Then underline other examples of relative clauses in the article.

1 *Remember the anchovy and tomato pizza* ***that you created?*** ___

2 *Remmi,* ***who lives in the USA,*** *is just 16.* ___

a) This relative clause identifies exactly which thing or person we are talking about.

b) This relative clause just gives us extra information about the thing or person we are talking about.

REMEMBER

- A relative clause tells us more about something. It starts with *which* (for things), *who* (for people), *that* (for people and things), *whose* (for possession), *where* (for places) or *when* (for time).
- A **defining relative clause** identifies which thing or person we are talking about. Without the relative clause, we don't know who we are referring to and the sentence may not make complete sense: *The pizza* ***that I made*** *was delicious!*
- In a defining relative clause, we don't use a comma and we can use *that* instead of *who* or *which*. We can also leave out the relative pronoun when it is the object of the clause: *The pizza I made was delicious!*
- In a **non-defining relative clause**, we already know which thing or person we are talking about and the relative clause just gives us extra information: *Pizza,* ***which is originally from Italy,*** *is one of my favourite dishes.*
- In a non-defining relative clause, we use a comma and we can't use *that* instead of *who* or *which*. We can't leave out the relative pronoun.

▶ See Grammar reference, Unit 6, page 153

1 Choose the correct relative clause.

1 a) My dad who does most of the cooking makes great curries.
b) My dad, who does most of the cooking, makes great curries.

2 a) The French dish that I absolutely love is *crème brûlée*.
b) The French dish, that I absolutely love, is *crème brûlée*.

3 a) I've been finding out about Remmi Smith, who is a young Chinese-American chef.
b) I've been finding out about Remmi Smith who is a young Chinese-American chef.

4 a) This is the restaurant where we ate last week.
b) This is the restaurant, where we ate last week.

2 Write a word from the box in each gap to complete the sentences. There may be more than one correct answer.

that | when | where | which | who | whose

1 The meal ___________ you made for us last night was delicious!

2 Do you remember the time ___________ you put sugar in the soup instead of salt?

3 Remmi Smith, ___________ show is called *Cook Time with Remmi*, loves cooking.

4 This is the restaurant ___________ we celebrated my mum's birthday.

5 Anchovies, ___________ I love, go really well on pizza.

6 Are there any celebrity chefs ___________ you admire?

3 Rewrite the sentences using the information given. Use a relative clause in each sentence.

1 Jamie Oliver was born in Essex. Essex is a county in England.

2 He first worked in the kitchens of a restaurant. His parents owned the restaurant.

3 His many cookery shows have appeared on TV around the world. They include *Jamie's School Dinners* and *Jamie at Home*.

4 *Jamie's School Dinners* tried to improve the quality of food. The food is served in schools.

5 It was hard to get pupils to eat well. The pupils didn't like eating vegetables.

6 In the end, he was successful and the government agreed to spend more on school meals. The government pays for school meals.

60 ▶ **Workbook Unit 6:** Grammar 1, page 46, exercises 1, 2, 3

Every Grammar lesson presents a different grammar point.

The *Grammar in context* box introduces the grammar lesson by asking students to identify the target structures in a context they have already seen.

Exercises are staged so as to be progressively more challenging as students work through the lesson.

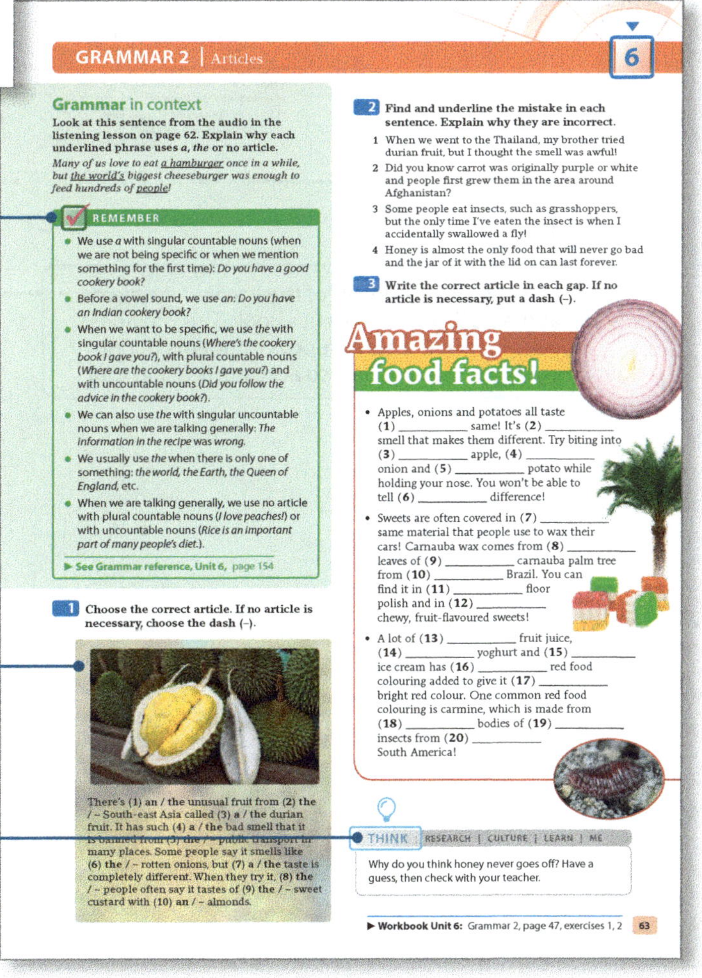

GRAMMAR 2 | Articles 6

Grammar in context

Look at this sentence from the audio in the listening lesson on page 62. Explain why each underlined phrase uses *a*, *the* or no article.

Many of us love to eat a hamburger once in a while, but the world's biggest cheeseburger was enough to feed hundreds of people!

REMEMBER

- We use *a* with singular countable nouns (when we are not being specific or when we mention something for the first time): *Do you have a good cookery book?*
- Before a vowel sound, we use *an*: *Do you have an Indian cookery book?*
- When we want to be specific, we use *the* with singular countable nouns (*Where's the cookery book I gave you?*), with plural countable nouns (*Where are the cookery books I gave you?*) and with uncountable nouns (*Did you follow the advice in the cookery book?*).
- We can also use *the* with singular uncountable nouns when we are talking generally: *The information in the recipe was wrong.*
- We usually use *the* when there is only one of something: *the world, the Earth, the Queen of England*, etc.
- When we are talking generally, we use no article with plural countable nouns (*I love peaches!*) or with uncountable nouns (*Rice is an important part of many people's diet.*).

▶ See Grammar reference, Unit 6, page 154

1 Choose the correct article. If no article is necessary, choose the dash (–).

There's (1) an / the unusual fruit from (2) the / – South-east Asia called (3) a / the durian fruit. It has such (4) a / the bad smell that it is banned from (5) the / – public transport in many places. Some people say it smells like (6) the / – rotten onions, but (7) a / the taste is completely different. When they try it, (8) the / – people often say it tastes of (9) the / – sweet custard with (10) an / – almonds.

2 Find and underline the mistake in each sentence. Explain why they are incorrect.

1 When we went to the Thailand, my brother tried durian fruit, but I thought the smell was awful!

2 Did you know carrot was originally purple or white and people first grew them in the area around Afghanistan?

3 Some people eat insects, such as grasshoppers, but the only time I've eaten the insect is when I accidentally swallowed a fly!

4 Honey is almost the only food that will never go bad and the jar of it with the lid on can last forever.

3 Write the correct article in each gap. If no article is necessary, put a dash (–).

Amazing food facts!

- Apples, onions and potatoes all taste (1) ___________ same! It's (2) ___________ smell that makes them different. Try biting into (3) ___________ apple, (4) ___________ onion and (5) ___________ potato while holding your nose. You won't be able to tell (6) ___________ difference!
- Sweets are often covered in (7) ___________ same material that people use to wax their cars! Carnauba wax comes from (8) ___________ leaves of (9) ___________ carnauba palm tree from (10) ___________ Brazil. You can find it in (11) ___________ floor polish and in (12) ___________ chewy, fruit-flavoured sweets!
- A lot of (13) ___________ fruit juice, (14) ___________ yoghurt and (15) ___________ ice cream has (16) ___________ red food colouring added to give it (17) ___________ bright red colour. One common red food colouring is carmine, which is made from (18) ___________ bodies of (19) ___________ insects from (20) ___________ South America!

THINK | RESEARCH | CULTURE | LEARN | ME

Why do you think honey never goes off? Have a guess, then check with your teacher.

▶ **Workbook Unit 6:** Grammar 2, page 47, exercises 1, 2 63

Remember boxes on the grammar pages present additional information in a clear way for students to remember, and end with a signpost to the *Grammar reference* at the back of the Student's Book, where further explanations and examples are provided.

Whenever possible, short texts are included on the grammar pages, to give your students the opportunity to see and practise grammar in realistic contexts.

Grammar personalisation activities suggest ways to use the grammar in a personal context.

STUDENT'S BOOK | Vocabulary lesson

The Vocabulary lesson in each unit has three separate word sets, one of which is always topic vocabulary.

Each lesson has three clearly-labelled vocabulary areas.

Topic vocabulary sections increase students' lexical knowledge in topics that commonly appear in exams.

Word formation tasks appear regularly to extend students' word knowledge as well as serving to prepare them for common exam tasks.

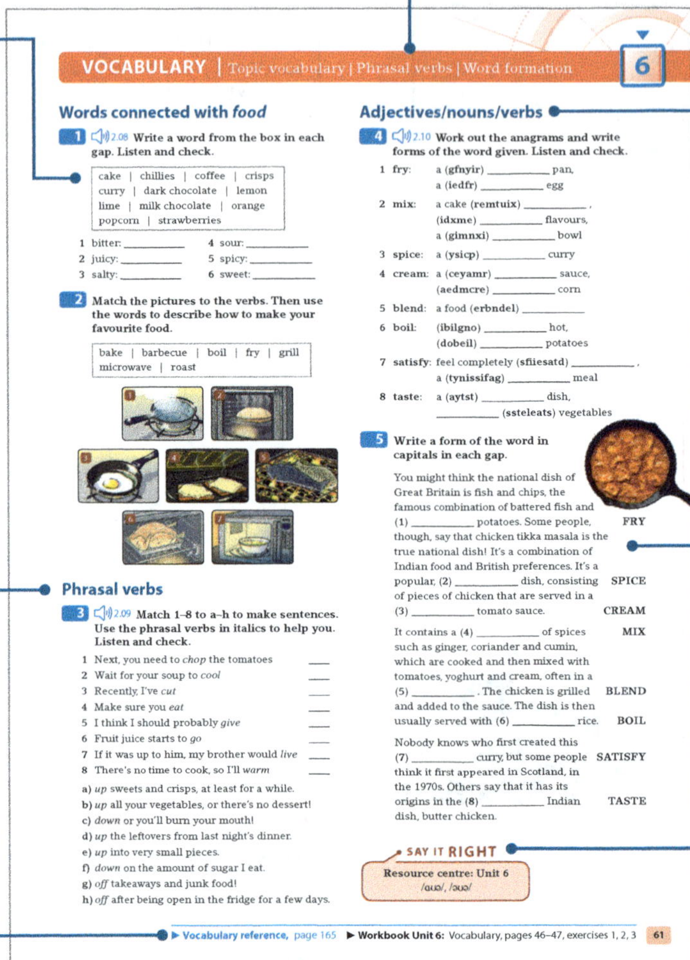

VOCABULARY | Topic vocabulary | Phrasal verbs | Word formation 6

Words connected with *food*

1 2.08 **Write a word from the box in each gap. Listen and check.**

cake | chillies | coffee | crisps | curry | dark chocolate | lemon | lime | milk chocolate | orange | popcorn | strawberries

1 bitter: ______
2 juicy: ______
3 salty: ______
4 sour: ______
5 spicy: ______
6 sweet: ______

2 Match the pictures to the verbs. Then use the words to describe how to make your favourite food.

bake | barbecue | boil | fry | grill | microwave | roast

Phrasal verbs

3 2.09 **Match 1–8 to a–h to make sentences. Use the phrasal verbs in italics to help you. Listen and check.**

1 Next, you need to *chop* the tomatoes ___
2 Wait for your soup to *cool* ___
3 Recently, I've *cut* ___
4 Make sure you *eat* ___
5 I think I should probably *give* ___
6 Fruit juice starts to *go* ___
7 If it was up to him, my brother would *live* ___
8 There's no time to cook, so I'll *warm* ___

a) *up* sweets and crisps, at least for a while.
b) *up* all your vegetables, or there's no dessert!
c) *down* or you'll burn your mouth!
d) *up* the leftovers from last night's dinner.
e) *up* into very small pieces.
f) *down* on the amount of sugar I eat.
g) *off* takeaways and junk food!
h) *off* after being open in the fridge for a few days.

Adjectives/nouns/verbs

4 2.10 **Work out the anagrams and write forms of the word given. Listen and check.**

1 **fry**: a **(gfnyir)** ______ pan, a **(iedfr)** ______ egg
2 **mix**: a cake **(remtuix)** ______, **(idxme)** ______ flavours, a **(gimnxi)** ______ bowl
3 **spice**: a **(ysicp)** ______ curry
4 **cream**: a **(ceyamr)** ______ sauce, **(aedmcre)** ______ corn
5 **blend**: a food **(erbndel)** ______
6 **boil**: **(ibilgno)** ______ hot, **(dobeil)** ______ potatoes
7 **satisfy**: feel completely **(sfiiesatd)** ______, a **(tynissifag)** ______ meal
8 **taste**: a **(aytst)** ______ dish, ______ **(ssteleats)** vegetables

5 Write a form of the word in capitals in each gap.

You might think the national dish of Great Britain is fish and chips, the famous combination of battered fish and (1) ______ potatoes. Some people, though, say that chicken tikka masala is the true national dish! It's a combination of Indian food and British preferences. It's a popular, (2) ______ dish, consisting of pieces of chicken that are served in a (3) ______ tomato sauce. — FRY, SPICE, CREAM

It contains a (4) ______ of spices such as ginger, coriander and cumin, which are cooked and then mixed with tomatoes, yoghurt and cream, often in a (5) ______ . The chicken is grilled and added to the sauce. The dish is then usually served with (6) ______ rice. — MIX, BLEND, BOIL

Nobody knows who first created this (7) ______ curry, but some people think it first appeared in Scotland, in the 1970s. Others say that it has its origins in the (8) ______ Indian dish, butter chicken. — SATISFY, TASTE

SAY IT RIGHT
Resource centre: Unit 6
/aʊə/, /ɔʊə/

▶ Vocabulary reference, page 165 ▶ **Workbook Unit 6:** Vocabulary, pages 46–47, exercises 1, 2, 3 61

Phrasal verbs are taught regularly to extend students' vocabulary as well as serving to prepare them for language that commonly appears in exams.

Exercises are set within realistic and familiar contexts, with a strong real-world focus to make the language as meaningful and relevant to students as possible.

Every unit contains a *Say it right* feature, which develops a specific aspect of pronunciation that appears in one of the lessons. The worksheet for this is available on the Resource Centre.

Lessons include details of the *Vocabulary reference* at the back of the Student's Book. This provides reference materials to support students during vocabulary tasks and also acts as a revision tool.

TOPIC VOCABULARY | Words connected with *food*

Word	Example sentence
bake (v)	Why don't we bake a cake this afternoon?
barbecue (v)	When you barbecue the fish, make sure it doesn't burn.
bitter (adj)	I don't like the taste of dark chocolate – it's too bitter.
boil (v)	Let the water boil for a minute before you put the eggs in the pan.
fry (v)	Fry the potatoes in a little oil and then add salt and pepper.
grill (v)	Chop the tomatoes while I grill the chicken.
juicy (adj)	These oranges are nice and juicy.
microwave (v)	I microwaved my bowl of soup and it got too hot!
roast (v)	I'm going to roast some beef for Sunday lunch.
salty (adj)	I love salty food, such as anchovies and olives.
sour (adj)	Add a bit of sugar to the tomato sauce if it's too sour.
spicy (adj)	I need a glass of water – this curry is too spicy!
sweet (adj)	My mum says I shouldn't eat too much sweet food.

STUDENT'S BOOK | Listening lesson

The Listening lesson in each unit focuses on a specific exam skill and always includes an exam task.

All class audio material is available on CDs as well as being provided on the Resource Centres.

Listening lessons always feature a specific exam skill and provide support and guidance to help students develop the skill further.

The initial task helps students to start thinking about the topic of the lesson in more depth.

The *Optimise your exam* box in the Listening lessons always gives students advice on how to approach this kind of task.

Every Listening lesson includes an exam task which allows students an opportunity to apply the advice given in the preceding *Optimise your exam* box.

The Exam skill boxes in Listening lessons focus on specific sub-skills needed to achieve success in listening.

Personalisation tasks at the end of the Listening lessons relate to the unit topic, giving students a chance to develop the topic further.

There is a reference to the relevant Workbook pages at the end of each Listening lesson.

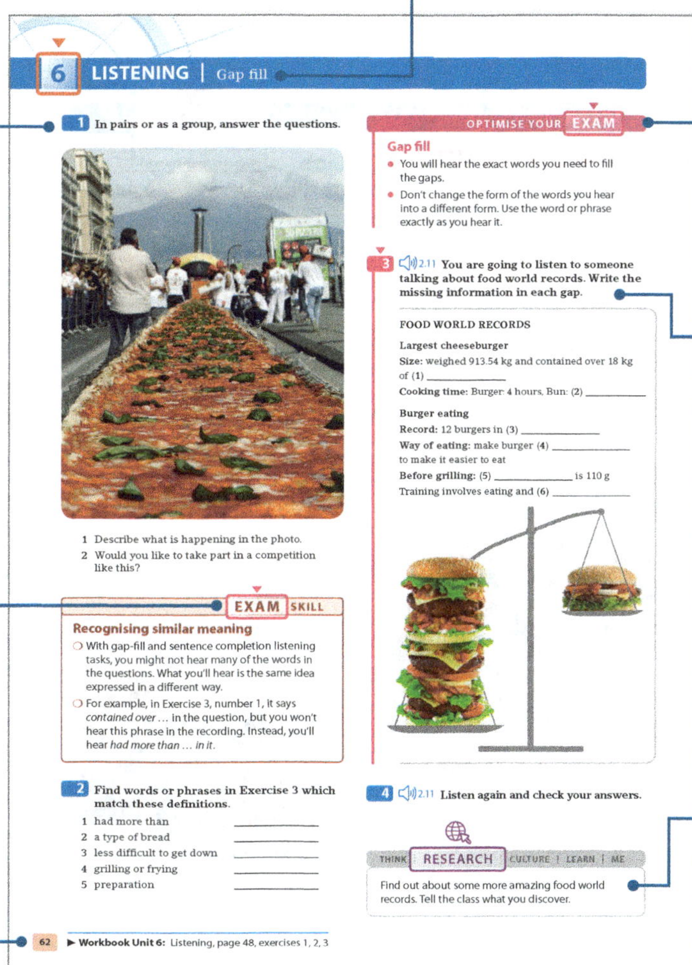

6 LISTENING | Gap fill

1 In pairs or as a group, answer the questions.

1 Describe what is happening in the photo.
2 Would you like to take part in a competition like this?

EXAM SKILL

Recognising similar meaning

- With gap-fill and sentence completion listening tasks, you might not hear many of the words in the questions. What you'll hear is the same idea expressed in a different way.
- For example, in Exercise 3, number 1, it says *contained over …* in the question, but you won't hear this phrase in the recording. Instead, you'll hear *had more than … in it.*

2 Find words or phrases in Exercise 3 which match these definitions.

1 had more than ________
2 a type of bread ________
3 less difficult to get down ________
4 grilling or frying ________
5 preparation ________

OPTIMISE YOUR EXAM

Gap fill

- You will hear the exact words you need to fill the gaps.
- Don't change the form of the words you hear into a different form. Use the word or phrase exactly as you hear it.

3 2.11 You are going to listen to someone talking about food world records. Write the missing information in each gap.

FOOD WORLD RECORDS

Largest cheeseburger
Size: weighed 913.54 kg and contained over 18 kg of (1) ________
Cooking time: Burger: 4 hours. Bun: (2) ________

Burger eating
Record: 12 burgers in (3) ________
Way of eating: make burger (4) ________ to make it easier to eat
Before grilling: (5) ________ is 110 g
Training involves eating and (6) ________

4 2.11 Listen again and check your answers.

THINK | RESEARCH | CULTURE | LEARN | ME

Find out about some more amazing food world records. Tell the class what you discover.

62 ► Workbook Unit 6: Listening, page 48, exercises 1, 2, 3

STUDENT'S BOOK | Speaking lesson

Talk2Me video in every Speaking lesson

Speaking lessons include a video which features target functional language.

Speaking lessons focus on one of four task types which students will need to develop in preparation for a speaking test.

All Speaking lessons suggest using an optional Flipped classroom approach, in which students watch the video and complete some exercises at home in order to prepare for the lesson.

All Speaking lessons include a *Talk2Me* video, featuring three teenage friends. Each video relates to the unit topic and models functional language through scripted interactions between the friends, which students then practise and use in their final task.

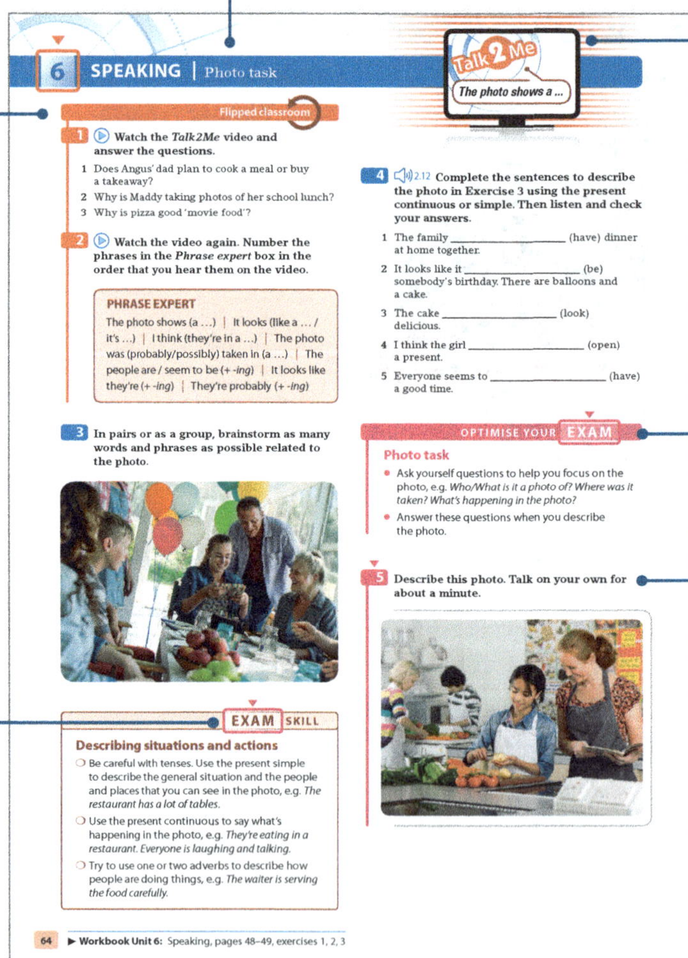

6 SPEAKING | Photo task

Talk2Me — The photo shows a ...

Flipped classroom

1 Watch the *Talk2Me* video and answer the questions.

1 Does Angus' dad plan to cook a meal or buy a takeaway?
2 Why is Maddy taking photos of her school lunch?
3 Why is pizza good 'movie food'?

2 Watch the video again. Number the phrases in the *Phrase expert* box in the order that you hear them on the video.

PHRASE EXPERT

The photo shows (a ...) | It looks (like a ... / it's ...) | I think (they're in a ...) | The photo was (probably/possibly) taken in (a ...) | The people are / seem to be (+ -ing) | It looks like they're (+ -ing) | They're probably (+ -ing)

3 In pairs or as a group, brainstorm as many words and phrases as possible related to the photo.

EXAM SKILL

Describing situations and actions

- Be careful with tenses. Use the present simple to describe the general situation and the people and places that you can see in the photo, e.g. *The restaurant has a lot of tables.*
- Use the present continuous to say what's happening in the photo, e.g. *They're eating in a restaurant. Everyone is laughing and talking.*
- Try to use one or two adverbs to describe how people are doing things, e.g. *The waiter is serving the food carefully.*

4 2.12 Complete the sentences to describe the photo in Exercise 3 using the present continuous or simple. Then listen and check your answers.

1 The family ______ (have) dinner at home together.
2 It looks like it ______ (be) somebody's birthday. There are balloons and a cake.
3 The cake ______ (look) delicious.
4 I think the girl ______ (open) a present.
5 Everyone seems to ______ (have) a good time.

OPTIMISE YOUR EXAM

Photo task

- Ask yourself questions to help you focus on the photo, e.g. *Who/What is it a photo of? Where was it taken? What's happening in the photo?*
- Answer these questions when you describe the photo.

5 Describe this photo. Talk on your own for about a minute.

64 ▶ Workbook Unit 6: Speaking, pages 48–49, exercises 1, 2, 3

The *Optimise your exam* box develops the lesson skill in order to prepare students for the exam task that follows.

The lesson ends in a speaking-test task consolidating the skill developed on this page.

The Exam skill box in the Speaking lesson highlights one of the sub-skills that are required for success in speaking tests.

STUDENT'S BOOK | Language in Use lesson

All Language in Use lessons provide comprehensive coverage of all aspects of grammar and vocabulary that students need in order to prepare for exams.

Every Language in Use lesson is based on a specific task type that students may be tested on in common exams.

Exam skills are language-focused for exam preparation, but also for students' general language development.

The *Optimise your exam* box develops the lesson skill in order to prepare students for the exam task that follows.

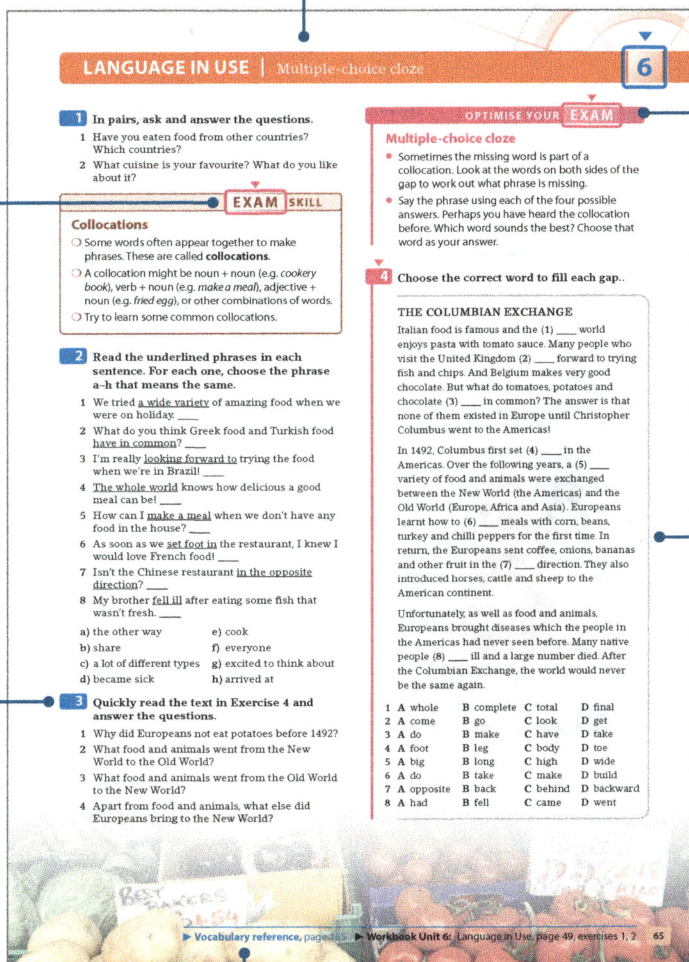

LANGUAGE IN USE | Multiple-choice cloze

6

1 In pairs, ask and answer the questions.

1 Have you eaten food from other countries? Which countries?
2 What cuisine is your favourite? What do you like about it?

EXAM SKILL

Collocations

- Some words often appear together to make phrases. These are called **collocations**.
- A collocation might be noun + noun (e.g. *cookery book*), verb + noun (e.g. *make a meal*), adjective + noun (e.g. *fried egg*), or other combinations of words.
- Try to learn some common collocations.

2 Read the underlined phrases in each sentence. For each one, choose the phrase a–h that means the same.

1 We tried a wide variety of amazing food when we were on holiday. ____
2 What do you think Greek food and Turkish food have in common? ____
3 I'm really looking forward to trying the food when we're in Brazil! ____
4 The whole world knows how delicious a good meal can be! ____
5 How can I make a meal when we don't have any food in the house? ____
6 As soon as we set foot in the restaurant, I knew I would love French food! ____
7 Isn't the Chinese restaurant in the opposite direction? ____
8 My brother fell ill after eating some fish that wasn't fresh. ____

a) the other way
b) share
c) a lot of different types
d) became sick
e) cook
f) everyone
g) excited to think about
h) arrived at

3 Quickly read the text in Exercise 4 and answer the questions.

1 Why did Europeans not eat potatoes before 1492?
2 What food and animals went from the New World to the Old World?
3 What food and animals went from the Old World to the New World?
4 Apart from food and animals, what else did Europeans bring to the New World?

OPTIMISE YOUR EXAM

Multiple-choice cloze

- Sometimes the missing word is part of a collocation. Look at the words on both sides of the gap to work out what phrase is missing.
- Say the phrase using each of the four possible answers. Perhaps you have heard the collocation before. Which word sounds the best? Choose that word as your answer.

4 Choose the correct word to fill each gap..

THE COLUMBIAN EXCHANGE

Italian food is famous and the (1) ____ world enjoys pasta with tomato sauce. Many people who visit the United Kingdom (2) ____ forward to trying fish and chips. And Belgium makes very good chocolate. But what do tomatoes, potatoes and chocolate (3) ____ in common? The answer is that none of them existed in Europe until Christopher Columbus went to the Americas!

In 1492, Columbus first set (4) ____ in the Americas. Over the following years, a (5) ____ variety of food and animals were exchanged between the New World (the Americas) and the Old World (Europe, Africa and Asia). Europeans learnt how to (6) ____ meals with corn, beans, turkey and chilli peppers for the first time. In return, the Europeans sent coffee, onions, bananas and other fruit in the (7) ____ direction. They also introduced horses, cattle and sheep to the American continent.

Unfortunately, as well as food and animals, Europeans brought diseases which the people in the Americas had never seen before. Many native people (8) ____ ill and a large number died. After the Columbian Exchange, the world would never be the same again.

	A	B	C	D
1	whole	complete	total	final
2	come	go	look	get
3	do	make	have	take
4	foot	leg	body	toe
5	big	long	high	wide
6	do	take	make	build
7	opposite	back	behind	backward
8	had	fell	came	went

▶ Vocabulary reference, page 165 ▶ Workbook Unit 6: Language in Use, page 49, exercises 1, 2

65

Many common exam tasks are covered: multiple-choice cloze, open cloze, word formation and sentence transformation.

Exercises build up throughout the lesson, preparing students for the final exam task.

Any extra material in the *Vocabulary reference* which is relevant to the Language in Use lesson is signposted at the bottom of the page.

Every unit ends with a two-page Writing lesson.

6 WRITING | A letter / An email

Writing lessons focus on the different types of writing that students may be expected to produce in an exam situation.

1 In pairs or groups, answer the questions.

1 Describe the photos. What occasion do you think it might be?
2 What was the last family party you went to? Describe it.

EXAM SKILL

Making suggestions

- When you write an informal letter or email, you sometimes need to make suggestions to the person you're writing to, perhaps because they have asked for your ideas or advice.
- Use words and phrases such as *Maybe/Perhaps you should/could …, How/What about -ing …?, If I were you, I'd …, One thing you could do is …, Don't forget to …* .

The Exam skill box develops key language functions that students will need to apply in writing tasks.

2 Read this email and answer the questions.

Hi Charlie,
It was great to hear from you. I'm glad you got the game you wanted!
Your family party sounds like it's going to be a lot of fun. I've got a few ideas that might help.
One thing you could do is make a bowl of chilli con carne. It's a Mexican dish that is really popular. You could make it spicy if your family like spicy food! Why not serve it with rice?
What about making different sandwiches? They're easy to make and you could give people a choice. Don't forget to make some without meat.
Good luck with your party!
Love,
Monica

1 Why does Charlie want suggestions?
2 What two reasons does Monica give for suggesting chilli con carne?
3 What three points does Monica make about sandwiches?

Every Writing lesson includes a model, which students can use to inform and guide their own writing when they complete the exam task later in the lesson.

3 Read the email again and find six places where the writer makes suggestions. Write the phrases the writer uses here.

1 ____
2 ____
3 ____
4 ____
5 ____
6 ____

OPTIMISE YOUR EXAM

A letter / An email

- It is just as important to plan an informal letter/email as it is to plan a formal letter/email.
- Make a note of all your ideas so you remember to include them. If you have to make suggestions, write down the things you are going to suggest before you start writing.

In Writing lessons, the *Optimise your exam* box provides guidance and advice to help students prepare for the lesson exam task.

66

4 Look at this writing task and make notes to answer the questions.

This is part of an email you received from an English friend.

> Help! My class is having a party and I have to make some food for it! What dishes should I include? Can you suggest something from your country I could make?

Write your email.

Students analyse the task and make notes to prepare for the writing in each unit.

5 Plan Make a paragraph plan.

Part	Purpose	Useful phrases	My notes
First line	greet the person you are writing to	*Dear …,* *Hi …!*	
Paragraph 1	thank the other person for their letter and refer to a piece of news	*Thanks for your letter.* *It was great to hear from you.* *I'm glad you're having a party.*	
Paragraph 2	refer to their request, say you have some ideas/suggestions	*You asked me about …, I've got a few ideas that might help.*	
Paragraph 3	make some suggestions and explain	*One thing you could do is …,* *You could …,* *What about -ing …?* *How about -ing …?*	
Paragraph 4			
Closing expressions 1	wish them luck, ask them to reply, say goodbye	*Good luck with …!* *Write soon!* *Bye for now!*	
Closing expressions 2	express friendship	*Love,* *Lots of love,* *Best wishes,*	
Your name	first name		

6 Write Write your email in an appropriate style. Write about 100 words.

7 Check Before you hand in your email, complete this checklist.

Checklist

- I've written an informal email.
- I've followed my paragraph plan.
- I've made some suggestions for dishes for the party.
- I've started and ended my email in the right way.
- I've checked my grammar and spelling.

▶ Writing reference, page 173 ▶ Workbook Unit 6: Writing, page 50, exercises 1, 2, 3, 4 and Progress check 6, page 51 67

After writing, students are encouraged to check their work carefully.

There is a Checklist at the end of every Writing lesson so that students take responsibility for reviewing and assessing their work.

In the *Writing reference*, there are model writing texts for each task type. The Workbook offers further writing practice.

STUDENT'S BOOK | Progress check

There is a two-page Progress check after every two units.

PROGRESS CHECK UNITS 5–6

GRAMMAR AND VOCABULARY

The *Progress checks* cover grammar and vocabulary from the preceding two units.

1 Choose the correct word or phrase.

1 I **can / could** read when I was three years old.
2 I don't think you **should / might** watch this film. It's scary!
3 You **don't have to / mustn't** come shopping with me, but you can if you want to.
4 I hope we'll **can / be able to** visit you again soon.
5 I **can / could** get a new phone for my birthday – if I'm lucky!
6 My mum's gone shopping, but she **should / can** be back soon.
7 Fran **mustn't / can't** be away on holiday. I saw her this morning!

__/7

2 Write a relative pronoun or adverb in each gap. Use each one only once.

1 That's the restaurant ________ they make great salads.
2 Do you remember the time ________ Liam fell in the lake?
3 My best friend, ________ mum is a food journalist, is excellent at cooking.
4 I can't find the recipe ________ you gave me.
5 My best friend, ________ is a top chef, is going to be on a cookery show.
6 Pasta, ________ is my favourite food, is easy to prepare.

__/6

3 Match to make collocations.

1 set ___ a) world
2 fall ___ b) variety
3 look ___ c) foot in
4 a wide ___ d) direction
5 the whole ___ e) forward to
6 the opposite ___ f) ill

__/6

4 If a word or phrase in bold is correct, put a tick. If it's incorrect, rewrite it correctly in each gap.

1 It took me about two weeks to completely **make** over that cold. ________
2 It was so hot in the school assembly, I nearly **passed** out. ________
3 I've got a terrible headache. I hope I'm not **arriving** down with flu. ________
4 You can't **live** off junk food! You have to eat fruit and vegetables regularly. ________
5 The cakes are still hot. Wait for them to **cold** down first. ________
6 **Happy** up! It's not the end of the world. It's just an English test. ________
7 Don't go to school if you don't **feel** up to it. ________
8 We should all **reduce** down on how much sugar we consume. ________

__/8

68

5 Write *do*, *have*, *make* or *take* in each gap.

1 ________ care of
2 ________ an effort
3 ________ fun of
4 ________ homework/housework
5 ________ flu
6 ________ up your mind
7 ________ your teeth/hair
8 ________ a mistake

__/8

6 Write a form of the word in capitals in each gap.

1 Have you made a ________ yet? DECIDE
2 This soup is ________ hot. I can't eat it yet! BOIL
3 That cake was really ________! Can I have some more, please? TASTE
4 The doctor gave me a ________ for antibiotics. PRESCRIBE
5 Pour the oil into a ________ pan. FRY
6 I'm not very keen on ________ food. SPICE
7 The ________ at the event was fantastic! ENTERTAIN
8 What ________ do we need to go camping? EQUIP

__/8

7 Write the correct article in each gap. If no article is necessary, put a dash (–).

1 The hotel provides ________ accommodation for up to 300 people.
2 Do you need ________ orange to make that dessert?
3 ________ bandages are what you use to wrap around an injury.
4 We went to ________ best Japanese restaurant in town last night.
5 ________ honey is 80% sugars and 20% water.
6 I can't find ________ blender. I used it last night!
7 Do you have ________ food delivery subscription? You receive food and recipes every week.

__/7

Total score __/50

There is a total of 50 marks for every *Progress check*.

EXAM SKILLS

Tick the statements that are true for you. Review the skills in the unit if you need more help.

I can ...	Unit/page
☐ locate information in an online article	Unit 5 p48
☐ understand agreement and disagreement in a conversation	Unit 5 p52
☐ talk about habits	Unit 5 p54
☐ understand how nouns are formed and use them in word formation exercises	Unit 5 p55
☐ use narrative tenses in a story	Unit 5 p56
☐ identify synonyms in a profile	Unit 6 p58
☐ recognise similar meaning in a short talk	Unit 6 p62
☐ describe situations and actions in a photo	Unit 6 p64
☐ form collocations and use them in a multiple-choice cloze exercise	Unit 6 p65
☐ make suggestions in an informal letter / an email	Unit 6 p66

69

Every *Progress check* ends with an *Exam skills can-do* checklist. This gives students the opportunity to assess what they can now do, having completed two more units of their Student's Book, and also provides references of where to look if there are any areas students feel they need to review.

STUDENT'S BOOK | Optimise your exams

The 12-page *Optimise your exams* section at the back of the Student's Book brings together exam strategies for each of the key skills, plus advice on how to perform well under exam conditions.

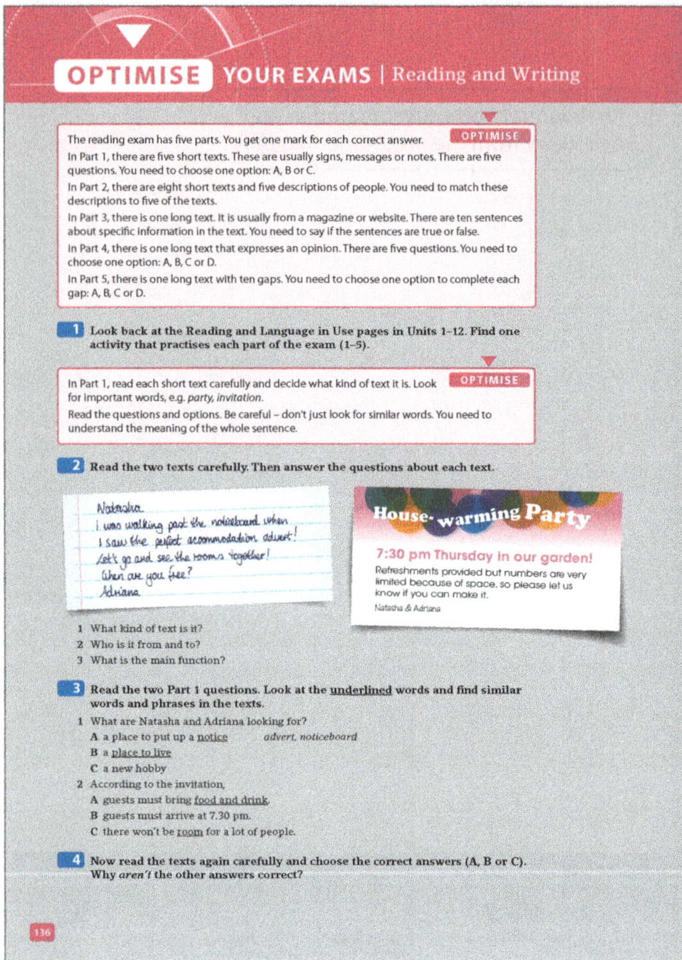

OPTIMISE YOUR EXAMS | Reading and Writing

OPTIMISE
The reading exam has five parts. You get one mark for each correct answer.
In Part 1, there are five short texts. These are usually signs, messages or notes. There are five questions. You need to choose one option: A, B or C.
In Part 2, there are eight short texts and five descriptions of people. You need to match these descriptions to five of the texts.
In Part 3, there is one long text. It is usually from a magazine or website. There are ten sentences about specific information in the text. You need to say if the sentences are true or false.
In Part 4, there is one long text that expresses an opinion. There are five questions. You need to choose one option: A, B, C or D.
In Part 5, there is one long text with ten gaps. You need to choose one option to complete each gap: A, B, C or D.

1 Look back at the Reading and Language in Use pages in Units 1–12. Find one activity that practises each part of the exam (1–5).

OPTIMISE
In Part 1, read each short text carefully and decide what kind of text it is. Look for important words, e.g. *party, invitation*.
Read the questions and options. Be careful – don't just look for similar words. You need to understand the meaning of the whole sentence.

2 Read the two texts carefully. Then answer the questions about each text.

Natasha
I was walking past the noticeboard when I saw the perfect accommodation advert! Let's go and see the rooms together! When are you free?
Adriana

House-warming Party
7:30 pm Thursday in our garden!
Refreshments provided but numbers are very limited because of space, so please let us know if you can make it.
Natasha & Adriana

1 What kind of text is it?
2 Who is it from and to?
3 What is the main function?

3 Read the two Part 1 questions. Look at the underlined words and find similar words and phrases in the texts.

1 What are Natasha and Adriana looking for?
  A a place to put up a notice *advert, noticeboard*
  B a place to live
  C a new hobby
2 According to the invitation,
  A guests must bring food and drink.
  B guests must arrive at 7.30 pm.
  C there won't be room for a lot of people.

4 Now read the texts again carefully and choose the correct answers (A, B or C). Why *aren't* the other answers correct?

136

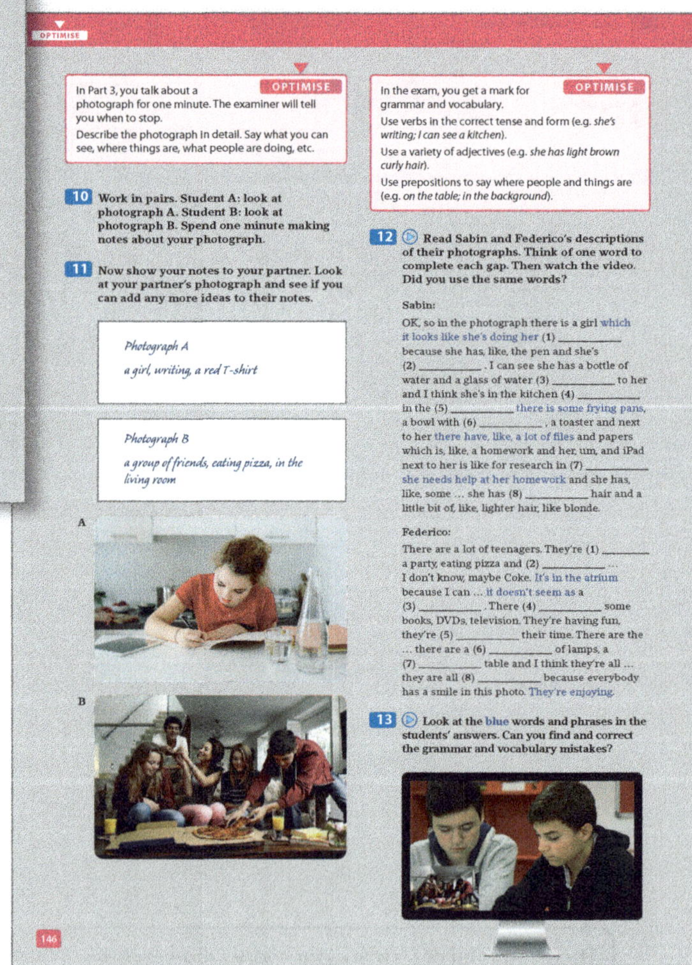

OPTIMISE

OPTIMISE
In Part 3, you talk about a photograph for one minute. The examiner will tell you when to stop.
Describe the photograph in detail. Say what you can see, where things are, what people are doing, etc.

10 Work in pairs. Student A: look at photograph A. Student B: look at photograph B. Spend one minute making notes about your photograph.

11 Now show your notes to your partner. Look at your partner's photograph and see if you can add any more ideas to their notes.

Photograph A
a girl, writing, a red T-shirt

Photograph B
a group of friends, eating pizza, in the living room

A

B

OPTIMISE
In the exam, you get a mark for grammar and vocabulary.
Use verbs in the correct tense and form (e.g. *she's writing; I can see a kitchen*).
Use a variety of adjectives (e.g. *she has light brown curly hair*).
Use prepositions to say where people and things are (e.g. *on the table; in the background*).

12 Read Sabin and Federico's descriptions of their photographs. Think of one word to complete each gap. Then watch the video. Did you use the same words?

Sabin:
OK, so in the photograph there is a girl which it looks like she's doing her (1) ________ because she has, like, the pen and she's (2) ________. I can see she has a bottle of water and a glass of water (3) ________ to her and I think she's in the kitchen (4) ________ in the (5) ________ there is some frying pans, a bowl with (6) ________, a toaster and next to her there have, like, a lot of files and papers which is, like, a homework and her, um, and iPad next to her is like for research in (7) ________ she needs help at her homework and she has, like, some ... she has (8) ________ hair and a little bit of, like, lighter hair, like blonde.

Federico:
There are a lot of teenagers. They're (1) ________ a party, eating pizza and (2) ________ ... I don't know, maybe Coke. It's in the atrium because I can ... it doesn't seem as a (3) ________. There (4) ________ some books, DVDs, television. They're having fun, they're (5) ________ their time. There are the ... there are a (6) ________ of lamps, a (7) ________ table and I think they're all ... they are all (8) ________ because everybody has a smile in this photo. They're enjoying.

13 Look at the blue words and phrases in the students' answers. Can you find and correct the grammar and vocabulary mistakes?

146

Optimise your exams features:

- Sections dedicated to each of the exam papers.
- Exercises to improve students' understanding of common exam tasks.
- Clear targeted advice on how to approach specific exam tasks.
- Exercises to encourage analysis of sample answers.
- Details of common FAQs regarding specific exam papers.
- A Speaking test video in which real candidates complete an authentic Speaking test, to watch and analyse.
- Sample writing plans to compare and critique.
- Information about how the test is marked.
- Advice on how much time to spend on different parts of the exams.

There is a bank of reference material at the back of the Student's Book, designed to support students as they work through the lessons, and also intended to act as a revision tool when required.

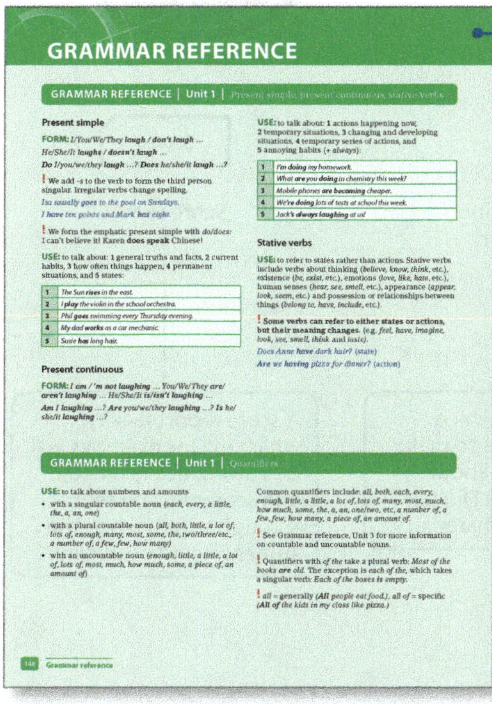

The *Grammar reference* pages provide more detailed explanations of the grammar points covered in every unit, along with example sentences showing how the structures can be used.

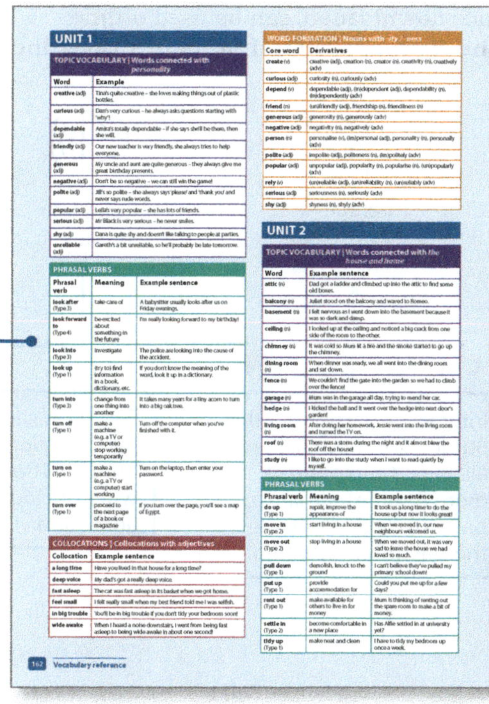

All three vocabulary sections from each unit are expanded upon in the *Vocabulary reference*. The sections on Topic vocabulary, Phrasal verbs, Collocations, Word patterns and Idioms all include example sentences. The Word formation sections from the Vocabulary lessons include a list of derivatives.

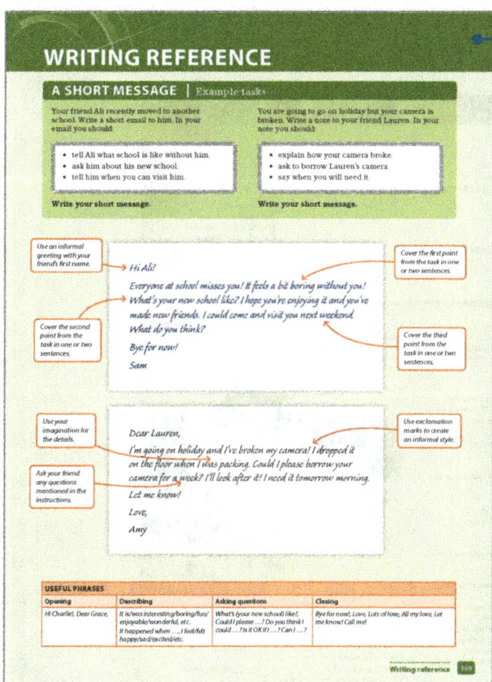

There is a model text for each writing genre, with annotations to highlight key points that students need to remember. Every *Writing reference* page also includes a bank of 'Useful phrases'.

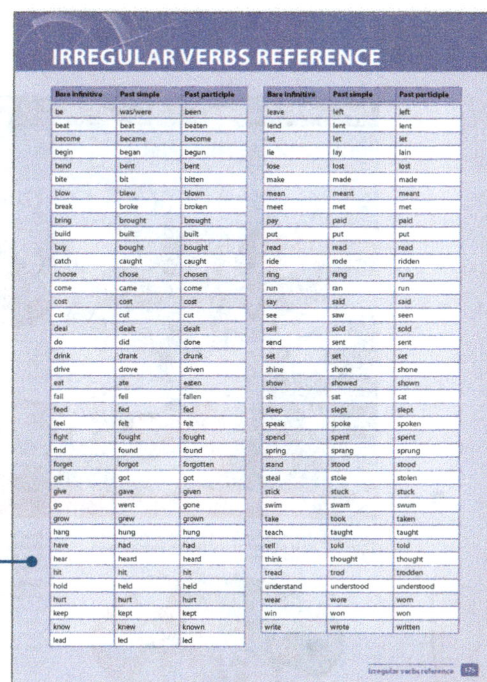

A list of irregular verbs used throughout the Student's Book is provided at the end of the reference material.

DIGITAL STUDENT'S BOOK SB

Includes an access code for the Student's Resource Centre

The *Optimise* Digital Student's Book offers students the possibility of an interactive learning experience, which engages the class as a whole and enables lessons to be dynamic and motivating. The material is easily downloadable and, once downloaded, can be used offline.

The *Optimise* Digital Student's Book includes:

Interactive Student's Book Activities
Interactive versions of the Student's Book activities, allowing the option of more flexible learning both inside and outside the classroom situation.

Complete class audio / **Integrated video**
Easy-to-navigate digital reproduction of the Student's Book pages which includes embedded audio and video material.

Note-taking function
A notes facility, which enables students to make their own notes about all aspects of the Digital Student's Book material.

Score report
A score report facility, which means exercises will be automatically marked and scores will be sent through to you when the student next goes online.

PRESENTATION KIT

Includes digital versions of the Student's Book and Workbook

You can use the *Optimise* Presentation Kit in the classroom to promote interactive, heads-up lessons, allowing for the option of collaborative learning. The Presentation Kit provides you with a versatile, digital presentation and teaching tool. Built-in functionality enables you to annotate and customise your presentation in advance, making the lesson more suited to the needs of your class. The Presentation Kit can be easily downloaded and, once downloaded, can be used offline.

The *Optimise* Presentation Kit includes:

Interactive Student's Book activities
Interactive versions of the Student's Book activities, giving you the opportunity to complete activities and check answers as a whole class.

Complete Class and Workbook audio / **Integrated video**
All class audio and video material, which can be played instantly by clicking on the hotspots throughout the Presentation Kit material.

Student's Book and Workbook Answer key feature
Answer keys for the Student's Book and Workbook are embedded within each activity, meaning you can show the next answer at the touch of a button. Additional answer key pop-ups are also provided, with suggested answers for open activities.

Note pad feature
A notes facility, enabling you to add your own comments on the material. This helps you deliver more effective and engaging lessons.

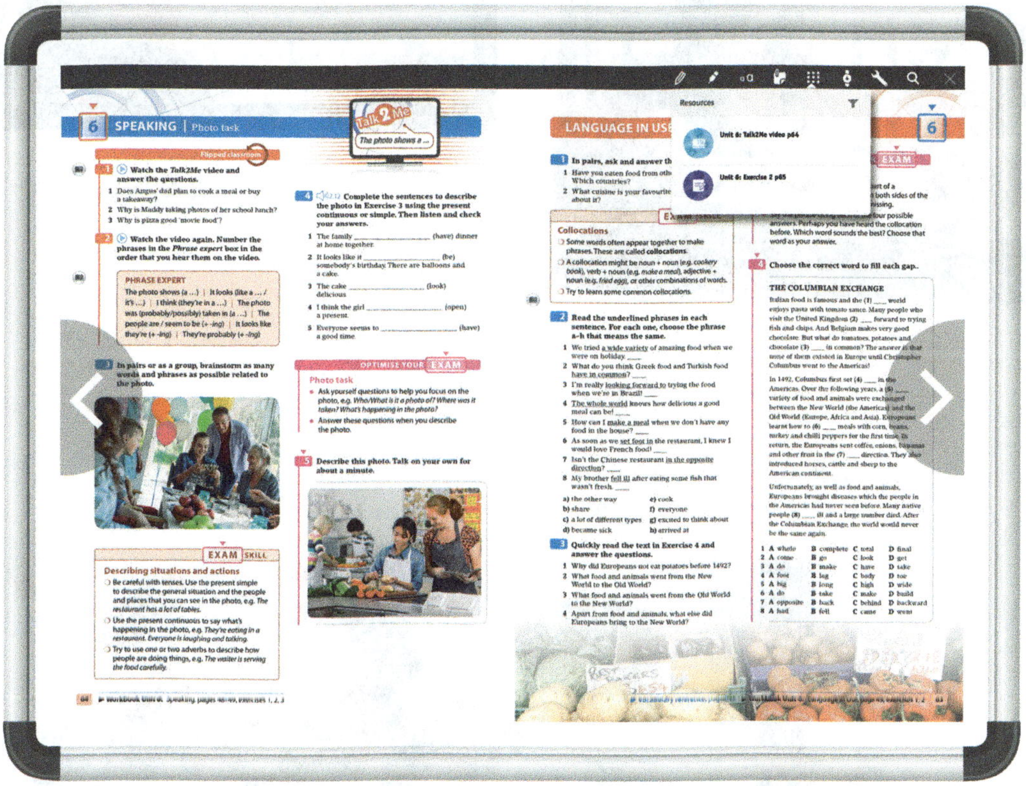

VIDEOS

Use in class or for self-study

Optimise videos provide comprehensive support for students to develop their speaking skills. The course features two different video strands, both of which are flexible and versatile resources that can be used in a number of different ways to support and extend listening and speaking skills.

Talk2Me

1 *Talk2Me* videos

Every Speaking lesson includes a *Talk2Me* video. These exciting videos feature three teenagers Angus, Maddy and Jamie in a series of episodes about their everyday lives.

The videos present key functional language in a natural and original context.

Flipped classroom

Flipped classroom option

You can choose to use the Flipped classroom approach for these videos and set them for homework. Students watch the videos and complete the exercises in the Student's Book at home to prepare for the Speaking lesson. This allows more class time to activate the functional language and develop fluency for the exam task.

Classroom option

Of course, the videos can be watched together as a class with students completing the exercises individually or sharing their ideas with other students.

The videos are available on the Resource Centre and are accompanied by additional worksheets, transcripts and answer keys.

2 Speaking test videos

Optimise includes Speaking test videos as part of the *Optimise your exams* section. The videos provide students with a chance to observe the performance of candidates doing complete Speaking tests under exam conditions.

Watching and discussing the video also enables students to have a greater understanding of the format and processes involved in speaking tests, giving them more confidence and helping them to feel better prepared for the exam.

WORKBOOK | Reading lesson

Each Workbook unit has eight pages, with a section for each separate lesson in the Student's Book, and one page for an end of unit Progress check.

Complete *Optimise Practice test* at the back of the Workbook

6 A piece of cake!

READING | Multiple choice

→Student's Book, pages 58–59

All exam skills match the corresponding Student's Book lesson.

Every unit includes a reference to the corresponding Student's Book lesson.

1 Read these words and phrases from Exercise 2. Write a word or phrase from the text that means the same in each gap.

1 started ______
2 making cakes in your kitchen ______
3 adolescents ______
4 advice ______
5 old ______
6 all over the world ______

2 Read the text. For questions 1–5, choose the answer (A, B, C or D) which you think fits best according to the text.

1 Fraser Doherty
- A has always made jam with his grandmother.
- B learnt to make jam and his life changed completely.
- C really enjoyed cooking in his parents' kitchen.
- D initially sold his products only to farmers.

2 What happened when Fraser was 16?
- A He talked to people at a supermarket chain.
- B He developed a jam without any sugar in it.
- C He started his own company.
- D He had the idea for his most popular product, *SuperJam*.

3 What is *BakeLab*?
- A A place where Fraser makes new cake recipes.
- B Jars that include cake ingredients and different types of tea.
- C Cakes that have jam as one of the ingredients.
- D Prepared ingredients for making cakes in your own kitchen.

4 What is part of the extra money from *SuperHoney* sales used for?
- A To help adolescents to find out how to prepare honey.
- B To buy bees for local community groups.
- C To design new and better beehives for producing honey.
- D To promote the product to supermarkets worldwide.

5 What does the writer say about the *SuperJam Tea Parties*?
- A Fraser tells young businesspeople how they can improve.
- B Over 500 old people go to each of the tea parties.
- C The tea parties are organised in all over the world.
- D Fraser gives talks about how he became successful.

Exercises check students' comprehension of the reading text and are designed to develop students' reading skills.

3 Find words and phrases 1–8 in the text and then match them to the definitions a–h.

1 experimented (*v*) ___
2 flavours (*n*) ___
3 approached (*v*) ___
4 turned him down (*phr v*) ___
5 profits (*n*) ___
6 beehives (*n*) ___
7 community (*n*) ___
8 entrepreneurs (*n*) ___

a) extra money you have from sales after you have covered all costs
b) the distinctive taste of food or drink
c) a group of people who live in the same place
d) tried new things to find out what results they will have
e) structures for keeping bees, from which you collect their honey
f) people who use money to start a business
g) didn't accept an offer
h) spoke to someone about something for the first time

New vocabulary from the Workbook reading text is highlighted.

44

Engaging images attract students' attention and interest in the text.

A piece of cake! 6

SUPERJAM

Have you ever cooked with your grandparents? Fraser Doherty did, and it changed his life! When he was 14, he learnt to make jam with his gran and loved it so much that he started doing it every day after school and at weekends. He experimented with different flavours and soon he was making 1,000 jars a week in his parents' kitchen. Fraser, known as *JamBoy*, sold his jams at local farmers' markets.

Fraser's jams, which contained no sugar, sold really well, so he set up his own business at age 16. A year later Fraser approached Waitrose supermarkets, hoping they would sell his jams. Waitrose turned him down, but they gave Fraser some great advice which he followed and, as a result, *SuperJam* was born. Waitrose then agreed to sell his jams and they quickly became popular. In one Edinburgh store, people bought 1,500 jars in just one day!

Since then, Fraser hasn't stopped. He created *BakeLab*, home-baking mixes where all the ingredients are included in a jar, and *SuperTea*, a range of teas to go with his cakes and jams. He also sells *SuperHoney* and part of the profits from this are used to buy beehives for local community groups which then teach young people to make honey. His products are now available in over 2,000 supermarkets around the world, in countries including Australia, Russia and Finland.

Fraser has also written two books, *The SuperJam Cookbook* and *SuperBusiness*, which is full of tips for young entrepreneurs. Every year, he also finds time to organise over 100 *SuperJam Tea Parties* all over Britain for elderly people, with around 600 participants at each one. Not surprisingly, he is also a popular speaker at events worldwide. Everyone wants to know the secret of his success – and his jam recipes!

45

The Reading lessons feature a full-length reading text.

Grammar lessons throughout the Workbook reflect the material covered in the Student's Book and provide students with more opportunities to consolidate and practise the structures.

The page number of the Student's Book *Grammar reference* is included in the Workbook so that students can refer back if they need to.

6 GRAMMAR 1 | Relative clauses

→Student's Book, page 60 →Grammar reference, Unit 6, Student's Book, page 153

1 Complete the sentences with the correct relative pronoun. If there is more than one correct answer, write both answers.

1 The cake __________ my dad made won first prize in the competition.
2 The girl __________ babysits for my little brother is teaching him to bake.
3 The shop __________ I bought this recipe book sells lots of cookery books.
4 The café, __________ is near my house, only serves organic food.
5 Giada De Laurentiis, __________ TV show I often watch, has her own catering business.
6 I've been reading about Sam Stern, __________ is a famous chef and writer.
7 That was the year __________ I learnt to cook!
8 Jamie Oliver, __________ cookbook I often use, is a famous British chef.

2 Add brackets ( ) around the relative pronouns that can be left out.

1 The chef who came to our school to give cooking lessons was great!
2 The man that I saw in the supermarket owns the restaurant near our house.
3 The recipe book which you gave me for my birthday is really good.
4 The restaurant, which opened last week, has had great reviews.
5 The waitress who I talked to was very helpful.
6 All the students who take cookery lessons enjoy them.

3 Rewrite the sentences using the information given. Use a relative clause in each sentence.

1 Our local food festival started four years ago. I can remember it.
____
2 The food festival was on last weekend. The food festival was really good.
____
3 I watched a celebrity chef. He made a delicious curry.
____
4 There were lots of stalls. The stalls sold different kinds of food.
____
5 There was a pop-up restaurant. You could eat Italian food there.
____
6 The organisers say it's been the most successful year ever. The organisers worked very hard.
____

6 VOCABULARY | Topic vocabulary | Phrasal verbs | Word formation

→Student's Book, page 61 →Vocabulary reference, Unit 6, Student's Book, page 165

The corresponding page of the *Vocabulary reference* is included throughout the Workbook wherever relevant.

1 Complete the sentences with the words in the box.

bitter | juicy | salty | sour | spicy | sweet

1 The pears are so __________ ! Wash your hands after eating one.
2 I don't like __________ food so I rarely eat puddings or cakes.
3 Kate loves __________ food, such as olives and crisps.
4 Plain yoghurt can be as __________ as lemons.
5 Leafy vegetables such as kale and some herbs can be __________ .
6 A lot of Indian and Mexican food is __________ because it contains chillies.

46

Each of the three vocabulary sections is covered separately in the Workbook, giving your students another chance to reinforce their lexical knowledge.

A piece of cake! 6

2 Choose the correct word or phrase to complete each sentence.

1 I was eating too much chocolate so I've cut down ____ the amount I eat.
a) off b) out c) on
2 The milk had gone ____ because it had been left out of the fridge. It smelt awful!
a) off b) down c) up
3 I gave ____ eating sweets for a month and felt much better for it!
a) off b) down c) up
4 The sauce is too hot – let it cool ____ for a few minutes.
a) off b) down c) down on
5 There's some pizza left from yesterday if you want to warm it ____ .
a) off b) up c) down
6 We live ____ the fruit and vegetables that we grow in our garden.
a) off b) up c) down
7 If you want to help, you can chop the potatoes ____ into small pieces.
a) down b) up c) off
8 Eat ____ , or your food will get cold.
a) down b) out c) up

3 Write a form of the word in capitals in each gap to complete the text.

10:05 AM

Jade Dragon ★★★★

Fancy a great Chinese meal? Try the Jade Dragon restaurant! If you think Chinese food is boring and (1) __________ , then think again! We ate there yesterday and we really loved the food. I had *Chicken Chow Mein* – it's a (2) __________ of vegetables that are (3) __________ with garlic, ginger and noodles and chicken in a wok (a kind of Chinese (4) __________ pan). I don't like hot food, so I was pleased this had great flavour without being too (5) __________ .
My friend had a coconut shrimp dish. There were plenty of shrimps in a (6) __________ coconut sauce, which he said was absolutely delicious! It came with plain, (7) __________ rice. We were both really (8) __________ with the food and the service. We'd certainly go again!

TASTE
MIX
FRY
FRY
SPICE
CREAM
BOIL
SATISFY

Every grammar section contains two or three exercises, and where possible texts are included, giving students another chance to see the unit grammar in a realistic context.

6 GRAMMAR 2 | Articles

→Student's Book, page 63 →Grammar reference, Unit 6, Student's Book, page 153

A second grammar section in the Workbook corresponds to the second grammar lesson in the Student's Book.

1 Choose the correct article. If no article is necessary, choose the dash (–).

Many people love (1) **the / –** pineapples, but they are not native to Britain. Historians believe (2) **a / the** fruit originated in Brazil and was brought to Europe by (3) **an / the** explorer Christopher Columbus, who was probably one of (4) **the / –** first Europeans to taste it. Around 1900, James Dole, (5) **an / the** American businessman, started (6) **a / the** business growing pineapples in Hawaii, which quickly became (7) **the / –** largest pineapple farm in (8) **a / the** world. Thanks to Dole, pineapples became popular and cheap enough for (9) **the / –** people worldwide to buy. Next time you buy (10) **a / the** pineapple, think of Dole!

2 Write the correct article in each gap. If no article is necessary, put a dash (–).

Teen Cooks is (1) __________ interesting documentary in which (2) __________ world-famous chef Ricky Andalcio teaches two teenagers to cook. (3) __________ teenagers have to learn how to prepare (4) __________ basic family meals. They are not allowed to use (5) __________ frozen food or microwave anything – they have to cook everything from raw ingredients! Their families must eat (6) __________ meals they cook. At (7) __________ end of (8) __________ two-week course, the teenagers have to make (9) __________ three-course meal for 20 people!

47

Exercises in the Workbook are staged so as to be progressively more challenging.

WORKBOOK | Listening lesson | Speaking lesson | Language in Use lesson

The listening exam skill in the Student's Book is practised again in the Workbook.

6 LISTENING | Gap fill

→ Student's Book, page 62

1 Look at the photos of food festivals and answer the questions.

1 Match photos 1–3 to festival names a–c.

a) Gilroy Garlic Festival ____ b) The Monkey Buffet ____ c) Chinchilla Melon Festival ____

1 

2 

3 

2 What do you think happens at these festivals?

____

____

____

2 Find words and phrases in Exercise 3 which match these definitions.

1 things we eat __________
2 dress up in __________
3 is on for __________
4 physical activities __________
5 presentations __________
6 organised by __________

3 13 You are going to listen to someone talking about unusual food festivals. Write the missing information in each gap.

At the **Monkey Buffet Festival**, which started in 1989, the monkeys eat (1) ______________ of food. Thousands of tourists come to the festival. (2) ______________ wear costumes and the entertainment includes music and dancing.

The Australian **Chinchilla Melon Festival** lasts (3) ______________ and you can do many sports including melon (4) ______________ as well as melon bungee jumping and melon throwing! There's plenty of other entertainment and food markets.

The **Gilroy Garlic Festival** takes place every July and has practical demonstrations of cooking by (5) ______________, competitions and live music. You can eat many different foods prepared with garlic. The festival is run by over 4,000 (6) ______________ and has raised millions for charity.

The Workbook listening exercises have their own dedicated audio material, available on the Resource Centres and on the Online Workbook.

Workbook exercises give students more practice in exam-type tasks.

6 SPEAKING | Photo task

→ Student's Book, page 64

1 Look at the photo and tick what you can see.

Places
kitchen ☐
restaurant ☐
home ☐
dining room ☐

People
school friends ☐
family ☐
father and daughter ☐
father and son ☐

Action
chopping ☐
eating ☐
cooking ☐
preparing food ☐

2 Read a description of the photograph in Exercise 1 and put the verbs into the correct tense.

This photo (1) ______________ (**show**) a father and son at home in a modern kitchen. They (2) ______________ (**wear**) T-shirts and they (3) ______________ (**look**) relaxed and happy. The father (4) ______________ (**watch**) his son prepare some food. There (5) ______________ (**be**) some peppers and carrots. The son (6) ______________ (**have got**) a knife and he (7) ______________ (**chop**) some tomatoes on a board, which (8) ______________ (**make**) of wood. It looks like the father (9) ______________ (**talk**), so perhaps he is telling his son what to do. In the background, there (10) ______________ (**be**) a pan and a frying pan on the cooker. In the foreground, there are some more knives.

48

As the Workbook is designed for independent use, the speaking lessons consist of written exercises specifically designed to provide essential preparation that will further improve students' speaking skills.

A piece of cake! 6

3 Look at the photo and write a description.

____

____

____

____

____

____

____

6 LANGUAGE IN USE | Multiple-choice cloze

→ Student's Book, page 65

1 Read the underlined phrases in each sentence. Then choose the best meaning a–h.

1 What do pizzas and pasta have in common? They're both Italian foods. ____
2 It takes a long time to prepare this dish, but it's worth it. ____
3 The shop has a wide variety of cheeses from all over the world. ____
4 Don't laugh – this is something you should take seriously. ____
5 I've been to the market to buy fresh ingredients and now I'm going to make a meal. I hope you're hungry! ____
6 We want to have a healthy lifestyle, so we have a good diet and exercise regularly. ____
7 Many people say the national dish in Britain is fish and chips. ____
8 I like looking at cookery books to get interesting recipes. ____

a) prepare the food for lunch or dinner
b) many different types
c) books with instructions on preparing dishes
d) the most typical food of a country
e) give careful attention to
f) share
g) a way of life that is good for your health
h) requires a lot of time

Workbook exercises give students the chance to examine and practise language in more detail.

2 Choose the correct word to fill each gap.

Grubs up!

What do beetles, caterpillars, bees and ants have in (1) ____, apart from being insects? They are the most frequently eaten bugs. Eating insects isn't unusual – around two billion people regularly eat them as part of a healthy (2) ____.

The idea of eating bugs might horrify you, but it's something you should (3) ____ seriously because it has many advantages. Insects are an excellent source of protein and vitamins and they're full of healthy fats and iron. They're also good for the environment because they don't take a (4) ____ time to grow and they are very good at converting food into body weight – crickets only need 2 kg of food to produce a kilo of meat, whereas cows need far more. Lastly, insect farming could provide jobs and income for people in developing countries.

Insects are surprisingly tasty and there is a (5) ____ variety to choose from! For example, sago grubs taste like bacon and apparently tarantula spiders taste like chicken. There are now plenty of (6) ____ books in the market so you can (7) ____ a delicious meal with insects if you fancy trying them out. You never know, beetles and chips could replace fish and chips as our new (8) ____ dish!

	A	B	C	D
1	A share	B common	C similarity	D characteristic
2	A habit	B living	C lifestyle	D food
3	A have	B do	C make	D take
4	A wide	B long	C huge	D forever
5	A plenty	B big	C wide	D full
6	A food	B kitchen	C cookery	D cooking
7	A be	B do	C make	D take
8	A national	B country	C tradition	D popular

49

The Language in Use lessons in the Workbook include an exam-type task, so students get a further opportunity to apply the language skills they developed in the Student's Book lesson.

6 WRITING | A letter / An email

→ Student's Book, pages 66–67 → Writing reference, Student's Book, page 173

Details of the *Writing reference* in the Student's Book are included, so students can easily refer back to it.

1 Choose the correct words to complete the exam skill advice.

1 It **is / isn't** important to plan an informal email or letter.
2 Note down **one or two / all** of your ideas so you remember to include them.
3 If you have to make suggestions, write down the things you are going to suggest **before / after** you start writing.

Writing lessons begin by re-focusing students on the exam advice given in their Student's Book.

From: Marta
To: Harry

Hi Harry,

Thanks for your email, it was great to hear from you.

Your food project for Spanish class sounds like it's going to be fun. You asked me for suggestions for good recipes for traditional food. I've got a few ideas – see what you think!

What about making a Spanish omelette? It's easy to make and everyone can have a small piece – you could also add vegetables like peppers for variety. Why not serve it with some olives and salad?

Good luck with the project. Write and tell me how it went. Bye for now!

Love,

Marta

The Workbook includes a model answer in addition to the one found in the Student's Book.

2 Read the email and find three suggestions.

______
______
______
______
______
______
______
______

3 Read the exam task and complete the suggestions.

This is part of an email you received from your British friend:

> I'm going to visit your country in the summer holidays. What are the national dishes? Can you suggest some dishes my family should definitely try?

Write your **email**.

1 Why don't you ______?
2 You could ______.
3 What about ______?
4 Don't forget to ______.
5 One thing you could ______.

Exercises in the Workbook will help students to consolidate and develop their writing skills in general.

4 Complete the paragraph plan for the exam task in Exercise 3.

Part	Purpose	My notes
First line	greet the person you are writing to	
Paragraph 1	thank the person for their email and refer to a piece of news	
Paragraph 2	refer to their visit and say you have some ideas/suggestions	
Paragraph 3	talk about the national dishes in your country	
Paragraph 4	make suggestions for things the family should try	
Closing expressions	wish them luck with the trip, ask them to reply, express friendship and say goodbye	

Students are not always required to do a complete writing task in the Workbook. Instead they will sometimes be asked to write or complete sentences, write a paragraph or complete a paragraph plan.

50

A piece of cake! 6

PROGRESS CHECK

Every Workbook lesson ends with a one-page *Progress check*.

1 Write one word in each gap to complete the sentences. If no word is necessary, put a dash (–). Sometimes there is more than one correct answer.

1 Christopher Columbus, ______ first brought potatoes and chocolate to Europe, was an explorer.
2 I watched ______ fascinating documentary about the history of food advertising.
3 I remember the time ______ I forgot to put eggs in the cake I was making. It tasted awful!
4 Maria, ______ father owns a restaurant, wants to be a top chef one day.
5 I love ______ strawberries, but I can't stand most sweet foods.
6 I don't think people should eat food on ______ public transport.
7 Did you like ______ recipe that I sent to you?
8 The programme ______ I listened to on the radio had some great ideas for growing your own food.

2 Choose the correct words or phrases.

1 I fancy something savoury and salty, I think I'll have some **cake / chillies / crisps**.
2 Can you pass me a **mixture / mixing / mixed** bowl to put the ingredients in?
3 The milk tastes **salty / juicy / sour**. I think it's gone off.
4 We had a fantastic meal, we were really **satisfy / satisfying / satisfied** with the new restaurant.
5 I need to buy a new **fry / frying / fried** pan because my old one is broken.
6 **Cream / Creamy / Creamed** corn is a popular dish in the USA.
7 The curry had no flavour at all, it was really **tasty / tasteless / taste**.
8 There is a **big / wide / large** variety of food to choose from the menu.
9 I missed the party because I **fell / dropped / slipped** ill the day before.
10 You don't have to do anything, I'll **do / make / have** the meal.
11 Lunch is almost ready, I just need to warm **down / on / up** the soup so it's nice and hot.
12 We've been eating too many cakes, we should **cut / put / get** down on sugar.
13 First, **chop up / cool down / eat up** the onion into small pieces, then fry it.
14 It's not a good idea to live **up / down on / off** fast food.

The *Progress Check* always has one exercise based on the vocabulary from the unit, and one exercise based on the unit grammar.

Cumulative progress 1 2 3 4 5 6 7 8 9 10 11 12

3 Choose the correct word or phrase for each gap.

Good food choices

Fast food is very popular. However, it contains large amounts of carbohydrates, unhealthy fats, salt and added sugar, so it has (1) ____ nutritional value. So, how can you encourage people to (2) ____ healthier food choices? Campaigns (3) ____ focus on the health benefits of a good diet have had little effect. Now, researchers have come (4) ____ with a new method.

They worked with a group of teenagers and instead of (5) ____ them to stop eating junk food, they gave them information about the food industry and advertising. The researchers (6) ____ the group how junk foods are prepared to encourage people to eat too much and how junk-food adverts are specifically designed to attract young people. The teenagers didn't like the fact that (7) ____ food industry was trying to control their behaviour. After this, (8) ____ they didn't know the researchers were studying their behaviour, they were more likely to choose healthy snacks and water than biscuits and fizzy drinks. The technique has been equally successful with adults too.

1 A few B much C little D amount of
2 A give B make C have D do
3 A who B whose C where D which
4 A up B in C around D off
5 A telling B tell C to tell D told
6 A have showed B are showing C showed D show
7 A a B the C an D –
8 A in spite of B despite C however D even though

51

The final part of the *Progress check* is a *Cumulative progress* exercise, which includes vocabulary and grammar items from any of the preceding units.

ONLINE WORKBOOK OWB

For students **PLUS** Gradebook for teachers

The *Optimise* Online Workbook includes all the print Workbook content in a fully-interactive digital format, which students can use for independent self-study.

The *Optimise* Online Workbook includes:

- Interactive Workbook activities
- Complete Workbook audio
- Automated marking for instant feedback
- Gradebook

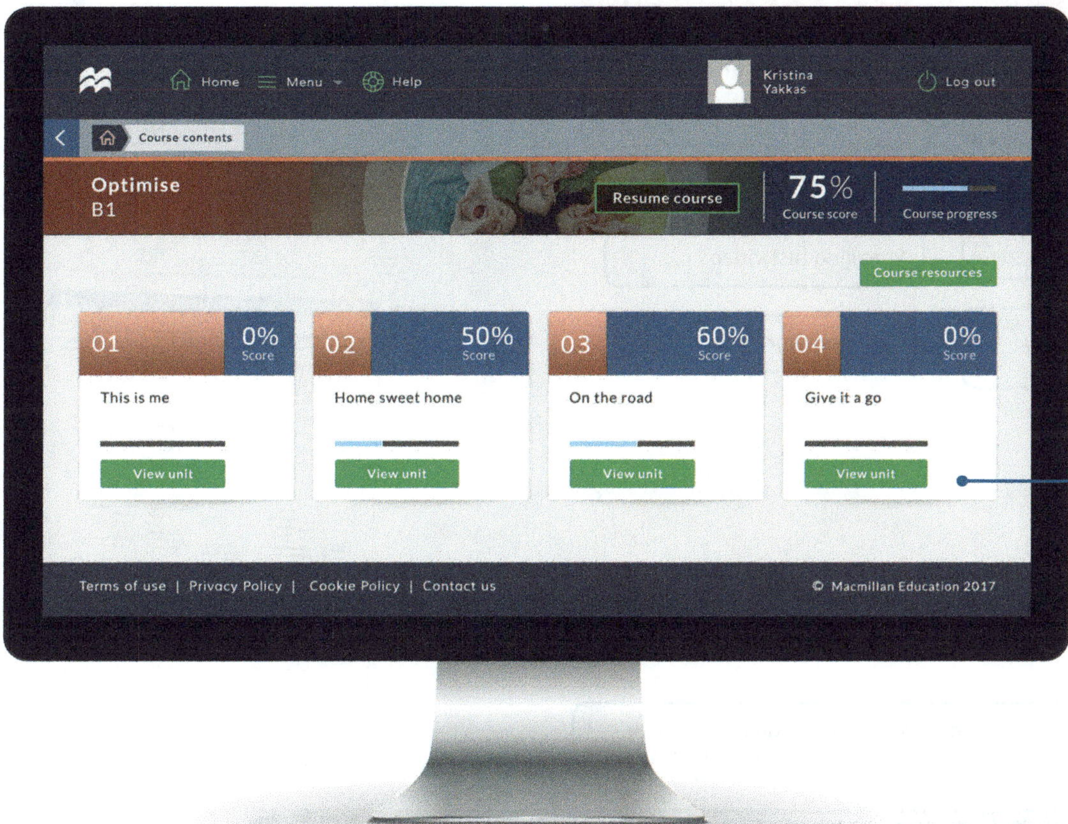

The automatic Gradebook facility will save you valuable marking time.

The Online Workbook enables you to manage multiple classes in a single location, and the content-locking facility gives you control over how you manage the tasks for your class.

Students have the chance to make multiple attempts at answering questions, enabling them to effectively consolidate their learning.

Scores are automatically collated and clearly displayed in the Gradebook, so it is easy to compare students and classes. Students' progress can be monitored at a glance, highlighting areas where they may require additional support.

The messaging and notification features allow you to correspond with your students, send homework reminders, and notify your classes when scores are available.

Detailed feedback on scores and progress creates a highly personalised self-study environment.

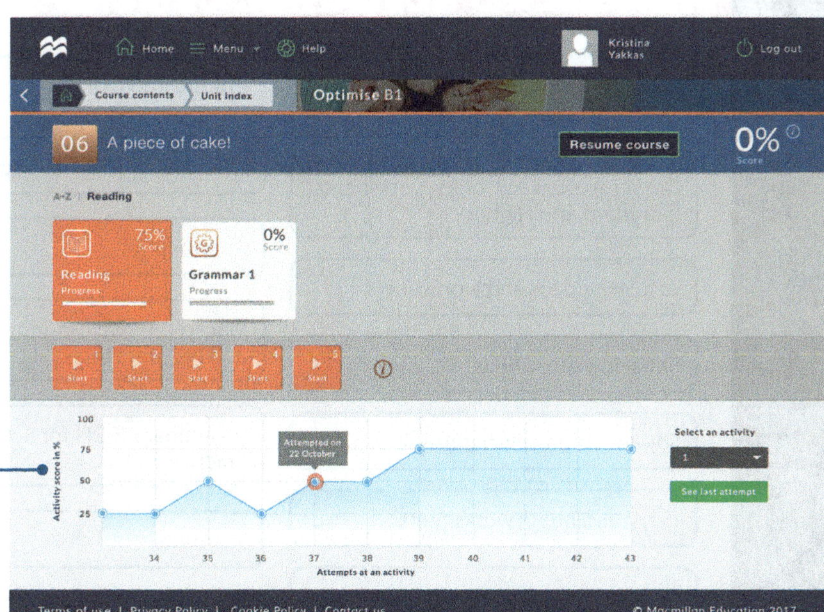

TEACHER'S AND STUDENT'S RESOURCE CENTRES

For teachers and students

The *Optimise* Resource Centres offer a huge bank of additional downloadable material and tests that have been designed to comprehensively support and enhance the core Student's Book and Workbook material.

For students, the Student's Resource Centre provides complementary materials to consolidate learning and encourage independent study.

STUDENT'S RESOURCE CENTRE

- *Optimise your grammar* worksheets (Standard and Higher)
- *Optimise your vocabulary* worksheets (Standard and Higher)
- *Talk2Me* videos and worksheets
- *Say it right* pronunciation worksheets
- Culture and CLIL worksheets
- Speaking test videos
- Class and Workbook audio

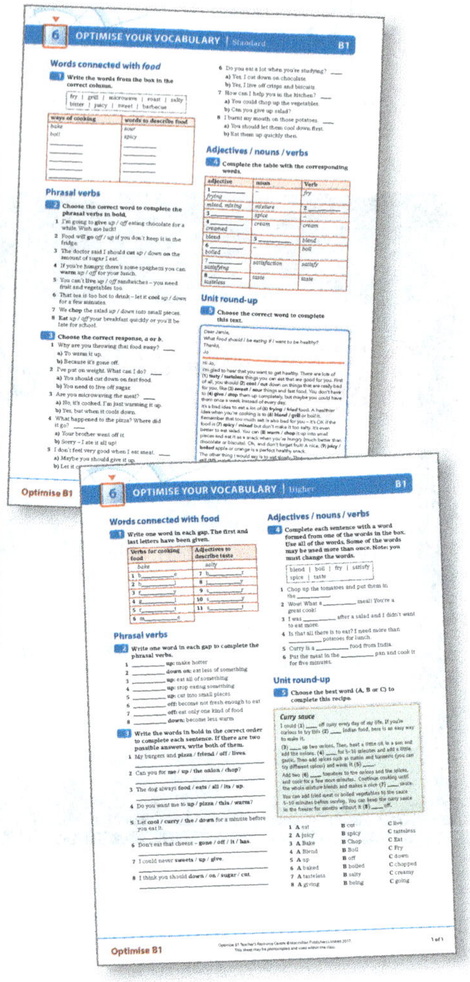

The Teacher's Resource Centre is your go-to place for resources to deliver dynamic lessons, assign for homework, and to support you in the classroom.

TEACHER'S RESOURCE CENTRE

- *Optimise your grammar* worksheets (Standard and Higher)
- *Optimise your vocabulary* worksheets (Standard and Higher)
- *Talk2Me* videos and worksheets
- Speaking test videos
- *Say it right* pronunciation worksheets
- *Everyday English* worksheets
- Grammar communication worksheets
- Culture and CLIL worksheets
- Class and Workbook audio
- Answer keys
- Placement and Diagnostic tests, Unit and Progress tests
- Preliminary (PET) for Schools Practice test
- Wordlists

TESTING MATERIALS

Complete testing package

Optimise provides an extensive range of testing materials, which can be used throughout the school year to assess your students' progress and to prepare them for exams.

Printable tests

Optimise offers a comprehensive range of printable tests, available on the Teacher's Resource Centre in PDF format.
All the *Optimise* tests correspond to the course level.
Tests are aligned closely to the CEFR and to competency levels for international and state exams.
Tests include:

- *Diagnostic* and *Placement tests*
- *Unit tests*, *Progress tests* and *End-of-year tests* (Standard and Higher)
- *Preliminary (PET) for Schools* practice tests:
  - an *Optimise Practice test* at the back of the Workbook
  - *Preliminary (PET) for Schools Practice test* on the Teacher's Resource Centre, which can be taken under test conditions.

Complete answer keys, audio and audioscripts are provided for all tests.

Test Generator

The *Optimise* Test Generator allows you to create customised tests from the pre-prepared Unit and Progress tests.

- Tests are aligned to CEFR levels.
- The content reflects Reading, Writing, Speaking and Listening tasks from international and state exams.
- The Test Generator comes with the option to save tests in progress and to preview them before printing.
- With Standard and Higher levels available, it also allows for maximum flexibility in choosing the test content.

Teacher support

PREPARING STUDENTS FOR EXAMS

Knowing your exam

- It's important that students become as familiar as possible with the different parts of the exam they are preparing for and understand what is required of them in each exam task.
- Carry out timed practice tests regularly with your students. As well as being excellent training, it's also an important way of highlighting specific areas for improvement.
- *Optimise* includes two Practice tests: one at the back of the Workbook and another on the Teacher's Resource Centre.
- After each test, draw up a class checklist of basic reminders or issues related to the exam.
- The *Optimise your exams* section at the back of the Student's Book provides a list of questions about different exam sections; this can be used for discussion and to create the class checklist.
- Many students associate exams with stress and panic, but if they are well prepared, students will generally feel more confident and that will show through in their performance.

Reading preparation

- It's important that students develop key strategies for dealing with a variety of question types. These include skimming, scanning, understanding implication, making deductions and locating information.
- Encourage students to refer to dictionaries or the *Grammar* and *Vocabulary references* at the back of the Student's Book. However, students also need to learn strategies for working independently, as reference material cannot be used in exams.
- Students should create an efficient system for recording all new vocabulary they learn. Encourage them to think about how they can record words and phrases in as much detail as possible.
- Remind students that spelling is important, especially in tasks that require students to complete sentences.
- Encourage students to read a variety of texts outside the classroom, e.g. online articles, graded readers, short stories and novels. This should help to increase their knowledge of vocabulary, grammatical structures and writing styles.
- Ask students to share ideas for recording and learning vocabulary, and to give short presentations about what they have read or learnt outside the classroom.

PREPARING STUDENTS FOR EXAMS

Writing preparation

- Writing in another language can be challenging for most young students, so make sure they choose tasks which are close to their interests or experiences whenever possible.
- Make sure students always read the question carefully and underline the key points. If they don't answer the question, or include all relevant information, they may lose marks.
- Remind students to think carefully about who they are writing for, and if the style required will be formal or informal.
- Encourage students to work in pairs or groups to discuss and brainstorm ideas in class and to make a clear plan before writing. This is especially useful for essays, where students may have to include some of their own ideas and opinions related to a topic.
- Timing is important in a real exam and practice under timed conditions in class is the best way to prepare students for writing tasks. If a longer piece of writing is to be completed, for example a story or an informal letter, students should spend some time planning, and leave some time at the end for re-reading and checking spelling and punctuation. They should avoid counting every word in the exam.
- Students need to write within the correct word limit. Under-writing may mean they haven't answered the whole question and overwriting can mean they have repeated ideas, included irrelevant information or not organised the piece of writing very well.
- Tell students to read each other's pieces of writing to give them ideas and develop their own writing further.

Listening preparation

- It's important that students develop key strategies for dealing with a variety of listening question types. These include selecting visual images while listening to short extracts; answering multiple-choice questions on a monologue or interview; completing a gap-fill while listening to a monologue or dialogue; answering true/false questions on a dialogue.
- Classroom discussions can help prior to doing a listening task. For example, ask students what they think the speakers will talk about, and if they will hear any specific information, such as times, names, dates and places.
- It can also be useful to vary the focus of a task in class before students attempt a set of exam questions. For example, students could listen once to give an overall summary of what was said on the audio, then listen again for specific information.
- When listening to monologues or interviews, students need to look carefully at multiple-choice options in questions and underline key words. This will help them to focus on the important points in a question and identify key words and phrases.
- When listening to longer extracts, encourage students to listen for the overall idea(s) first before they focus on the actual words and phrases. Make sure students listen to stressed or key words that have an important message, rather than focusing on every individual word.
- Encourage students to listen to audio material outside class, for example on English-language digital radio or TV stations. They also need to hear a variety of accents, styles and age groups.

Speaking preparation

- Some students may feel especially nervous about taking a speaking exam, so one way to reassure them is to make them familiar with the structure of the exam they are going to take.
- In some speaking exams, students are tested in pairs or groups of three and there are two examiners: one interlocutor, who speaks to the candidates and directs the test as well as giving marks, and one assessor, who marks the students on specific criteria.
- It is important for students to understand the different types of interaction that will take place. For example, students need to know when they will speak alone and when they will speak with their partner or with the interlocutor.
- All classroom activities that encourage students to discuss issues in pairs or groups will give them practice in skills they will need in an exam, such as starting and ending a discussion, asking for and giving opinions, agreeing and disagreeing, developing arguments, and giving examples and reasons for opinions.
- Remind students that they don't have to agree with each other when doing a speaking task, but that they should use appropriate language for disagreeing politely.
- When practising any activities for speaking, encourage students to speak clearly and to ask for clarification if they don't understand or aren't sure about something.
- Ask students to work in pairs or groups to create their own set of questions about topics, such as school and free time interests, family and friends, sports, travel, etc. They can compare questions and interview each other.
- Encourage students to expand on their ideas and give examples or reasons when speaking.
- Give students as much practice as possible in talking for the required amount of time for each part of the test. They can time each other in class in order to improve on this.
- Make sure students know there isn't a correct answer to a question and they don't need to be experts on a topic.
- When they are speaking with a partner, encourage them to help each other and be supportive. It's a good idea for students to practise different tasks with different classmates and also to spend time speaking to other students they feel comfortable with.

TEACHING MIXED-ABILITY CLASSES

Introduction

All classes have students of different abilities and with a range of different learning needs. The teacher's challenge is to engage the more advanced students at the same time as helping those who are finding lessons more difficult. Here are some practical tips to create a more inclusive classroom.

Group dynamics

Begin the whole class together with a lead-in activity to provide a sense of community and a foundation for the levelled tasks that will follow. Lead-in activities preview, present and practise language in a way that lends itself perfectly to whole-class, multi-level instruction. At the end of a lesson, always bring the class back together and assign a whole-class activity.

Group, pair and individual work

Vary the way students work in the class to address different levels and needs. Organise students to work in pairs, small groups and teams. It is less stressful for weaker students to work with other classmates because they have more time to think about tasks, and students can help and learn from each other.

In some schools, it may be possible to divide classes into two groups according to ability. The two groups can be given the same work to complete, or they can work on differentiated material.

Games and activities, such as brainstorming vocabulary, help to increase collaboration in the mixed-ability classroom. For example, ask students to work together to produce spidergrams as a way to help them remember topic vocabulary.

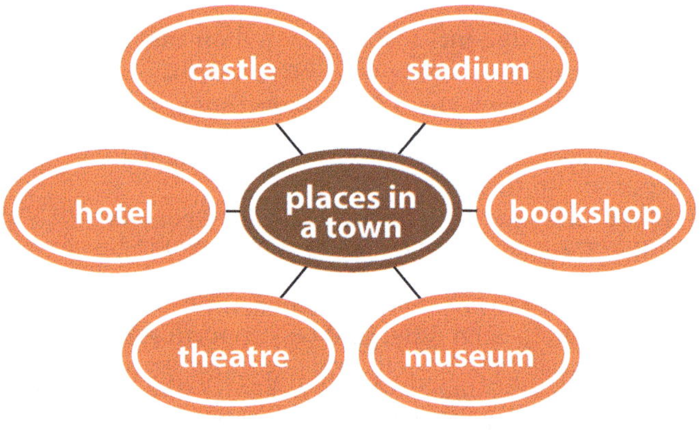

No matter what the level of the student, they all get better results through collaboration than they would have got by working on their own.

Pair work is usually successful in the mixed-ability classroom because it is easy to control and there is greater student participation. Depending on the task, decide how you organise your students into pairs: students with a similar level can work together at their own pace, or a stronger student can pair with a weaker student and help to support them. There are plenty of opportunities for pair work throughout *Optimise*.

Individual work allows for variations in speed and level. By giving a time limit rather than a quantity-of-work limit (e.g. *'Do as much as you can in three minutes.'* instead of, *'Do exercise 3.'*), students are able to work at their own pace.

Specific strategies for dealing with above-level students

- **Reading**

Set students more challenging work to keep the more advanced students motivated. For example, they could write their own comprehension questions to ask the class, select six new words from the reading text to write definitions for and learn, or create their own sentences or short texts using new vocabulary from the reading text.

Ask more advanced students to write or say a short summary of the text with their books closed.

- **Grammar and Vocabulary**

Ask stronger students to deduce the meaning of new words from the context and to elicit grammar rules by looking at the language in context.

Demand a higher level of fluency and accuracy from the students.

Encourage students to support weaker classmates by explaining the grammar point to them or by clarifying the meaning of a new vocabulary item.

- **Listening**

Ask students to summarise what they heard after listening to it the first time (as a whole class or in pairs).

Encourage students to write their own comprehension questions to ask the class.

- **Speaking**

Demand a higher level of fluency and accuracy and ask students to justify and defend their opinions.

Practise paraphrasing and brainstorm other phrases to use in the functional language.

Encourage students to write their own dialogues to act out in pairs.

- **Writing**

Indicate where something could be said in a more interesting or more complex way, and give creative tasks that students can do at their level.

Encourage peer correction by asking them to look at each other's work and suggest improvements. However, where more advanced students are reviewing work from below-level students, always make sure they are sensitive and constructive in their advice.

TEACHING MIXED-ABILITY CLASSES

Specific strategies for dealing with below-level students

- **General classroom organisation**

Make sure weaker students don't sit at the back, where it's more difficult for you to make eye contact with them.

Give clear instructions and check students have understood the task before they begin. For more complex tasks, ask stronger students to do an example of the task to check understanding.

- **Reading**

Ask weaker students easier questions, alternating with harder questions for stronger students.

Simplify multiple-choice tasks by reducing the number of options. Then gradually increase to exam level.

- **Grammar and Vocabulary**

Simplify gap-fill tasks by introducing optional answers, so students can identify the correct answer rather than having to produce it.

Be selective in your error correction and praise students for what they have managed to do, regardless of what others have produced.

Use homework to address weaknesses and consolidate classwork by using the mixed-ability Grammar and Vocabulary worksheets on the Teacher's Resource Centre.

- **Listening**

Pause the audio regularly to check understanding and explain if anything remains unclear. For more difficult texts, provide audioscripts after the first two listenings.

- **Speaking**

Provide useful phrases and model answers for less-able students to use as a basis for their answers.

- **Writing**

Additional model answers can assist students with their writing tasks. For students who need more support, provide a gapped or jumbled model answer for them to complete or put in order instead of asking them to write a text from scratch.

Mixed-ability features in *Optimise*

The **Mixed-ability** features in the *Optimise* Teacher's Book help to engage different groups of students using the same class material as the starting point, but with multi-level instruction. This way, you avoid increased preparation time, and the student group can still work together for most of the class.

As well as the **Mixed-ability** features in the *Optimise* Teacher's Book, the **Optional extension** and **Fast finishers** boxes also offer teachers a range of suggestions for ways to differentiate activities for stronger students.

Mixed ability

Break the text into chunks and give less confident students the option of only reading some of the text and answering fewer questions. If stronger students finish early, ask them to write a short summary of the text.

Optional extension

In pairs, students tell each other what they think they'd like to do as a job one day. They then write a list of tips for each other using *must*, *mustn't*, *have to*, *need to*, *don't have to*, *should*, *ought to*, *may*, *might*, *could*. Students then tell their partner and see if he/she agrees with their advice.

Fast finishers

Ask students who finish early to say which features they would expect to see in the two text types they didn't need (*a magazine advert* and *a reminder*). When everyone has finished this activity, students could read out their answers to the rest of the class.

Suggested answers

A magazine advert – colourful design, bright colours, good slogan, large font size

A reminder – short text, maybe capital letters, imperative form, instructions

The *Optimise* Teacher's Resource Centre provides additional Grammar and Vocabulary worksheets in addition to the Unit and Progress tests, all available at two levels (Standard and Higher).

The *Optimise* Test Generator also allows teachers to custom-build their own tests according to their students' needs.

Encourage students to use the Online Workbook. Students get immediate feedback on their work and they can do the tasks as many times as necessary in order to get them correct. It's perfect for students of all abilities.

TEACHING TIPS

Here are some useful teaching tips for you to refer to throughout the school year.

Encouraging language development

Optimise B1, positioned at CEFR level B1, provides your students with an excellent opportunity to consolidate and build on the language they have learnt up to this point. The material is rich with new vocabulary and presents comprehensive coverage of a full range of grammar structures. Lessons include a wide range of strategies that you can use to help your students develop their language. Exploiting all this material in as many ways as possible will help to consolidate the language and make students comfortable and confident about using it in other contexts.

Useful expressions

One important aspect of language development which you can help your students focus on at this level is learning expressions. Expressions are high-frequency, multi-word phrases that function as a unit. Very often, expressions are pronounced as if they were one word. Fixed expressions, such as expressions of opinion, perform specific functions and they can't always be defined by looking them up in a dictionary as individual words. Such expressions are important in helping students improve their fluency. If they can learn these fixed expressions, students can develop language competency by transferring them to a variety of different contexts.

It is often the case that students learn these expressions, use them in the class and then go back to using just one expression they were already familiar with. Point out to students they can gain more points in an oral exam if they use a variety of expressions.

Developing accuracy and fluency in speaking

Accuracy is the ability to produce correct sentences with correct grammar and vocabulary. Fluency is the ability to read, speak or write easily, smoothly and with the correct intonation. The accuracy/fluency question depends on the purpose of the activity students are doing in the class. Controlled and semi-controlled speaking practice such as drills and information exchanges are working on accuracy. More open discussion should focus on fluency.

In general, try not to correct speaking too often in class as it interrupts the student's train of thought and can undermine their confidence. It's important to encourage students to talk and to keep talking. It's useful to note down errors while students are speaking then to take a few minutes at the end of class for a quick feedback session.

Memory and learning

Students are far more likely to remember words that they have analysed or focused on in some way than words they have learnt in isolation. If they have learnt the word in context and have fully understood it, rather than just learning it based upon a definition, it is much easier for students to remember the word in the long-term. Ask your students how they learn words best – do they need to hear them, see them written down or write them down themselves? Some students memorise vocabulary by associating new words with ideas or anecdotes. Good learners create mnemonic devices such as short phrases, tunes or poems to support their learning. In order to internalise vocabulary, students should also review vocabulary regularly. For strong lexical ability, students need to study vocabulary in context and that is best done by reading in English. Try to encourage your students to do this as much as possible. You could invite them to bring English books and magazines to class for group discussion or presentations. When your students come across a new word, encourage them to look at its place in the sentence, and to look at the words that appear either side of it. Remind them to think about the context and who the text is written for, and to look out for word patterns. They should always try to deduce meaning, but where they can't, point out that it's fine to use a dictionary as a tool for vocabulary building.

Teacher-talking time

As a teacher, you're always aware of how much time you spend speaking during the lesson. This is especially important in speaking lessons, where the key purpose is to encourage students to speak. That's not to say your speech isn't invaluable in providing models for pronunciation, functional language and appropriate discourse. But sometimes a large amount of teacher-talking time can slow the pace of a lesson and students can lose concentration and become bored or disinterested.

Some useful strategies to avoid this are:

- Wait for an answer when you ask a question. Students need 'thinking' time.
- Ask open-ended questions (e.g. *Wh-* questions) to encourage students to give longer answers, e.g. *What did you do last weekend?* instead of *Did you have a good weekend?*
- Vary the way students get feedback: they can check activities in pairs, for example.
- Encourage students to give explanations instead of giving them yourself.
- Present students with clear examples and guided questions so that they do not need to be 'told'. Guided discovery is a better and more rewarding way for students to learn.
- A useful guideline is to limit your talking to 30% of class time and no more than ten minutes at a time.

TEACHING TIPS

Pairwork

Pairwork is another opportunity for students to practise their speaking skills. Pairwork activities enable all students to have much more speaking time than if each student had an individual turn at speaking. When students are working in pairs, it also provides teachers with a chance to walk round and listen, and to give advice to students in a more discreet and personal way, rather than in front of the whole class.

If you ask students to work in pairs, they are likely to pair up with their friends or the person they sit nearest. It's a good idea to put students into 'new' pairs from time to time, so they can work with classmates of different abilities and with different approaches.

Certain speaking skills are necessary when working with another person, so it's useful to teach phrases that help students interrupt politely (*Yes, I agree, but … / May I … So you think …*, etc.).

Another idea to put students at their ease when they're speaking is to play some quiet music in the background. This helps students feel less self-conscious.

Personalisation

Students are more likely to want to speak when they are speaking about something they personally know about, are interested in or have experienced. Personalisation is important in learning a second language as it makes language more meaningful and therefore memorable to learners. There are plenty of personalisation opportunities throughout *Optimise*. Where possible, extend and adapt other activities to give students even more speaking opportunities.

Developing writing skills

Students are required to produce different genres of writing whilst preparing for exams. Nevertheless, the basic steps for all writing tasks are the same. This is reinforced by the approach used throughout *Optimise* – ***Plan, Write, Check***.

There are some extra points to keep in mind when helping students with writing tasks:

Before beginning to write, students need to consider the purpose of the text and who the text is for, as both things will affect the tone (*formal or informal*).

During the ***Plan*** phase, students should brainstorm ideas (they can make lists, mind maps, or use question words as prompts: *Why? What? Where? When? How? Who?*). Students then need to choose and order their final ideas. It is important to encourage students to spend time on this stage as it makes the writing task easier.

Next is the ***Write*** phrase. Students write a first draft as quickly as they can, including all the main points from the brainstorming phase. They should make sure they include all required information and that they fully answer the question.

The final stage is the ***Check*** phase, where students need to look closely at spelling, grammar, punctuation and word choice. They can use the *Optimise* **Checklist** for this.

Classroom management

It can be particularly challenging with larger class groups to keep all students engaged in the lesson.

Here are some ideas to consider:

- Move around and teach the class from different points in the classroom to give the students the feeling of being in the middle of the 'action' rather than an observer. Moving around the class makes the room feel smaller and encourages student involvement. It also means students who are furthest away from the front of the classroom can feel more involved.
- Check understanding regularly, and give students feedback to clarify points they haven't understood.
- Set up some class routines (weekly homework assignments of 30 minutes, class discussions every Friday, etc.). Where possible, involve students in deciding what these routines should be.
- Find ways to link what students have learnt to the exam, so they can clearly see their progress and the fact that they are achieving a common goal.
- Give regular short tests and dictations.
- Change the pace of the lesson from time to time and change delivery methods (speaking, using IWB, playing video, etc.)
- Start lessons by writing a lesson outline on the board so students know what to expect.
- Give fast finishers something to do (see the unit teaching notes for suggestions) or direct them to the Workbook.

Games

As a useful change of pace, and sometimes to refocus students, games can be an excellent teaching tool. Students generally enjoy games and tend to remember more as a result. Vocabulary games are helpful for practising and reviewing language. Always make the 'rules' clear, and check understanding before playing the game. For example, after explaining what to do, ask the students to explain the game back to you. Or demonstrate the game by playing it yourself with a few students while the others watch.

When planning games you need to consider what your aims and objectives are. Games are particularly useful for reviewing work from the previous lesson, checking what students know before teaching a new language item, practising a new language item you have just presented, warming up at the beginning of the lesson or filling in at the end of a lesson. There are a variety of games suggested throughout the *Optimise* teaching notes.

LISTENING	SPEAKING	LANGUAGE IN USE	WRITING
Understanding the situation Multiple choice (extracts)	Talking about yourself Interview Talk2Me	Identifying phrasal verbs Multiple choice cloze	Starting and ending a letter/an email A letter / An email
Predicting Multiple choice	Saying where things are Photo task Talk2Me	Result clauses Sentence transformation	Asking questions A short message
Listening for feelings and attitude True/false	Making suggestions Collaborative task Talk2Me	Using particles to create phrasal verbs Open cloze	Choosing positive and negative points A review
Recognising similar meanings Multiple choice	Explaining likes and dislikes Discussion Talk2Me	Connectors of contrast Sentence transformation	Describing personal experience A short message
Understanding agreement and disagreement True/false	Talking about habits Interview Talk2Me	Words formed from verbs Word formation	Using narrative tenses A story
Recognising similar meaning Gap fill	Describing situations and actions Photo task Talk2Me	Collocations Multiple choice cloze	Making suggestions A letter / An email
Understanding relevant information Multiple choice (extracts)	Asking questions Discussion Talk2Me	Nouns connected with people Word formation	Using direct speech A story
Predicting missing information Gap fill	Discussing alternatives Collaborative task Talk2Me	*-ing* and infinitives Sentence transformation	Writing descriptions A story
Listening for attitude and opinion Multiple choice	Talking about other people Interview Talk2Me	Verbs with similar meaning Multiple-choice cloze	Giving opinions A short message
Selecting relevant information Gap fill	Listening and responding Discussion Talk2Me	*wish* and *if only* Open cloze	Describing how to do something An article
Understanding implication Multiple choice (extracts)	Expressing uncertainty Photo task Talk2Me	Spelling of irregular forms Word formation	Using given information A short message
Thinking logically True/false/not stated	Reaching a decision Collaborative task Talk2Me	Auxiliary verbs Open cloze	Giving reasons An essay

▶ SPEAKING / ▶ SPEAKING TEST VIDEO p 144–147

Student's Resource Centre

- *Talk2Me* videos
- Speaking test videos
- *Optimise your grammar* worksheets
- *Optimise your vocabulary* worksheets
- *Say it right* pronunciation worksheets
- Culture and CLIL worksheets
- Class and Workbook audio

1 This is me

UNIT AIMS

Exam preparation in Unit 1:

- skim a magazine interview for general meaning
- listen to understand the situation in conversations
- talk about yourself
- identify phrasal verbs and use them in a multiple-choice cloze text
- use phrases to start and end an email or letter

TEACHER'S PRESENTATION KIT

- *Talk2Me* videos
- Speaking test videos
- Class and Workbook audio
- Workbook pages and answer key

UNIT OVERVIEW

Student's Book / Digital Student's Book SB		Workbook / Online Workbook OWB
LESSON / EXAM TASK	EXAM SKILLS / LANGUAGE FOCUS	CONSOLIDATION
Reading **Multiple choice**	Skimming A magazine interview	Workbook, pp 4–5, Exercises 1, 2, 3 Unit 1, Reading, Exercises 1, 2, 3
Grammar 1	Present simple, present continuous, stative verbs	Workbook, p 6, Exercises 1, 2 Unit 1, Grammar 1, Exercises 1, 2
Vocabulary	Words connected with *personality* Nouns with *-ity / -ness* Collocations with adjectives	Workbook, pp 6–7, Exercises 1, 2 Unit 1, Vocabulary, Exercises 1, 2
Listening **Multiple choice (extracts)**	Listening to understand the situation	Workbook, p 8, Exercises 1, 2, 3 Unit 1, Listening, Exercises 1, 2, 3
Grammar 2	Quantifiers	Workbook, p 7, Exercises 1, 2, 3 Unit 1, Grammar 2, Exercises 1, 2, 3
Speaking **Interview**	Talking about yourself	Workbook, pp 8–9, Exercises 1, 2, 3 Unit 1, Speaking, Exercises 1, 2, 3
Language in Use **Multiple-choice cloze**	Phrasal verbs	Workbook, p 9, Exercises 1, 2, 3, 4 Unit 1, Language in Use, Exercises 1, 2, 3, 4
Writing **A letter / An email**	Starting and ending a letter / an email	Workbook, p 10, Exercises 1, 2, 3, 4 Unit 1, Writing, Exercises 1, 2, 3, 4
		Workbook, p 11, Progress check and Cumulative progress Progress check and Cumulative progress

Additional material

PRESENTATION KIT	TEACHER'S/STUDENT'S RESOURCE CENTRE RC	TEST GENERATOR
Talk2Me video *Well, she's …*	**Unit 1 worksheets:** *Optimise your grammar* (Standard and Higher), *Optimise your vocabulary* (Standard and Higher), *Talk2Me* video, *Say it right* **Units 1–2 worksheets:** CLIL, Culture, Everyday English (TRC only), Grammar communication (TRC only)	Unit Test 1 (Standard and Higher)

READING

Multiple choice | A magazine interview

→ Student's Book, pages 4–5

Lesson aims

- Improve skimming skills
- Practise a multiple-choice exam task

Lead-in

Elicit the meaning of the unit title ***This is me*** and ask students in open class what they think the lesson is going to be about (*personal identity*). Then ask them why they think the teenagers in the photo are touching hands (*to signify their friendship*).

1 In pairs or as a group, students complete the exercise. Check students know the meaning of *freckles* /ˈfrek(ə)lz/ (small brown spots on your skin). Elicit answers from around the class.

Suggested answers

Hair and facial hair: beard, blond(e), light-haired, curly/long/short/straight/wavy hair

Face and complexion: brown/green eyes, glasses, light/dark-skinned, smiley

Height and build: athletic, slim, plump, fat, overweight, thin

Appearance and personality: trendy, bright, cheeky, funny, generous, hardworking, honest, kind, likeable, lively, popular, quiet, shy, smart, sociable, trustworthy, untidy

Language note

Adjectives

Remind students that the basic position for adjectives is before the noun and that they are never plural.

Many adjectives describe qualities that can exist in different degrees, such as size, height and weight. These adjectives are often called gradable adjectives because they can be used in comparative and superlative forms or with grading adjectives, such as *very*, *a little*, *a bit*, to show that a person or a thing has more or less of a particular quality.

EXAM SKILL

Skimming

Ask students to read the tips.

- Remind students that in reading exams, they will need to use different types of reading techniques. Explain that skimming is a technique we use when we read a magazine article to check whether it is something we want to read. When we skim a text, we read faster than when we read each word; we do not read everything, so this increases our reading speed.
- Point out key skimming techniques: reading the title and the introduction and each paragraph very quickly to get an overall understanding before they read the comprehension questions. Remind students to look at any illustrations or photos to give them clues about the text.
- Students will practise this technique in Exercise 3.

2 Ask students to complete the exercise. They could then tell their partner the words and phrases, and say why they chose them.

Answers

Students' own answers

3 Focus students' attention on the photos and title, and elicit what they think the article is going to be about. Ask them to complete the exercise. Time this activity (three minutes) and give updates, e.g. *One minute to go … Only 30 seconds left*, to encourage them to read quickly. Check answers in open class and elicit what techniques students used to help them quickly find the answers.

Answers

1 F **2** T **3** T **4** T **5** F **6** F

OPTIMISE YOUR EXAM

Multiple choice

Ask students to read the tips.

- Remind students that sometimes a text may overtly state the writer's purpose, but often they will have to choose an option (A, B, C or D) based on their informed impression. Question 4 in the exam task will allow them to practise this technique.
- Point out that the questions always follow the order of the text.
- Remind them that they should try not to leave any questions unanswered.

▼ Exam task

4 1.01 **Note: The reading text is also available on the audio CD. You may want to have students listen and read the text before doing the exam task.**

Ask students to complete the exercise. Have them compare in pairs before you check answers in open class. Elicit evidence for the answers.

Answers

1 D (*I listen to the description of the criminal and turn the description into a picture … No, I also draw historical figures.*)

2 A (*When a witness says that a person wears glasses, for example, we can bring up on screen different styles of glasses …*)

3 C (*We often work with people who are upset, so we help them remember clearly and give us enough detail.*)

4 D (*It's really useful, and there are some great computer programs we can use … Faces obviously change as we get older.*)

Fast finishers

Ask students to note down if they think being a forensic artist is an interesting job and give reasons why or why not. When all the students have finished the activity, discuss in open class.

Cultural note

Forensic artists can create a facial approximation in a number of ways which include 2D (drawing), 3D (sculpture) and computerised technology. They need to maintain accurate case records and they may need to testify in court. There are very few full-time forensic artist jobs.

5 Ask students to complete the exercise individually. Check their answers.

Answers

1 bring, up **2** witness **3** successful **4** expert **5** turn, into **6** get older **7** fascinating **8** upset

Fast finishers

Students who complete the task early can think of antonyms and synonyms for the words and expressions in Exercise 5.

THINK | RESEARCH | CULTURE | LEARN | ME

Students complete the task in class or for homework. In pairs or groups, they could read out their descriptions for others to comment on and ask follow-up questions.

Extra support

Elicit words and expressions for describing how people's appearance can change over the years, e.g. *bald, lines, dyed hair*. Write them on the board for students to refer to in this activity.

Optional extension 1.01

Play the recorded reading text and ask students to underline all the adjectives. Elicit their answers.

Answers

forensic, simple, successful, historical, ancient, fascinating, useful, great, different, good, upset, curly, wavy, better, older, interesting, shy, lively, sociable

Homework

OWB

Assign students Reading exercises 1, 2 and 3 on pages 4–5 of their Workbook.

GRAMMAR 1

Present simple, present continuous, stative verbs

→ Student's Book, page 6 SB

Lesson aims

- Review and practise the correct usage of the present simple and continuous
- Learn the difference between stative and action verbs

Lead-in

Write these four categories on the board and ask students to add as many verbs as they can to each category: *Verbs of feeling (emotion), Verbs of thinking, Verbs of the senses, Verbs of possession*. Give a three-minute time limit.

In a less confident class, write these verbs on the board for students to categorise and elicit an example for each category: *prefer, like, mind, sounds, know, own, mean, hear, think, looks, see, love, hate, have, understand.*

Suggested answers

Verbs of feeling (emotion), e.g. *love, like, hate, mind*

Verbs of thinking, e.g. *know, think, understand, prefer, mean*

Verbs of the senses, e.g. *sounds, looks, see, hear*

Verbs of possession, e.g. *have, own*

Grammar in context

Ask students to complete the task. Refer them to the information in the *Remember* box if they aren't sure. Check answers in open class.

Remind students that they can find more information in the Grammar reference, Unit 1, page 148. This should be the first source they refer to when they have any questions or doubts.

Answers

1 d **2** a **3** e **4** c **5** b

Language note

The emphatic form is not a tense but is logically included in this section. It uses *do/does* or *did* with the base form of the verb. It is used to give greater emphasis to the idea expressed by the verb and is often used in conversation, for example when one speaker is contradicting another: *'I don't think he works very hard.' 'Well, I think he* ***does*** *work hard.'*

Emphatic forms are used only in the present and past tense. In spoken English, the auxiliary is usually pronounced with heavier stress than usual.

Remind students that we usually make questions in the present simple by adding the auxiliary *do* or *does* (exceptions are the verb *to be* and modal verbs such as *can*). In short answers we repeat the auxiliary, e.g. *Does she draw? Yes, she* ***does*** */ No, she* ***doesn't***. Remind students of intonation patterns in *Yes/No* questions.

Stative verbs generally fall into four groups: verbs of feeling, verbs of thinking, verbs of the senses, verbs of possession.

Optional extension

In pairs, students make sentences similar to the examples for each point in the *Remember* box. Ask students to read out their sentences in open class. If appropriate, ask students to come up and write them on the board and discuss as a class if they are correct. Encourage them to make questions and negative sentences from their examples.

1 Ask students to complete the exercise. Check their answers.

Answers

1 lives (present simple for general facts)
2 we're (present simple for general facts)
3 has (present simple – state)
4 usually wears (present simple – habits and routines)
5 Emma's smiling (present continuous – descriptions of pictures)
6 always seems (present simple – state)
7 doesn't speak (present simple – habits and routines)
8 Emma's shopping (present continuous – actions happening now)

2 Ask students to complete the exercise. Check answers in open class.

Answers

1 doesn't look **2** isn't **3** doesn't wear [generally] / isn't wearing [in the picture] **4** doesn't smile **5** often seems **6** does have **7** often tells **8** 's wearing **9** loves **10** almost always arrives **11** doesn't live **12** is watching / 's watching

3 Ask students to complete the exercise. Have them compare in pairs before you check answers in open class.

Answers

1 Who has (got) long hair?
2 Is Emma smiling in the photo?
3 Do either of them seem shy?
4 Does Paulina usually ride a bike to school?
5 Students' own answers

4 In pairs, students complete the exercise. In a less confident class, model an example dialogue in open class.

Answers

Students' own answers

Homework OWB

Assign students Grammar 1 exercises 1 and 2 on page 6 of their Workbook.

VOCABULARY

Topic vocabulary | Word formation | Collocations

→ Student's Book, page 7 SB

Lesson aims

Understand the correct usage of:

- words connected with *personality*
- nouns ending in *-ity* and *-ness*
- adjective collocations

Lead-in

Write these phrases on the board or dictate them: *is honest, is a good listener, does what I say, wears nice clothes, cheers you up when you're sad, is funny, is kind, has lots of money, does the right thing, only talks to me, gives me presents, cares about other people.*

In pairs, students discuss which qualities are most important to them in a friend. Elicit answers from different students around the class.

Words connected with *personality*

1 1.02 Ask students to complete the exercise. Play the audio for them to listen and check their answers.

Answers/Audioscript

1 Someone who is *negative* is not enthusiastic about something.
2 Someone who is *creative* is imaginative, artistic and talented.
3 Someone who is *curious* wants to find out and learn about things.
4 Someone who is *unreliable* doesn't do what they say they will.
5 Someone who is *dependable* is someone you can trust and rely on.
6 Someone who is *friendly* is pleasant and helps other people.
7 Someone who is *popular* is liked by lots of people.
8 Someone who is *generous* gives a lot of their time to people.
9 Someone who is *polite* behaves in a very nice way.
10 Someone who is *serious* is very careful and doesn't laugh a lot.
11 Someone who is *shy* is nervous and embarrassed around people.

2 In pairs or small groups, students complete the exercise. Elicit answers in open class.

Suggested answers

1 Someone who is *friendly* is pleasant, warm, helpful and kind. Someone who is *popular* is liked by lots of other people.
2 Someone who is *generous* gives things (e.g. help, money, gifts, etc.) to other people. Someone who is *polite* is respectful, doesn't say rude things and has good manners.
3 Someone who is *serious* doesn't laugh or smile much. Someone who is *shy* is quiet, nervous, not confident and uncomfortable with other people.

Refer students to the Vocabulary reference, page 162, for more information on topic vocabulary.

Nouns with *-ity / -ness*

3 1.03 Ask students to complete the exercise. Elicit answers in open class. Then play the audio for them to listen and check their answers.

Answers/Audioscript

1 friend, friendship, friendliness **2** politeness **3** seriousness **4** shyness

Language note

The suffix *-ship* is used to create abstract nouns denoting different kinds of relationships. It indicates a state or condition (e.g. *citizenship, leadership, membership*).

The suffix *-ness* is one of a number of noun suffixes. It is used to make nouns from adjectives, although not every adjective can be modified in this way. Highlight the spelling change to adjectives that end in *-y* with more than one syllable, e.g. *ready – readiness, happy – happiness.*

The suffix *-ity* means state or quality.

Note that *personal – personality* is different from the other words as the meaning of the noun is completely different to that of the adjective. *Personal* = used about your own feelings or beliefs; *personality* = the part of you that makes you behave in a particular way, e.g. *friendly, shy,* etc.

SAY IT RIGHT

/ə/ TRC

For the *Say it right* pronunciation activity and instructions, go to the Teacher's Resource Centre.

4 Ask students to complete the exercise. Have them check in pairs before you elicit answers in open class.

Answers

1 negativity **2** shyness **3** personality **4** friendship **5** generosity **6** curiosity

Refer students to the Vocabulary reference, page 162, for more information on word formation.

Collocations with adjectives

5 1.04 Remind students what collocations are before they do the activity (a combination of words that are frequently used together and they 'sound right' to native speakers). In this exercise, students develop their intuition for how words work together.

Ask students to complete the exercise. Play the audio for them to listen and check their answers.

Answers/Audioscript

1 (e) big trouble **2** (d) fast asleep **3** (f) feel small **4** (a) wide awake **5** (c) long time **6** (b) deep voice

6 Ask students to complete the exercise. Check answers in open class and ask what mistakes Leah made. (*Leah arrived late and then she fell asleep.*)

Answers

1 big trouble **2** wide awake **3** fast asleep **4** deep voice **5** feel small **6** long time

Fast finishers

Students make a list of babysitting tips. When you have checked the answers for Exercise 6, ask students to share their ideas in open class. Ask them if they have ever done any babysitting and, if so, to describe their experiences. Try and start a discussion on the key characteristics babysitters need to have.

Refer students to the Vocabulary reference, page 162, for more information on collocations.

THINK | RESEARCH | CULTURE | LEARN | ME

In pairs or small groups, students complete the task. Elicit answers in open class.

Homework

OWB

Assign students Vocabulary exercises 1 and 2 on pages 6–7 of their Workbook.

LISTENING
Multiple choice (extracts)

→ Student's Book, page 8 SB

Lesson aims

- Learn how to understand a situation in a conversation
- Practise a multiple-choice (extracts) exam task

Lead-in

Write these questions on the board:

What are good topics of conversation when you meet someone for the first time?

How can you make a good first impression?

In pairs, students discuss the questions. Elicit answers in open class and discuss any differences.

Suggested answers

Usual topics of initial conversation (small talk) are free time, hobbies, school/work, weather, family, nationality.

Ways to make a good first impression include being on time, a warm smile, being open and confident, appropriate dress.

1 In pairs or as a group, students complete the exercise. Elicit ideas from the class and accept all sensible suggestions.

Suggested answers

a new student in class, a game show, a radio interview, joining a sports team, at a party, in a lecture/meeting, on holiday, meeting your friend's family, during your homestay on a language study trip

EXAM SKILL

Understanding the situation

Ask students to read the tips.

- Students should first listen for a general understanding (top-down listening). This refers to the use of background knowledge in helping to understand the meaning of the message. Background knowledge consists of the situation and topic. Once the topic has been established, students can use any topic vocabulary they know to help them 'match' what they are listening to to their expectations so they get a general picture. Encourage students to try to answer questions the first time they hear the recording and then use the second time to check their work and fill in any missing answers.

2 1.05 Play the track for students to listen and complete the exercise. Have them compare in pairs before you check answers in open class. Accept all sensible suggestions and encourage students to give reasons for their answers.

Answers

Situation 1: a teacher and students, in a classroom, a new student called Jared (*key words: term, everyone*)

Situation 2: at a party (*music in background*)

Situation 3: on a game/quiz show (*quiz show jingle – key words: 'Question The Answers', show, win, contestant*)

Situation 4: in radio/TV interview / discussion programme (*show jingle – key word: studio*)

OPTIMISE YOUR EXAM

Multiple choice (extracts)

Ask students to read the tips.

- In multiple-choice tasks, students can expect to listen to a wide range of spoken materials, in both informal and neutral settings, on a range of everyday topics. Recorded materials may include announcements, interviews and discussions about everyday life.
- Point out that predicting words and ideas from looking at the pictures can help students identify relevant points in a listening exam.
- The incorrect options are usually mentioned in some way in the recording, but as distractors. It can help if students notice similarities in two of the options because the correct answer is normally between those two.
- Remind students to be careful if they hear words like *but* or *however*. This often means that the speaker is going to qualify a previous statement.

Exam task

3 1.06 Play the track for students to listen and complete the exercise. Remind them that they have to choose the correct picture and that they can listen to the audio twice.

Don't check answers at this stage as students will listen again to check in Exercise 4.

4 1.06 Play the track again for students to check their answers. In open class, discuss the specific clues that helped them choose their answers.

Answers

1 B (*They're both great jobs, but I want to be a dancer when I'm older.*)

2 A (Boy: *A drink of something? Maybe some lemonade?* Girl: *That's sounds nice, thanks.*)

3 C (*… but right now I've got a couple of mice at home called Charlie and Benny and they keep me company.*)

4 B (*Geography, actually.*)

Extra support

Play the track again for students to note down the distracting information in the incorrect options for each question. This is useful in helping students understand how examiners set traps for listeners. Even if students think they know the answer to a question, they should also think about why the other answers are not correct. This will help them build good listening habits and become more aware of how distractors work in listening exams.

Answers

1 My mum's a computer programmer and my dad's a nurse.

2 Boy: Can I get you something to eat? There's some great pizza in the kitchen.
Girl: I'm fine. I'm not hungry, thanks.
Boy: Do you fancy dancing?
Girl: I don't think so, thanks. I'll just stay here.

3 My dream is to have a farm one day with lots of horses in the fields, and I love cats and rabbits, of course – my brother's got several –

4 Presenter: In some ways, Josephine's just a normal university student studying – what is it? Maths? / … a physics book about space and time and the wonders of the universe …

THINK | **RESEARCH** | CULTURE | LEARN | ME

Ask students to complete the task. In a less confident class, elicit questions students can ask and write them on the board for students to refer to. You could get them to walk around and survey as many other students as they can. Ask them to prepare themselves for the survey with a pencil and their Student's Book to lean on while they are writing answers. When they have finished, students write up their results and then present them to the class.

Homework

Assign students Listening exercises 1, 2 and 3 on page 8 of their Workbook. OWB

GRAMMAR 2
Quantifiers

→ Student's Book, page 9 SB

Lesson aims

- Learn to identify quantifiers for talking about numbers and amounts
- Practise using quantifiers

Lead-in

Write the phrases from this dialogue in a jumbled order on the board:

Hi, I'm Mike.
Nice to meet you. I'm Samantha.
Can I get you something to eat?
I'm fine. I'm not hungry, thanks.
Do you fancy dancing?
I don't think so, thanks. I'll just stay here.
A drink of something?
That's sounds nice, thanks.
I'll be right back!

In pairs, students order the dialogue. Elicit answers from different students around the class. Ask students to act out the dialogue in pairs.

Grammar in context

Ask students to complete the task. Check their answers and ask them to read more about quantifiers in the *Remember* box.

Remind students that they can find more information in the Grammar reference, Unit 1, page 148.

Answers

1 yes
2 no (*most of the* would be correct)
3 no (*each of the questions* would be correct)
4 no (*not all listeners* would be correct)

Language note

Quantifiers

If we are talking about a specific group of people or things, we can use *of the …*, e.g. *All of the children went to university.* (= *all of the children in the class/family*, etc.).

The *of* is often dropped after *both of*, e.g. *She has eaten **both** apples. / She has eaten **both the apples**.* (less common – *She has eaten **both of the apples**.*).

When we talk about two people or things, we use the quantifiers *both, either* and *neither*, e.g. *Both the cinemas were closed. / Neither of the cinemas was open. / I don't think either of the cinemas was open.* Highlight that nouns with *either* and *neither* have a singular verb.

1 Ask students to complete the exercise. Have them compare in pairs before you check answers in open class.

Answers

1 girl, has **2** students, has **3** each **4** Most **5** both of

2 Elicit what is happening in the cartoon in open class. Ask students to complete the exercise. Have them compare in pairs before you check answers in open class.

Answers

1 Both (of the) police officers are wearing uniforms / a uniform.
2 All (of) the men are standing up.
3 Most of the men are tall.
4 The woman is/isn't looking carefully at every man.
5 The woman is/isn't looking carefully at each of the men.
6 The woman is talking to both of the police officers.

3 Ask students to complete the exercise. Check answers in open class.

Answers

1 Every **2** all of **3** of **4** Some **5** others/some **6** all **7** both **8** enough

Mixed ability

Give less confident students the first letter for each answer, or do the first couple of items with them. Ask stronger students to write two comprehension questions. They can read them out to test other students' understanding of the text once everyone has finished the exercise.

Homework OWB

Assign students Grammar 2 exercises 1, 2 and 3 on page 7 of their Workbook.

Assign students the Flipped classroom tasks on page 10 of their Student's Book if you'd like them to prepare for the next lesson. To complete this task, students need to watch the *Talk2Me* video which can be found on the Resource Centre.

SPEAKING
Interview

→ Student's Book, page 10 SB

Lesson aim

- Answer personal questions

The *Talk2Me* video in this unit focuses on talking about yourself and your life. People talk about where they live, their friends, studies and what activities they enjoy doing in their free time. Students answer some comprehension questions and then listen out for key expressions. The video can be used in one of two ways:

Flipped classroom

Flipped classroom option

Using this approach, students watch the video and complete the exercises for homework. This prepares students for the speaking lesson by introducing them to the topic and the key phrases to use in the exam task. Teachers who use this method will find they have more class time to spend on activating the target language and developing fluency for the final task.

***Talk2Me* worksheet**

Ask students to also complete the *Talk2Me* worksheet on the Resource Centre for more detailed comprehension exercises and more practice of the key phrases.

Classroom option

Lead-in

Write these jumbled questions on the board:
favourite your What's drink?
usually to you the same café go Do?
your like else you doing free What do in time?

Ask students to order the questions. Check their answers and ask students to take turns to ask and answer the questions in pairs. Elicit answers from different students around the class.

Answers

What's your favourite drink?
Do you usually go to the same café?
What else do you like doing in your free time?

1 Ask students to read the questions. Play the *Talk2Me* video for students to complete the exercise. Play the video again, if necessary, before checking their answers.

Answers

1 hot chocolate **2** five/5 years **3** No, Maddy's drink is the smallest. Jamie's is the biggest.

2 Play the *Talk2Me* video again, so students can underline the phrases in the *Phrase expert* box. Pause the video from time to time if necessary. Check answers in open class.

Answers

Yes, I've … for …, My favourite (thing) is definitely …, Well, it's …, I don't have a lot of free time, but …, I'd say I'm …

***Talk2Me* worksheet**

Ask students to also complete the *Talk2Me* worksheet on the Resource Centre for more detailed comprehension exercises and more practice of the key phrases.

Answers

The transcript and answer key for the *Talk2Me* video exercises and Worksheet can be found on the Teacher's Resource Centre.

3 In pairs or groups, students ask and answer the questions. Elicit answers from different students around the class.

Answers

Students' own answers

EXAM SKILL

Talking about yourself

Ask students to read the tips.

- In the first part of an official speaking exam, the examiner may ask the candidate to spell all or part of his or her name or the name of their town/city as well as other 'getting to know you' questions.
- Point out to students that they are not expected to talk to each other in this first stage. However, remind them to listen to each other. If they can include a phrase, such as *Like Samuel, I also live …*, they will impress the examiner.
- Students should follow up their answers and expand on how often they go, who they go with and why they go, etc. Remind students that it's a good idea to work with a friend to practise or record themselves and listen to the recording before actually doing the exam.

4 1.07 Play the track for students to listen and complete the exercise. Check answers in open class.

Answers

	Nisha	Alfie
1	✓ Gupta	✓ Dugmore
2	✓ G-U-P-T-A	✓ D-U-G-M-O-R-E
3	✓ Tiltbury (near Manchester)	✓ Manchester
4	✗ Yes, I do.	✓ Yes, I've studied English for nearly six years now.
5	✗ Yes, I do.	✗ I really enjoy it.
6	✗ Maths	✓ My favourite school subject is probably history, but I really like languages too.
7	✓ … chatting online with my friends and listening to music in my room.	✓ … sports. In the winter I play football and in the summer I play cricket.
8	✓ I don't have a best friend exactly, as I have many friends. But Charlotte is a very close friend.	✗ He's called Ben.

Mixed ability

Elicit what students could have said when their answers were too short and didn't provide full answers. Write students' suggestions on the board for less confident students to refer to in the next activity.

Suggested answers

4 (Nisha) Yes, I do. I study English for four hours a week.
5 (Nisha and Alfie) Yes, I do. It's one of my favourite subjects.
6 (Nisha) Maths is my favourite subject. I get good marks and I think it's very useful.
8 (Alfie) He's called Ben. He lives near my house and we play football together.

OPTIMISE YOUR EXAM

Interview

Ask students to read the tips.

- Students can also be asked a couple of questions about their past, present and future in the first part of the exam. They should think about the types of topics and questions they may be asked and have ideas ready. Students will practise this task in exercises 5 and 6.
- It's better not to memorise long replies because students sound unnatural. Remind students to focus on good pronunciation and intonation.

5 Ask students to look at the questions in Exercise 4 and think about their answers. Encourage them to write a few notes.

Answers

Students' own answers

Exam task

6 In pairs or groups, students complete the task. Elicit interesting or surprising answers from different students around the class.

Optional extension

Find someone who … Students stand up and walk round asking personal questions. Remind students to give longer answers when possible. You could put some music on in the background while students are doing this activity.

Homework

OWB

Assign students Speaking exercises 1, 2 and 3 on pages 8–9 of their Workbook.

LANGUAGE IN USE

Multiple-choice cloze

→ Student's Book, page 11

SB

Lesson aims

- Focus on phrasal verbs
- Practise a multiple-choice cloze exam task

Lead-in

Play ***Noughts and crosses***. Draw a large three-by-three grid on the board. Number the boxes 1 to 9 and write some of the quantifiers from the Grammar 2 lesson in the boxes (*all, both, each, enough, little, lots of, many, most, much*). Divide the class into two teams, X and O. Flip a coin to see which team goes first. In order for the team to receive the X or the O for the box they have chosen, they must make a correct sentence using the quantifier. Alternate between the teams until one team has a line of three Xs or Os, or it is a draw.

1 Focus students' attention on the photo on the page and ask them to describe what they can see (*a robot doing housework*). In pairs or as a group, ask students to complete the exercise. Elicit answers from different students around the class.

Answers

Students' own answers

Cultural note

Robots are becoming more technologically advanced and autonomous. They can learn how to do dangerous, complex jobs faster and better than humans and save money. Their precision makes them perfect for a wide variety of jobs. The car industry uses robots to help with building cars. They are also used in space and underwater exploration. Robot-assisted surgery is changing how surgeons work, as they can perform remote surgery without being in the operating room.

Remember

Ask students to read the information.

Phrasal verbs are very common in spoken English and informal writing. They can be transitive (i.e. they need someone or something after the verb) or intransitive (i.e. they stand alone). As well as knowing whether or not a phrasal verb is transitive or intransitive, students also have to become familiar with the idea of separable (the verb and extra word(s) that make it a phrasal verb can be separated) and inseparable (we do not split the main verb from the other words in the phrasal verb).

Refer students to the Vocabulary reference, page 162, for more information on phrasal verbs.

2 Ask students to complete the exercise. Have them compare in pairs before you elicit answers in open class.

Answers

1 look **2** Turn **3** turn **4** looking **5** turn **6** Turn **7** looking **8** looking

Mixed ability

Ask more advanced students to discuss the meaning of each of the phrasal verbs in Exercise 2. Give less confident students definitions (see below) in a jumbled order and ask them to match them to the phrasal verbs. Individually, students then write personalised sentences with two or three of the verbs. In pairs, students read out their sentences without saying the phrasal verb (they could substitute this for a 'beep' sound) for their partner to guess.

1 find out information by looking somewhere (look up)
2 the change from working to not working (turn off)
3 change the page / go to the next page of a book/magazine, etc. (turn over)
4 take care of by watching/looking to make sure no-one's in trouble, etc. (look after)
5 change/transform from one thing into another (turn into)
6 the change from not working to working (turn on)
7 look into the future (at something good that will happen) (look forward to)
8 investigate (by looking at the situation) (look into)

3 Ask students to complete the exercise. Check the answer in open class.

Answer

c

4 Ask students to complete the exercise. Check their answers.

Answers

Questions **1, 2, 3, 8**

OPTIMISE YOUR EXAM

Multiple-choice cloze

Ask students to read the tips.

- Phrasal verbs are frequently tested in multiple-choice cloze exam tasks, but it is hard to predict which ones. Students need to look out for missing verbs or prepositions/particles.
- Encourage students to think about why the other three answers are not correct, even if they are happy that they know the correct answer. This will build good vocabulary habits.
- Remind students that when they have finished the task, they should read the text again and make sure the text makes sense with all their answers in place.

Exam task

5 Ask students to complete the exercise. Check answers in open class.

Answers
1 B **2** B **3** A **4** D **5** C **6** D **7** B **8** B

Homework OWB
Assign students Language in Use exercises 1, 2, 3 and 4 on page 9 of their Workbook.

WRITING
A letter / An email

→ Student's Book, pages 12–13 SB

Lesson aims

- Focus on language for starting and ending a letter / an email
- Plan and write a letter

Lead-in

Play ***Hangman*** with some of the words from the unit. Invite students to come to the front to lead the game, if it's appropriate.

1 In pairs or as a group, students answer the questions. Elicit answers in open class.

Answers
Students' own answers

EXAM SKILL

Starting and ending a letter / an email

Ask students to read the tips.

- Remind students that letters and emails start and end with typical opening and closing sentences and usually refer back to the letter or email to which they are replying.
- Students are often asked to write back to someone they know fairly well. In addition to giving news, letters and emails are often used to request information, congratulate people, give advice and ask questions.

For more information on letters and emails, refer students to the Writing reference, page 173.

2 Ask students to complete the exercise. Check their answers and remind them they must always pay attention to accurate spelling and punctuation.

Answers
1 start; Thanks **2** end; Anyway, soon **3** end; best **4** start; Dear

3 Ask students to read the letter and discuss the questions in pairs or groups. Elicit answers in open class.

Answers
1 that she passed her swimming test, that she's doing a project at school on families (and wants some information from Sasha on families in her country)
2 She'll probably thank Sasha for the information about families in her country. She'll probably ask Sasha if she passed her piano exam.
3 swimming test: paragraph 1, project: paragraph 2
thank Sasha: no particular paragraph, but Sasha gives information in paragraphs 2 and 3, and offers more help if required in paragraph 4, piano exam: paragraph 4

OPTIMISE YOUR EXAM

A letter / An email

Ask students to read the tips.

- There are a lot of similarities between informal letters and conversation. Informal letters ask a lot of questions, show interest and enthusiasm, and imagine a lot of shared information.
- At this level, students are typically asked to write an informal letter or email. Elicit examples of key features of informal language that students can use to show their examiner that they are confident at writing in a conversational style:
  phrasal verbs
  informal vocabulary (*I guess you loved the pics.*)
  contractions but not abbreviated language that we can find in emails
  question tags
  short sentences
  connectors that are more specific to spoken language, e.g. *Well …, By the way …, Anyway …, Actually …*

Exam task

4 Students complete the exercise. Walk round, monitoring students and helping with any vocabulary for their notes.

5 Plan Ask students to complete the paragraph plan using their notes from Exercise 4. You may want to look at students' plans, if this is possible, to check them and give advice and suggestions for improvement before students write.

6 Write Students write their letter in about 100 words, in an appropriate style. Depending on time, it may be a good idea to set this and the subsequent checklist exercise for homework.

7 Check Students complete the checklist before they hand in their letter.

Homework OWB
Assign students Writing exercises 1, 2, 3 and 4 on page 10 of their Workbook and Progress check 1 on page 11.

2 Home sweet home

UNIT AIMS

Exam preparation in Unit 2:

- understand different types of texts
- predict information in an interview
- say where things are
- understand result clauses and apply them in a sentence-transformation exercise
- use personal questions in a short message

TEACHER'S PRESENTATION KIT

- *Talk2Me* videos
- Speaking test videos
- Class and Workbook audio
- Workbook pages and answer key

UNIT OVERVIEW

Student's Book / Digital Student's Book SB		Workbook / Online Workbook OWB
LESSON / EXAM TASK	EXAM SKILLS / LANGUAGE FOCUS	CONSOLIDATION
Reading **Multiple choice**	Understanding text type A short message	Workbook, pp 12–13, Exercises 1, 2, 3, 4 Unit 2, Reading, Exercises 1, 2, 3, 4
Grammar 1	Past simple and past continuous	Workbook, p 14, Exercises 1, 2, 3 Unit 2, Grammar 1, Exercises 1, 2, 3
Vocabulary	Words connected with *the house and home* Phrasal verbs Word patterns	Workbook, pp 14–15, Exercises 1, 2, 3 Unit 2, Vocabulary, Exercises 1, 2, 3
Listening **Multiple choice**	Predicting	Workbook, p 16, Exercises 1, 2, 3, 4 Unit 2, Listening, Exercises 1, 2, 3, 4
Grammar 2	*used to* and *would*	Workbook, p 15, Exercises 1, 2 Unit 2, Grammar 2, Exercises 1, 2
Speaking **Photo task**	Saying where things are	Workbook, pp 16–17, Exercises 1, 2, 3 Unit 2, Speaking, Exercises 1, 2, 3
Language in Use **Sentence transformation**	Result clauses	Workbook, p 17, Exercises 1, 2, 3 Unit 2, Language in Use, Exercises 1, 2, 3
Writing **A short message**	Asking questions	Workbook, p 18, Exercises 1, 2, 3 Unit 2, Writing, Exercises 1, 2, 3
Progress check	Check language progress for Units 1 and 2	Workbook, p 19, Progress check and Cumulative progress Progress check and Cumulative progress

Additional material

PRESENTATION KIT	TEACHER'S / STUDENT'S RESOURCE CENTRE RC	TEST GENERATOR
Talk2Me video *In the background ...*	**Unit 2 worksheets:** *Optimise your grammar* (Standard and Higher), *Optimise your vocabulary* (Standard and Higher), *Talk2Me* video, *Say it right* **Units 1–2 worksheets:** CLIL, Culture, Everyday English (TRC only), Grammar communication (TRC only)	Unit Test 2 (Standard and Higher)

READING
Multiple choice | A short message

→ Student's Book, pages 14–15 SB

Lesson aims

- Focus on understanding different text types
- Practise a multiple-choice exam task

Lead-in

Elicit the difference between 'house' and 'home'. (*The main difference is that* house *refers to a building in which someone lives; in contrast, a* home *has more of an emotional aspect – the place where you live and you feel you belong to.*) Focus students' attention on the photo and ask them to describe it in open class. Use this opportunity to pre-teach vocabulary in Exercise 1 if necessary.

1 In pairs or groups, students complete the exercise. Elicit answers from different students around the class.

Answers
Students' own answers

Extra support

Read out these definitions of types of homes for students to match to the words in the box in Exercise 1.
a house which is not joined to another house (detached)
a house which is joined to another house on one side (semi-detached)
a large building with homes on different levels (block of flats)
a house in the British countryside (cottage)

EXAM SKILL

Understanding text type

Ask students to read the tips.

- In reading exams, students will come across different kinds of factual texts, such as notices and advertisements, each with its own features, purposes and conventions.
- Giving students adequate experience with different kinds of texts can help them understand more rapidly that reading comprehension is not a function of understanding every word but rather of developing strategies for selecting and identifying verbal and non-verbal cues, strategies essential in both oral and written communication. Having this context at the beginning of a reading task helps students understand the tone, style and purpose of the text.
- Point out that students will practise this skill in Exercise 2.

2 Ask students to complete the exercise. Elicit answers from different students around the class and ask what helped them decide on their answers (tone, style, design, font, choice of words, etc.).

Answers
Text 1 f Text 2 d Text 3 g Text 4 a Text 5 b

Fast finishers

Ask students who finish early to say which features they would expect to see in the two text types they didn't need (*a magazine advert* and *a reminder*). When everyone has finished this activity, students could read out their answers to the rest of the class.

Suggested answers
A magazine advert – colourful design, bright colours, good slogan, large font size
A reminder – short text, maybe capital letters, imperative form, instructions

3 Ask students to complete the exercise. Set a two-minute time limit to stop them reading in too much detail at this stage. Elicit answers in open class.

Answers
1 They are students at a summer school in another country.
2 Yes, they do, because they are having a house-warming party to celebrate.

OPTIMISE YOUR EXAM

Multiple choice

Ask students to read the tips.

- It can be helpful for students to predict their own answer before actually looking at the answer choices. These are designed and worded to all sound plausible, so they could distract them from their original understanding of the question.
- If they find themselves overly justifying an answer, it's probably not the correct one. Generally, wrong answers are too specific, too broad, describe a relationship in reverse order or just present a totally unrelated concept. A good rule of thumb is to avoid extremes. Words like *never* or *always* are not usually present in the correct answer.
- Remind students to make sure they can back up all their answers with evidence direct from the text. They mustn't choose an answer that 'feels' right; the answer must be derived from and supported by the text itself.

Exam task

4 1.08 **Note: The reading text is also available on the audio CD. You may want to have students listen and read the text before doing the exam task.**

Ask students to complete the exercise. Have them compare in pairs before you check answers in open class. Elicit evidence for the answers.

Answers
1 A (*All meals and cleaning, but not laundry, included.*)
2 B (*Let's go and see the rooms together! When are you free?*)
3 B (*… did you notice any bedroom lamps? … can buy some if not.*)
4 C (*I don't need the cooking things … look after them for me for the future!*)
5 B (*… please let us know if you can make it.*)

5 Ask students to complete the exercise. Check their answers and elicit the meaning of the secret word.

Answers

1 accommodation **2** furnished **3** laundry **4** flatmate
5 refreshments **6** house-warming (party)

Secret word: roommate (someone you share a room with)

THINK | RESEARCH | CULTURE | LEARN | ME

Students complete the task in class or for homework. In pairs or groups, students could read out their ideas for others to comment on and ask follow-up questions.

Optional extension

Brainstorm ideas for a perfect roommate in class together. Feed in ideas, such as *clears up, has a similar timetable to you, pays the bills on time, takes out the rubbish, always cooks*, etc.

In pairs, students use the ideas to write an advert and describe their perfect roommate.

Homework OWB

Assign students Reading exercises 1, 2, 3 and 4 on pages 12–13 of their Workbook.

GRAMMAR 1
Past simple and past continuous

→ Student's Book, page 16 SB

Lesson aims

- Understand the correct usage of the past simple and past continuous
- Practise using the past simple and past continuous

Lead-in

Tell students a short personalised story using both the past simple and past continuous. Tell the story twice. The first time students just listen, and the second time they note down the key points. Ask them to retell the story in pairs. Elicit the story from students around the class and check how familiar they are with the tenses.

Example story: *I got two tickets to the opening night of* A Monster Calls *the other day. I texted my friend and told her to meet me outside the cinema at a café on the corner. It was raining when I arrived, so I went inside the café. Guess what! I met an old friend from school. We were having a coffee together when the phone rang. It was my friend – she couldn't come. She said she was having problems with her car. I asked my friend if he was free. He said yes and we had a great time.*

Grammar in context

Ask students to complete the task. Refer them to the information in the *Remember* box if they aren't sure. Check answers in open class and ask them to explain their choice.

Remind students that they can find more information in the Grammar reference, Unit 2, page 149.

Answers

d, because the action of walking was interrupted by the action of seeing the notice

Language note

Highlight that the past continuous describes situations that go on for some time, e.g. *I was dancing* and *He was playing*, but the past simple describes actions that happen quickly, e.g. *rang* and *fell*.

Point out the important difference between these two sentences:

*When they arrived, Sue **was doing** her homework.* (Sue started doing her homework before they arrived.)

*When they arrived, Sue **did** her homework.* (Sue started doing her homework after they arrived.)

Note that *when* is most often followed by the past simple, e.g. *I saw him when I **went** to the park*, whereas *while* is usually followed by the past continuous, e.g. *I saw him while I **was running** in the park. While* expresses the idea of 'during that time'.

Remind students that stative verbs cannot be used in any continuous tenses.

Extra support

In pairs, students make sentences similar to the examples above for each point in the *Remember* box. Ask them to read out their sentences in open class. If appropriate, ask students to come up and write them on the board and discuss as a class if they are correct. Encourage them to make questions and negative sentences from their examples.

1 Ask students to complete the exercise. Check their answers and ask them to explain their choices.

Answers

1 moved **2** was raining **3** didn't have **4** invited **5** visited
6 was decorating

2 Ask students to complete the exercise. Have them compare in pairs before you check answers in open class.

Answers

1 She was putting up a poster when the phone rang.
2 They were playing a video game when the lights suddenly went off.
3 He was doing his homework when the party upstairs began.
4 We were walking home when it started to rain.

Optional extension

In groups of three, students write one of the sentences from Exercise 2 on a sheet of paper. Tell them to fold the paper so the sentence cannot be seen and pass the paper to their right. Tell students to write a sentence to say what happened next. Remind them to use the past simple and/or the past continuous. Tell them to fold the paper and pass it to their right. Ask students to write what happened in the end. Students read out their stories. They could choose a story to improve on: adding links, more adjectives, adding past continuous for atmosphere, etc.

3 Ask students to complete the exercise. Have them compare in pairs before you check answers in open class. Ask if they would like to live in a house like the one in this exercise and to say why or why not.

Answers

1 were planning **2** had **3** built **4** came **5** created **6** were designing **7** realised **8** found

Homework

Assign students Grammar 1 exercises 1, 2 and 3 on page 14 of their Workbook.

OWB

VOCABULARY

Topic vocabulary | Phrasal verbs | Word patterns

→ Student's Book, page 17

SB

Lesson aims

Understand the correct usage of:

- words connected with *the house and home*
- phrasal verbs
- verb forms after expressions, e.g. *be worth, be keen on, depend on,* etc.

Lead-in

Write these verbs on the board and ask students to write their past tense form in the correct column, according to the pronunciation of the *-ed* ending (/t/, /d/ or /ɪd/): *start, turn, watch, decide, like, cook, rain, listen, love, plant, play, stay, work, hate, want, need, kiss, wash.*

Elicit the rules and drill the pronunciation of each past tense form.

Answers

/t/ watched, liked, cooked, worked, kissed, washed

If the verb ends with a voiceless sound (*-f, -p, -k, -s, -sh, -ch, -x, -h*), we say /t/.

/d/ turned, rained, listened, loved, played, stayed

If the verb ends with a voiced vowel sound or consonant (*-b, -g, -l, -m, -n, -th, -v, -z*), we say /d/.

/ɪd/ started, decided, planted, hated, wanted, needed

If the verb ends in *-d* or *-t*, we say /ɪd/. This is the sound that really matters in oral speech.

Words connected with *the house and home*

1 1.09 Ask students to complete the exercise. Play the audio for them to listen and check their answers.

Answers/Audioscript

1 attic **2** roof **3** ceiling **4** balcony **5** fence **6** living room **7** dining room **8** basement **9** study **10** garage **11** hedge **12** chimney

Refer students to the Vocabulary reference, page 162, for more information on topic vocabulary.

Phrasal verbs

2 1.10 Ask students to complete the exercise. Play the audio for them to listen and check their answers.

Answers/Audioscript

1 I didn't like this house when we first *moved in* but now I love it!

2 When we moved house, it took me a long time to make friends and *settle in*.

3 I *was tidying up* my bedroom when I found some old comics I didn't know I had!

4 Come and stay for a few days! We can *put* you *up* in the spare room.

5 You could *rent* your flat *out* while you're on holiday and make some money.

6 Jake couldn't afford the rent so he had to *move out*.

7 I can't believe they're going to *pull down* the house I was born in! It'll be gone forever!

8 My parents bought an old house so they can *do* it *up* and make it attractive again.

Mixed ability

Before students do the exercise, you could read out these definitions in a jumbled order for the phrasal verbs in the box in Exercise 2:

do up – *repair something old*
move in – *start living in a different house*
move out – *leave the house where you live*
pull down – *destroy a building because it's dangerous*
put up – *let someone stay in your house*
rent out – *allow a room that you own to be used by someone who pays you regularly for it*
settle in – *become familiar with a new way of life*
tidy up – *clean*

Students write down the phrasal verb. In pairs, students compare their answers. Read the definitions out again and this time, challenge more advanced students to write down your definition. Check answers in open class.

3 Ask students to complete the exercise. Have them check in pairs before you elicit answers in open class.

Answers

1 move out **2** moved in **3** am settling in / have settled in **4** tidy up

Refer students to the Vocabulary reference, page 162, for more information on phrasal verbs.

Word patterns

4 1.11 Ask students to complete the exercise. Play the audio for them to listen and check their answers.

Answers/Audioscript

1 It's *worth visiting* a new neighbourhood before you buy a house there.
2 I'm not *keen on* living on the 20th floor of a block of flats!
3 I think that your happiness *depends on* where you live.
4 I *told* you *to tidy* your room *up* and it's still a mess!
5 We had to *stop* the neighbours *from* playing loud music!
6 When we moved house, my parents *made* me *have* the smallest bedroom!

Refer students to the Vocabulary reference, page 163, for more information on word patterns.

SAY IT RIGHT

Stress in compound nouns

TRC

For the *Say it right* pronunciation activity and instructions, go to the Teacher's Resource Centre.

Homework

OWB

Assign students Vocabulary exercises 1, 2 and 3 on pages 14–15 of their Workbook.

LISTENING
Multiple choice

→ Student's Book, page 18 SB

Lesson aims

- Learn about predicting what you might hear before listening
- Listen for detail to decide if questions are true or false
- Practise a multiple-choice exam task

Lead-in

Focus students' attention on the photos in Exercise 1. Elicit descriptions and ask why they think people choose to live in this type of housing. Pre-teach vocabulary that students are going to need for this lesson:
Photo 1 – *yurt, nomadic lifestyle*
Photo 2 – *underground, cool air, dig*
Photo 3 – *stilts, protection from bad weather, safety, floods*

1 In pairs or as a group, students complete the exercise. Check answers by asking different students around the class. Elicit if they know of other countries where people live in the same type of housing.

Answers

1 Mongolia **2** Tunisia **3** the Philippines

EXAM SKILL

Predicting

Ask students to read the tips.

- Prediction helps students when they listen because it prepares them for what they are about to hear. Whether their predictions are correct or not, the process helps them to know what to expect and helps them to start thinking about the topic even before they hear anything. Remind students that we make predictions all the time. When listening to a foreign language we can use two main types of information to help predict what is going to be said next:

  Background knowledge
  Background – general knowledge of the world; knowledge of the foreign culture; specific subject knowledge.

  Knowledge of context
  Context – the situation (who is speaking, where and when); the 'co-text' – what has been said so far.
- Point out that students have described types of housing and this should help them predict what type of information they are going to listen to.
- If students predict the sort of things they are going to hear in the listening test, they can reduce the amount they need to listen out for during the test. Students usually have 30 seconds before the first listening to look at the questions and options and think of what they're going to listen to. Remind students that this strategy, predicting information, helps them identify relevant points and reject irrelevant information.

2 Ask students to complete the exercise and then compare in pairs.

3 1.12 Play the track for students to listen and check their answers.

Answers

1 T **2** T **3** F **4** T **5** T

OPTIMISE YOUR EXAM

Multiple choice

Ask students to read the tips.

- Students often make the mistake of writing the first answer they hear. Remind them to listen for gist – the key words – the first time and build a general image in their mind of the opinion and attitude of the speakers. In the second listening, remind students that they should listen for any key words and synonyms and eliminate the options they think are incorrect.
- Highlight that the speaker may discuss all the options but will highlight one as the key point. Students should listen out for words like *but* … and *though* … which signal that the speaker is homing in on what is important to him/her.
- Exam questions usually involve 'paraphrasing': sentences with the same meaning as the options but with different words. Using synonyms is one of the main methods of paraphrasing. It is a very important skill that will help students in all areas of an exam.

Exam task

4 1.12 Play the track for students to listen and complete the exercise. Play the track again for them to check their answers. In open class, discuss the specific clues that helped students choose their answers.

Answers

1 A (*My interest in houses, though, was really started by my dad getting a new job in China.*)

2 A (*I thought it was going to be smoky, and a bit frightening, but it wasn't at all. It was really peaceful and I actually slept very well.*)

3 B (*… you can step into the cool air and get away from the sun.*)

4 C (***The real reason**, though, is that there are often floods in the area.* – Highlight this connector that signals the speaker is about to say the most significant point.)

5 B (*… go back to Ireland and design a house using some of the things I learnt.*)

Extra support

Ask students to listen again and note down the distracting information for the incorrect options. Alternatively, give students the audioscript and ask them to underline the distracting information.

Answers

1 I used to want to be an architect. / I would often watch programmes about unusual buildings on television.
2 One family invited me to spend the night with them in their yurt. I thought it was going to be smoky, and a bit frightening, but it wasn't at all.
3 It's perfectly safe, although it's very hot work digging out the rooms.
4 That can be useful for keeping rats out of the house. / It also creates a space under the house for animals like sheep.
5 I've just finished a tour visiting houses in countries all around the world, and I've written a book.

Homework

Assign students Listening exercises 1, 2, 3 and 4 on page 16 of their Workbook.

OWB

GRAMMAR 2
used to and *would*

→ Student's Book, page 19

SB

Lesson aims

- Understand the correct usage of *used to* and *would*
- Practise using *used to* and *would*

Lead-in

In pairs, students find out things about their partner's childhood (e.g. *I lived in a small flat.*). Encourage students to use the past simple and elicit answers in open class.

Grammar in context

Ask students to complete the task. Check their answers and ask them to read more about *used to* and *would* in the *Remember* box.

Remind students that they can find more information in the Grammar reference, Unit 2, page 149.

Answers

1 T **2** F **3** T **4** F

Language note

Highlight that neither *used to* nor *would* can be used to refer to single actions in the past. For example, it would not be possible to use either form in this sentence: *I moved to Barcelona in 2012.*

When students describe habitual actions and temporary or repeated events in the past, it's a good idea to try to vary their choice between *used to*, *would* and the past simple to make their descriptions more interesting, e.g. *I **used to** live quite near my school, so every day I **would** walk there with my friends.*

An important difference between *used to* and *would* is that *would* is not used with stative verbs, such as *love, be, understand* and *feel*. The use of *would* is more restricted than that of *used to*. Advise students that if they aren't sure which one to use, it's best to choose *used to*.

Remind students that the contracted form of *would* is *'d*.

1 Ask students to complete the exercise. Have them compare in pairs before you check answers in open class.

Answers

1 both **2** both **3** did you **4** used to **5** didn't use to **6** did you

Language note

Point out that two verbs, *live* and *work*, are not usually listed as stative verbs, but they can be used to describe states. When they describe more temporary situations, they act like dynamic verbs and we tend to use a continuous tense:

*She**'s living** with her parents until she can find a new flat.* (temporary situation)

But when they describe permanent or long-lasting states, they act like stative verbs and we use a simple tense. They can go with *used to* to talk about the past, but not *would*:

He used to live in Spain, but now he lives in France.

~~*He would live in Spain, but now he lives in France.*~~

Highlight that both *love* and *be* are state verbs and remind students that stative verbs often describe states which last for quite a long time.

2 Ask students to complete the exercise. Have them compare in pairs and expand their answers before you check answers in open class. Elicit some examples. Ask students if they can replace *used to* with *would* in their sentences.

Answers

Students' own answers

3 Ask students to complete the exercise. Check answers in open class.

Answers

1 used to **2** didn't use to **3** would / used to **4** didn't use to **5** didn't use to **6** Didn't they use to **7** would / used to **8** would / used to

THINK | RESEARCH | **CULTURE** | LEARN | ME

Ask students to complete the task. Alternatively, they could prepare this for homework and read their descriptions to each other in pairs at the start of the next lesson.

Homework OWB

Assign students Grammar 2 exercises 1 and 2 on page 15 of their Workbook.

Assign students the Flipped classroom tasks on page 20 of their Student's Book if you'd like them to prepare for the next lesson. To complete this task, students need to watch the *Talk2Me* video which can be found on the Resource Centre.

SPEAKING
Photo task

→ Student's Book, page 20 SB

Lesson aim

- Describe photographs

The *Talk2Me* video in this unit focuses on describing where things are. In the audio tracks, people discuss what is happening in a photo and talk about where different objects are in a photo. Students answer some comprehension questions and then listen out for expressions to say where things are. The video can be used in one of two ways:

Flipped classroom

Flipped classroom option

Using this approach, students watch the video and complete the exercises for homework. This prepares students for the speaking lesson by introducing them to the topic and the key phrases to use in the exam task. Teachers who use this method will find they have more class time to spend on activating the target language and developing fluency for the final task.

***Talk2Me* worksheet**

Ask students to also complete the *Talk2Me* worksheet on the Resource Centre for more detailed comprehension exercises and more practice of the key phrases.

Classroom option

Lead-in

Divide the students into two teams. Call out letters randomly (don't use the letter X) and ask teams to think of a word they've learnt so far which begins with that letter. Students put up their hand if they know a word. Choose the first student who puts their hand up and ask him/her to say the word then spell it. If it is correct, their team gets a point. Play for a set time. At the end, the team with the most points wins.

1 Ask students to read the questions. Play the *Talk2Me* video for students to complete the exercise. Play the video again, if necessary, before checking their answers.

Answers

1 They are looking for something to eat / a tin of biscuits which has been hidden.

2 3/4 years old

3 Beginning: tidy, there's a note on the table
Middle: untidy, messy from baking, flour on the table
End: clean/tidy with cookies on the table

2 Play the *Talk2Me* video again, so students can underline the phrases in the *Phrase expert* box. Pause the video from time to time if necessary. Check answers in open class.

Answers

on the right, at the top, to the left of the ..., above the ..., behind the ..., in front of the ...

***Talk2Me* worksheet**

Ask students to also complete the *Talk2Me* worksheet on the Resource Centre for more detailed comprehension exercises and more practice of the key phrases.

Answers

The transcript and answer key for the *Talk2Me* video exercises and Worksheet can be found on the Teacher's Resource Centre.

3 In pairs or as a group, students ask and answer the questions. Elicit answers from different students around the class.

Suggested answers

1 A teenage boy listening to music in his bedroom; he is in the foreground and on the right of the picture. He's lying on his bed. In the background on the left there is a desk with a lamp, laptop and small set of shelves on it. In the background near the desk there is a larger set of shelves with books on them. In front on the desk there is an orange chair. Behind the desk there is a window with orange curtains.

2 Students' own answers

Optional extension

Give students further practice for saying where things are using the phrases in the *Phrase expert* box. In pairs, ask students to describe the position of an object in the classroom without saying what it is for their partner to guess from the description of the positioning of the object.

EXAM SKILL

Saying where things are

Ask students to read the tips.

- In speaking exams, students often need to describe photographs that depict everyday situations and give a simple description of what they can see in their photograph. This part of the exam allows candidates to demonstrate a wide range of vocabulary and their ability to organise language in a long turn lasting approximately one minute.
- In this task, students need to do three things: refer to the picture, describe the picture, and speculate about the picture. In this lesson, students learn key expressions to refer to the objects in a photo.

4 1.13 Play the track for students to listen and complete the exercise. Check answers in open class.

Answers/Audioscript

This is a photo of two blonde girls in a living room. They're sitting on a sofa and both of them are using their laptops. In the background, on the left, there's a small picture on the wall. In the background behind the sofa, there are two red lamps. Between the lamps there's a big picture on the wall. On the left, next to the sofa, there are two small tables. On one of the tables, there's a plant and on the other one, there's a small lamp and some candles. On the sofa, to the left of the girls there are two green cushions and on the sofa to the right of the girls there are two more cushions. In the foreground, on the floor in front of the sofa, there's a bright orange rug. In the foreground on the right, you can see part of another sofa.

5 Ask students to complete the task. Elicit if students' drawings were the same or different.

Answers

Students' own answers

OPTIMISE YOUR EXAM

Photo task

Ask students to read the tips.

- Students should give a general description of the scene, e.g. *This photograph shows … In this photo I can see … This is a photo of some people … .*
- Students should then move on to give specific details. A good description will include something about the people, the place, the action and what is in the background (*Where are they? What are they doing? Who are they? How old are they? What are their feelings? What are they wearing?*).
- Remind students to talk in sentences and not just produce a list of items they can see.

6 Individually, students complete the task. Encourage less confident students to make some notes.

Exam task

7 In pairs, students take turns to describe the photo. Remind them to time each other so that they speak for at least one minute.

Homework OWB

Assign students Speaking exercises 1, 2 and 3 on pages 16–17 of their Workbook.

LANGUAGE IN USE

Sentence transformation

→ Student's Book, page 21 SB

Lesson aims

- Focus on result clauses
- Practise a sentence-transformation exam task

Lead-in

In groups, ask students to write the unit theme *House and Home* in the centre of a blank page. Encourage them to make a 'vocabulary network' with related ideas branching out in all directions, categorised into sub-themes, e.g. *types of houses, furniture, rooms, associated phrasal verbs, adjectives and expressions,* etc. Students can look back over the unit for ideas, and add drawings and lots of colour. Set a five minute time limit and walk round, helping students if necessary. In a less confident class, ask students for their ideas and make a collective mind map on the board.

1 In pairs, ask students to complete the exercise. Elicit answers from different students around the class.

Suggested answers

1 A boat that looks like people live on it – it's on a canal in the middle of a town.

2 Positive points: lower cost, freedom, simplify your life, closer to nature, etc. Negative points: small, cold, poor internet connection, not safe, etc.

Remember

Ask students to read the information.

We can use *too* before an adjective, e.g. *It's **too** hot*, or before an adverb, e.g. *You walk **too** quickly.* Before a noun, we use *too much* (uncountable nouns) or *too many* (countable nouns), e.g. *I drank **too much** lemonade. I ate **too many** sandwiches.*

We can also use *too much* after a verb, e.g. *I ate **too much**.*

We use *enough* before a noun, e.g. *We have **enough** pens,* but after an adjective or verb, e.g. *He isn't tall **enough** to go on all the rides.*

Sentences with *too* and *enough* are often followed by *to* + verb infinitive, e.g. *I'm not tall enough **to reach** that book.* = *I'm too short **to reach** that book.*

So means *very*, e.g. *It's **so** hot! So* is generally used before an adjective or an adverb, e.g. *He's **so** clever! He plays the guitar **so** well!*

In modern English, *so* is increasingly being used before nouns and verbs, e.g. *That top is **so** last year!* (= That top is last year's fashion.).

Such also means *very*. *Such* is used before an adjective and noun, e.g. *They are **such** bright students. A/an*, if necessary, go after *such*, not before, e.g. *That's **such a** pretty scarf!* NOT ~~*That's a such pretty scarf!*~~

So and *such* can be used with a *that* clause, to show a result of the first clause, e.g. *I was **so** tired **that** I slept for hours. It was **such** a nice day **that** we decided to go for a swim.*

Remind students that they can find more information in the Grammar reference, Unit 2, page 150.

Fast finishers

Ask students to make sentences similar to the examples for each point in the *Remember* box. Ask students to read out their sentences and discuss as a class if they are correct. Encourage them to make questions and negative sentences from their examples.

2 Ask students to complete the exercise. Have them compare in pairs before you check answers in open class.

Answers

1 such **2** so **3** so **4** such **5** so **6** such

3 Ask students to complete the exercise. Elicit if they agree or disagree with the statements and try to develop an open-class discussion.

Answers

1 a **2** b **3** c **4** a **5** c

OPTIMISE YOUR EXAM

Sentence transformation

Ask students to read the tips.

- In the Cambridge English: Preliminary (for Schools) exam, sentence transformations are in Part 1 of the Writing paper. Many students consider this to be the hardest part in official exams. Remind them that they will practise this type of task in this lesson and many more times during the course. You could do the first one in Exercise 4 together in open class.
- Good spelling is essential in this task. In many official exams, a misspelt word means no marks for that question.

Exam task

4 Ask students to complete the exercise. Check answers in open class.

Answers

1 a great life **2** too young **3** such bad weather **4** is enough wood **5** so small

Homework

Assign students Language in Use exercises 1, 2 and 3 on page 17 of their Workbook.

OWB

WRITING
A short message

→ Student's Book, pages 22–23 SB

Lesson aims

- Focus on asking questions politely
- Plan and write a short message

Lead-in

Write the language functions we usually use for writing a short message on sticky notes and stick them to the board, e.g. *greeting, inviting, reminding, congratulating, apologising, arranging a meeting, offering, saying yes, saying no, asking for advice, saying goodbye*. Divide the class into teams. Ask a volunteer from each team to choose a note and give an example of the language function. If they are correct, their team keeps the note and if not, they return it to the board. The team with the most notes wins the game.

1 In pairs or as a group, students discuss the questions. Elicit answers in open class.

Suggested answers

1 Text messages, emails, sticky notes, etc.

2 To invite, remind, congratulate, apologise, arrange a meeting, offer, ask for advice, etc.

EXAM SKILL

Asking questions

Ask students to read the tips.

- Remind them that *Would you mind …?* means *Is it a problem for you?*, so the polite answer when we say 'yes' is *Not at all* or *Of course not.*
- Direct questions can sound impolite. Questions with *can* are made more polite by using *could*, e.g. *Could you pick up a book for me?* and *would*, e.g. *Would you go to the shops for me?* Another way of making direct questions more polite is to add *please* at the end of the question.
- Using indirect question forms is an especially polite way of asking questions. Indirect questions begin with a phrase (*Would you mind + -ing*), e.g. *Would you mind going to the bank for me?*

For more information on short messages, refer students to the Writing reference, page 169.

2 Ask students to complete the exercise. Check answers in open class.

Answers

1 second sentence (*We're not going far, just two miles away to another part of town.*)

2 third sentence (*I feel sad about leaving my old bedroom but excited too!*)

3 fourth sentence (*Would you mind helping me pack?*)

3 Ask students to complete the exercise. Check answers in open class.

Answers

Students should tick: a, b, e, f

OPTIMISE YOUR EXAM

A short message

Ask students to read the tips.

- Remind students that in official exams, their message is supposed to be understood without difficulty, but they are not expected to be 100% accurate in their grammar and spelling. It's OK to make some minor mistakes, as long as the message is clear.
- Point out that there is a word limit. If students exceed the limit, they are probably writing information that is irrelevant to the task. On the other hand, if they don't reach the word limit, it's likely that they are missing some essential information.

Exam task

4 Ask students to complete the exercise. Check answers in open class.

Answers

What your new home is like? (Should be: What is your new home like?)

What are you think? (Should be: What do you think?)

Rafael misunderstands the third instruction.

5 Plan Ask students to complete the exercise. Check answers in open class.

Answers

Students' own answers

Exam task

6 Ask students to complete the exercise. Check answers in open class.

Answers

1 Students should tick: b, c, d

2 Students should tick: a, b, c

3 Students should tick: a, b, d

7 Plan Ask students to complete the paragraph plan. You may want to look at students' plans, if this is possible, to check them and give advice and suggestions for improvement before students write.

8 Write Students write the short messages in exercises 4 and 6 in 35–45 words and in an appropriate style. Depending on time, it may be a good idea to set this and the subsequent checklist exercise for homework.

9 Check Students complete the checklist before they hand in their messages.

Homework OWB

Assign students Writing exercises 1, 2 and 3 on page 18 of their Workbook and Progress check 2 on page 19.

Answers PROGRESS CHECK Units 1–2

Exercise 1
1 meet **2** are you crying **3** doesn't **4** do you play **5** I don't know

Exercise 2
1 was looking, found **2** didn't go / did not go, was feeling / felt **3** were we talking, came

Exercise 3
1 c **2** e **3** a **4** b **5** d

Exercise 4
1 used **2** play **3** ✓ **4** Did **5** ✓

Exercise 5
1 so **2** enough **3** such **4** too **5** enough

Exercise 6
1 forward **2** in **3** up **4** up **5** into **6** from making **7** on **8** seeing **9** trying **10** tidy

Exercise 7
1 personality **2** friendship **3** creativity **4** shyness **5** generosity **6** unreliable **7** politeness

Exercise 8
1 fast **2** deep **3** wide **4** hedge **5** big **6** attic **7** balcony

3 On the road

UNIT AIMS

Exam preparation in Unit 3:

- understand difference in true/false tasks
- listen for feeling and attitude in short extracts
- make suggestions in a collaborative task
- understand how to use particles to create phrasal verbs in an open-cloze exercise
- choose positive and negative points in a review

TEACHER'S PRESENTATION KIT

- *Talk2Me* videos
- Speaking test videos
- Class and Workbook audio
- Workbook pages and answer key

UNIT OVERVIEW

Student's Book / Digital Student's Book SB		Workbook / Online Workbook OWB
LESSON / EXAM TASK	**EXAM SKILLS / LANGUAGE FOCUS**	**CONSOLIDATION**
Reading **True/false**	Understanding difference A class project	Workbook, pp 20–21, Exercises 1, 2, 3, 4 Unit 3, Reading, Exercises 1, 2, 3, 4
Grammar 1	Present perfect simple and continuous	Workbook, p 22, Exercises 1, 2, 3 Unit 3, Grammar 1, Exercises 1, 2, 3
Vocabulary	Words connected with *holidays* Adjectives with *un- / im- / il- / ir- / dis-* Word patterns	Workbook, pp 22–23, Exercises 1, 2, 3 Unit 3, Vocabulary, Exercises 1, 2, 3
Listening **True/false**	Listening for feelings and attitude	Workbook, p 24, Exercises 1, 2, 3 Unit 3, Listening, Exercises 1, 2, 3
Grammar 2	Countable and uncountable nouns	Workbook, p 23, Exercises 1, 2, 3 Unit 3, Grammar 2, Exercises 1, 2, 3
Speaking **Collaborative task**	Making suggestions	Workbook, pp 24–25, Exercises 1, 2, 3 Unit 3, Speaking, Exercises 1, 2, 3
Language in Use **Open cloze**	Particles in phrasal verbs	Workbook, p 25, Exercises 1, 2, 3 Unit 3, Language in Use, Exercises 1, 2, 3
Writing **A review**	Choosing positive and negative points	Workbook, p 26, Exercises 1, 2, 3, 4 Unit 3, Writing, Exercises 1, 2, 3, 4
		Workbook, p 27, Progress check and Cumulative progress Progress check and Cumulative progress

Additional material

PRESENTATION KIT	TEACHER'S / STUDENT'S RESOURCE CENTRE RC	TEST GENERATOR
Talk2Me video *What do you think about …?*	**Unit 3 worksheets:** *Optimise your grammar* (Standard and Higher), *Optimise your vocabulary* (Standard and Higher), *Talk2Me* video, *Say it right* **Units 3–4 worksheets:** CLIL, Culture, Everyday English (TRC only), Grammar communication (TRC only)	Unit Test 3 (Standard and Higher)

READING

True/false | A class project

→ Student's Book, pages 26–27 SB

Lesson aims

- Focus on understanding different ways of saying something
- Practise a correct/incorrect exam task

Lead-in

Elicit the meaning of the unit title ***On the road*** (*on a journey*) in open class and ask students what they can see in the photographs (*a camel / cable cars / gondolas in Venice / a motorbike / a number of mini taxis in Cuba*). Then ask them what they think the lesson will be about (*travel and transport*) and ask one or two students in open class to describe a recent journey they went on and what sort of transportation they used.

1 In pairs or as a group, students complete the exercise. Elicit answers from different students around the class.

Suggested answers

aeroplane/plane/airplane (US)/aircraft, ambulance, bicycle/bike, bus, car, caravan, coach, ferry, fire engine, hang-glider, helicopter, horse, hot-air balloon, lorry, motorbike, police car, ship, spaceship, (speed/motor/sailing) boat, taxi, train, tram, truck, van, yacht

2 Ask students to complete the exercise. Draw their attention to the model sentence to help them construct their definition.

3 Ask students to complete the exercise. Set a two-minute time limit to stop them from reading in too much detail at this stage. Elicit answers in open class.

Answers

1 a new means of transport

2 They've started, but they haven't finished.

3 It'll be much faster.

EXAM SKILL

Understanding difference

Ask students to read the tips.

- Vocabulary tests are highly predictive of performance in reading exams. It is a good idea to teach students words with associated meanings together. Learning vocabulary is not just a question of mastering the form, meaning and use. It is also linking the item to the whole network of previously learnt words, to provide not just breadth (the number of words a student, at least superficially, knows) but also depth – knowledge of the various aspects of a word.
- Giving opposite similar words to convey meaning is a quick way of explaining meaning, but be careful. Using *thin* as a synonym for *skinny*, for example, can be quite effective, but there is a difference in connotation.

4 Ask students to complete the exercise. Elicit answers in open class.

Suggested answers

1 We can't go at the speed of light in real life.

2 They've started, but they haven't finished.

3 Thirty minutes is 'half the time it currently takes by plane'. In other words, it takes one hour.

OPTIMISE YOUR EXAM

True/false

Ask students to read the tips.

- Remind students that in this type of exercise, they need to look for meanings and not just words. This really does get easier if they get used to seeing this pattern. The key words in the statements only tell students where to look, not what the answer is.
- The questions will probably use synonyms rather than the words in the text. The more practice they do, the better they'll get at finding the answers by recognising the similar 'key words' in the statements and in the text and discarding redundant information.

Exam task

5 1.14 **Note: The reading text is also available on the audio CD. You may want to have students listen and read the text before doing the exam task.**

Ask students to complete the exercise. Have them compare in pairs before you check answers in open class. Elicit the key phrases in the text that helped them decide on their answers.

Answers

1 F (*... most planes today are unable to travel that fast ...*)

2 F (The information in the text says it *sounds like something out of Star Wars ...* as an example of sci-fi.)

3 F (*In fact, a team of scientists and engineers have already started to build it.*)

4 F (The information in the text says who Elon Musk is, but it does not say that the writer has met him, therefore the statement is incorrect.)

5 T (*That's almost the speed of sound!*)

6 F (The information in the text says ... *Today, the fastest trains in the world only travel at about half that speed* and students must calculate 600 km.)

7 F (The information in the text says Captain America's shield was made of vibranium, but it does not say it is a character.)

8 F (*It's designed for journeys of 1,600 kilometres or less.*)

9 T (The text says that he's raised money in the past ... *he's already experienced in raising millions of dollars*, so it is likely that he can do this again.)

10 T (*... I'm looking forward to hearing more about it over the next few years.*)

Mixed ability

Break the text into chunks and give less confident students the option of only reading some of the text and answering fewer questions. If stronger students finish early, ask them to write a short summary of the text.

6 Ask students to complete the exercise. Check answers in open class.

Answers

1 affordable **2** billion **3** sci-fi **4** passengers **5** environmentally friendly **6** currently **7** supersonic **8** revolutionise

Extra support

Pair up students and give each student half the words in Exercise 6. Ask them to compare before you elicit the definitions in open class.

THINK | RESEARCH | CULTURE | LEARN | ME

Students could discuss the questions in pairs before you elicit students' opinions in open class.

Optional extension 1.14

Play the recorded reading text and ask students to underline adverbs, adjectives (not including numbers), comparative adjectives and a superlative adjective. Elicit their answers in open class.

Answers

Adverbs: fast, today, soon, already, currently

Adjectives: impossible, supersonic, exciting, new, solar powered, environmentally friendly, safe, affordable, fast, long, strong, special, carbon, superhero, extra strong, successful, next

Comparative adjectives: faster, slower, longer, older

Superlative adjective: fastest

Homework OWB

Assign students Reading exercises 1, 2, 3 and 4 on pages 20–21 of their Workbook.

GRAMMAR 1
Present perfect simple and continuous

→ Student's Book, page 28 SB

Lesson aims

- Understand the correct usage of the present perfect simple and continuous
- Practise using the past simple, present perfect simple and present perfect continuous

Lead-in

Play ***Grammar tennis***. Write on the board the infinitive form of some verbs students have seen in the unit so far, e.g. *do, have, take, make, read, start, finish, fly, invent, sit, build, carry, think, choose*, etc. Divide the class into two teams, A and B. Ask a volunteer from team A to 'serve' one of the infinitives on the board to a student on team B. This student must say the past participle form to win a point. If he/she gets it wrong, they get a second chance (like the second service in tennis). If he/she still gets it wrong, elicit the correct form and write it on the board. It is now team A's turn to respond to the service and give the past simple form of the same infinitive. Team A only has one chance. Then team B serves an infinitive. The first team to get five points is the winner.

Grammar in context

Ask students to complete the task. Refer them to the information in the *Remember* box if they aren't sure. Check answers in open class and ask them to explain their choice.

Remind students that they can find more information in the Grammar reference, Unit 3, pages 150–151.

Answers

1 Have **2** I've **3** been working **4** has

Language note

In both the present perfect simple and continuous, our reference point is the present.

Remind students that there is often very little difference between the present perfect simple and the present perfect continuous, e.g. ***I've lived*** *here for five years*, and ***I've been living*** *here for five years*. Both tenses show a connection to the present. However, we use the present perfect continuous when we want to emphasise the process and duration of an action and say how long something has been happening up to now. If the action is very short, we cannot use the continuous form.

Highlight that when a verb describes a state and not an action, we don't use the continuous tenses.

1 Ask students to complete the exercise. Check their answers and ask them to explain their choices.

Answers

1 booked **2** heard **3** stayed **4** been writing, finished (the present perfect continuous for a situation over a period of time up to the present / for an action continuing up to the present moment)

2 Ask students to complete the exercise. Have them compare in pairs before you check answers in open class.

Answers

1 for **2** since **3** already **4** still **5** yet **6** ever

Language note

We can use the present perfect + *for* to show how long a situation has been going on and the present perfect + *since* to show when a situation started. *Since* can only be used with perfect tenses. *For* can also be used with the past simple.

Just is usually used with the present perfect and it means 'very recently'. It comes between the auxiliary verb (*have*) and the past participle.

Yet is used to talk about something which is expected to happen. It means 'up until the present time or implied time'. It is used in questions and negatives and usually comes at the end of the sentence.

Still is used to talk about something that hasn't finished, especially when we expected it to finish earlier. It usually comes in the middle of a sentence.

Already is used to say that something has happened early – or earlier than it might have happened. It usually comes in the middle of a sentence.

Highlight that we often use *been to*, instead of *gone to* when we refer to completed visits, e.g. *Sue's just* ***gone to*** *the supermarket. She'll be back in about 10 minutes.* (Sue hasn't returned from the supermarket yet.) / *Sue's just* ***been to*** *the supermarket. She bought some bread.* (Sue has returned from the supermarket.).

Optional extension

Ask students to write two true sentences and one false sentence about themselves using the adverbs in Exercise 2. In pairs or small groups, they read out their sentences for their partner to guess which sentences are true or false.

Extra support

Dictate or read these sentences aloud to the class:

1 She's ____ to visit Jack. She'll be back home tomorrow. (gone)

2 Have you ever ____ to Paris? (been)

3 You're late. Where have you ____ ? (been)

4 My brother's ____ to Thailand. He's staying there for three weeks. (gone)

Say 'beep' for the gap and ask students to write *been* or *gone* in their notebooks. Have them compare in pairs before you check answers in open class.

3 Ask students to complete the exercise. Have them compare in pairs before you check answers in open class.

Suggested answers

1 has had his motorbike for four years. **2** you (ever) been to Madrid before? **3** haven't stayed in a hostel (before). **4** have been waiting for you since one o'clock!

Mixed ability

When checking the answers to Exercise 3, divide the class into A and B pairs, mixing up higher- and lower-level students. Tell Student A to read out the first sentences and the word in brackets. Student B tries to formulate the second sentence without looking at their notes. If the answer is correct, Student B continues. If they make a mistake, Student A has a turn, starting again from sentence 1. The aim of the game is for both students to go through all the sentence transformations in one go without making any mistakes.

4 Ask students to complete the exercise. Have them compare in pairs before you check answers in open class.

Answers

1 Have you ever been **2** you've probably travelled / you probably travelled **3** you haven't been **4** you've probably heard **5** opened **6** have been travelling / have travelled **7** has changed **8** have opened **9** have closed **10** have got on / have been getting on **11** has actually counted **12** have calculated

Fast finishers

Write these ordinal and cardinal numbers and dates on the board and ask students to say what they refer to in the text: *third, 1863, 150, 1884, 24, 3 million, half a million.*

Homework OWB

Assign students Grammar 1 exercises 1, 2 and 3 on page 22 of their Workbook.

VOCABULARY

Topic vocabulary | Word formation | Word patterns

→ Student's Book, page 29 SB

Lesson aims

Understand the correct usage of:

- words connected with *holidays*
- the negative prefixes *un-, im-, il-, ir-* and *dis-*
- word patterns with gerunds and infinitives

Lead-in

Ask students to describe what they can see in the photo. Write these questions on the board and ask students to discuss in pairs:

Have you ever been abroad? Where did you go?

What's your most memorable school trip? Tell your partner why it was memorable.

Elicit interesting and unusual answers from around the class.

Words connected with *holidays*

1 1.15 Ask students to complete the exercise. Play the audio for them to listen and check their answers.

Answers/Audioscript

1 *package* holiday: a holiday where flights and accommodation are included in the price

2 *cruise*: a holiday on board a big ship

3 *camping* trip: a holiday where you sleep in a tent

4 guided *tour*: when an expert shows you round a tourist attraction

5 *business* trip: whens someone travels as part of their job

6 school *trip*: when students visit a place away from school

2 Ask students to complete the exercise. Check answers in open class.

Answers

1 business trip **2** cruise **3** guided tour **4** package holiday **5** school trip **6** camping trip

Fast finishers

Write these definitions for words from exercises 1 and 2 on the board:

1 an act of travelling from one place to another, especially a long distance (journey)

2 a town or a city where ships load and unload (port)

3 the area or place that can be seen (view)

4 a long journey, especially by boat or into space (voyage)

5 a collection of tents or caravans (camp)

Ask students to find words in exercises 1 and 2 that match the definitions. When everyone has finished Exercise 2, ask them to test the other students in the class.

3 1.16 Ask students to complete the exercise. Play the audio for them to listen and check their answers. Elicit one more item for each category from the class, e.g. *hotel, travel agent, sun cream.*

Answers/Audioscript

places to stay: campsite, hostel, resort

people: backpacker, guest, sightseer, tour guide, tourist

things to take on holiday: currency, guidebook, luggage, passport

Refer students to the Vocabulary reference, page 163, for more information on topic vocabulary.

Adjectives with *un- / im- / il- / ir- / dis-*

4 1.17 Ask students to complete the exercise. Play the audio for them to listen and check their answers.

Answers/Audioscript

1 uncertain **2** unable **3** uncomfortable **4** unhelpful **5** dishonest **6** illegal **7** unhappy **8** impatient **9** unpopular **10** impossible **11** disabled **12** unfair **13** irresponsible **14** untidy

Language note

A prefix is placed at the beginning of a word to change its meaning. In this exercise, students are presented with a variety of prefixes that mean 'not' or 'the opposite of'. The most common prefixes are *un-* and *dis-*.

Highlight that in the prefixes *il-*, *ir-* and *im-*, the spelling often changes to match the first letter of the base word. This sometimes results in a double letter:
il- before words starting with *l*, e.g. *legible / illegible*

ir- before words starting with *r*, e.g. *relevant / irrelevant*

im- before words starting with *m* but also in front of words starting with *p*, e.g. *mature / immature, polite / impolite*

5 Ask students to complete the exercise. Check answers in open class.

Answers

1 illegal (also accept: irresponsible) **2** uncomfortable **3** disabled **4** impossible **5** unhelpful

Refer students to the Vocabulary reference, page 163, for more information on word formation.

Word patterns

6 1.18 Ask students to complete the exercise. Play the audio for them to listen and check their answers.

Answers/Audioscript

1 Will you have time *to look* round the Colosseum while you're in Rome?

2 We spent a lot of time *lying* on the beach. It was so relaxing!

3 Are you interested *in coming* on a camping trip in the summer?

4 I'm really looking forward to *going* on the sightseeing tour next week!

5 I'm not keen *on* having a job that involves lots of business trips.

6 I don't know why they prevented us *from going* in that room in the castle.

7 Are you ready *for* your holiday next week? Have you packed yet?

8 Please don't make us *go* on another guided tour tomorrow!

Refer students to the Vocabulary reference, page 163, for more information on word patterns.

SAY IT RIGHT

/dʒ/, /ŋ/ and /g/ TRC

For the *Say it right* pronunciation activity and instructions, go to the Teacher's Resource Centre.

Homework OWB

Assign students Vocabulary exercises 1, 2 and 3 on pages 22–23 of their Workbook.

LISTENING
True/false

→ Student's Book, page 30 SB

Lesson aims

- Listen for feelings and attitude
- Practise a true/false exam task

Lead-in

Write these groups of words on the board and, in pairs, ask students to decide on the odd word out in each list:

journey, voyage, cruise, excursion

tent, caravan, camper van, hostel

sightseer, backpacker, travel agent, tourist

passport, tickets, money, sunglasses

Check answers in open class and ask students to give reasons for their answers.

Suggested answers

excursion – it means a short trip, all the others are longer

hostel – all the others you can find on a campsite

travel agent – it's the only job; all the others are words for people on holiday

sunglasses – all the others are essential travelling items

1 Focus students' attention on the photo and ask them to describe what is happening. (*There's a mum and her children waiting in an airport lounge. They look bored. They might be delayed.*) Ask students if they have ever had this experience.

In pairs or as a group, students complete the exercise. Elicit answers from different students around the class.

Suggested answers

1 delays, cancellations, accommodation not as expected, bad weather, illness, lose tickets/passport, etc., accidents, etc.

2 Students' own answers

EXAM SKILL

Listening for feelings and attitude

Ask students to read the tips.

- Elicit what the word *attitude* means (*someone's opinions or feelings about something, especially as shown by their behaviour*) and brainstorm related words, e.g. *negative, positive, aggressive.*
- Attitude questions often deal with information that's given not just by *what* the speaker says, but also by *how* they say it. In listening exam tasks, students should listen out for the speaker's intonation as well as word choice to give them clues about the speaker's feelings and relationship toward the subject he/she is discussing.
- Remind students that listening for intonation means listening for tone, pitch, volume and speed, as well as the words. The sound of a speaker's voice can tell them a lot about the speaker's attitude.
  - We use a higher pitch and rising intonation to express surprise.
  - We use a falling intonation and a depressed tone to express disappointment.
  - We usually use falling intonation, an irritated tone and speak in a loud voice when we are annoyed and angry.
  - We speak fast with an enthusiastic tone to express we are impatient for something good to start – the pitch goes up at the end of the sentence.

Optional extension

Write this sentence on the board: *It's not what you say, it's how you say it!* Ask students if they agree. Elicit how we can change or affect the meaning of a sentence by the way we say things.

Now write *bananas* on the board and elicit different attitudes that will mean we say the word in a different tone, e.g. enthusiastic, amazed, bored, angry, surprised, frustrated, relaxed. Ask students to say *bananas* in pairs and try to guess each other's attitude.

2 Ask students to complete the exercise. You could do the first one together, if appropriate. Elicit answers from different students around the class and accept all sensible suggestions.

Answers

1 a **2** b **3** a **4** b

OPTIMISE YOUR EXAM

True/false

Ask students to read the tips.

- Remind students that underlining key words in the questions will give them helpful clues (the relationship between the speakers, what they are talking about, where they are, what the speaker wants to achieve, etc.).
- Remind students that the speaker's words do not match the exact words in the statements. Encourage them to read and reread the statements before they listen. It will help them focus on the aspects of the text they need to listen out for and identify synonyms or similar words explained in another way (paraphrasing).
- Highlight that sometimes, however, the speaker does use exactly the same words as appear in the question. Point out that these are normally distractors. They must select the correct answer, not the first one they hear.

▾ Exam task

3 1.19 Play the track for students to listen and complete the exercise. Don't check answers yet as they will listen again in Exercise 4.

4 1.19 Play the track for students to listen again. Check answers in open class. Elicit the key words or phrases that helped them decide on their answers.

Answers

1 F (*Well, I didn't mind at first …*)

2 T (*I kept looking at the departures board* – Highlight the verb pattern *keep doing something* to describe doing something many times.)

3 F (*… I spent about three hours going round the shops – I'm sure I went in each shop at least four times!* – She doesn't say she was uncertain about which shop to look around first.)

4 F (*I took two huge suitcases with me … I've never carried so much luggage on holiday before!* He says they are heavy but doesn't say that he couldn't carry them.)

5 F (*Oh no! That's annoying.* She doesn't say that she is annoyed, she says the situation is annoying.)

6 T (*I couldn't believe my luck!* Highlight Daniel's enthusiastic intonation.)

THINK | RESEARCH | CULTURE | LEARN | **ME**

In pairs, students complete the task. Elicit answers in open class.

Homework

Assign students Listening exercises 1, 2 and 3 on page 24 of their Workbook. OWB

GRAMMAR 2
Countable and uncountable nouns

→ Student's Book, page 31 SB

Lesson aims

- Understand the correct usage of countable and uncountable nouns
- Practise using the correct verbs and quantifiers with countable and uncountable nouns

Lead-in

In groups, ask students to write the unit theme *Travel and transport* in the centre of a blank page. Encourage them to make a 'vocabulary network' with related ideas branching out in all directions categorised into sub-themes, e.g. *types of transport, adjectives related to holidays, words connected to holidays*, etc. then divided into further sub-themes, e.g. *places to stay, things to take, things to do on holiday, people*, etc. Students can look back over the unit for ideas and add drawings and lots of colour. Set a five-minute time limit and walk round, helping students if necessary. In a less confident class, ask students for their ideas and make a collective mind map on the board.

Grammar in context

Ask students to complete the task. Check their answers and ask them to read more about countable and uncountable nouns in the *Remember* box.

Remind students that they can find more information in the Grammar reference, Unit 3, page 151.

Answers
1 U **2** C **3** U **4** U **5** U **6** C

Language note

Highlight that some uncountable nouns are plural words. They have no singular form with the same meaning and cannot be used with numbers, e.g. *My clothes* ***are*** old (other examples are *police, customs, thanks, trousers, jeans, pyjamas, pants, scissors, spectacles, glasses*, etc.).

1 Ask students to complete the exercise. Have them compare in pairs before you check answers in open class.

Answers
1 was **2** were **3** were **4** was **5** was **6** was

2 Ask students to complete the exercise. Have them compare in pairs before you check answers in open class.

Answers
1 many **2** much **3** amount **4** lots **5** less **6** Few

3 Ask students to describe the photo and elicit suggestions from the class. Tell them it's part of a hotel. Students then skim read the text and say what is strange about the four hotels in the text.

Ask students to complete the exercise. Check answers in open class.

Answers
1 ✓ **2** s **3** ✓ **4** ✓ **5** s **6** ✓ **7** ✓ **8** s **9** ✓ **10** ✓

Homework OWB

Assign students Grammar 2 exercises 1, 2 and 3 on page 23 of their Workbook.

Assign students the Flipped classroom tasks on page 32 of their Student's Book if you'd like them to prepare for the next lesson. To complete this task, students need to watch the *Talk2Me* video which can be found on the Resource Centre.

SPEAKING
Collaborative task

→ Student's Book, page 32 SB

Lesson aim

- Making suggestions

The *Talk2Me* video in this unit focuses on making suggestions. Students answer some comprehension questions and then listen out for different ways to make suggestions. They also learn key expressions for what to say if they don't understand something in a speaking exam. The video can be used in one of two ways:

Flipped classroom

Flipped classroom option

Using this approach, students watch the video and complete the exercises for homework. This prepares students for the speaking lesson by introducing them to the topic and the key phrases to use in the exam task. Teachers who use this method will find they have more class time to spend on activating the target language and developing fluency for the final task.

Talk2Me **worksheet**

Ask students to also complete the *Talk2Me* worksheet on the Resource Centre for more detailed comprehension exercises and more practice of the key phrases.

Classroom option

Lead-in

Write the word *Holidays* on the board and elicit different types of holiday (*wildlife holidays, beach holidays, walking holidays, cultural holidays, family holidays*). Ask students to discuss which holiday they prefer in pairs or small groups. Elicit answers from students around the class and discuss the advantages and disadvantages of each type of holiday.

1 Ask students to spend a minute or two reading the questions. Play the *Talk2Me* video for students to complete the exercise. Play the video again, if necessary, before checking their answers.

Suggested answers

1 been to the beach (every day), swimming in the sea, eating out

2 The younger kids want to go to the zoo. The older kids want to go to the shopping centre. The grown-ups want to go to the museum.

3 The museum is closed.

2 Play the *Talk2Me* video again, so students can underline the phrases in the *Phrase expert* box. Pause the video from time to time if necessary. Check answers in open class.

Answers

Maybe we/they could …, … might be a good idea, How about …? What do you think about …?

Talk2Me worksheet

Ask students to also complete the *Talk2Me* worksheet on the Resource Centre for more detailed comprehension exercises and more practice of the key phrases.

Answers

The transcript and answer key for the *Talk2Me* video exercises and Worksheet can be found on the Teacher's Resource Centre.

3 In pairs or groups, students ask and answer the questions. Elicit answers from different students around the class.

Suggested answers

1 The girl is skateboarding. The boys are playing football.

2 skateboarding: a skateboard, a helmet, knee pads, trainers
football: football, football boots, a goal/net, football kit

EXAM SKILL

Making suggestions

Ask students to read the tips.

- Students are assessed on their discussion skills and how well they can make and respond to suggestions, talk about alternatives and make recommendations.
- Highlight that we use words like *perhaps*, *maybe*, *possibly*, modal verbs and conditional forms when we make suggestions in order to sound more polite and modest. By presenting an idea or message in a way that makes it easy for the listener to receive, we improve communication.

4 1.20 Play the track for students to listen and complete the exercise. Check answers in open class.

Answers

1 knee pads, gloves, tool box, football scarf

2 skateboard, cycling helmet, ticket to a football match

5 1.20 Play the track again for students to listen and complete the exercise. Check answers in open class.

Answers

… hasn't he? What do you think about …? … aren't they? They could …, … so it may be a good suggestion. … might be a good idea. (So) perhaps …, Well, how about …

OPTIMISE YOUR EXAM

Collaborative task

Ask students to read the tips.

- Students should have a plan for what they can say to help them if they don't know all the words they need. Elicit strategies students can use, e.g. they can give examples, describe its purpose or function (*it's used to* + infinitive / *it's used for* + *-ing*), give a description using relative clauses (*it's a person who … it's a thing that*), say a synonym or an antonym or use phrases to approximate (*it's a kind of / it's a sort of*).
- At the start of this stage of a speaking exam, students can ask the examiner to repeat a question or an instruction. Then students interact with each other and the examiner listens to their discussion but does not participate in it.

6 In pairs, students complete the task. Elicit answers from students around the class.

Answers

a (cycling) helmet – it protects your head if you fall and hit it
(a pair of) knee pads – they protect your knees if you fall and hit them
(a pair of) (cycling) gloves – they help you grip onto the handlebars
(a pair of) (football) tickets – they let you in to a venue to watch a special event or sport
a skateboard – you stand on it while skateboarding
a tool kit – you use the things in it to repair a bike, wheel, etc.
a (football) team scarf – you wear it to keep warm and to show which team you support

Exam task

7 In pairs, students complete the task. Elicit answers from students around the class. Walk round, monitoring students and noting down errors and good use of language.

Optional extension

Ask students to give themselves a mark from 1 to 5 on their performance in the activity in Exercise 7. Give feedback; highlight good language students used and go over errors in open class. Then ask students to swap partners and do this activity again. This time they should focus on scoring a higher mark.

Homework

OWB

Assign students Speaking exercises 1, 2 and 3 on pages 24–25 of their Workbook.

LANGUAGE IN USE
Open cloze

→ Student's Book, page 33 SB

Lesson aims

- Focus on particles in phrasal verbs
- Practise an open-cloze exam task

Lead-in

Put students in small teams for an ***A–Z race***. They have to think of a means of transport for each letter of the alphabet, except for *x*. Set a five-minute time limit and ask students to stop when the time is up and count their words. The team with the most correct words wins the game.

Suggested answers

aeroplane, boat, caravan, donkey, express train, ferry, gondola, helicopter, icebreaker, jet, kayak, limousine, motorbike, narrow boat, ocean liner, powerboat, quad bike, racing car, submarine, taxi, unicycle, van, wagon, yacht, zeppelin

1 In pairs or as a group, students to complete the exercise. Elicit answers from different students around the class.

Answers

Students' own answers

Remember

Ask students to read the information.

2 Ask students to complete the exercise. Have them compare in pairs before you check answers in open class.

Answers

1 down **2** up **3** off **4** off **5** up **6** in **7** off **8** up

Language note

In this exercise, students see two types of phrasal verbs: intransitive (with no object), e.g. *What time does the plane **take off**? Let's **set off**. They **turned up** early. When do we **check in**? The car **broke down**. **Speed up**!*

Transitive verbs whose object is either after the verb or after the particle, e.g. *I'll **pick** the car **up** at 6. / I'll **pick up** the car at 6.* If the object is a pronoun, the object must come between the verb and the particle, e.g. *I'll **pick** him **up** / **drop** him **off** at 6.* (NOT ~~*I'll pick up him at 6.*~~).

Refer students to the Vocabulary reference, page 163, for more information on phrasal verbs.

3 Ask students to complete the exercise. Elicit answers in open class.

Suggested answers

1 a flying car **2** 800 km **3** two

OPTIMISE YOUR EXAM

Open cloze

Ask students to read the tips.

- In an exam, students should always read the text for general understanding first. They did this in Exercise 3. Remind them that when they have finished the task, they should read the text again and make sure it makes sense with all their answers in place.
- Point out that they can expect to be tested on many different things in gapped texts, but most of the gaps are usually grammatical words, not topic vocabulary, except phrasal verbs. Different phrasal verbs have different grammar and they are frequently tested in cloze exam tasks. Students need to look out for missing verbs or prepositions/particles.

▾ Exam task

4 Ask students to complete the exercise. Check answers in open class.

Answers

1 have **2** off/out **3** up **4** off **5** has (also accept: have) **6** checking **7** up **8** in

Homework

OWB

Assign students Language in Use exercises 1, 2 and 3 on page 25 of their Workbook.

WRITING
A review

→ Student's Book, pages 34–35 SB

Lesson aims

- Focus on choosing positive and negative points
- Plan and write a review

Lead-in

Write these facts about Athens on the board: *Greek, The Parthenon Temple, The Agora, 1896, 2004*. In pairs, ask students to think of the questions that give them the answers on the board. Elicit answers in open class. Ask if anyone has been to Athens or travelled to Greece, and ask them to share their experience in open class.

Suggested answers

What language is spoken in Greece?
What is one of the city's famous monuments? / What can you visit in Athens?
What was the name of the main marketplace in Athens?
When were the first modern Olympic Games held in Athens?
When were the last Summer Olympic Games held in Athens?

1 Focus students' attention on the photo and ask them to complete the exercise. Elicit answers in open class.

Suggested answers

1 People would visit the place to eat in the café (especially if they like seafood), buy takeaway food and souvenirs, get tourist information, take children to the playground.
2 Students' own answers

2 Ask students to read the review and complete the exercise in pairs or as a group. Check answers in open class.

Answers

1 Athens Clue; in Athens (Greece) **2** different scenarios **3** find and solve clues (to escape from a room) **4** €15 each **5** positive **6** great for people who love solving problems, great fun, worth the cost, great for people who like challenges **7** expensive, some clues too hard, not suitable for people who don't speak English well, not suitable for less than two people, too difficult for younger children

EXAM SKILL

Choosing positive and negative points

Ask students to read the tips.

- People reading a review want to know about the writer's personal experience, so they can determine if they'd like to visit that place, see the film, etc.
- Positive and negative aspects may include objective statements (*It was quite difficult to find, but …*) and subjective views based on personal opinion and points of view (*… it's the best experience for teenagers in Athens!*). Point out that it is not enough to tell the reader that the place is amazing, boring, exciting, etc. They need to show why they think that way by giving examples and offering reasons for their opinion.

For more information on writing reviews, refer students to the Writing reference, page 171.

3 In pairs or as a group, students complete the exercise. Ask them to give reasons for their opinions.

Suggested answers

1 No – it's only suitable for groups of two or more.
2 Yes – it's perfect for teenagers and people who like challenges.
3 No – they're too young.
4 No – it will cost more than that.
5 No – it's only suitable for people who speak English well.

OPTIMISE YOUR EXAM

A review

Ask students to read the tips.

- All good reviews follow a similar structure: an overview, positive and negative aspects, and a verdict or recommendation. Point out that, in real life, readers often look at the last paragraph of a review first to see what the general verdict is. Remind students to make sure their review gives a clear verdict.
- In a review, students will need to entertain their target audience as well as inform them about a place, a restaurant or a film. Highlight the personal and youth-friendly style of the review in Exercise 2. The review catches the reader's attention by opening with rhetorical questions, e.g. *Are you on holiday in Athens? Are you keen on solving puzzles?*, and addresses the reader as *you*. The writer uses a broad range of vocabulary, e.g. *scenarios, mysterious* and *race against time*.

Exam task

4 Ask students to complete the exercise. Check answers in open class.

Answers

Students' own answers

5 Plan Ask students to complete the paragraph plan using their notes from Exercise 4. You may want to look at students' plans, if this is possible, to check them and give advice and suggestions for improvement before students write.

6 Write Students write their review in about 100 words, in an appropriate style. Depending on time, it may be a good idea to set this and the subsequent checklist exercise for homework.

7 Check Students complete the checklist before they hand in their review.

For more information on reviews, refer students to the Writing reference, page 171.

Homework OWB

Assign students Writing exercises 1, 2, 3 and 4 on page 26 of their Workbook and Progress check 3 on page 27.

4 Give it a go

UNIT AIMS

Exam preparation in Unit 4:

- scan an online guide to find specific information
- recognise similar meanings in a multiple-choice listening exercise
- explain likes and dislikes in a discussion
- understand connectors of contrast and apply them in a sentence-transformation exercise
- describe personal experience in a short message

TEACHER'S PRESENTATION KIT

- *Talk2Me* videos
- Speaking test videos
- Class and Workbook audio
- Workbook pages and answer key

UNIT OVERVIEW

Student's Book / Digital Student's Book SB		Workbook / Online Workbook OWB
LESSON / EXAM TASK	EXAM SKILLS / LANGUAGE FOCUS	CONSOLIDATION
Reading **Multiple matching**	Scanning An online guide	Workbook, pp 28–29, Exercises 1, 2, 3 Unit 4, Reading, Exercises 1, 2, 3
Grammar 1	*will* and *be going to*	Workbook, p 30, Exercises 1, 2, 3 Unit 4, Grammar 1, Exercises 1, 2, 3
Vocabulary	Words connected with *outdoor activities* Phrasal verbs Collocations connected with *free time*	Workbook, pp 30–31, Exercises 1, 2, 3 Unit 4, Vocabulary, Exercises 1, 2, 3
Listening **Multiple choice**	Recognising similar meanings	Workbook, p 32, Exercises 1, 2 Unit 4, Listening, Exercises 1, 2
Grammar 2	Present simple and present continuous for the future	Workbook, p 31, Exercises 1, 2 Unit 4, Grammar 2, Exercises 1, 2
Speaking **Discussion**	Explaining likes and dislikes	Workbook, pp 32–33, Exercises 1, 2, 3 Unit 4, Speaking, Exercises 1, 2, 3
Language in Use **Sentence transformation**	Connectors of contrast	Workbook, p 33, Exercises 1, 2, 3 Unit 4, Language in Use, Exercises 1, 2, 3
Writing **A short message**	Describing personal experience	Workbook, p 34, Exercises 1, 2, 3, 4 Unit 4, Writing, Exercises 1, 2, 3, 4
Progress check	Check language progress for Units 3 and 4	Workbook, p 35, Progress check and Cumulative progress Progress check and Cumulative progress

Additional material

PRESENTATION KIT	TEACHER'S / STUDENT'S RESOURCE CENTRE RC	TEST GENERATOR
Talk2Me video *I'm a big fan of …*	**Unit 4 worksheets:** *Optimise your grammar* (Standard and Higher), *Optimise your vocabulary* (Standard and Higher), *Talk2Me* video, *Say it right* **Units 3–4 worksheets:** CLIL, Culture, Everyday English (TRC only), Grammar communication (TRC only)	Unit Test 4 (Standard and Higher) Progress Test (Standard and Higher)

READING
Multiple matching | An online guide

→ Student's Book, pages 36–37 SB

Lesson aims

- Focus on scanning
- Practise a multiple-matching exam task

Lead-in

Elicit the meaning of the unit title ***Give it a go*** (*to try something to see if you like it or can do it*). *'Give it a go'* is a typical British response to *'I'm not sure I'd like it.'* Elicit what students think the lesson is going to be about (*new experiences, leisure*).

1 Ask students to complete the exercise. Elicit answers from different students around the class.

Ask if anybody has experienced wearing a virtual reality headset and, if so, what it was like.

Answers

1 A teenager is playing a game wearing a virtual reality headset.

2 Students' own answers

2 Ask students to complete the exercise. Elicit answers in open class.

Answers

1 d **2** e **3** a **4** c **5** b

EXAM SKILL

Scanning

Ask students to read the tips.

- Scanning is a strategy for speed reading in order to find specific information in a text. Students won't have time to read every text in detail in a reading exam, so scanning can help them quickly locate the answers.
- Elicit situations where students need to find a particular piece of information quickly within a large amount of text (e.g. *a word in a dictionary, a sports score in a newspaper*, etc.). Highlight key techniques, such as keeping the concept clearly in mind as you scan, and using words in bold, italics, a different font size, font or colour to help locate specific information. Many students find that using a highlighter pen helps them to concentrate and enhances their understanding.
- Remind them to always start by reading the introduction to the task and the title of the text, and then read the text just to get an overall impression and understanding of it.

3 Ask students to complete the exercise. Set a two-minute time limit to stop them from reading in too much detail at this stage. Elicit answers in open class.

Answers

1 C, H **2** B, C, G **3** E **4** G **5** D, E **6** F **7** A **8** G

OPTIMISE YOUR EXAM

Multiple matching

Ask students to read the tips.

- This type of task focuses on detail, opinion, specific information, implication (things that are implied or suggested in the text).
- Remind students that questions and texts are not necessarily in the same order and they should also be aware that important information may come in different parts of the same paragraph.
- Remind students to use paraphrasing of ideas rather than individual words in the questions to help them identify the answer in the text. Underlining the key words in each question and the options will help them identify synonyms in the text. This will, in turn, help students decide on their answer.
- In class, always ask your students to tell you why a particular part of the text matches a question. This helps them check their choices carefully.

▼ Exam task

4 1.21 **Note: The reading text is also available on the audio CD. You may want to have students listen and read the text before doing the exam task.**

Ask students to complete the exercise. Have them compare in pairs before you check answers in open class. Elicit the key phrases in the texts that helped students decide on their answers.

Mixed ability

In a less confident class, ask students to underline the key words in the question in Exercise 4 and identify key phrases for the first teenager to help them look for their answer in the text. Ask them to think of synonyms and related phrases. (*Which activity from the text would be <u>most suitable</u> for these teenagers? Write the answer in each gap. / 1 Grace enjoys <u>finding out about the past</u> and is interested in <u>learning about how things work</u>. She is also interested in <u>business</u>.*)

Answers

1 B (*... classic games on games consoles from the last 40 years. While you are playing, you'll learn about the way gaming has developed into the multi-billion pound industry it is today.*)

2 H (*Watching a film in a D-BOX seat will blow your mind! ... Both in the cinema ... or at home ..., it puts you in the middle of the action ...*)

3 A (*... virtual reality rollercoaster in the UK ... Riders actually travel on a real rollercoaster ... You will think you are flying beyond the stars, around black holes and through distant galaxies!*)

4 G (*Google Cardboard allows people to experience virtual reality for very little cost. Apart from games, other apps allow you to experience activities such as hang-gliding and deep-sea diving.*)

5 E (*... you can enjoy ... concerts from anywhere in the world. The system records a live event and then creates a virtual version online.*)

Fast finishers

Students write a profile for the type of person who would enjoy one of the other activities in the text (C, D and F). They can read out their profiles for others to match to an activity in the text.

5 Ask students to complete the exercise. Check answers in open class.

Answers
1 float **2** exact **3** mind **4** app **5** gamers **6** frightening

THINK | RESEARCH | CULTURE | LEARN | **ME**

Students could discuss the questions in pairs before you elicit their opinions in open class.

Homework OWB
Assign students Reading exercises 1, 2 and 3 on pages 28–29 of their Workbook.

GRAMMAR 1
will* and *be going to

→ Student's Book, page 38 SB

Lesson aims

- Understand the correct usage of *will* and *be going to*
- Practise using *will* and *be going to*

Lead-in

Write the following on the board: *My intentions for the rest of the year (things I want to do but haven't arranged). My predictions about technology.* Write some example sentences, e.g. *I'm going to buy an electric bicycle this year. I think virtual reality will become part of daily life for billions of people.*

Have students talk for a minute about each topic and make sure they are clear about the difference between *predictions* (a forecast, what someone thinks might or will happen in the future) and *intentions* (plans). Elicit some examples in open class.

Grammar in context

Ask students to complete the task. Refer them to the information in the *Remember* box if they aren't sure. Check answers in open class and ask them to explain their choice.

Remind students that they can find more information in the Grammar reference, Unit 4, page 151.

Answers
1 b **2** a

Language note

We can use a variety of future forms to express different meanings. We cannot be certain about what happens in the future, so the choice of future form depends on the speaker's intention or mood. *Will* is the most common way to talk about the future. Remind students that we often use the contracted form of *will* in spoken English. *'ll* is pronounced with the dark /l/ sound like the /l/ in *full* rather than *light*.

Another less common alternative to *will* is *shall*. Elicit the negative of *shall* (*shall not* or *shan't*). Point out that *shall* for future reference is restricted to first-person pronouns (*I* and *we*) and that *shall* is more commonly used for making offers, e.g. *Shall I bring you some sandwiches?*

Remind students that we use *gonna* /gʌnə/ in informal contexts, especially in speaking and in song lyrics. We write *gonna* to show how to pronounce it, e.g. *Are you gonna try and come as soon as you can? / Are you going to try and come as soon as you can?*

1 Ask students to complete the exercise. Check answers in open class.

Answers
1 ✓ (*be going to* to talk about plans) **2** Shall (*shall* for suggestions) **3** ✓ (*going to* to make a prediction based on evidence) **4** ✓ (*will* to make a prediction – *I expect that you will love it.*) **5** 'm/am going to (*going to* to express intention) **6** ✓ (*will* for a decision made at the time of speaking)

2 Ask students to describe what activity is featured in the advertisement. Elicit if anybody has ever tried paintballing and ask them to share their experiences in open class.

Ask students to complete the exercise. Have them compare in pairs before you check answers in open class.

Answers
1 will / are going to (both can be used for prediction) **2** will (Point out that it is more natural to use *will* here and there is no evidence for the prediction.) **3** will (*will* to talk about offers and promises) **4** will (*will* to talk about offers and promises) **5** is going to (*going to* to make predictions based on evidence) **6** are you going to (*going to* to ask about plans in the future)

Cultural note

Paintballing was developed in the 1980s in the USA. Players have to eliminate their opponents by hitting them with paintballs shot from a paintball gun. The game's focus is on teamwork and strategy and there are many different game types. All players are required to wear safety gear as paintballing can be dangerous.

3 Ask students to complete the exercise. Have them compare in pairs before you check answers in open class.

Ask if paintballing is popular in their country and if they have played or know someone who has played it. Elicit other fun, outdoor activities that people book for a party or celebration.

Answers
1 am/'m going to (*be going to* for plans) **2** will/'ll / am/'m going to (*will* for general predictions or *be going to* for plans) **3** Shall (*shall* for suggestions) **4** will/'ll (*will* for a spontaneous decision at the moment of speaking) **5** is/'s going to (*going to* for when you think something is very likely) **6** Are you going to (*going to* for intentions) **7** will/'ll / is/'s going to (*will* to give general information about the future or *be going to* for plans) **8** will/'ll (*will* for a spontaneous decision at the moment of speaking)

Homework OWB
Assign students Grammar 1 exercises 1, 2 and 3 on page 30 of their Workbook.

VOCABULARY
Topic vocabulary | Phrasal verbs | Collocations

→ Student's Book, page 39 SB

Lesson aims
Understand the correct usage of:
- words connected with *outdoor activities*
- phrasal verbs
- collocations connected with *free time*

Lead-in

Ask students if they prefer indoor or outdoor activities, and elicit a few ideas for activities they do. Encourage interesting and unusual answers.

They could then try to classify a few activities, e.g. *outdoor = hiking, camping / indoor = basketball, bowling, five-a-side football*, etc.

Words connected with *outdoor activities*

1 1.22 Ask students to complete the exercise. Play the audio for them to listen and check their answers. Remind students that in this exercise the *-ing* form of the verb is used like a noun to name activities.

Answers/Audioscript
1 hiking **2** horse-riding **3** ice skating **4** rock climbing **5** sailing **6** skiing **7** snowboarding **8** sky-diving

2 In pairs, students complete the exercise. Elicit answers in open class. Highlight that this is a typical question in official oral examinations.

Answers
Students' own answers

Refer students to the Vocabulary reference, page 163, for more information on topic vocabulary.

Phrasal verbs

3 1.23 Ask students to complete the exercise. Play the audio for them to listen and check their answers.

Answers/Audioscript
1 (b) I've got some free time so I'm going to *take up* sailing. – start doing (a new hobby)
2 (f) I've recently started to *work out* at the gym three times a week. – exercise
3 (a) The bad weather means they are going to *call off* the tennis competition. – cancel
4 (h) Are you going to *go out* this evening or help me clean the house? – leave your house to meet friends, etc.
5 (c) At the weekend, my brother and I *stay up* and watch TV. – don't go to bed until later than usual
6 (g) Let's *get together* on Sunday and I'll tell you all about my hiking trip. – meet, spend time together
7 (d) My family and I try to *eat out* together at least once a month. – go to a restaurant
8 (e) I'm really tired, so I'll probably *sleep in* tomorrow morning. – stay in bed in the morning longer than usual

4 Ask students to complete the exercise. Walk round, monitoring and helping students with language if necessary. Ask them to compare their sentences in pairs and elicit any interesting or unusual sentences in open class.

Answers
Students' own answers

Fast finishers

In pairs, students read out their sentences without saying the phrasal verb (they could substitute this for a 'beep' sound) for their partner to guess.

Refer students to the Vocabulary reference, page 164, for more information on phrasal verbs.

Collocations connected with *free time*

5 1.24 Ask students to complete the exercise. Play the audio for them to listen and check their answers.

Answers/Audioscript
1 I'd love to *have a go at* snowboarding because it looks like a lot of fun.
2 Do you like *spending time with* friends at the weekend?
3 It's important to *make time for* your interests.
4 You should *take a break from* work and try to relax.
5 We *had a good time* on the camping trip.
6 The next time we *have the day off* school, let's go ice skating.

Refer students to the Vocabulary reference, page 164, for more information on collocations.

THINK | **RESEARCH** | CULTURE | LEARN | ME

Ask students to complete the task. If you don't have access to the internet in the classroom, set this for homework and ask students to present their research at the start of the next class.

Homework OWB
Assign students Vocabulary exercises 1, 2 and 3 on pages 30–31 of their Workbook.

LISTENING
Multiple choice

→ Student's Book, page 40 SB

Lesson aims

- Learn to recognise similar meanings
- Practise a multiple-choice exam task

Lead-in

Play ***Noughts and crosses*** to recycle phrasal verbs and collocations from the previous lesson. Divide the class into two teams: X and O. Draw two three-by-three grids on the board. Write these phrasal verbs and collocations in each square of one of the grids, in random order: *have a day off, have a go, spend time with, make time for, take a break from, sleep in, work out, take up, call off.* Each team must think of a grammatically correct sentence using the phrasal verb / collocation in the square they choose to win, e.g. *I've got the day off school tomorrow.* If they win a square, write X or O in the same square of the second grid. The first team to get a line in a row wins the game.

1 Focus students' attention on the photo and elicit where the people are. Ask them to speculate about what sort of film the people are watching. (*They are in a cinema, but it looks like a restaurant or a club. They seem to be watching a black-and-white film, maybe it's a classic old movie.*)

In pairs or as a group, students complete the exercise. Elicit answers in open class. Ask students to share their experiences in class if they have had a similar experience at a cinema like the one in the photo.

Answers

Students' own answers

Optional extension

Brainstorm associated words and phrases for the theme *cinema* and pre-teach some of the vocabulary students will need in this lesson. Check that they understand what the words mean and how they are pronounced, e.g. *on the big screen, movie, seats, buy a ticket, go along to a venue, open-air cinema, silent movies, headsets, 3D glasses, special effects, cinema-goers.*

EXAM SKILL

Recognising similar meanings

Ask students to read the tips.

- Remind students that the speaker's words do not match the exact words in the statements. Encourage them to read the statements before they listen. It will help them focus on the aspects of the text they need to listen out for and identify synonyms or similar words explained in another way (paraphrasing).
- Highlight that students should also think of words with opposite as well as similar meanings and related words in the same thematic group. They need to think of words that are related to the idea in the question. They will work on this in Exercise 2.

2 Ask students to complete the exercise. You could do the first one together, if appropriate. Elicit answers in open class.

Answers

1 A **2** X **3** X **4** B **5** C **6** X

OPTIMISE YOUR EXAM

Multiple choice

Ask students to read the tips.

- An awareness of how listening tasks work and what distractors are can really help improve students' listening score. Put simply, a distractor is the 'trick' answer – the one you think that may be right if you don't read the whole question. A common mistake students make is to pick their answer and stick to it. Remind them that they should be ready to challenge their first ideas in the second listening.
- Students should get used to answering all the questions, even if they are not sure of the correct answer – they've probably understood more than they think.

Exam task

3 1.25 Play the track and ask students to complete the exercise. Don't check answers yet as they will listen again in Exercise 4.

4 1.25 Play the track again for students to listen and check their answers. Check answers in open class. Elicit the key words or phrases that helped them decide on their answers.

Answers

1 B (*Servers come to the cars and you can buy popcorn and drinks to have while you watch.*)

2 C (*… your seat moves, you feel air and water on your face and you smell scents connected to what you can see on the screen.*)

3 B (*… and go along to the venue, without knowing what to expect.*)

4 C (*… One thing that stops people having open-air cinemas is the noise. However, with wireless headsets, silent cinema solves that problem.*)

5 A (*… but some others find it annoying when people use their phones in the cinema. That's partly because phones are bright in a dark cinema, and make noises.*)

6 C (*You can send messages during the film and your messages appear on the screen, next to the film.*)

Extra support

Play the audio again for students to listen out for why the other options are not correct, or give them the audioscript to underline the distracting information. Ask students to work in pairs or small groups, and check answers in open class. Remind them that they can sometimes answer multiple-choice questions by elimination using this skill.

Answers

1 A She says *You drove into the parking area and stayed in your car to watch …*, but she's talking about the 1950s. C She says *you don't need to be able to drive*, similar to the key words in 'need a driving licence'.

2 A She says *where you wear special glasses and things look very real*, but she's talking about 3D cinema, not 4D. B She says you *might feel all the crashes in your seat*, which would be uncomfortable, but she says *They're great fun for a group* and she's going back again.
3 A She says *You buy your ticket for the film you want to see*, i.e. you know what film you are going to see. C She doesn't say anything about the people you might meet there. She talks about the organisers, but we don't know if they are at the event.
4 A She doesn't say specifically that you can hear everything the characters say, just a general comment *everyone hears the dialogue and the music through headphones*. B She doesn't say that you can talk to your friends, she just says *You can sit with your friends*.
5 B She talks about phones making noises – not about people who speak loudly to their friends. C She doesn't say anything about social media.
6 A Students have to infer that it is probably distracting as messages appear on the screen while you are watching the film. B The messages on the screen are the audience's opinions about the film, not subtitles.

THINK | RESEARCH | CULTURE | LEARN | ME

In pairs or as a group, students complete the task. Elicit answers in open class.

Homework

OWB

Assign students Listening exercises 1 and 2 on page 32 of their Workbook.

GRAMMAR 2
Present simple and present continuous for the future

→ Student's Book, page 41 SB

Lesson aims

- Understand the correct usage of the present simple and present continuous for the future
- Practise using the present simple and present continuous for the future

Lead-in

Ask students to complete these sentences with verbs in the present simple or present continuous:

1 What time ______ (the train to Cambridge/leave)?

2 What ______ (you/do) tomorrow afternoon?

3 The film ______ (start) at 8:45 pm.

4 I ______ (visit) a friend this weekend.

Monitor carefully to see if students are familiar with these future forms.

Answers

1 does the train to Cambridge leave **2** are you doing **3** starts **4** am/'m visiting

Grammar in context

Ask students to complete the task. Check their answers and ask them to read more about the present simple and present continuous for the future in the *Remember* box.

Remind students that they can find more information in the Grammar reference, Unit 4, page 152.

Answers

1 b **2** a

Language note

It can help students to remember that the present continuous is used for fixed arrangements if you call this use 'the diary tense' (we use it to talk about the sort of future events that you might write in your diary, e.g. ***I'm meeting** Sarah on Saturday at 10 am.*).

Point out that when we use the present simple to talk about a future event, the sentences usually contain words like: *to be, open, close, begin, start, end, finish, arrive, come, leave, return*, e.g. *The plane leaves at 9 pm.*

1 Ask students to complete the exercise. Have them compare in pairs before you check answers in open class.

Answers

1 starts **2** does ... start **3** Are ... seeing **4** is/'s driving **5** comes **6** doesn't leave **7** isn't meeting **8** am/'m going

2 Ask students to describe what they can see in the photo. (*There are three teenagers – one with a tablet, another with a laptop and another looking at a smartphone.*) Check students know the meaning of the word *blog* (a regular record of your thoughts, opinions or experiences that you put on the internet) and focus their attention on the title of the text. Elicit what they think the text is going to be about.

Ask students to complete the exercise. Have them compare in pairs before you check answers in open class.

Answers

1 am/'m catching **2** leaves **3** is/'s taking **4** are meeting **5** are/'re going **6** 's/is / are/'re playing **7** starts **8** are/'re having **9** are/'re recording **10** am/'m writing

3 In pairs, students complete the exercise. Elicit answers from different students around the class.

Answers

Students' own answers

Extra support

In a less confident class, ask students to prepare their answers in written form before they do this as a speaking activity. Walk round, monitoring and helping students where necessary. Give feedback after the activity on good language and write common errors on the board for students to correct in open class.

THINK | RESEARCH | CULTURE | **LEARN** | ME

Ask students to complete the task. Alternatively, they could prepare this for homework and discuss the blogs they have found in open class at the start of the next lesson.

Homework

OWB

Assign students Grammar 2 exercises 1 and 2 on page 31 of their Workbook.

Assign students the Flipped classroom tasks on page 42 of their Student's Book if you'd like them to prepare for the next lesson. To complete this task, students need to watch the *Talk2Me* video which can be found on the Resource Centre.

SPEAKING
Discussion

→ Student's Book, page 42 SB

Lesson aim

- Explaining likes and dislikes

The *Talk2Me* video in this unit focuses on likes and dislikes. In the audio tracks, people explain their likes and dislikes and give reasons for their answers. Students answer some comprehension questions and then listen out for linking words and phrases for giving reasons. The video can be used in one of two ways:

Flipped classroom

Flipped classroom option

Using this approach, students watch the video and complete the exercises for homework. This prepares students for the speaking lesson by introducing them to the topic and the key phrases to use in the exam task. Teachers who use this method will find they have more class time to spend on activating the target language and developing fluency for the final task.

***Talk2Me* worksheet**

Ask students to also complete the *Talk2Me* worksheet on the Resource Centre for more detailed comprehension exercises and more practice of the key phrases.

Classroom option

Lead-in

Play the game ***First to five*** to revise useful vocabulary from the unit. Say different word categories for pairs or small groups to race against each other to think of five words for each one. When they have five, they shout out 'First to five'. Check their answers. If they are correct, they get a point. The pair or group with the most points wins the game.

Suggested categories: *different types of cinema, words connected to the cinema, sporting activities, technology, phrasal verbs connected to the theme* leisure.

1 Ask students to read the questions. Play the *Talk2Me* video for students to complete the exercise. Play the video again, if necessary, before checking their answers.

Answers

1 social media

2 Have a night off to chill out and hang out with their best friends. Turn off their phones.

3 They decide to go to the party.

2 Play the *Talk2Me* video again, so students underline the phrases in the *Phrase expert* box. Pause the video from time to time if necessary. Check answers in open class.

Answers

Angus: None of us are big fans of milkshake. (*this is said as a joke*) / I prefer to just chill out on a Friday night. / That's because you're so busy.

Maddy: I really like my phone. / We don't really like dancing. / I'm not a big fan of all the reminders.

Jamie: I'm not keen on pizza with loads of cool friends. / I don't mind the reminders so much but sometimes social media gets me down a bit.

***Talk2Me* worksheet**

Ask students to also complete the *Talk2Me* worksheet on the Resource Centre for more detailed comprehension exercises and more practice of the key phrases.

Answers

The transcript and answer key for the *Talk2Me* video exercises and Worksheet can be found on the Teacher's Resource Centre.

3 In pairs or as a group, students ask and answer the questions. Elicit answers from different students around the class.

Suggested answers

1 In one photo there are three girls. Two are ice skating and pulling the other on a sledge. In the other photo a boy is watching something on a tablet. He is listening to it with headphones.

2 Students' own answers

EXAM SKILL

Explaining likes and dislikes

Ask students to read the tips.

- To be awarded top marks, students need to show the examiner they have a range of vocabulary and should try not to repeat the same words or expressions. Remind students that they will impress the examiner if they ask about their partner's likes and dislikes, e.g. *How do you feel about that?* and react to each other's likes and dislikes, e.g. *Me too, I'm crazy about skateboarding.*
- Remind students that *very much* and *a lot* always come after the things they like, e.g. *I like skateboarding a lot* NOT ~~*I like a lot skateboarding*~~.

4 1.26 Play the track for students to listen and complete the exercise. Check answers in open class.

Answers
A Layla 3 Rory 2
B Layla 3 Rory 1

5 1.26 Play the track again for students to listen and complete the exercise. Check answers in open class.

Answers
Students should tick: 2, 3, 4, 6

Mixed ability

Play the track again for students to note down activities Layla and Rory like and dislike doing and the reasons they give. Check their answers and write the activities and key expressions on the board for students to refer to in the next activity.

Answers

Layla: I love watching films, so I go to the cinema whenever I can. I'm a big fan of fantasy films. The reason is that you can relax and forget about the real world. … I also like swimming. It's really good exercise, so I go to the pool two or three times a week. … I'm not very keen on being cold. Oh … except skiing. I did it once and I loved it. I'm going again this winter.

Rory: Personally, I like doing sport in my free time. I play basketball a lot. … I prefer outdoor activities like rock climbing. … I'm not a big fan of winter sports.

OPTIMISE YOUR EXAM

Discussion

Ask students to read the tips.

- Highlight that candidates score well in this section of the exam if they make positive contributions that extend the discussion as far as possible, before coming to a conclusion. Highlight how Layla and Rory kept the conversation going in Exercise 4 by responding to what their partner says and asking follow-up questions, showing that they are listening and interested (*Do you like swimming? Where do you go to do it?*).
- Remind students that they can also make suggestions and talk about what they would like to do in the future. Refer how Layla and Rory did this in their discussion in Exercise 4 (*You could go camping and stay the whole weekend though … I'm going again this winter.*).

Exam task

6 In pairs, students complete the task. Elicit answers from different students around the class.

Homework OWB
Assign students Speaking exercises 1, 2 and 3 on pages 32–33 of their Workbook.

SAY IT RIGHT

Long vowels TRC

For the *Say it right* pronunciation activity and instructions, go to the Teacher's Resource Centre.

LANGUAGE IN USE
Sentence transformation

→ Student's Book, page 43 SB

Lesson aims

- Focus on connectors for contrasting ideas
- Practise a sentence-transformation exam task

Lead-in

Write these sports on the board: *sky-diving, skiing, skateboarding, snowboarding, running, skating, swimming, ice hockey.* In pairs or small groups, students rank the sports in order of danger. Elicit answers in open class and ask students to justify their choices. In a less confident class, write some prompt phrases on the board to help them in this speaking activity:

I don't agree. X is much more dangerous than Y, because …
I agree. X is as dangerous as Y, because …
I think X is a bit more dangerous / a bit less dangerous than Y, because …

1 In pairs, students complete the exercise. Elicit answers from different students around the class.

Answers
Students' own answers

Language note

Point out that students are often asked to talk about a life experience in official oral examinations. The question is in the present perfect, e.g. ***Have you ever done*** *an extreme sport?*, so students should answer in this tense but then go on to describe details of experiences they have had in the past simple, e.g. *Yes, I have. I* ***went*** *snowboarding last year.* Remind students to use their imagination and even if they don't have any past experience to talk about, they can say what they would like to do.

Remember

Ask students to read the information.

We can use these linking words (conjunctions) when we want to connect two contrasting ideas in the same sentence or we want to link one idea to another one which is surprising or unexpected. These conjunctions emphasise a contrast more than *but* and they will get students more marks in their writing and speaking exams if they can use a wide variety of forms.

Even though is a slightly stronger form of *although*. We can use both at the beginning or in the middle of a sentence: *Although / Even though the weather is bad, London's the best city in the world. / London's the best city in the world, although / even though the weather is bad.*

We can use *though* (but not *although* or *even though*) with a meaning similar to *however* or *nevertheless*. In these cases, we usually put it at the end of a clause, e.g. *'It's a bit expensive.' 'It's nice, though.'*.

The only difference between *in spite of* and *despite* is the *of*. They can go in the middle or at the beginning of a sentence: *I love London despite / in spite of the bad weather. In spite of / Despite the bad weather, I love London.*

Remind students that they can find more information in the Grammar reference, Unit 4, page 152.

2 Ask students to complete the exercise. Have them compare in pairs before you check answers in open class.

Answers
1 although / even though **2** despite / in spite of **3** Despite / In spite of **4** Although / Even though **5** although / even though **6** Despite / In spite of

3 Ask students to complete the exercise. Elicit answers in open class.

Answers
1 a **2** b **3** a **4** b

OPTIMISE YOUR EXAM

Sentence transformation

Ask students to read the tips.

- These connectors are commonly used for sentence transformations because they have very similar functions, but their application is a little different.
- Ask students to read the information about doing sentence transformations and elicit the correct answer to the first question in Exercise 4 as an example. Emphasise the importance of including all the information and point out that not doing this is a common way for students to lose marks.

Exam task

4 Ask students to complete the exercise. Check answers in open class.

Answers
1 though **2** the fact **3** in spite **4** (her) feeling **5** despite / in spite of **6** despite the fact

Homework

OWB

Assign students Language in Use exercises 1, 2 and 3 on page 33 of their Workbook.

WRITING
A short message

→ Student's Book, pages 44–45 SB

Lesson aims

- Focus on language for describing personal experience
- Plan and write a short message

Lead-in

Write the adjectives that appear in this lesson on the board and check the meaning by asking students to think of synonyms: *annoyed, brilliant, disappointing, excited, fantastic, scary, thrilled, wonderful, worried, awesome.* In pairs or small groups, ask students to take turns to mime the adjectives for others to guess.

1 In pairs or groups, students complete the exercise. Elicit answers from different students around the class.

Answers
Students' own answers

EXAM SKILL

Describing personal experience

Ask students to read the tips.

- *Guess what?* is often a great way to start because notes are normally written in an informal style and students have very limited space.
- Students should try to use as wide a variety of tenses as possible in a very short text.
- Elicit adjectives that students can use to talk about personal experiences, e.g. *A memorable / amazing / shocking / unforgettable experience (that/which) I had is …* Remind them that they should reflect on the situation and carefully choose no more than one or two strong adjectives to help them get their point across.
- Remind students that *experience* is an uncountable noun when we are talking about knowledge or skill, e.g. *Do you have any babysitting experience?* However, in this context, *experience* is the countable form for when we are talking about incidents that affect us, e.g. *Bungee jumping is quite an experience.*

For more information on writing short messages, refer students to the Writing reference, page 169.

2 Ask students to complete the exercise. Check answers in open class.

Elicit the purpose of the first sentence in the text – to describe the situation as outlined in the task. Highlight the informal closing in this note: *Let me know.*

Answers
1 Ed's skates are broken. **2** He wants to borrow Matt's skates. **3** The competition is on Saturday.

3 Ask students to complete the exercise. Check answers in open class.

Answers
1 F **2** E **3** E **4** F **5** E **6** E **7** F **8** E **9** F **10** E

Language note

-ed adjectives are used to talk about a person's feelings or opinions (these are the *receivers* of feelings) and *-ing* adjectives are used to describe things, people, places, activities (these are the *sources* or the *causes* of the feelings).

Extra support

Give students an example sentence with an adjective from Exercise 3 and write it on the board: *Doing something annoying makes you feel annoyed.* Drill similar sentences with the other *-ed/-ing* adjectives (*disappointing, excited, thrilled, worried*). Ask students to write three or four questions about places, people, things, events and activities using the adjectives, e.g. *What do you find really annoying?* In pairs, students take turns to ask and answer the questions.

OPTIMISE YOUR EXAM

A short message

Ask students to read the tips.

- Remind students that they should spend only about 10 minutes maximum on this task in an official writing exam.
- They won't lose marks for small spelling and grammar errors in this task, but highlight that students often make mistakes in this section by using *ever* in positive statements (~~*I have ever tried in-line skating.*~~), or not using the past simple as soon as a time expression in the past is given (~~*I have had a problem with my motorbike this week.*~~).

Language note

Students may have to use a passive form to describe the situation. Ask students to look for the passive form in the note in Exercise 2 (*my skates are broken*) and revise how we make a passive structure in English (subject + *be* + past participle) to describe an action performed by another person or by yourself. The person doing the work does not have to be named.

Exam task

4 Ask students to complete the exercise. Check answers in open class.

Answers

1 I'm really excited because I'm entering a bike race. ✓ I've got a bike race this weekend! ✓ **2** (suggested answers) It's got a puncture, the brakes don't work … **3** (suggested answer) Could I please borrow your bike? **4** Students' own answers

Language note

Students are often asked to write a note to borrow something, e.g. *Can I borrow your bike?* Remind them that they can impress the examiner if they use *lend* in their note back to their friend instead of *borrow*, e.g. *Can you lend me your bike?* Revise the difference between the two verbs: *lend* – to give something to someone else to use for a period of time, *borrow* – to receive something from someone else for a period of time.

5 Plan Ask students to complete the paragraph plan using their notes from Exercise 4. You may want to look at students' plans, if this is possible, to check them and give advice and suggestions for improvement before students write.

Exam task

6 Ask students to complete the task. Elicit which card is better and ask students to give reasons for their answer.

Answer

The first card simply copies all the language from the task with no attempt to put it into the writer's own words. Erin doesn't tell Emma anything about the experience of horse-riding and deals with each of the points in a very simple way. It is also too short.

The second card is better. Erin describes the experience and uses her own words. She also adds one or two relevant details to make the card seem more real.

7 Plan Ask students to make a plan for the task in Exercise 6.

8 Write Students write the short messages in exercises 4 and 6 in 35–45 words and in an appropriate style. Depending on time, it may be a good idea to set this and the subsequent checklist exercise for homework.

9 Check Students complete the checklist before they hand in their messages.

Homework

OWB

Assign students Writing exercises 1, 2, 3 and 4 on page 34 of their Workbook and Progress check 4 on page 35.

Answers PROGRESS CHECK Units 3–4

Exercise 1
1 Shall **2** am/'m going to **3** am/'m having **4** ✓ **5** I'll get

Exercise 2
1 has been making **2** have/'ve never been **3** hasn't bought **4** Have you seen **5** have/'ve been waiting

Exercise 3
1 d **2** f **3** a **4** b **5** c **6** e

Exercise 4
1 ✓ **2** in **3** have **4** going **5** ✓ **6** from taking **7** yourselves

Exercise 5
1 up **2** off **3** out **4** down **5** up **6** off/out **7** up

Exercise 6
1 Although **2** even though **3** in spite **4** Despite

Exercise 7
1 illegal **2** dishonest **3** uncomfortable **4** untidy **5** impatient **6** unfair

Exercise 8
1 many **2** much **3** few **4** piece **5** little

Exercise 9
1 passport **2** luggage **3** passenger **4** mind **5** exact

5 In good health

UNIT AIMS

Exam preparation in Unit 5:

- locate information in an online article
- understand agreement and disagreement phrases in a discussion
- talk about habits in an interview
- understand words formed from verbs and use them in a word-formation exercise
- use narrative tenses in a story

TEACHER'S PRESENTATION KIT

- *Talk2Me* videos
- Speaking test videos
- Class and Workbook audio
- Workbook pages and answer key

UNIT OVERVIEW

Student's Book / Digital Student's Book SB		Workbook / Online Workbook OWB
LESSON / EXAM TASK	EXAM SKILLS / LANGUAGE FOCUS	CONSOLIDATION
Reading **True/false/not stated**	Locating information An online article	Workbook, pp 36–37, Exercises 1, 2, 3, 4 Unit 5, Reading, Exercises 1, 2, 3, 4
Grammar 1	Modals (1): ability, obligation, advice, permission	Workbook, p 38, Exercises 1, 2, 3 Unit 5, Grammar 1, Exercises 1, 2, 3
Vocabulary	Words connected with *health and illness* Phrasal verbs Collocations with *have, take, make* and *do*	Workbook, pp 38–39, Exercises 1, 2, 3 Unit 5, Vocabulary, Exercises 1, 2, 3
Listening **True/false**	Understanding agreement and disagreement	Workbook, p 40, Exercises 1, 2, 3 Unit 5, Listening, Exercises 1, 2, 3
Grammar 2	Modals (2): possibility, probability, certainty	Workbook, p 39, Exercises 1, 2, 3 Unit 5, Grammar 2, Exercises 1, 2, 3
Speaking **Interview**	Talking about habits	Workbook, pp 40–41, Exercises 1, 2, 3 Unit 5, Speaking, Exercises 1, 2, 3
Language in Use **Word formation**	Words formed from verbs	Workbook, p 41, Exercises 1, 2, 3 Unit 5, Language in Use, Exercises 1, 2, 3
Writing **A story**	Using narrative tenses	Workbook, p 42, Exercises 1, 2, 3, 4 Unit 5, Writing, Exercises 1, 2, 3, 4
		Workbook, p 43, Progress check and Cumulative progress Progress check and Cumulative progress

Additional material

PRESENTATION KIT	TEACHER'S / STUDENT'S RESOURCE CENTRE RC	TEST GENERATOR
Talk2Me video *That depends on …*	**Unit 5 worksheets:** *Optimise your grammar* (Standard and Higher), *Optimise your vocabulary* (Standard and Higher), *Talk2Me* video, *Say it right* **Units 5–6 worksheets:** CLIL, Culture, Everyday English (TRC only), Grammar communication (TRC only)	Unit Test 5 (Standard and Higher)

READING

True/false/not stated | An online article

→ Student's Book, pages 48–49 SB

Lesson aims

- Focus on locating key information
- Practise a true/false/not stated exam task

Lead-in

Focus students' attention on the photo and ask them to describe it in open class (*a girl balancing on a rock by the edge of a lake*) and highlight that this denotes health and well-being. Draw students' attention to the unit title and elicit what they think the lesson is going to be about (*health*). Then ask in what ways people can stay healthy (e.g. *to exercise, to eat a healthy and balanced diet*).

1 In pairs or as a group, students complete the exercise. Elicit answers in open class. Highlight that *vet* is short for *veterinarian* (US) and *veterinary surgeon* (UK).

Answers

1 doctor **2** vet **3** dentist **4** nurse **5** chemist **6** paramedic

Fast finishers

Ask students to describe one of the jobs in Exercise 1 without saying what it is, for their partner to guess.

2 Ask students to complete the exercise. Set a two-minute time limit to prevent them from reading in too much detail at this stage. Elicit answers in open class.

Answers

1 b **2** a **3** a **4** c **5** b **6** c

EXAM SKILL

Locating information

Ask students to read the tips.

- Remind students that they also need to understand what the statement as a whole means as well as the key words. Important words to underline are also qualifying phrases, such as *some, usually, often, always, at least* and *occasionally*. These words are there to test if you have read the whole statement because they can change the meaning. Point out that students have to read the appropriate part of the text very carefully in order to understand what the writer means.
- Highlight that 'not stated' doesn't mean there are no words in the statements that match words in the text, but that they don't have enough information to answer the question as a whole.

3 Ask students to complete the exercise. Elicit answers in open class.

Suggested answers

1 Animals … usually stay there forever / We treat them, then release them back into the wild when they're healthy again

2 volunteers have to pay extra for meals / food and accommodation are part of the package

3 Members of the public often get in touch / Sometimes, someone in their garden, or someone walking or riding in the countryside, spots an animal in trouble. They contact us

4 rescue at least one injured deer each week / if you see two people carrying an injured deer on a stretcher

5 usually helps domestic animals / trapped animals, often pets

6 Foster parents receive training before they can look after the animals. / many go to volunteer foster parents. These people take an animal into their home for a short time

OPTIMISE YOUR EXAM

True/false/not stated

Ask students to read the tips.

- Students often find this type of reading task the most difficult of all. The biggest problem here is the *not stated* option because students are not sure what to look for. Highlight that *not stated* or *not given* doesn't mean there aren't any words in the statements that match words in the text, but that there isn't enough information to answer the question as a whole. Most students have not had much practice with questions like this and spend too much time making sure that it is *not stated* and this affects the rest of their test.
- Remind students that there will be at least one of all three answers. If they haven't got at least one *true, false* or *not stated*, they have probably got an answer wrong and they should go back and check.

▼ Exam task

4 2.01 **Note: The reading text is also available on the audio CD. You may want to have students listen and read the text before doing the exam task.**

Ask students to complete the exercise. Have them compare in pairs before you check answers in open class. Confirm the phrases they chose in Exercise 3.

Answers

1 F (*We treat them, then release them back into the wild when they're healthy again …*)

2 F (*… food and accommodation are part of the package.*)

3 T (*Sometimes, someone in their garden, or someone walking or riding in the countryside, spots an animal in trouble. They contact us …*)

4 NS (Although the text says … *if you see two people carrying an injured deer* it doesn't talk about how many are rescued each week.)

5 T (*… often pets.*)

6 NS (Although the text says many go to volunteer foster parents it does not mention training.)

Mixed ability

Break the text into three parts (questions 1–2, 3–4, 5–6) and give less confident students the option of only reading about one organisation and answering two questions. Students can then share their information about the other texts. If stronger students finish early, ask them to write a one-line description of each voluntary organisation. When everyone has finished, ask them to read out their descriptions for others to identify which organisation they are talking about.

5 Ask students to complete the exercise. Check answers in open class.

Answers

1 care, after **2** release **3** accommodation **4** stretcher **5** trapped **6** permanent

Extra support

Give less confident students the words in a jumbled order, e.g. *release, permanent, after, stretcher, accommodation, care, trapped.*

Cultural note

Britain is an animal-loving nation and there are many animal welfare groups concerned with the health, and protection of animals. The best known of these are the Royal Society for the Prevention of Cruelty to Animals (RSPCA) in England and Wales, the USPCA in Northern Ireland and the Scottish SPCA and the RSPB for protecting birds. The RSPCA takes in over 16,000 wild animals each year and the charity receives a call every 30 seconds. The most frequent enquiry is how to help an injured animal.

THINK | RESEARCH | **CULTURE** | LEARN | ME

Students could discuss the questions in pairs before you elicit their answers in open class.

Optional extension 2.01

Play the recorded reading text and ask students to underline words and phrases connected to animal welfare and the names of animals. Check answers by eliciting synonyms and definitions in open class.

Answers

Animal welfare: sick and injured, taking care of, animals in need, feed the animals, build and clean the cages, give … love and attention, looks after ill or hurt wild animals, treat, release … back into the wild, (to be) healthy again, rescue, treatment, an animal in trouble, an animal that needs help, on a stretcher, to be in good hands, trapped animals, an animal that needs rescuing, medical care, badly hurt, well enough

Names of animals: deer, foxes, badgers, squirrels, monkeys, tortoises, sloths, ocelots, leopards, tropical birds, toucans, parrots

Homework

OWB

Assign students Reading exercises 1, 2, 3 and 4 on pages 36–37 of their Workbook.

GRAMMAR 1

Modals (1): ability, obligation, advice, permission

→ Student's Book, page 50 SB

Lesson aims

- Focus on modals to talk about ability, obligation, advice and permission
- Practise using modals

Lead-in

Ask students if they own a pet and, if so, what type of animal it is. Brainstorm rules, obligations and advice for owning a dog, and write the key ideas on the board. In pairs or small groups, ask students to write full sentences about owning a dog with a suitable modal verb, e.g. *You should take your dog for a walk every day.* Walk round, monitoring students as they work. Elicit answers in open class. If they seem familiar with modals, quickly work through the *Grammar in context* box as an open-class activity.

Grammar in context

Ask students to complete the task. Refer them to the information in the *Remember* box if they aren't sure. Check answers in open class and ask them to explain their choice.

Ask students to think of personalised sentences of their own using modals in the box. Elicit a few examples around the class.

Remind students that they can find more information in the Grammar reference, Unit 5, pages 152–153.

Answers

1 A **2** P **3** O **4** O **5** L **6** AD **7** A

Language note

Point out that when we talk about general past ability (not a specific ability) we use *could / could not*, e.g. *When I was younger, I **could** play football very well (but I can't now).*

Point out that *could* isn't enough to indicate the past on its own; we need the context of a time expression, e.g. *years ago*, to let us know it is the past, e.g. *He **could** run fast **years ago**.*

Have to and *need to* are often used in the same context, but *need to* is often used to express something that is less urgent, something in which you have a choice. Remind students we can also say *have got to* as well as *have to*, e.g. ***I've got to** get up early every day for school.*

Must and *have to* mean the same when we are talking about rules and external obligations, but we generally use *must* when we feel something is necessary (internal obligation), e.g. *I **must** do more exercise, I need to get fit.*

Ought / oughtn't to can be used in the same way as *should / shouldn't*, but *should* is more common, especially in negatives and questions, e.g. *You **shouldn't** get your hair wet if you have a cold / **Should** you go outside if it's cold?*

Extra support

In pairs, ask students to make sentences in the past and future similar to the examples for each point in the *Remember* box. Ask them to read out their sentences in open class. If appropriate, ask them to come up and write them on the board and discuss as a class if they are correct. Encourage them to make questions and negative sentences from their examples.

1 Ask students to complete the exercise. Check answers in open class and ask them to explain their choices.

Draw their attention to the silent letter *l* in *should* and *shouldn't* and the silent *t* in *mustn't*. Drill the pronunciation of these two forms.

Answers

1 couldn't (past ability) **2** mustn't (present obligation) **3** has to (present obligation) **4** shouldn't (past advice) **5** will be able to (future ability)

Extra support

Ask students to match the sentences in Exercise 1 with the grammatical rules in the *Remember* box (see Answers).

2 Ask students to complete the exercise. Have them compare in pairs before you check answers in open class. Elicit any differences in meaning.

Suggested answers

1 wasn't allowed to (permission); didn't (past simple – a fact); wasn't able to (ability)

2 can't (permission); shouldn't, ought not to (advice)

3 must (obligation); ought to, should (advice)

4 mustn't, wasn't allowed to (obligation); couldn't (permission)

5 can (ability): should, ought to (advice); must, has to, will have to (obligation)

3 Focus students' attention on the photo and ask them what they think the job is and what they think it involves (*a paramedic* – paramedics care for the sick or injured, respond to emergency calls, perform medical services and transport patients to hospitals; people's lives often depend on their quick reaction and competent care).

Ask students to complete the exercise. Have them compare in pairs before you check answers in open class. Accept all sensible suggestions.

Suggested answers

1 have to / must **2** don't have to / don't need to **3** should / ought to **4** can **5** shouldn't **6** can't / cannot **7** be able to **8** mustn't / shouldn't / can't **9** have to / need to / must / should / ought to **10** can **11** has to / needs to / must **12** can / are able to

Mixed ability

Give less confident students a limited set of answers in a jumbled order (*has to, should, are able to, don't have to, shouldn't, be able to, can × 2, have to, can't, mustn't, need to*). Tell more confident students to think of all the possible answers for each gap.

THINK | RESEARCH | CULTURE | LEARN | ME

Discuss the question in open class.

Suggested answers

It's satisfying helping people (especially taking people home) and every day is different. It's limited (they don't provide important medical care), the days are long and it can be stressful when there is an accident.

Optional extension

In pairs, students tell each other what they think they'd like to do as a job one day. They then write a list of tips for each other using *must, mustn't, have to, need to, don't have to, should, ought to, may, might, could*. Students then tell their partner and see if he/she agrees with their advice.

Homework OWB

Assign students Grammar 1 exercises 1, 2 and 3 on page 38 of their Workbook.

VOCABULARY

Topic vocabulary | Phrasal verbs | Collocations

→ Student's Book, page 51 SB

Lesson aims

Understand the correct usage of:

- words connected with *health and illness*
- phrasal verbs
- collocations with *have, take, make* and *do*

Lead-in

In open class, discuss what students would do in the situations below, using the question *If this happened to someone, what would you do?*

fell over and cut him/herself, had a nose bleed, had a high temperature, fell over and was in pain

Talking about ailments or illnesses can be a sensitive issue for some students. Using the 'one step removed' approach by using hypothetical situations can therefore be useful.

Suggested answers

apply an ice pack, ring for an ambulance, stop the bleeding, loosen clothing, apply cool, wet cloths to wrists and neck, calm the person down, wash the wound

Words connected with *health and illness*

1 2.02 Ask students to complete the exercise. Play the audio for them to listen and check their answers.

Answers/Audioscript

the body: ankle, blood, bone, chin, knee, shoulder, skin

problems and illness: ache, cold, cough, cut, flu, hurt, infection, injure, pain

treatments and help: bandage, medicine, operation, prescription

Fast finishers

Ask students to add two more items to each column in the table in Exercise 1. When everyone has finished, ask them to read out their extra items for others to say in which category they think they go.

2 Ask students to complete the exercise. Check answers in open class.

Answers

1 hurt/injured **2** bone **3** hurts **4** bandage **5** prescription **6** pain

Refer students to the Vocabulary reference, page 164, for more information on topic vocabulary.

Phrasal verbs

3 2.03 Ask students to complete the exercise. Play the audio for them to listen and check their answers.

Answers/Audioscript

1 (h) recover from: It took me a week to *get over* my cold.

2 (b) become ill with: Janie's *come down with* flu so she won't be coming to school this week.

3 (e) gain, add extra: My dad's on a diet because he *put on weight* over the summer.

4 (d) feel well enough for: I know you've got a bad stomach ache, but do you *feel up to* having some lunch?

5 (f) kill (a very sick animal): Our 22-year-old cat's very ill, so the vet might have to *put her down*. It's very sad.

6 (c) faint, become unconscious: I felt really lightheaded at school this morning and nearly *passed out*.

7 (a) become happier: *Cheer up*! Don't look so sad.

8 (g) make sad or miserable: It really *gets* me *down* when people don't look after animals properly.

Fast finishers

Ask students to write two true sentences and one false sentence about themselves using the phrasal verbs from Exercise 3. In pairs or small groups, they read out their sentences for their partner to guess which sentences are true or false.

Refer students to the Vocabulary reference, page 164, for more information on phrasal verbs.

Collocations with *have, take, make* and *do*

4 2.04 Ask students to complete the exercise. Have them compare in pairs before you play the audio for them to listen and check their answers.

Answers/Audioscript

1 have/take a bath/shower **2** make/take a decision **3** have a headache **4** make a mistake **5** make an effort **6** take care of someone **7** have flu or a cold/cough **8** make fun of someone **9** have/take medicine **10** do/take some exercise **11** have surgery or an operation **12** make up your mind **13** make your bed **14** do homework/housework **15** do your teeth/hair

5 Ask students to complete the exercise. Check answers in open class.

Suggested answers

1 Karen's made/taken a decision. / Karen's made up her mind.

2 Aidan's doing the housework.

3 Toby made a mistake.

4 Helen's going to have an operation / have surgery (on her knee).

5 My sister does / takes some exercise every morning.

6 Greg's really made an effort.

Refer students to the Vocabulary reference, page 164, for more information on collocations.

Optional extension

Ask students to write example sentences for some of the other phrases in Exercise 4, e.g. *have/take a bath/shower, have a headache, take care of someone*, etc. Walk round the classroom, monitoring students and helping with language if necessary. Ask students to compare their sentences in pairs.

Homework

OWB

Assign students Vocabulary exercises 1, 2 and 3 on pages 38–39 of their Workbook.

LISTENING
True/false

→ Student's Book, page 52 SB

Lesson aims

- Listen for phrases that express agreement and disagreement
- Practise a true/false exam task

Lead-in

In pairs or small groups, ask students to list all the items you can find in a first-aid kit. Elicit answers in open class.

Suggested answers

bandages, scissors, plasters, latex gloves, gauze, wipes, ice pack

1 Focus students' attention on the photos and ask them to describe what is happening. (*We can see some teenagers on a first-aid course, learning how to give CPR [cardiopulmonary resuscitation], an arm in plaster and a first-aid kit.*) Ask students if they have ever gone on a first-aid course and, if so, to share their experiences in open class.

In pairs or as a group, students complete the exercise. Encourage them to use the words in the box and a dictionary if necessary. Elicit answers from different students around the class.

Suggested answers

1 On a first-aid course, you learn to be able to recognise life-threatening situations and to offer vital assistance before more experienced help arrives. Some of the topics covered are CPR, how to put someone in the recovery position, how to deal with allergic reactions and what to do if someone is unconscious. You also learn how to use a first-aid kit to deal with a broken arm or leg, or a head injury and bleeding, such as a nose bleed.

2 Students' own answers

EXAM SKILL

Understanding agreement and disagreement

Ask students to read the tips.

- If students know the key words and signs of agreement and disagreement in a conversation, they will be able to rapidly tune in when a speaker is discussing other people's ideas and decide if he/she agrees or disagrees with them. This skill is useful in listening exams and will help them improve their performance in oral exams.
- Remind students that a response can give helpful clues as to whether the speaker has positive, negative or mixed reactions about the subject being discussed. In addition, highlight that often in listening exams, the first information sounds like the speakers are disagreeing but, in fact, later on they agree, or vice versa.

2 Ask students to complete the exercise. You could do the first one together, if appropriate. Elicit answers from different students around the class and accept all sensible suggestions.

Answers

1 A **2** D **3** D **4** D

Optional extension

Write these topics on the board: *the best way to stay healthy, the most important first-aid tip*. In pairs, students take turns to make simple statements about the topics and agree or disagree with each other using the expressions in Exercise 2. Remind them to justify their opinions.

OPTIMISE YOUR EXAM

True/false

Ask students to read the tips.

- Remind students that they also need to understand what the statement as a whole means as well as the key words. Opinions are often (though not always) preceded with terms, such as *I think*, or with adjectives, comparatives and superlatives, such as *good, better, the best*.
- Most questions will be about people's ideas, feelings and opinions, so paying attention to the interviewee's response can give helpful clues as to whether they have positive, negative or mixed reactions about the subject being discussed.

Exam task

3 2.05 Play the track for students to listen and complete the exercise. Don't check answers yet as they will listen again in Exercise 4.

4 2.05 Play the track for students to listen and check their answers. Check answers in open class. Elicit the key words or phrases that helped them decide on their answers.

Answers

1 F (Kate: ... *they haven't given them to us yet. We should get them in a couple of weeks.*)

2 T (Kate: *The opposite actually! The time flew by. I wanted it to be longer!*)

3 F (Kate: *And I learnt so many different skills.* Adam: *I'm surprised.*)

4 F (Kate: *We didn't actually see any real blood!* Highlight how we use *actually* to emphasise that something is surprising.)

5 F (Adam: *That can't be very useful in real life though.* Kate: *You'd be surprised how many thousands of people have survived because of CPR.*)

6 T (Adam: *Well, you never know, I may do it soon too. It does sound interesting!*)

THINK | RESEARCH | **CULTURE** | LEARN | ME

In pairs, students complete the task. Elicit answers in open class.

Homework OWB

Assign students Listening exercises 1, 2 and 3 on page 40 of their Workbook.

GRAMMAR 2

Modals (2): possibility, probability, certainty

→ Student's Book, page 53 SB

Lesson aims

- Focus on modals to talk about possibility, probability and certainty
- Practise using modals

Lead-in

Play ***First to five*** to revise useful vocabulary related to the unit theme of health. Pairs or small groups race against each other to think of five words for each of five categories. When they have five full lists, they shout out 'First to five'. Check their answers. For each correct list, they get a point. The pair or group with the most points wins the game.

In a less confident class, write the five categories on the board and dictate a few examples for them to categorise. In small groups, students add as many new words as they can for each category in a five-minute time limit.

Suggested categories: *Related adjectives (injured), Related nouns (accident), Body (bone), Problems and illnesses (infection), People (paramedic).*

Grammar in context

Ask students to complete the task. Refer them to the information in the *Remember* box if they aren't sure. Check answers in open class.

Remind students that they can find more information in Grammar reference, Unit 5, page 153.

Answers
1 PR **2** C **3** C **4** P **5** P

Language note

These modal verbs are often known as modals of speculation and deduction. We use them when we talk about possibility or probability, e.g. when we are making a guess or drawing a logical conclusion (*The bone must be broken.*).

May expresses a greater degree of certainty than *might* and is not used to introduce a question, e.g. ***Could/Might*** *Kate be studying now?* NOT ~~*May Kate be studying now?*~~ We can also say *Do you think …?* or *Is it likely that …?*

Couldn't expresses negative deduction, not possibility, e.g. *He* ***couldn't*** *be at home now (because he's gone on holiday).*

Extra support

Write these percentages on the board in a line: *90%, 70%, 50%, 50%, 70%, 90%.* Elicit modal verbs of possibility, probability and certainty and example sentences with the verb *work* and write them next to the cline.

Suggested answers

I'm 90% certain it's possible/likely/true. (must)	*It must work.*
I'm 70% certain it's possible. (should, ought to)	*It ought to work.*
I'm 50% certain it's possible. (may, might, could)	*It may work.*
I'm 50% certain it's impossible. (may not, might not)	*It may not work.*
I'm 70% certain it's impossible. (shouldn't)	*It shouldn't work.*
I'm 90% certain it's impossible / not true. (can't)	*It can't work.*

1 Focus students' attention on the photo in Exercise 1 and ask what illness they think the girl is suffering from (*hay fever*). Ask what they know about hay fever and if they experience it themselves.

Ask students to complete the exercise. Have them compare in pairs before you check answers in open class.

Answers
1 must **2** might **3** may **4** could **5** can't **6** could **7** should

2 Ask students to complete the exercise. Have them compare in pairs before you check answers in open class. Accept all sensible suggestions.

Suggested answers
1 The injured girl must have hurt/twisted her ankle.
2 The operator may be asking for information about the injury.
3 The boy on the phone might be calling for an ambulance.
4 The friends ought to stay together / phone her parents.
5 The injured girl might not be able to walk.
6 The injury could be serious.

THINK | **RESEARCH** | CULTURE | LEARN | ME

Ask students to complete the task. In pairs, they take turns to read out their sentences for their partner to guess who the family member or friend might be. If there is not enough time in class, set this for homework. Students can read out their sentences in pairs at the start of the next class.

Homework

OWB

Assign students Grammar 2 exercises 1, 2 and 3 on page 39 of their Workbook.

Assign students the Flipped classroom tasks on page 54 of their Student's Book if you'd like them to prepare for the next lesson. To complete this task, students need to watch the *Talk2Me* video which can be found on the Resource Centre.

SPEAKING
Interview

→ Student's Book, page 54 SB

Lesson aim

- Answer personal questions

The *Talk2Me* video in this unit focuses on talking about how often they do something. People talk about things they do regularly and temporary situations happening now or around now. Students answer some comprehension questions and then listen out for key expressions. The video can be used in one of two ways:

Flipped classroom

Flipped classroom option

Using this approach, students watch the video and complete the exercises for homework. This prepares students for the speaking lesson by introducing them to the topic and the key phrases to use in the exam task. Teachers who use this method will find they have more class time to spend on activating the target language and developing fluency for the final task.

Talk2Me **worksheet**

Ask students to also complete the *Talk2Me* worksheet on the Resource Centre for more detailed comprehension exercises and more practice of the key phrases.

Classroom option

Lead-in

Dictate or write these questions on the board:

When was the last time you came down with something?
What gets you down more: a cold, a sore throat or a headache?
Who takes care of you when you are unwell?
Do you look after yourself?
Do you feel up to eating if you have flu?

In pairs or small groups, students take it in turns to ask and answer each other questions. Walk round, helping students if necessary. When students have finished talking, elicit some answers from different students around the class.

1 Ask students to read the questions. Play the *Talk2Me* video for students to complete the exercise. Play the video again, if necessary, before checking their answers.

Answers

1 Angus is unwell. He has a sore throat, headache, high temperature and feels weak. He feels 'awful'.

2 It hurts when he coughs and tries to drink something.

3 Louise is a doctor and a friend of Angus' dad. She suggests antibiotics, a few days off school and ice cream.

2 Play the *Talk2Me* video again, so students can underline the phrases in the *Phrase expert* box. Pause the video from time to time if necessary. Check answers in open class.

Answers

In the morning/afternoon ..., I usually/often ..., I ... all the time, quite often, It depends on ..., ... don't ... very often ..., We'd like to ... more often, but ...

Talk2Me worksheet

Ask students to also complete the *Talk2Me* worksheet on the Resource Centre for more detailed comprehension exercises and more practice of the key phrases.

Answers

The transcript and answer key for the *Talk2Me* video exercises and Worksheet can be found on the Teacher's Resource Centre.

3 In pairs or groups, students ask and answer the questions. Elicit answers from different students around the class.

Answers

Students' own answers

EXAM SKILL

Talking about habits

Ask students to read the tips.

- Highlight that students can prepare for talking about how often they do activities by making a list of daily activities and deciding how often they do them. Remind them they will score high marks if they use a variety of adverbs of frequency and expressions correctly.
- Elicit that adverbs of frequency are usually before the main verb or between the auxiliary and the main verb, but they come after the verb *to be*.

4 2.06 Play the track for students to listen and complete the exercise. Check answers in open class.

Answers

1 b **2** d **3** c **4** a

5 2.06 Play the track again for students to listen and complete the exercise. Check answers in open class.

Answers

1 On schooldays, at the weekend

2 once or twice a week, (usually) at the weekend

3 rarely, (maybe) once a month, every day

4 every six months, (at the moment), once every three or four weeks

OPTIMISE YOUR EXAM

Interview

Ask students to read the tips.

- Highlight that students will impress their examiner if they can contrast the present simple and present continuous to describe general and temporary situations. However, remind students that they need to sound natural and spontaneous; they can have ideas ready, but they shouldn't memorise long replies to typical questions.
- Remind students that we use the present simple with stative verbs. We can't use any continuous tense (including the present continuous tense, of course) with stative verbs, e.g. verbs for talking about emotions, thinking, existing, appearing, possession and the senses, e.g. *want, need, like, love, hate, prefer, believe, think, know, realise, understand, recognise, suppose, be, exist, appear, look, seem, belong, have (for possession), own, feel, smell, taste.*

Exam task

6 In pairs, students complete the task. Elicit interesting or surprising answers from different students around the class.

Optional extension

Find someone who ... Students stand up and walk around asking questions in Exercise 4. Remind students to give extended answers. You could put some music on in the background while students are doing this activity.

Homework

Assign students Speaking exercises 1, 2 and 3 on pages 40–41 of their Workbook. OWB

LANGUAGE IN USE

Word formation

→ Student's Book, page 55 SB

Lesson aims

- Focus on word formation with suffixes *-ment* and *-ion*
- Practise a word-formation exam task

Lead-in

Divide the class into tag teams. One student from each team must run to the board and write illnesses or ailments on the board and return to tag the next person of the team, who does the same thing as the first player. The team that writes the most correct answers in two minutes wins the game.

Draw students' attention to the photo at the top of the page and ask them what is happening.

1 In pairs or as a group, students complete the exercise. Elicit answers from different students around the class.

Suggested answers

1 Colds: hot water and lemon, lots of fluids, rest, depending on the type of cold you can take some medication; Stomach ache: chamomile tea, hot-water bottle, eat rice or bananas, take some medication

2 Colds: put an onion by your bed, eat chilli peppers, listen to jazz music; Stomach ache: drink carrot juice, eat ginger and mint

Remember

Ask students to read the information.

Often, the suffix causes a spelling change to the original word, e.g.

*beau**ty**, du**ty*** + *-ful* → *beauti**ful**, duti**ful*** (*-y* changes to *-i*)

*heav**y**, read**y*** + *-ness* → *heavi**ness**, readi**ness*** (*-y* changes to *-i*)

*ab**le**, possib**le*** + *-ity* → *ab**il**ity, possib**il**ity* (*-le* changes to *-il*)

*permi**t**, omi**t*** + *-ion* → *permi**ss**ion, omi**ss**ion* (*-t* changes to *-ss*)

Point out that students can guess by adding various prefixes and suffixes until they get something that sounds right and obeys the rules of word formation. Often, while they are doing this, they find the one that 'sounds right' and suddenly realise that they were familiar with it after all. This routine should also be used when you go through the answers.

Refer students to the Vocabulary reference, page 165, for more information on word formation.

2 Ask students to complete the exercise. Have them compare in pairs before you check answers in open class.

Answers

-ment: agreement, amazement, enjoyment, entertainment, equipment, excitement, improvement, treatment

-ion: accommodation, communication, decision, infection, operation, organisation, prescription, protection

3 Ask students to complete the exercise. Elicit answers in open class.

Answers

1 writing lyrics, making recordings, watching music videos, singing **2** It helps reduce stress, which helps your body heal faster. It can help some children and teenagers express themselves, and help with other parts of their lives too. **3** ill **4** gap 3

OPTIMISE YOUR EXAM

Word formation

Ask students to read the tips.

- Suffixes are often tested in key word transformation tasks, such as Exercise 4. Remind students that within a task there are usually three or four conversions from verb to noun and possibly one negative or a plural form.
- Remind students to read through the whole text again with their answers completed to make sure it makes sense and sounds correct. The type of mistake they will often pick up at this point is not changing words to the negative to fit in with the meaning of the text. By reading the whole text they will see that it is grammatically correct, but it doesn't make sense in the context.

Exam task

4 Ask students to complete the exercise. Check answers in open class.

Answers

1 prescription **2** operation **3** treatments **4** entertainment **5** illness **6** communication **7** enjoyment **8** improvement

SAY IT RIGHT

Changing stress

TRC

For the *Say it right* pronunciation activity and instructions, go to the Teacher's Resource Centre.

Homework

OWB

Assign students Language in Use exercises 1, 2 and 3 on page 41 of their Workbook.

WRITING
A story

→ Student's Book, pages 56–57 SB

Lesson aims

- Focus on using narrative tenses
- Plan and write a story

Lead-in

Play ***Back to the board***. Divide the class into two teams. Ask a volunteer from the first team to sit in a chair with his/her back to the board, facing the class. Write a word from the unit so far on the board so that the volunteer can't see the word. His/her team must give clues for him/her to guess the word in less than a minute. A correct guess gets a point for their team. Swap teams and repeat the procedure five times with each team, changing the volunteer every time. The team with the most points wins the game.

1 Focus students' attention on the photo and elicit what has just happened. (*A teenager has just fallen off a skateboard.*) Ask students to complete the exercise. Elicit answers in open class.

Suggested answers

1 You can bruise yourself or break or fracture a bone.
2 Students' own answers

2 Ask students to complete the exercise. Elicit answers from different students around the class.

Answers

1 knew, was, was, liked, thought, set off, shouted, hit, went, went, fell, were, was, asked, shouted, said, filmed
2 Four verbs are in the past continuous: *was standing* (background information), *was filming* (background information, and action taking place at that moment), *was flying* (action taking place), *wasn't moving* (action taking place).
3 'It's seven steps' 'I can do this.', 'Danny, are you OK?', 'I'm fine.' They're all in direct speech.
4 'I've done it!' Yes, it's in direct speech.
5 'Call an ambulance!', '... tell me you filmed it!' Yes, they're in direct speech.

EXAM SKILL

Using narrative tenses

Ask students to read the tips.

- Highlight that direct speech, e.g. *'Do you remember me?'* makes stories more interesting and shows a good use of punctuation marks and capitalisation. Students will learn more about the rules for direct speech in Unit 7.
- The past simple is the 'standard' narrative tense. It describes the main events and sequences of events in a story. However, point out that the past simple is not only used for single, momentary actions. It is also used to describe events that occurred over longer periods of time and actions which were repeated over an extended period, but are now ended, e.g. *He made hundreds of trips in the ambulance as a paramedic.*
- Elicit words that go with the different tenses, e.g. *when* with past simple and past continuous, *while / during / as / just as* with the past continuous, *after / before* with past simple, etc.
- We use narrative tenses to tell stories and anecdotes. Learning how to write a good short story will also help improve students' spoken accuracy and fluency.

Language note

There are some rules to follow when writing direct dialogue in narratives:

- We use inverted commas to indicate the words that are spoken by the characters, e.g. *'Help me!' she exclaimed.* Remind students to make sure the reader knows who is doing the talking, e.g. *'Can I go now?' Sue asked.*
- If what is said is not a question or exclamation, we use a comma and not a full stop before the second inverted comma, e.g. *'I didn't go to school yesterday,' said Tammy.*
- Students can use other reporting verbs apart from *say* to impress an examiner like *cry, suggest, complain, ask, insist, reply, warn, promise,* etc.

For more information on writing stories, refer students to the Writing reference, page 172.

3 Ask students to complete the exercise. Check answers in open class.

Answers

1 didn't want **2** had **3** were kneeling (note: 'knelt' is incorrect because three others were already on top of them) **4** were **5** climbed **6** had **7** don't like **8** thought **9** didn't want **10** started

OPTIMISE YOUR EXAM

A story

Ask students to read the tips.

- The exam question may give students the opening or closing sentence or ask them to write about a true event. They must include this in their story. They are usually asked to write a story based on a general theme or common experience.
- Remind students that a good story has a catchy title, a simple plot, careful paragraphing and a chronological order of events. They will earn higher marks if they use interesting vocabulary, a range of tenses and good linking words and time phrases to show where their story is going.
- Remind students that short sentences create suspense, which makes their story more interesting.

Exam task

4 Ask students to complete the exercise. Check answers in open class.

Answers

Students' own answers

5 Plan Ask students to complete the paragraph plan using their notes from Exercise 4. You may want to look at students' plans, if this is possible, to check them and give advice and suggestions for improvement before students write.

6 Write Students write their story in about 100 words, in an appropriate style. Depending on time, it may be a good idea to set this and the subsequent checklist exercise for homework.

7 Check Students complete the checklist before they hand in their story.

Homework

OWB

Assign students Writing exercises 1, 2, 3 and 4 on page 42 of their Workbook and Progress check 5 on page 43.

6 A piece of cake!

UNIT AIMS

Exam preparation in Unit 6:

- identify synonyms in an article
- recognise similar meaning of words in a gap-fill exercise
- describe situations and actions in a photo task
- understand when to use collocations in a multiple-choice cloze exercise
- make suggestions in a letter / an email

TEACHER'S PRESENTATION KIT

- *Talk2Me* videos
- Speaking test videos
- Class and Workbook audio
- Workbook pages and answer key

UNIT OVERVIEW

Student's Book / Digital Student's Book SB		Workbook / Online Workbook OWB
LESSON / EXAM TASK	EXAM SKILLS / LANGUAGE FOCUS	CONSOLIDATION
Reading **Multiple choice**	Identifying synonyms An article	Workbook, pp 44–45, Exercises 1, 2, 3 Unit 6, Reading, Exercises 1, 2, 3
Grammar 1	Relative clauses	Workbook, p 46, Exercises 1, 2, 3 Unit 6, Grammar 1, Exercises 1, 2, 3
Vocabulary	Words connected with *food* Phrasal verbs Adjectives/nouns/verbs	Workbook, pp 46–47, Exercises 1, 2, 3 Unit 6, Vocabulary, Exercises 1, 2, 3
Listening **Gap fill**	Recognising similar meaning	Workbook, p 48, Exercises 1, 2, 3 Unit 6, Listening, Exercises 1, 2, 3
Grammar 2	Articles	Workbook, p 47, Exercises 1, 2 Unit 6, Grammar 2, Exercises 1, 2
Speaking **Photo task**	Describing situations and actions	Workbook, pp 48–49, Exercises 1, 2, 3 Unit 6, Speaking, Exercises 1, 2, 3
Language in Use **Multiple-choice cloze**	Collocations	Workbook, p 49, Exercises 1, 2 Unit 6, Language in Use, Exercises 1, 2
Writing **A letter / an email**	Making suggestions	Workbook, p 50, Exercises 1, 2, 3, 4 Unit 6, Writing, Exercises 1, 2, 3, 4
Progress check	Check language progress for Units 5 and 6	Workbook, p 51, Progress check and Cumulative progress Progress check and Cumulative progress

Additional material

PRESENTATION KIT	TEACHER'S / STUDENT'S RESOURCE CENTRE RC	TEST GENERATOR
Talk2Me video *The photo shows a …*	**Unit 6 worksheets:** *Optimise your grammar* (Standard and Higher), *Optimise your vocabulary* (Standard and Higher), *Talk2Me* video, *Say it right* **Units 5–6 worksheets:** CLIL, Culture, Everyday English (TRC only), Grammar communication (TRC only)	Unit Test 6 (Standard and Higher)

READING
Multiple choice | An article

→ Student's Book, pages 58–59 SB

Lesson aims
- Identify synonyms
- Practise a multiple-choice exam task

Lead-in

Elicit the meaning of the unit title ***A piece of cake!*** (something that is very easy, e.g. *A: How did you do in the exam? B: I got an A. The exam was a piece of cake!*). Elicit example sentences using this expression in open class. Ask them what they think the lesson is going to be about (*food*).

1 In pairs, students complete the task. Set a three-minute time limit and encourage students to race against each other to see who can think of the most food items. Elicit answers from different students around the class.

Answers
Students' own answers

Extra support

In a less confident class, brainstorm different types of food and write them on the board. Match at least one food item to each category from the healthy-eating plate in open class. Students then continue to classify each food item in pairs.

EXAM SKILL

Identifying synonyms
Ask students to read the tips.

- Paraphrasing statements in the exam task – retelling the information without changing the original idea – can help students understand the key idea and quickly locate words that have the same meaning in the text. Point out that paraphrasing is like rapping or talking to yourself, students can learn the acronym **RAP** for this key exam technique (**R**ead the question, **A**sk yourself what the main idea is, **P**ut it in your own words.).
- Remind students to watch out for 'word-spotting' in this task. Exact word matches are often a trap. If a key word in the text is exactly the same as the word in the question, it's almost certainly not the answer. They should also be careful of partial matches and find a sentence in the text that matches **all** the key words instead.
- Students often overuse common words due to their lack of knowledge of specific synonyms. Helping students choose synonyms that are appropriate for a given context encourages them to use more descriptive words in their speech and writing, as well as giving them a deeper understanding of how written texts work. Point out to students that they will practise this technique in Exercise 2.

2 Ask students to complete the exercise individually. Set a time limit of two minutes to stop students from focusing on the text in detail at this stage. Elicit answers by asking different students around the class.

Answers
1 well known **2** preparing **3** recipes **4** meals for her family **5** videoed **6** make their own food

OPTIMISE YOUR EXAM

Multiple choice
Ask students to read the tips.

- Remind students that sometimes they will have to choose an option (A, B, C or D) based on information in two or more paragraphs. The first question in Exercise 3 will allow them to practise this technique. To choose the best answer, students need to carefully read both paragraphs 1 and 2 in order to back up their answer with enough evidence from the text.
- Highlight how important it is to understand the questions. All the options in the second question give correct information about Remmi, but only one answers the question. They are worded so that they all sound possibly correct and could distract you from your original understanding of the question. Wrong answers might be off by even one word and students need to eliminate these. The right answer needs to be 100% right.
- If students have no idea what the answer is, remind them to guess. They have a 25% chance of getting the answer right!

Exam task

3 2.07 **Note: The reading text is also available on the audio CD. You may want to have students listen and read the text before doing the exam task.**

Ask students to complete the exercise and have them compare in pairs before you check answers in open class. Elicit evidence for the answers.

Answers

1 C (*For most of us, it takes a long time to learn how to make something tasty, but not for Remmi Smith. Still a teenager, she's already creating fantastic dishes … By the age of seven, Remmi … could cook complete meals for her family.*)

2 A (*From the age of four, Remmi helped in the kitchen by preparing vegetables.*)

3 A (*A local cable channel broadcast them.*)

4 C (*… when young people make their own food, they care more about what they eat.*)

5 D (*For a monthly subscription, you receive snacks, which include … and fun cooking activities that help you develop a healthy lifestyle.*)

4 Ask students to complete the exercise individually. Check their answers.

Answers
1 tasty **2** cookery **3** foodie **4** cable **5** delicious **6** subscription

THINK | RESEARCH | CULTURE | LEARN | **ME**

Students complete the task in class or for homework. In pairs or groups, students could read out their answers for others to comment on and ask follow-up questions.

Optional extension 2.07

Mind maps are a useful way to record vocabulary. Write *food* on the board and include branches with the following subheadings: *food, adjectives, verbs, related words, expressions*. Have students copy this on their notebooks. Play the recorded reading text and ask students to underline all the words and expressions related to food and cooking. They then add the words to their mind map, organised in categories with subheadings. Students can add words and expressions as they come across them during the unit.

Answers

Food: anchovy, pizza, salad dressing, vegetables, paella, strawberries, kebabs, sandwich, fruit bars, popcorn

Adjectives: tasty, healthy

Verbs: prepare, cook, make (your own) food, eat

Related words: dishes, cookery shows, meals, school cafeterias

Expressions: to be a foodie, take healthy eating seriously, create a healthy meal, develop a healthy lifestyle

Cultural note

Public Health England is responsible for the *Eatwell Guide*, developed from evidence-based scientific knowledge and government recommendations on foods, nutrients and health. The *eatwell plate* is based on the five food groups and it illustrates the proportions in which we should eat foods from these groups to provide a balanced diet.

Being overweight and obesity are prevalent in British adolescents. For example, in 2013 in England, 34% of boys and 39% of girls aged 13–15 were overweight or obese. UK National survey data show adolescents are still consuming too much saturated fat, added sugars and salt and not enough fruit, vegetables, oily fish or fibre. A proportion of teenagers (especially girls) have low intakes of some vitamins and minerals (in particular vitamin A, iron, calcium, zinc and iodine). A healthy diet is important for growth, maintaining a healthy weight and lowering the risk of developing heart disease, type 2 diabetes and some cancers.

Homework

OWB

Assign students Reading exercises 1, 2 and 3 on pages 44–45 of their Workbook.

GRAMMAR 1
Relative clauses

→ Student's Book, page 60 SB

Lesson aims

- Identify the correct usage of relative clauses
- Practise using defining and non-defining relative clauses

Lead-in

Play ***Noughts and crosses*** to revise relative clauses. Divide the class into two teams, one team is noughts (O) and the other team is crosses (X). Draw a three-by-three grid on the board and write a relative pronoun (*who, that, which, where, when, whose*) in each square, followed by + or – to indicate affirmative or negative sentences. Teams take turns to choose a square and say a correct sentence using the relative pronoun to win the square. The first team to win three squares in a row wins the game.

Grammar in context

Ask students to complete the task and refer them to the information in the *Remember* box if they are not sure. Check their answers and ask students to say whether the other sentences they find in the article are defining or non-defining relative clauses.

Remind students that they can find more information in the Grammar reference, Unit 6, page 153.

Answers

1 a **2** b

Examples from the text:

She's also becoming well known for her Italian salad dressing, *which is delicious*. (non-defining)

By the age of seven, Remmi was a real foodie *who could cook complete meals for her family*. (defining)

Remmi, *who was born in China*, began making videos for fun. (non-defining)

That show focused on Remmi's main interest, *which is getting teenagers to take healthy eating seriously*. (non-defining)

Remmi works with a company in the USA *which shows her videos in school cafeterias*. (defining)

Remmi believes that young people can create a healthy meal for their family *which doesn't cost a lot*. (defining)

In fact, strawberries, *which are Remmi's favourite food*, appear in other recipes, including strawberry sandwich! (non-defining)

For a monthly subscription, you receive snacks, *which include fruit bars and popcorn*, and fun cooking activities *that help you develop a healthy lifestyle*. (non-defining)

Language note

- The relative pronoun *whom* instead of *who* is formal and is more common in written English.
- Defining relative clauses with *who, which* and *that* as the subject pronoun can have the pronoun replaced with a participle. This makes the sentence shorter and easier to understand, e.g. *I told you about the girl who lives next door. / I told you about the girl living next door.*
- Non-defining relative clauses have a variety of uses in written English. As well as adding descriptive information, they are often used to indicate that one event happened after another, e.g. *He called out to the girl, who ran away.*
- Sometimes, non-defining relative clauses are used to make a comment about the situation described in a main clause, rather than someone or something mentioned within it, e.g. *She felt really upset about the exam, which was understandable.*
- Non-defining clauses can be introduced by expressions like *all of, many of* + relative pronoun, e.g. *There are a lot of friends in this class, many of whom I have known for years.*

1 Ask students to complete the exercise. Have them compare their answers in pairs before you check in open class. Ask students to justify their answers using the information in *Grammar in context* and elicit if other relative pronouns are possible in each sentence.

Answers

1 b (non-defining) **2** a (defining, *which* also possible) **3** a (non-defining) **4** a (defining)

Extra support

When checking answers, model each sentence and drill the pronunciation in open class. Highlight the pause at the commas in non-defining relative clauses compared to defining relative clauses, which have no commas and no pause.

2 Ask students to complete the exercise. Check their answers in open class.

Answers

1 which/that **2** when **3** whose **4** where **5** which **6** who/that

3 Ask students to complete the exercise. Students compare in pairs before you check in open class.

Answers

1 Jamie Oliver was born in Essex, which is a county in England.

2 He first worked in the kitchens of a restaurant which his parents owned.

3 His many cookery shows, which include *Jamie's School Dinners* and *Jamie at Home*, have appeared on TV around the world.

4 *Jamie's School Dinners* tried to improve the quality of food which/that is served in schools.

5 It was hard to get pupils, who didn't like eating vegetables, to eat well.

6 In the end, he was successful and the government, which pays for school meals, agreed to spend more on them.

Fast finishers

For more practice of non-defining relative clauses, students work in pairs asking each other questions to find out two pieces of information about their partner. Students then join the two pieces of information into one sentence using a relative clause. Check their answers in open class.

Optional extension

Ask students to write short simple sentences with information about their favourite food using relative pronouns. Students then pass their sentences on to their partner, who adds extra information to the sentences using non-defining relative clauses.

Cultural note

Jamie Oliver MBE is a British celebrity chef born in 1975, in Clavering, UK. He is known for his TV shows, cookbooks and restaurants. As a child he worked in his parents' restaurant, which greatly influenced his career direction. He attended Westminster Catering College and then gained valuable experience working at several reputable restaurants. His break into television came when he appeared in a documentary while working at the River Café in London. From there, he gained fame after hosting a hit cooking show, *The Naked Chef*. In a documentary TV series, Oliver ran the kitchen meals in Kidbrooke School, Greenwich, for a year. He was shocked by the unhealthy food being served to schoolchildren, and the lack of healthy alternatives on offer. His campaign to improve the standard of Britain's school meals eventually persuaded the British Government to spend £280m on school dinners.

Homework OWB

Assign students Grammar 1 exercises 1, 2 and 3 on page 46 of their Workbook.

VOCABULARY

Topic vocabulary | Phrasal verbs | Word formation

→ Student's Book, page 61 SB

Lesson aims

Understand the correct usage of:

- words connected with *food*
- phrasal verbs
- word formation

Lead-in

Personalised presentations by the teacher provide a good language model for students and can be highly memorable. Remember it need not be a monologue – you can tell your students to interrupt and ask questions as you go.

Tell students about your favourite food and how you make it. Tell the story twice and ask students to note down the ingredients, instructions and any utensils you use. Ask them to retell the recipe in pairs. Elicit the recipe from students around the class and also some of their favourite dishes.

Words connected with *food*

1 2.08 Ask students to complete the exercise. Play the audio for students to listen and check their answers.

Answers/Audioscript

1 bitter: coffee, dark chocolate **2** juicy: orange, strawberries **3** salty: crisps, popcorn **4** sour: lemon, lime **5** spicy: chillies, curry **6** sweet: cake, milk chocolate

2 Ask students to complete the exercise. Elicit answers in open class.

Answers

1 boil **2** bake **3** fry **4** grill **5** barbecue **6** roast **7** microwave

Students' own answers

Refer students to the Vocabulary reference, page 165, for more information on topic vocabulary.

Phrasal verbs

3 2.09 Ask students to complete the exercise. Play the audio for students to listen and check their answers.

Answers/Audioscript

1 e **2** c **3** f **4** b **5** a **6** h **7** g **8** d

1 Next, you need to *chop* the tomatoes *up* into very small pieces.

2 Wait for your soup to *cool down* or you'll burn your mouth!

3 Recently, I've *cut down* on the amount of sugar I eat.

4 Make sure you *eat up* all your vegetables, or there's no dessert!

5 I think I should probably *give up* sweets and crisps, at least for a while.

6 Fruit juice starts to *go off* after being open in the fridge for a few days.

7 If it was up to him, my brother would *live off* takeaways and junk food!

8 There's no time to cook, so I'll *warm up* the leftovers from last night's dinner.

Extra support

In pairs or as a group, ask students to discuss the meaning of each of the phrasal verbs in Exercise 3.

Answers

1 chop up: cut into pieces **2** cool down: to become cooler **3** cut down: reduce **4** eat up: finish **5** give up: stop doing something you do regularly **6** go off: to be no longer fresh **7** live off: depend on **8** warm up: make food or drink warm

Refer students to the Vocabulary reference, page 165, for more information on phrasal verbs.

Adjectives/nouns/verbs

4 2.10 Ask students to complete the exercise. Play the audio for students to listen and check their answers. In many Language in Use exam papers there is a task where students use the root of a word and write a word in the same word family to fill a gap in a text. Students will practise this skill in Exercise 5.

Answers/Audioscript

1 fry: a frying pan, a fried egg

2 mix: a cake mixture, mixed flavours, a mixing bowl

3 spice: a spicy curry

4 cream: a creamy sauce, creamed corn

5 blend: a food blender

6 boil: boiling hot, boiled potatoes

7 satisfy: feel completely satisfied, a satisfying meal

8 taste: a tasty dish, tasteless vegetables

Cultural note

Creamed corn is a soup or sauce made by pulping corn kernels and collecting the milky residue from the corn. It is a common part of Midwestern and Southern American cuisine and is typically sold in cans.

5 Ask students to complete the exercise. Walk around the classroom to assist students and check for accuracy. Check their answers in open class.

Answers

1 fried **2** spicy **3** creamy **4** mixture **5** blender **6** boiled **7** satisfying **8** tasty

Optional extension

In pairs, students prepare a questionnaire using the phrasal verbs and vocabulary from the lesson. Elicit a few examples, e.g. *Could you live off just vegetables? Do you think you should cut down on something in your diet?* Walk round, monitoring students and helping them when necessary. Students then swap pairs and take it in turns to ask each other their questions. Elicit interesting or unusual information students have found out from their questionnaires.

Refer students to the Vocabulary reference, page 165, for more information on word formation.

SAY IT RIGHT

/aʊə/, /əʊə/ TRC

For the *Say it right* pronunciation activity and instructions, go to the Teacher's Resource Centre.

Homework OWB

Assign students Vocabulary exercises 1, 2 and 3 on pages 46–47 of their Workbook.

LISTENING
Gap fill

→ Student's Book, page 62 SB

Lesson aims

- Recognise similar meaning
- Practise a gap-fill exam task

Lead-in

Play a game to recycle the phrasal verbs from the previous lesson (*chop up, cool down, cut down, eat up, give up, go off, live off, warm up*). Split the class into four or five teams. Call out a phrasal verb and ask teams to think of a grammatically correct sentence using the verb. The first team to produce a correct sentence gets a point. After you have used all the phrasal verbs, the team with the most points is the winner.

1 In pairs or as a group, students ask and answer the questions. Elicit ideas from different students around the class.

Answers

1 The photo shows an extremely long pizza. Chefs are cooking the pizza in a huge oven and crowds of people are watching them.
2 Students' own answers

EXAM SKILL

Recognising similar meaning

Ask students to read the tips.

- Highlight that students should use the time allowed before each recording to read through the text, so they are prepared for what they hear. Remind them to get into the habit of reading not only the text in front of the gap, but also the text which follows the gap, which may affect their answer.
- Remind students that in the reading lesson in this unit they worked on synonyms, thinking of words with similar meanings. In this lesson, students see how this skill can provide a lot of information about what they are going to hear, predict the type of information that is missing and help them identify more quickly relevant points in a listening exam. Point out to students that they will practise this technique in Exercise 2.

2 Ask students to complete the exercise. Do the first one together, if appropriate. Elicit answers around the class.

Answers

1 contained over **2** bun **3** easier to eat **4** cooking **5** training

OPTIMISE YOUR EXAM

Gap fill

Ask students to read the tips.

- Students should know that the missing information follows the order of the listening. They must write the exact words they hear and, in many official exams, use capital letters onto the answer sheet to get points in this type of exam task.
- In most listening exams at this level, answers do not exceed three words in length and minor spelling errors are usually not penalised if the candidate's intention is clear and unambiguous. Candidates are asked to spell words which are below the B2 level.
- Highlight that they should always check that what they write fits grammatically in a gap, e.g. singular or plural and that it makes sense in the complete sentence.

Exam task

3 2.11 Play the track for students to listen and complete the exercise. Don't check answers at this stage as students will listen again to check in Exercise 4.

4 2.11 Play the track again for students to check their answers. Remind them to always write something in the gap. Elicit answers in open class.

Answers

1 (American) cheese (*… 24 kilos of tomatoes, more than 18 kilos of American cheese …* The word 'tomatoes' signals the list of ingredients.)

2 7/seven hours (*Even the bread took seven hours to cook.* Highlight the synonym for *bun* here.)

3 3/three minutes (*He got through a dozen of them on a TV show! Competitors had three minutes to eat as many as they could.* Highlight the synonym for *dozen* (12) in the task.)

4 wet (*… most people have a special way of eating them. They make each one wet by dipping it in water. That makes it less difficult to get down.* Here students are primed for the information and must listen carefully to select the key word. Highlight the similar wording for *easier to eat.*)

5 (the/each) burger (*Before being grilled and then added to the bun, which weighs 50 grams, the burgers all have the same weight: 110 grams.* Highlight the non-defining relative clause which distracts the listener with extra information.)

6 exercising (*His preparation involves eating 6,000 calories a day and then exercising to avoid putting on weight.* Point out the *-ing* form that fits grammatically with *eating.*)

THINK | RESEARCH | CULTURE | LEARN | ME

Students work in small groups to discuss the questions. If you have internet access, students could do this in class. Alternatively, they could do this at home and present their information in the next class.

Homework

OWB

Assign students Listening exercises 1, 2 and 3 on page 48 of their Workbook.

GRAMMAR 2
Articles

→ Student's Book, page 63 SB

Lesson aims

- Focus on articles
- Practise using articles

Lead-in

Play ***First to five*** to revise useful vocabulary. Say different word categories (*healthy food items, relative pronouns, adjectives to describe food, ways of cooking, national dishes*). Small groups compete to think of five words for each one. When they have five, they shout 'First to five'. Check their words, giving one point for each correct answer. The group with the most points wins.

Grammar in context

Ask students to complete the task and refer them to the *Remember* box if they aren't sure. Check their answers, explaining why each underlined word or phrase uses *a*, *the* or no article.

Remind students that they can find more information in the Grammar reference, Unit 6, page 154.

Answers

a hamburger: we use *a* for a singular countable noun when we are not specific. **the world:** we use *the* because it refers to something there is only one of. **people:** we use no article with plural countable nouns when we are talking generally.

Language note

- Remind students that spelling is not a reliable indicator of when to use *a* or *an*. *An* goes in front of any word that begins with a pure vowel sound or a silent *h*, e.g. *an hour, an SOS*.
- The indefinite article is placed in front of a countable noun that is being mentioned for the first time. Once introduced, further references to it can be preceded by the definite article, e.g. *I have two children, a boy and a girl. The boy is 10 and the girl is two.*
- In English, an indefinite article is needed in front of professions, e.g. *She is a doctor.*
- *Little* and *few* are more positive when preceded by the indefinite article, e.g. *She has little money. / She has a little money.*
- Nouns preceded by superlative adjectives and ordinal numbers require the definite article, e.g. *It's the best idea I ever had. / He is the first one to go.*
- We use *the* with the names of musical instruments (*She plays the piano.*), currencies (*the US dollar*), newspapers (*The Guardian*), hotels (*The Hilton*) and also in proper names consisting of noun(s) and/or adjective(s) + noun (*the English Channel*).
- We use *the* with oceans, seas, rivers, island and mountain chains, deserts and noun forms of points of the compass, e.g. *the Mediterranean, the north-west of England.*
- We use *the* with countries whose names include words like *kingdom, states* or *republic*, e.g. *the United Kingdom* and countries which have plural nouns as their names, e.g. *the Netherlands, the Philippines.*
- No article is needed before *bed, court, hospital, prison, school, college, university*, etc. when these are used for their primary purpose, e.g. *I'm going to school.* If, however, you start talking about some place in particular, then the definite article is required, e.g. *You're sleeping in the bed by the door.*

1 Ask students to complete the exercise. Students compare in pairs before you check in open class.

Answers

1 an **2** – **3** the **4** a **5** – **6** – **7** the **8** – **9** – **10** –

2 Ask students to complete the exercise. Have students check in pairs before you check their answers in open class.

Answers

1 the Thailand (should be 'Thailand') **2** carrot (should be 'the carrot') **3** the insect (should be 'an insect') **4** the jar (should be 'a jar')

3 Ask students to complete the exercise. Check answers in open class.

Answers

1 the **2** the **3** an **4** an **5** a **6** the **7** the **8** the **9** the **10** – **11** – **12** – **13** – **14** – **15** – **16** – **17** a **18** the **19** – **20** –

THINK | RESEARCH | CULTURE | LEARN | ME

In pairs, students discuss the question. Elicit ideas in open class. (One reason honey never goes off in a sealed jar is because it contains very little moisture and bacteria cannot survive on the surface.)

Homework

OWB

Assign students Grammar 2 exercises 1 and 2 on page 47 of their Workbook.

Assign students the Flipped classroom tasks on page 64 of their Student's Book if you'd like them to prepare for the next lesson. To complete this task, students need to watch the *Talk2Me* video which can be found on the Resource Centre.

SPEAKING
Photo task

→ Student's Book, page 64 SB

Lesson aim

- Describing situations and actions

The *Talk2Me* video in this unit focuses on describing situations and actions. In the audio track, people talk about who or what is in a photo, where it was taken and what is happening. Students answer some comprehension questions and then listen out for the present simple or present continuous tense and adverbs. The video can be used in one of two ways:

Flipped classroom

Flipped classroom option

Using this approach, students watch the video and complete the exercises for homework. This prepares students for the speaking lesson by introducing them to the topic and the key phrases to use in the exam task. Teachers who use this method will find they have more class time to spend on activating the target language and developing fluency for the final task.

***Talk2Me* worksheet**

Ask students to also complete the *Talk2Me* worksheet on the Resource Centre for more detailed comprehension exercises and more practice of the key phrases.

Classroom option

Lead-in

Dictate or write these questions on the board:
How often do you eat out at a restaurant?
When did you last have a takeaway?
What was the last special meal you ate?
What do you usually do for school lunch?

In pairs or small groups, students take it in turns to ask and answer each other questions. Walk round, helping students if necessary. When students have finished talking, elicit some answers from different students around the class.

1 Ask students to read the questions. Play the *Talk2Me* video for students to complete the exercise. Play the video again, if necessary, before checking their answers.

Answers

1 buy a takeaway

2 She is doing a nutrition diary for food tech/homework.

3 Pizza is easy to eat and easy to share.

2 Play the *Talk2Me* video again, so students number the phrases in the *Phrase expert* box. Pause the video from time to time if necessary. Check answers in open class.

Answers

It looks like it's …, The photo shows a …, It looks like a …, The people seem to be enjoying …, The photo was probably taken in a …

Talk2Me worksheet

Ask students to also complete the *Talk2Me* worksheet on the Resource Centre for more detailed comprehension exercises and more practice of the key phrases.

Answers

The transcript and answer key for the *Talk2Me* video exercises and Worksheet can be found on the Teacher's Resource Centre.

3 In pairs or groups, students brainstorm as many words and phrases as they can think of related to the photo. Elicit answers from different students around the class.

Answers

(birthday) party, celebrate/celebration, dinner, family, balloons, (birthday) present, (birthday) cake, smiling, happy

EXAM SKILL

Describing situations and actions

Ask students to read the tips.

- Photos are often used for practising the present continuous, e.g. *What is happening in the photo?*, but it can be misleading to extend this to a description of the scene. A photo is like a moment, so if there is action in it, we use the present continuous because the action is happening right now in our mind as we look at the picture. If there isn't any action, we use *there is / there are* and the present simple. These two tenses are very natural for speaking about photos which you are showing to someone.
- Highlight that adverbs can often be identified by their *-ly* ending, e.g. *quickly, slowly.* They add more detail and interest and students will score high marks if they use them correctly to describe people doing things in a photo.

4 2.12 Students complete the exercise. Then play the track for students to listen and check their answers. Check answers in open class.

Answers/Audioscript

1 The family *is having* dinner at home together.

2 It looks like it's somebody's birthday. There are balloons and a cake.

3 The cake *looks* delicious.

4 I think the girl *is opening* a present.

5 Everyone seems to *be having* a good time.

Language note

Dynamic and stative verbs

Remind students that some verbs can function as dynamic and stative verbs, e.g.

Have

Stative: possession

I have a car. He has a dog.

Action: expressions with *have*

He's having fun (experiencing fun).

Look

Stative: appearance

That cake looks delicious!

Action: directing your eyes to something

He's looking at the camera.

OPTIMISE YOUR EXAM

Photo task

Ask students to read the tips.

- The Five Ws (and one H) is a concept used in journalism and is a very useful formula for developing a full description of a photo in a minute. The maxim of the Five Ws (and one H) is that information is only complete when we can answer a checklist of six questions: *Who? What? Where? When? Why?* and *How?*

Exam task

5 In pairs, students take it in turns to complete the task by describing the photo. Walk round, monitoring students and noting down good use of language and errors to go over in a feedback session at the end of the activity. Elicit interesting or surprising information about the photo from different students around the class.

Homework

Assign students Speaking exercises 1, 2 and 3 on pages 48–49 of their Workbook.

OWB

LANGUAGE IN USE
Multiple-choice cloze

→ Student's Book, page 65 SB

Lesson aims

- Focus on collocations
- Practise a multiple-choice cloze exam task

Lead-in

Write these international dishes on the board: *goulash, injera, curry, roast beef, tacos, sushi, moussaka, couscous, coq au vin, paella.*

In pairs, ask students to guess which countries the dishes come from. Elicit answers from around the class and ask students what they think the main ingredients for each dish are.

Answers
Hungary: goulash; Ethiopia: injera; India: curry; Britain: roast beef; Mexico: tacos; Japan: sushi; Greece: moussaka; Morocco: couscous; France: coq au vin; Spain: paella

1 Ask students to answer the questions. Elicit answers in open class.

EXAM SKILL

Collocations

Ask students to read the tips.

- Collocations are frequently tested in multiple-choice cloze exam tasks. Remind students that it is important to revise and practise the collocations they have learnt. Tell students they can record collocations in a variety of ways, according to personal preference: by topic (jobs, family, food, etc.), by key word (work, holiday, etc.) or by grammatical structure (noun + noun, verb + noun, adjective + noun).

Refer students to the Vocabulary reference, page 165, for more information on collocations.

2 Ask students to complete the exercise. Students compare in pairs before you elicit answers in open class.

Answers
1 c **2** b **3** g **4** f **5** e **6** h **7** a **8** d

Extra support

Ask students to write personalised sentences with the collocations from Exercise 2 individually. Then, in pairs, students take it in turns to read out their sentences without saying the collocation (they could substitute this for a 'beep' sound) for their partner to guess.

3 Ask students to complete the exercise. Check answers in open class.

Answers
1 Because they didn't exist in Europe. **2** tomatoes, potatoes, chocolate, corn, beans, turkey, chilli peppers **3** coffee, onions, bananas, other fruit, horses, cattle, sheep **4** diseases

OPTIMISE YOUR EXAM

Multiple-choice cloze

Ask students to read the tips.

- In an exam, students should always read the text for general understanding first, as they did in Exercise 3. Remind them that when they have finished the task, they should read the text again and make sure the text makes sense with all their answers in place.
- Remind them to look at the text before and after the gap. Multiple-choice cloze is a test of vocabulary rather than grammar. Tell students that they develop their intuition by saying the options to themselves. If one 'sounds right', they should go for it. They should only change an answer if they are 100% sure it is wrong. Point out that it is far more common to change a right answer than to change a wrong one.
- Students should not leave the answer sheet blank for any question. If they don't know the correct answer, they should always make a guess.

Exam task

4 Ask students to complete the exercise. Check their answers in open class.

Answers
1 A **2** C **3** C **4** A **5** D **6** C **7** A **8** B

Homework OWB

Assign students Language in Use exercises 1 and 2 on page 49 of their Workbook.

WRITING
A letter / An email

→ Student's Book, pages 66–67 SB

Lesson aims

- Focus on language for making suggestions
- Plan and write an informal email

Lead-in

Play ***Back to the board***. Ask for a volunteer to come to the front and stand with their back to the board. Write a word from the unit on the board. The student mustn't see what's written. Invite other students to give verbal clues to help the student in front of the board guess the word. The only rule is that they mustn't say the word written on the board. When the student guesses, repeat the exercise with a different volunteer and word.

1 In pairs or as a group, students answer the questions. Elicit answers in open class.

Suggested answers

1 The photos show different desserts. One photo has little cakes. One photo has an ice cream sundae with cream, sprinkles and cherries. The third photo shows a chocolate fountain with fruit on sticks for dipping. They could all be part of a birthday party. The little cakes and chocolate fountain could be for a wedding. The ice cream could be a treat for a special occasion like passing an exam. **2** Students' own answers

EXAM SKILL

Making suggestions

Ask students to read the tips.

- Students should make sure that their email or letter answers any questions in the email/letter they are replying to. Before students start writing, they should note the main point they want to make in each paragraph. It is important to cover all the points in order to get a good grade. They will work on this in Exercise 2.
- Point out that in this lesson students will look at ways of making suggestions that are useful for both writing and speaking exams.

2 Students complete the exercise. Check their answers in open class.

Answers

1 Because he is going to make food for a family party. **2** It's really popular. He could make it spicy. **3** They're easy to make. He could give people a choice. Don't forget to make some without meat.

Language note

Highlight that *Why not serve …?* uses the bare infinitive in a question and *What about making …?* uses the *-ing* form of the verb in a question.

3 Ask students to complete the exercise. Check answers in open class.

Answers

1 One thing you could do is **2** You could **3** Why not **4** What about **5** you could **6** Don't forget to

OPTIMISE YOUR EXAM

A letter / An email

Ask students to read the tips.

- Remind students that letters and emails have a simple format which is easy to follow.
- There are a lot of similarities between informal letters and conversation. Informal letters and emails usually show a lot of interest and enthusiasm.
- Remind students that they must always pay attention to accurate spelling and punctuation.

For more information on letter/email writing, refer students to the Writing reference, page 173.

Exam task

4 Ask students to complete the exercise individually. Monitor students for good use of language and errors to go over at the end of the activity.

Answers

Students' own answers

5 Plan Ask students to complete the paragraph plan using their notes from Exercise 4.

6 Write Students write their email in about 100 words. Depending on time, it may be a good idea to set this and the subsequent checklist exercise for homework.

7 Check Students complete the checklist before they hand in their email.

Homework

OWB

Assign students Writing exercises 1, 2, 3 and 4 on page 50 of their Workbook, and Progress check 6 on page 51.

Answers PROGRESS CHECK Units 5–6

Exercise 1
1 could **2** should **3** don't have to **4** be able to **5** could **6** should **7** can't

Exercise 2
1 where **2** when **3** whose **4** that **5** who **6** which

Exercise 3
1 c **2** f **3** e **4** b **5** a **6** d

Exercise 4
1 get **2** ✓ **3** coming **4** ✓ **5** cool **6** Cheer **7** ✓ **8** cut

Exercise 5
1 take **2** make **3** make **4** do **5** have **6** make **7** do **8** make

Exercise 6
1 decision **2** boiling **3** tasty **4** prescription **5** frying **6** spicy **7** entertainment **8** equipment

Exercise 7
1 – **2** an **3** – **4** the **5** – **6** the **7** a

7 Shop till you drop!

UNIT AIMS

Exam preparation in Unit 7:

- understand meaning from context in a newspaper article
- understand relevant information in short extracts
- ask questions in a discussion
- understand how to form words for people and apply this in a word-formation gap-fill exercise
- use direct speech in a story

TEACHER'S PRESENTATION KIT

- *Talk2Me* videos
- Speaking test videos
- Class and Workbook audio
- Workbook pages and answer key

UNIT OVERVIEW

Student's Book / Digital Student's Book SB		Workbook / Online Workbook OWB
LESSON / EXAM TASK	EXAM SKILLS / LANGUAGE FOCUS	CONSOLIDATION
Reading **True/false**	Understanding meaning from context A newspaper article	Workbook, pp 52–53, Exercises 1, 2, 3, 4 Unit 7, Reading, Exercises 1, 2, 3, 4
Grammar 1	Past perfect simple and continuous	Workbook, p 54, Exercises 1, 2, 3 Unit 7, Grammar 1, Exercises 1, 2, 3
Vocabulary	Words connected with *shopping* Phrasal verbs Idioms for *shopping and spending*	Workbook, pp 54–55, Exercises 1, 2, 3 Unit 7, Vocabulary, Exercises 1, 2, 3
Listening **Multiple choice (extracts)**	Understanding relevant information	Workbook, p 56, Exercises 1, 2, 3, 4 Unit 7, Listening, Exercises 1, 2, 3, 4
Grammar 2	Comparatives and superlatives	Workbook, p 55, Exercises 1, 2 Unit 7, Grammar 2, Exercises 1, 2
Speaking **Discussion**	Asking questions	Workbook, pp 56–57, Exercises 1, 2, 3 Unit 7, Speaking, Exercises 1, 2, 3
Language in Use **Word formation**	Nouns connected with *people*	Workbook, p 57, Exercises 1, 2 Unit 7, Language in Use, Exercises 1, 2
Writing **A story**	Using direct speech	Workbook, p 58, Exercises 1, 2, 3, 4, 5 Unit 7, Writing, Exercises 1, 2, 3, 4, 5
		Workbook, p 59, Progress check and Cumulative progress Progress check and Cumulative progress

Additional material

PRESENTATION KIT	TEACHER'S / STUDENT'S RESOURCE CENTRE RC	TEST GENERATOR
Talk2Me video *Do you agree that …?*	**Unit 7 worksheets:** *Optimise your grammar* (Standard and Higher), *Optimise your vocabulary* (Standard and Higher), *Talk2Me* video, *Say it right* **Units 7–8 worksheets:** CLIL, Culture, Everyday English (TRC only), Grammar communication (TRC only)	Unit Test 7 (Standard and Higher)

READING
True/false | A newspaper article

→ Student's Book, pages 70–71 SB

Lesson aims

- Understanding meaning from context
- Practise a true/false exam task

Lead-in

Draw students' attention to the photo and ask them what they think the lesson is going to be about (*shopping and services*). Elicit the meaning of the unit title ***Shop till you drop!*** (*It's an American idiom which means to go shopping until you are so tired you can't shop anymore.* Till *is a contraction of* until *and can be spelt* 'til.) Point out that *go shopping* is a general phrase and *do the shopping* is when you buy things you need, probably from the supermarket. Ask students if they think this would be an enjoyable experience and ask them to say why or why not.

1 In pairs or as a group, students complete the exercise. Elicit answers from different students around the class. If appropriate, ask students to come up to the board and write what they can buy in their favourite shops to check spelling.

Suggested answers

1 chemist's/pharmacy, supermarket, newsagent's, bakery, café, butcher's, jeweller's, grocer's, optician's, greengrocer's, fishmonger's, clothes shop, shoe shop, a department store, a boutique

2 Students' own answers

2 Ask students to complete the exercise. Set a two-minute time limit to prevent them from reading in too much detail at this stage. Elicit answers in open class.

Suggested answers

1 teenagers **2** lots of things, including (luxury) soaps and candles, accessories for the house and garden, clothing, comics, homemade cakes, art **3** attend performances (e.g. singing, dancing) and workshops (yoga and Zumba)

EXAM SKILL

Understanding meaning from context

Ask students to read the tips.

- Highlight that spending time looking up words in a dictionary can slow down reading. More importantly, in most exams, students are not allowed dictionaries.
- Point out that a better strategy is to use the context, the words and sentences surrounding a particular word, cultural knowledge and simple common sense to infer meaning. This skill not only helps increase students' vocabulary, it also helps them develop a deeper understanding of how written texts work and helps them improve their writing.

3 Ask students to complete the exercise. Elicit answers in open class.

Answers

1 a **2** b **3** b **4** b **5** b **6** a

OPTIMISE YOUR EXAM

True/false

Ask students to read the tips.

- Highlight that some questions ask students to 'read between the lines' when information is not directly stated, because the suggestion, rather than the actual words, carries the meaning. They need to find clues to get some answers and then add to those clues what they already know or have read. Helping students understand when information is implied will improve their skill in drawing conclusions and making inferences.
- Remind students that they should pay careful attention to 'little' words that qualify or change meaning, such as *only, sometimes, always*, etc.

Exam task

4 2.13 **Note: The reading text is also available on the audio CD. You may want to have students listen and read the text before doing the exam task.**

Ask students to complete the exercise. Have them compare in pairs before you check answers in open class. Elicit the key phrases in the text that helped them decide on their answers.

Answers

1 T (*On Saturdays and Sundays in the UK …*)
2 T (*… from loom bands to homemade cakes …*)
3 F (*I also sell my work in a shop, …*)
4 F (*They had heard about a successful event called the Vintage Village …* They didn't organise it, though.)
5 F (*For our first event, we had 70 applications! We immediately realised there were young people out there with the right skills and creative talent …* Highlight that the exclamation mark indicates a positive or negative emotion, e.g. surprise, anger or joy. The following sentence confirms that the surprise was positive for Joe and Tom.)
6 T (*Before, some town centres had been empty on Sundays. Now, they're fun and lively …*)
7 T (*The Teenage Market also welcomes performers. Singers … dance, yoga and Zumba workshops.*)
8 F (*To get involved … apply to take part in upcoming events.*)

Mixed ability

In pairs, less confident students read only three paragraphs each. Break the text into two parts (questions 1–4, 5–8). Students then share their information. For stronger students, write these definitions on the board. Then ask them to match the verbs and expressions in the text and questions in Exercise 4.

be involved in an activity with other people (take part in)
come somewhere without a firm arrangement (turn up)
take control of something (take over)
organise or control (run)
exchange products for money (sell)

5 Ask students to complete the exercise. Check answers in open class and elicit the key words that helped them decide on their answer.

Answer

B (*they'll be available soon*)

THINK | RESEARCH | CULTURE | LEARN | ME

Ask students to complete the task. They could present their profiles in small groups and vote on which stall they think would be most successful in a Teenage Market. If you don't have enough time, set this for homework. Students could present their profiles at the start of the next class.

Optional extension 2.13

Play the recorded reading text and ask students to underline words and phrases in the text connected with selling products. Elicit answers in open class.

Answers

shop online, shoppers, local outdoor market, browse, buy, market stalls, run by teenagers, sells, handmade, natural ingredients, a range of accessories, promote, products, a wide variety of products on offer, exhibit, selling his work, event, sellers, vintage items, spending money, entrepreneur, find customers, make sales

Cultural note

Farmers' markets – food markets where farmers and producers bring their produce for sale direct to the public – are becoming very popular and there are now over 240 in the UK. Customers now shop around more and the 'once-a-week big shop' is changing so that customers shop little and often. Customers enjoy the atmosphere and experience of farmers' markets and like buying good quality produce usually at competitive prices. The current movement towards more healthy eating has led to increased sales in locally sourced and organic products, especially fruit, vegetables, eggs and poultry. Farmers' markets strengthen local economies and the community and are good for the environment because food travels less far.

Homework OWB

Assign students Reading exercises 1, 2, 3 and 4 on pages 52–53 of their Workbook.

GRAMMAR 1
Past perfect simple and continuous

→ Student's Book, page 72 SB

Lesson aims

- Understand the correct usage of the past perfect simple and continuous
- Practise using the past perfect simple and continuous

Lead-in

Write on the board the infinitive form of some verbs students saw in the previous lesson, e.g. *do, take, sell, make, be, hear, have, give*, etc. Divide the class into two teams, A and B and play ***Grammar tennis***. Ask a volunteer from team A to 'serve' one of the infinitives on the board to a student on team B. This student must write the past simple and past participle form on the board to win a point. Then it is team A's turn to respond to the service and give the past simple and past participle of another infinitive. The first team to get five points is the winner.

Grammar in context

Ask students to complete the task. Refer them to the information in the *Remember* box if they aren't sure. Check answers in open class and ask them to explain their choices.

Remind students that they can find more information in the Grammar reference, Unit 7, page 154.

Answers

1 had heard **2** had been **3** had been selling

Sentence 1: It makes it clearer that they heard about it before they had the idea. **Sentence 2:** Yes. **Sentence 3:** Yes. Here, the use of the continuous just emphasises that the action was still in progress. We can also use *sold*.

Language note

We form the past perfect simple with *had* + past participle; we form the past perfect continuous with *had been* + *-ing* form.

Highlight the contracted form of *had* (*'d*). It is difficult for students to hear contractions and they must listen carefully for *'d/hadn't* and pay attention to the context to be sure of the tense being used.

Point out that using the past perfect continuous before another action in the past is a good way to show cause and effect, e.g. *I was tired because I* ***had been working*** *all day.*

1 Ask students to complete the exercise. Have them compare in pairs before you check answers in open class.

Answers

1 a **2** b **3** a **4** b **5** b **6** b

Cultural note

The Grand Bazaar in Istanbul is one of the largest and oldest covered markets in the world. It attracts between 250,000 and 400,000 visitors daily and is one of the world's most-visited tourist attractions.

2 Focus students' attention on the photo and ask them what they can see (*people shopping at market stalls in an old building – the Grand Bazaar in Istanbul*). Ask if they have visited Istanbul or have been to a similar market.

Ask students to complete the exercise. Have them compare in pairs before you check answers in open class.

Answers

1 went **2** had/'d never visited **3** had/'d expected / expected **4** had/'d been walking / had/'d walked **5** had been saying / had said **6** had/'d hoped / had/'d been hoping / hoped **7** had/'d been looking / had/'d looked **8** found **9** bought **10** had/'d been saving up / had/'d saved up

Fast finishers

Ask students to write similar sentences using the verbs from the gap fill.

Optional extension

Write these questions on the board. In pairs or small groups, students find the answers in the text in Exercise 2.

1 Which places did they visit in Istanbul?

2 How many shops are there in the Grand Bazaar?

3 What did they buy?

Answers

1 Topkapi Palace, the Blue Mosque and the Grand Bazaar **2** over 5,000 **3** He bought a watch and his mum bought a necklace.

Homework OWB

Assign students Grammar 1 exercises 1, 2 and 3 on page 54 of their Workbook.

VOCABULARY

Topic vocabulary | Phrasal verbs | Idioms

→ Student's Book, page 73 SB

Lesson aims

Understand the correct usage of:

- words connected with *shopping*
- phrasal verbs
- idioms connected with *shopping and spending*

Lead-in

Play ***First letter, last letter***. In small groups, a student starts the game by naming something you can buy in a shop, e.g. *a bag*. The next player has to name something they can buy in a shop that starts with the last letter of the previously named item, in this case, *g*, so *grapes* could be a good choice. Set a time limit of three minutes. The group that thinks of the most words in the time limit wins the game.

Words connected with *shopping*

1 2.14 Ask students to complete the exercise. Play the audio for them to listen and check their answers.

Answers/Audioscript

1 *change*: coins, or the money you get back when you buy something

2 *voucher*: an official piece of paper that you can use instead of money

3 *cash card*: people use this to take money out of a bank machine

4 If it's *half price*, it's usually 50% cheaper.

5 If it's a *bargain*, it's very cheap.

6 If it's on *special offer*, it's cheaper than usual.

7 If it's *second-hand*, someone has owned it before.

8 If it's *brand-new*, it hasn't been used before.

9 The bike isn't in stock, but we can *order* it for you.

10 This jumper's too small. Can I *exchange* it for a bigger one, please?

11 I got two of these for my birthday, so can I *return* one of them?

12 Are you going to buy the film or just *rent* it?

13 How much does this phone *cost*?

Refer students to the Vocabulary reference, page 165, for more information on topic vocabulary.

Phrasal verbs

2 2.15 Ask students to complete the exercise. Play the audio for them to listen and check their answers.

Answers/Audioscript

1 I'm going to *save up* my pocket money and buy a new comic.

2 If you *shop around*, I'm sure you'll find a bargain somewhere else.

3 These shoes are really uncomfortable so I'm going to *take* them *back*.

4 If you lend me the money for the ticket, I'll *pay* you *back* tomorrow.

5 My uncle doesn't earn much money, and he finds it difficult to *get by* on his salary.

6 We don't want to *run out of* snacks during the picnic, so let's get some more now.

7 With all the desserts, the bill will *add up to* at least €50.

8 I've got too many clothes so I'm going to *give* some *away* to charity.

Extra support

Write these definitions on the board for students to match to the phrasal verbs in Exercise 2. Ask them to write personalised sentences with two or three of the phrasal verbs.

1 use all of something and not have any left (run out of)

2 go to several shops before you decide what particular thing to buy (shop around)

3 give someone the same amount of money that you borrowed from them (pay back)

4 provide someone with something that you no longer want or need (give away)

5 keep money so that you can use it in the future (save up)

6 return something that you bought to the shop because it is broken or not suitable (take back)

7 have just enough money so that you can do what you need to do (get by)

8 calculate the total of several numbers or amounts (add up)

Refer students to the Vocabulary reference, page 166, for more information on phrasal verbs.

Idioms for *shopping and spending*

3 2.16 Ask students to complete the exercise. Play the audio for them to listen and check their answers.

Answers/Audioscript

1 (b) We're going to *shop till we drop* tomorrow! – go shopping for a long time
2 (a) The cheapest kind of shopping is *window shopping!* – looking but not buying
3 (a) Dana won the lottery so *she went on a spending spree* – bought lots of things
4 (a) Their youngest kid was rushing around *like a bull in a china shop!* – likely to cause damage
5 (a) I'm celebrating, so the pizza *is on me* tonight! – I'm paying

Language note

Elicit what an idiom is (*an expression whose meaning is different from the meaning of the individual words, e.g.* to have your feet on the ground *is an idiom meaning 'to be sensible'*). Highlight that using idioms isn't necessary in an exam, but they can make students' language sound more advanced and natural.

Refer students to the Vocabulary reference, page 166, for more information on idioms.

SAY IT RIGHT

Short vowels

TRC

For the *Say it right* pronunciation activity and instructions, go to the Teacher's Resource Centre.

Homework

OWB

Assign students Vocabulary exercises 1, 2 and 3 on pages 54–55 of their Workbook.

LISTENING
Multiple choice (extracts)

→ Student's Book, page 74 SB

Lesson aims

- Listen to understand relevant information
- Practise a multiple-choice (extracts) exam task

Lead-in

With their books closed, ask students to listen to you talking about your shopping habits and decide what two questions you are answering. Base your presentation on the questions in Exercise 1 (see model below as a guide). Ask students to compare their ideas in pairs and repeat if necessary. Elicit the two questions and ask students to look at Exercise 1 on page 74 to see if they were right.

Model presentation

*1 **I generally go shopping** to the retail park where there's every sort of shop available. **I usually spend time in** clothes shops. **Sometimes I go shopping** in small boutiques – it's more fun and they have original designs.*

*2 When I was younger, I was a bit of a shopaholic and **I used to go window shopping** all the time. Nowadays, however, **I don't like to window shop as much. I like to window shop a bit**, but then I wait three or four days before I go and buy things. It stops me spending so much money.*

1 Focus students' attention on the photo and ask them to describe what is happening. (*We can see some teenagers window shopping.*)

In pairs or as a group, students complete the exercise. Elicit answers from different students around the class.

Answers

Students' own answers

Mixed ability

Point out that these are both typical questions in oral exams. They ask about everyday shopping habits and likes and dislikes. Students should use the present simple and past simple, time phrases to say how often, and different ways to say they like or dislike something. They can also vary the grammar by using *If …* sentences. In a less confident class, write a few prompt sentences on the board (see words in bold in Model presentation in the *Lead-in*) for students to refer to during the activity. You could ask students to prepare their answers in note form before they do this as a speaking activity.

2 2.17 Play the track for students to listen and complete the exercise. Check answers in open class and elicit the key words that helped them decide on their answers.

Answers

1 d (*website*) **2** c (*… so you're not going to buy anything. … I like looking.*) **3** a (*how many stalls … you should think of having a stall.*) **4** b (*special offer … half price*)

EXAM SKILL

Understanding relevant information

Ask students to read the tips.

- The ability to infer meaning and situation correctly is an important listening skill. Question 1 from Exercise 4 *What do they decide to get Tim?*, for example, will probably require them to listen to two people giving their opinion and deciding on a gift for a third person (Tim).

3 2.18 Play the track for students to listen and complete the exercise. Have them compare in pairs before you check answers in open class. Elicit the key sentences which helped them decide on their answers.

Suggested answers

1 Dan's mum/mother (*What are you doing, Mum?*)
2 Dan's cousin (*your cousin Tim*)
3 Dan (*… he's two years younger than you.*)
4 Aisha's mum/mother (*… my mum's going to order some online for me.*)
5 the artist (of the painting) (*I talked to the artist – he's only thirteen!*)
6 his mum/mother (*I like these, Mum.*)
7 a shop assistant (*Let's find an assistant.*)

OPTIMISE YOUR **EXAM**

Multiple choice (extracts)

Ask students to read the tips.

- It is common that aspects of all the multiple-choice options will be mentioned in the audio to distract listeners in this task. Sometimes the correct answer is mentioned first and then the speakers discuss other options before coming back to their first idea. Remind students to listen for phrases, such as *Actually, I think you were right.* because this may signal that a speaker is reflecting on a previous opinion.

Exam task

4 Ask students to try and complete the exercise from memory. Remind them to guess if they are not sure. Don't check answers yet as they will listen again in Exercise 5.

5 2.18 Play the track for students to listen and check their answers. Check answers in open class. Elicit the key words or phrases that helped them decide on their answers.

Answers

1 C (Dan: *Get him a gift voucher.* They then discuss the other two options but eventually decide on this first option – Mum: *Actually, I think you were right. If we get him a gift card, he can choose his own book.*)
2 B (Mark: *Put the T-shirt back.* Aisha: *Hold on – I'm just going to see what I look like in it.* Highlight that the pronoun *it* confirms that it is a T-shirt and not the shorts, which would take the plural pronoun *them.*)
3 C (*A fantastic painting of a skyline. It was one of the best paintings I've ever seen.*)
4 A (Mum: *I'm sure I can use my credit card.* Jack: *Yes, of course you can.*)

Extra support

Play the track again and ask students to note down what the speakers say about the wrong options. Alternatively, hand out copies of the audioscript and ask them to underline the distracting information.

1 A Mum: *I was thinking of this video game.* Dan: *He wouldn't like that.* B Dan: *Why don't you get him a book?* Mum: *I don't know what he's already got.*
2 A Aisha mentions a jumper for Mark but not for her. C Aisha: *It goes well with these shorts here.* Mark: *You need some new shorts, don't you?* Aisha: *Yeah, but my mum's going to order some online for me.*
3 A Karen: *Did you see the handmade soap and candles? Some of them were lovely.* She likes the soap and candles, but she doesn't say she likes it more than anything else. B Dad: *My favourite was the cake stall!* Karen's dad liked the cakes most.
4 B Mum: … *I haven't got any cash on me.* C Mum: *I think I've got a voucher for this shop here somewhere.* Jack: *Oh look – it says here because it's a sale you can't use vouchers or gift cards.*

Optional extension 2.18

Do a ***Dictogloss***. Divide the class into small groups. Play conversation 2 again for students to note down exactly what Aisha and Mark say. Students then work in small groups to compare their notes and reconstruct the text.

Play the track if necessary. Students practise this role play in pairs.

This intensive listening task also practises writing and speaking skills and gives students opportunities to talk about both content and the language itself.

Homework

Assign students Listening exercises 1, 2, 3 and 4 on page 56 of their Workbook. OWB

GRAMMAR 2
Comparatives and superlatives

→ Student's Book, page 75 SB

Lesson aims

- Understand the correct usage of comparatives and superlatives
- Practise using comparatives and superlatives

Lead-in

Play ***First to five*** to revise useful vocabulary from the unit. Pairs or small groups race against each other to think of five words for each of five categories. When they have five full lists, they shout out 'First to five'. The pair or group with the most points wins the game.

Suggested categories: *types of shops, things you can buy in a market, words connected with shopping, phrasal verbs connected to shopping, idioms.*

Grammar in context

Ask students to complete the task. Refer them to the information in the *Remember* box if they aren't sure. Check answers in open class.

Remind students that they can find more information in the Grammar reference, Unit 7, page 155.

Answers

1 younger **2** than **3** best **4** more

Language note

Elicit what word comes after comparatives (*than*) and what word comes before superlatives (*the*).

The usual comparative and superlative forms of *old* are *older* and *oldest*. The alternative forms *elder* and *eldest* are generally restricted to talking about the age of people.

Highlight that if we want to talk about a quality which is smaller in amount relative to others, we use the forms *less* (the opposite of the comparative *more*) and *least* (the opposite of the superlative form *most*). *Less* is used to indicate that something or someone does not have as much of a particular quality as something or someone else, e.g. *This sofa is **less comfortable** than the other one. The least* is used to indicate that something or someone has less of a quality than any other person or thing of its kind, e.g. ***The least expensive** way to travel is by coach.*

1 Ask students to complete the exercise. Have them compare in pairs before you check answers in open class.

Answers
1 than **2** the **3** less **4** more **5** as **6** worst

2 Ask students to complete the exercise. Have them compare in pairs before you check answers in open class.

Answers
1 closer than **2** not as/so far (away) as **3** further (away) than **4** not as/so close as **5** the closest **6** the furthest

3 Elicit what students can see in the photo and point out that *shopping malls* is US English and they are called *shopping centres* in British English. Ask students if they go to malls to shop. Have them complete the exercise and compare in pairs before you check answers in open class.

Answers
1 the largest **2** the biggest **3** larger **4** the most dedicated **5** more enjoyable than **6** largest **7** the longest **8** (the) highest **9** longer than (note: *as long as* fits, but the instruction asks for comparative or superlative forms) **10** more interested **11** the best **12** (the) most powerful

Fast finishers

Ask students to write a couple of comprehension questions on the text in Exercise 3 to ask the class when everyone has finished, e.g. *Is West Edmonton Mall the largest shopping centre in the world? How many days do you need to visit all the shops? What can you do there apart from shop?*

THINK | RESEARCH | CULTURE | LEARN | **ME**

Ask students to complete the task. Ask some of them to share their experience in open class and ask them all to say or write comparative and superlative sentences about the shopping centres.

Homework

OWB

Assign students Grammar 2 exercises 1 and 2 on page 55 of their Workbook.

Assign students the Flipped classroom tasks on page 76 of their Student's Book if you'd like them to prepare for the next lesson. To complete this task, students need to watch the *Talk2Me* video which can be found on the Resource Centre.

SPEAKING
Discussion

→ Student's Book, page 76 SB

Lesson aim

- Asking questions

The *Talk2Me* video in this unit focuses on asking questions. People talk about shopping and ask each other questions. Students answer some comprehension questions and then listen out for questions and ways of giving opinions. The video can be used in one of two ways:

Flipped classroom

Flipped classroom option

Using this approach, students watch the video and complete the exercises for homework. This prepares students for the speaking lesson by introducing them to the topic and the key phrases to use in the exam task. Teachers who use this method will find they have more class time to spend on activating the target language and developing fluency for the final task.

Talk2Me worksheet

Ask students to also complete the *Talk2Me* worksheet on the Resource Centre for more detailed comprehension exercises and more practice of the key phrases.

Classroom option

Lead-in

Ask students to describe a time when they bought something for someone. Dictate or write these prompt questions on the board:

What did you buy?

Why did you buy it?

Did the person like it? Why / Why not?

In pairs or small groups, students take it in turns to ask and answer each other questions. Walk round, helping students if necessary. When students have finished talking, elicit some answers from different students around the class.

1 Ask students to read the questions. Play the *Talk2Me* video for students to complete the exercise. Play the video again, if necessary, before checking their answers.

Answers

1 He thinks it's a waste of time.

2 make-up, jeans, trainers

3 They're the most comfortable shoes he's ever worn.

4 They go to get milkshakes and find Jamie's trainers on a market stall. They meet up with Jamie and show him the trainers.

2 Play the *Talk2Me* video again, so students can decide who uses the phrases in the *Phrase expert* box. Pause the video from time to time if necessary. Check answers in open class.

Answers

Angus: I agree with you.

Jamie: What do you think? Why do you think that? Personally, I …, I'm not sure …, That's a good question!

Maddy: What's your opinion? How about you? Do you agree that …? I agree with you.

Talk2Me worksheet

Ask students to also complete the *Talk2Me* worksheet on the Resource Centre for more detailed comprehension exercises and more practice of the key phrases.

Answers

The transcript and answer key for the *Talk2Me* video exercises and Worksheet can be found on the Teacher's Resource Centre.

3 In pairs or groups, students ask and answer the questions. Elicit answers from different students around the class.

Answers

Students' own answers

EXAM SKILL

Asking questions

Ask students to read the tips.

- Highlight to students that if they can answer a question with only a *yes* or *no* response, then they are answering a close-ended type of question. Open-ended questions are ones that require more than one-word answers and encourage people to give more information. Ask students to decide which question generates the best answer: *Do you like shopping?* or *What do you like about shopping?* Point out to students that they can have an awkward and not very interesting discussion if they end up with a string of one-word answers.
- Remind students to listen carefully and give each other time to think and respond to questions.

4 2.19 Play the track for students to listen and complete the exercise. Check answers in open class.

Answers

1 What **2** Have **3** How **4** Are **5** Who

Mixed ability

Play the track again to give a second opportunity to less confident students. Ask more advanced students to note down the teenager's answer to the questions. Elicit answers in open class.

Answers

1 a necklace **2** a new bike **3** 150 euros **4** Boy: a new bike Girl: No, not at the moment. **5** her mum and dad

5 Ask students to complete the exercise. Check answers in open class and elicit *wh-* questions that they could ask instead.

Suggested answers

Questions 2 and 4 can be answered with *yes* or *no*. They could ask these questions instead: *2 What have you saved up for? 4 What are you saving up for at the moment?*

6 Ask students in pairs or groups to complete the exercise.

Answers

Students' own answers

OPTIMISE YOUR EXAM

Discussion

Ask students to read the tips.

- In many speaking exams, the last part is a discussion based on the theme of the photographs in the previous section. The candidates must talk together for about three minutes without the help of the examiner, who will only intervene if necessary. Usually there are two things to talk about (as they have seen in Exercise 6). Remind students to talk about both of them and give reasons and examples for their opinions. Students will score high marks if they support and include each other and add and build on each other's responses.
- Giving your opinion in the form of a question (*Do you think/agree that …?*) is a good way to express key ideas or opinions in an engaging way. These types of questions are useful for persuading a listener by drawing them in, rather than simply telling or stating your opinion as fact, with no opportunity for engagement. Students can practise this technique in Exercise 7.

Exam task

7 In pairs, students complete the task. Walk round, monitoring students and noting down good use of language and errors to go over in a feedback session at the end of the activity. Elicit interesting or surprising answers from different students around the class.

Homework

OWB

Assign students Speaking exercises 1, 2 and 3 on pages 56–57 of their Workbook.

LANGUAGE IN USE
Word formation

→ Student's Book, page 77 SB

Lesson aims

- Focus on nouns connected with *people*
- Practise a word-formation exam task

Lead-in

Play ***Twenty questions***. Ask students to guess a job that you are thinking of by asking at most 20 *Yes/No* type questions. If no-one guesses the answer after 20 tries, give them the answer. A 'yes' answer earns the questioner another chance to ask; a 'no' means the next player asks a question.

1 In pairs, students complete the exercise. Elicit answers from different students around the class.

Answers

Students' own answers

Remember

Ask students to read the information.

Many formerly gender-specific job titles have been replaced with gender-neutral job titles, and it's important students make use of these to show they are respectful of all people.

Remind students that we use *a/an* with names of jobs, e.g. *She is a doctor.*

Point out that when we ask someone about their *job*, we usually ask *What do you do?*, and not *What is your job?*

Refer students to the Vocabulary reference, page 166, for more information on word formation.

2 Ask students to complete the exercise. Have them compare in pairs before you check answers in open class.

Answers

1 assistant **2** buyer **3** cashier **4** customer **5** electrician **6** hairdresser **7** lawyer **8** librarian **9** manager **10** managing director **11** mechanic **12** optician **13** owner **14** receptionist **15** salesman/saleswoman/salesperson **16** seller **17** shopper **18** supervisor **19** visitor **20** waiter/waitress

OPTIMISE YOUR EXAM

Word formation

Ask students to read the tips.

- Suffixes are letters that are placed at the end of words to create new words. There are no hard and fast rules as to when these nouns have an *-or* ending and when they are written *-er*, so students should always check in a good dictionary if they are unsure.
- Students can note that while the *-er*, *-or* and *-ar* suffixes are often attached to verbs, the *-ist*, *-an*, *-ic* and *-ier* suffixes are usually attached to other nouns.

Exam task

3 Ask students to complete the exercise. Check answers in open class.

Answers

1 assistants **2** customers **3** waitresses **4** receptionist(s) **5** visitors **6** cashier **7** supervisor **8** lawyer

Optional extension

Ask students to find five part-time jobs and five skills teenagers need to be successful in the world of work in the text in Exercise 3.

Answers

shop assistant, waiter/waitress, hairdresser assistant, tour guide, cashier, tour guide

be good at maths, be responsible with money, have good social skills for dealing with the public, be hardworking, be able to follow instructions from supervisor

Homework

OWB

Assign students Language in Use exercises 1 and 2 on page 57 of their Workbook.

WRITING

A story

→ Student's Book, pages 78–79 SB

Lesson aims

- Focus on using direct speech in stories
- Plan and write a story

Lead-in

Write the steps involved in online shopping on the board and ask students to put them in the correct order (see numbers in brackets).

receive package (7)

track shipping (6)

choose payment and delivery method (4)

add items to the virtual basket (2)

browse through the online catalogue (1)

receive order confirmation (5)

visit the virtual checkout (3)

1 Focus students' attention on the photo and elicit what they think the person is doing (*They could be ordering something online on their tablet.*)

Ask students to complete the exercise. Elicit answers in open class.

Suggested answers

1 There's greater variety and items can be more available. There is more competition, so items and services can be bought at a lower price. It's quick, convenient and discreet. You can research products and services and compare prices and product details.

2 There are security concerns about payment portals and the information you are giving to retailers about yourself. You can't physically inspect products before you buy them. Sometimes goods arrive damaged, late or not at all.

EXAM SKILL

Using direct speech

Ask students to read the tips.

- Highlight that using direct speech, e.g. *'Do you remember me?'* can earn high marks in official writing exams because it shows a good use of punctuation and capitalisation.
- Direct speech helps to describe the characters and adds life to moments of action. The way people speak in stories tells the reader a lot about them. It can also help to provide excitement and tension in your story.
- Highlight that students will study the rules in Exercise 4.

2 Ask students to complete the exercise. Check answers in open class.

Answers

Paragraph 1: C
Paragraph 2: A
Paragraph 3: D
Paragraph 4: B

Fast finishers

Ask some comprehension questions about the story:

1 Who were Jo, Aidan and Tom buying a present for?
2 Why can't they buy the watch online?
3 What was the bad news?
4 What do you think they are going to do?

Answers

1 Their mum. **2** Because it's vintage and they have to buy it in this shop. **3** The shop was closed. **4** Students' own answers

3 Ask students to complete the exercise. Elicit possible titles from different students around the class.

4 Ask students to complete the exercise. Have them compare in pairs before you elicit answers in open class.

Answers

1 can **2** can't **3** start (Highlight that this is to make it clear who is speaking.) **4** comma **5** must (Highlight that it's important to be consistent.) **6** can't

Language note

It must be absolutely clear who is speaking. If there are only two speakers, you do not need to put *said X* or *said Y* after every speech. But you must put *said X* after the first speech that X makes, and *said Y* after the first speech that Y makes.

'What shall we do now?' asked Jo. Highlight that when the speech is separated from *asked Jo* by a question mark (or an exclamation mark), the question mark still behaves like a comma, and is followed by a small letter.

We usually use *asked X* or *said Y* in direct speech. Students can add variety if they use *respond, reply* or *answer*. However, this doesn't give us information about the tone of the speaker's voice or loudness. You could elicit verbs that show that the speaker was angry or was speaking in a loud or quiet voice, e.g. *order, command, shout, whisper,* etc.

OPTIMISE YOUR EXAM

A story

Ask students to read the tips.

- Elicit the key elements that make the short story in Exercise 2 successful and interesting.
- The writer uses short sentences to create suspense, there is a strong character description of Jo (she is the main organiser and we can see she is worried) and there is a simple, well-organised plot. There is a wide variety of adjectives and expressions (*race against time, vintage, ruined, good news, sign*) and tenses (present simple, imperatives, *shall*, past perfect, *will*, past simple).
- Point out that a good story always has a conflict of some sort. Remind students to draw on their own life experiences where possible.
- The first paragraph should set the tone for the rest of the story. Students must jump straight in with a catchy first paragraph to grab their examiner's attention.

For more information on writing stories, refer students to the Writing reference, page 172.

Exam task

5 Ask students to complete the exercise.

Answers

Students' own answers

Mixed ability

First discuss the questions after the task in Exercise 5 in open class. Elicit and brainstorm ideas. Write them on the board for students to refer back to when they write their story.

Who is he and what does he want? *A poor teenager who sees a second-hand guitar in a music shop? An older teenager/adult who sees an amazing car, house or yacht? A spoilt rich kid who wants to buy something because it is part of his/her collection? A millionaire who wants to buy an island? A shopaholic who has just come out of therapy?*

What is the conflict? *The character doesn't have enough money, borrows and gets into debt. The character can buy anything he or she wants, but it is not morally fair.*

6 Plan Ask students to complete the paragraph plan using their notes from Exercise 5. You may want to look at students' plans, if this is possible, to check them and give advice and suggestions for improvement before students write.

7 Write Students write their story in about 100 words, in an appropriate style. Depending on time, it may be a good idea to set this and the subsequent checklist exercise for homework.

8 Check Students complete the checklist before they hand in their story.

Homework OWB

Assign students Writing exercises 1, 2, 3, 4 and 5 on page 58 of their Workbook and Progress check 7, page 59.

8 A sense of style

UNIT AIMS

Exam preparation in Unit 8:

- identify synonyms in a project report
- predict missing information in a gap-fill exercise
- discuss alternatives in a collaborative task
- understand how *-ing* and infinitives are formed and use them in a sentence-transformation exercise
- write descriptions in a story

TEACHER'S PRESENTATION KIT

- *Talk2Me* videos
- Speaking test videos
- Class and Workbook audio
- Workbook pages and answer key

UNIT OVERVIEW

Student's Book / Digital Student's Book SB		Workbook / Online Workbook OWB
LESSON / EXAM TASK	EXAM SKILLS / LANGUAGE FOCUS	CONSOLIDATION
Reading **Matching headings to paragraphs**	Identifying synonyms A project report	Workbook, pp 60–61, Exercises 1, 2, 3 Unit 8, Reading, Exercises 1, 2, 3
Grammar 1	The passive	Workbook, p 62, Exercises 1, 2 Unit 8, Grammar 1, Exercises 1, 2
Vocabulary	Words connected with *clothes and accessories* Phrasal verbs Adjectives/nouns/verbs	Workbook, pp 62–63, Exercises 1, 2, 3 Unit 8, Vocabulary, Exercises 1, 2, 3
Listening **Gap fill**	Predicting missing information	Workbook, p 64, Exercises 1, 2 Unit 8, Listening, Exercises 1, 2
Grammar 2	Question tags	Workbook, p 63, Exercises 1, 2 Unit 8, Grammar 2, Exercises 1, 2
Speaking **Collaborative task**	Discussing alternatives	Workbook, pp 64–65, Exercises 1, 2, 3 Unit 8, Speaking, Exercises 1, 2, 3
Language in Use **Sentence transformation**	*-ing* and infinitives	Workbook, p 65, Exercises 1, 2, 3 Unit 8, Language in Use, Exercises 1, 2, 3
Writing **A story**	Writing descriptions	Workbook, p 66, Exercises 1, 2, 3, 4 Unit 8, Writing, Exercises 1, 2, 3, 4
Progress check	Check language progress for Units 7 and 8	Workbook, p 67, Progress check and Cumulative progress Progress check and Cumulative progress

Additional material

PRESENTATION KIT	TEACHER'S / STUDENT'S RESOURCE CENTRE RC	TEST GENERATOR
Talk2Me video *On the one hand …*	**Unit 8 worksheets:** *Optimise your grammar* (Standard and Higher), *Optimise your vocabulary* (Standard and Higher), *Talk2Me* video, *Say it right* **Units 7–8 worksheets:** CLIL, Culture, Everyday English (TRC only), Grammar communication (TRC only)	Unit Test 8 (Standard and Higher) Progress Test (Standard and Higher)

READING
Matching headings to paragraphs | A project report

→ Student's Book, pages 80–81 SB

Lesson aims

- Identify synonyms
- Practise a heading-paragraph-matching exam task

Lead-in

Elicit the meaning of the unit title ***A sense of style*** (an awareness of what is tasteful or fashionable; *to have a sense of style* means to be aware of your own individual fashion preferences and taste). Elicit example sentences from students, e.g. *Jane's sense of style is unique – I can't think of anyone who dresses like her!* Ask students what they think the unit is going to be about (*fashion*) and whether they think it's important.

Draw students' attention to the photo and ask them to describe what the activity is (*sewing*), what material is being used (*denim*) and what is being made (*jeans or a denim jacket*). Use this opportunity to pre-teach the vocabulary for materials in Exercise 1 if necessary.

1 In pairs or as a group, students complete the exercise. Elicit answers from different students around the class.

Suggested answers

I have a lot of cotton clothes that I wear in the summer. I have denim jeans and a jacket that I wear at the weekend. I don't wear leather or fur because I'm against animal cruelty. I have a silk dress that I wear on special occasions. In the winter, I wear thick wool jumpers when I go for walks.

Language note

If we talk about the parts or materials from which something is constructed, we can use both *made of* or *made out of*. We use *made from* when we talk about something that is manufactured, e.g. *Plastic is* ***made from*** *oil.* We use *made out of* when we talk about something that has been changed or transformed from one thing into another, e.g. *This bag has been* ***made out of*** *patches from recycled clothes.*

Extra support

Read out these definitions of the materials for students to match to the words in the box in Exercise 1:

thin smooth cloth made from the fibres produced by an insect (silk)

the soft hair that covers the body of some animals (fur)

thick hair that grows on sheep and some other animals (wool)

thick cotton cloth that is usually blue and is used especially to make jeans (denim)

cloth made from the white fibres of a plant (cotton)

a strong material made from animal skin that is used for making shoes, clothes, bags, etc. (leather)

EXAM SKILL

Identifying synonyms

Ask students to read the tips.

- As usual, students should look for key words in the text that are similar to the words in the headings. As a rule, nouns, adjectives, adverbs and main verbs carry meaning.
- Highlight, however, that in this reading exam task where students match headings to paragraphs, *paraphrasing* is also an important technique. Paraphrasing is when you take a sentence or a paragraph or text and express it in your own words. This can help them link the key ideas in the text with the headings.

2 Ask students to complete the exercise. Elicit answers in open class.

Answers

1 Jen **2** Grace **3** Lewis **4** Robert

Fast finishers

Elicit the key words in each idea and the matching phrases in each paragraph that helped students choose their answers.

Suggested answers

1 You can go **online** to **change** what companies do.
online – *organising a campaign on social media / I've already started a Facebook page*
change – *do something about*

2 Use your clothes **for longer** and in **different ways**.
for longer – *make your clothes last longer*
different ways – *taking better care of them / recycle it / recycling point / finding a way to reuse*

3 Exchanging clothes **with other people** can help.
Exchanging – *clothes-swapping event / take along all the clothes … and then swap them*
with other people – *get together with your friends*

4 Making clothes can **damage the environment**.
Making – *are made of / produce*
damage the environment – chemicals / ends up in rivers / fossil fuel / dumped in rivers / adding to pollution / huge environmental problems!

OPTIMISE YOUR EXAM

Matching headings to paragraphs

Ask students to read the tips.

- In the 'heading-paragraph-matching' task, students may not have time to read the whole text carefully. They need generalisation skills to help find the main ideas in a text – the gist – in ways that save time and get good results.
- Highlighting specific discourse features typical of the text genre is a practical way to direct learners' attention to where core meaning can be found. The text genre here, a report, typically has clear topic sentences.
- Highlight that the author often begins or ends a paragraph with the main idea, which is located in what's called a topic sentence. Sometimes, however, a paragraph builds up to its main idea, and sometimes the main idea is implied instead of stated.

Exam task

3 2.20 **Note: The reading text is also available on the audio CD. You may want to have students listen and read the text before doing the exam task.**

Ask students to complete the exercise. Have them compare in pairs before you check answers in open class.

Answers
A 1 **B** 6 **C** 2 **D** 3 **E** 4

Extra support

Elicit the key idea in each paragraph that helped students choose their answers. Help them notice how the people who write the reading test used paraphrasing to make the questions.

1 Modern spending habits – The key idea is in the middle of this paragraph: *However, many of us are starting to think more carefully about how our clothes are made and the cost to the environment.*

2 New to you – The idea is implicit in the text – students can 'read between the lines' that the T-shirt feels new: *I swapped an old top I never wear for a T-shirt that really suits me!*

3 Creative clothing ideas – The paragraph builds up to the main idea of how to reuse clothes; the match between *creative* and the phrase *a bit of imagination* in this sentence helps students know this is the correct answer: *With a sewing kit and a bit of imagination, that old T-shirt with a hole in it that you never wear anymore could become a trendy scarf or a headband!*

4 Making wise choices – The idea in this heading is indirectly stated in this paragraph where the writer lists wise or 'ethical' choices.

5 Expensive mistakes – Although paragraph A mentions cost, this heading does not match any of the ideas in the five paragraphs.

6 One dangerous example – The idea is implicit in this paragraph which looks *into one item of clothing – denim* and how it can cause *huge environmental problems.*

4 Ask students to complete the exercise. Check answers in open class.

Answers
1 outfit **2** item of clothing **3** dye **4** reuse, recycle **5** trendy **6** fit **7** suit(s) **8** alter

Mixed ability

Provide the first letter for each gapped word for weaker students. More advanced students can think of synonyms for the words in Exercise 4. At the end of the activity, ask them to share their synonyms with others in the class.

Suggested answers
1 set of clothes / clothing / get-up **2** article of clothing **3** colour/tint **4** reprocess, reclaim, convert **5** stylish **6** to be the right size **7** look good, complement **8** modify, remodel

Cultural note

According to statistics, the clothing industry is the second largest polluter in the world (oil is the first). We buy billions of new clothes every year, and there has been an increase of 400% compared to what we bought 20 years ago. Dyes and other chemicals pollute rivers and seas, and clothes travel thousands of miles by container ships to get from the countries where they're manufactured (60% of world clothing is made in developing countries) to the retail outlets of the West.

5 Ask students to complete the exercise. Check answers in open class.

Answers
1 suits **2** dye **3** outfit **4** trendy **5** fit **6** alter

Optional extension 2.20

Play the recorded reading text and ask students to underline words and phrases in the text connected with fashion. Elicit their answers in open class.

Suggested answers
fashion, outfit, latest styles, clothes, fashion industry, clothing, jeans, denim, cotton, dyed, dye, 'stonewashed', faded, clothes-swapping event, fit, old top, really suits, to be the same size, alter (the) clothes, thrown away, sewing kit, T-shirt, hole, trendy scarf, headband, 'ethical fashion'

THINK | RESEARCH | CULTURE | LEARN | ME

In pairs or small groups, students complete the task. Elicit answers from different students around the class and try to open to a class discussion if possible.

Homework OWB
Assign students Reading exercises 1, 2 and 3 on pages 60–61 of their Workbook.

GRAMMAR 1
The passive

→ Student's Book, page 82 SB

Lesson aims

- Understand the correct usage of the passive
- Practise using the passive

Lead-in

Write these questions on the board:

How often do you buy clothes?

Do you buy clothes for fashion, price or ethical reasons?

What were you wearing yesterday?

Have you ever made your own clothes?

In pairs, students take turns to ask and answer the questions. Elicit interesting or unusual answers from around the class.

Grammar in context

Ask students to complete the task. Refer them to the information in the *Remember* box if they aren't sure. Check answers in open class.

Remind students that they can find more information in the Grammar reference, Unit 8, page 155.

Answers

Jeans are made of denim, which is a form of cotton.

The cotton is then dyed (usually blue), and the dye often ends up in rivers.

Other examples:

… about how our clothes are made and the cost …

… volcanic stones are used to hit the denim. Those stones are shipped around the world, often using fossil fuel and, when they break, they are dumped in rivers, adding to pollution.

Often, clothes are thrown away after being worn only a few times.

First of all, we can check how the clothes we want to buy were made.

Language note

Many passive sentences do not contain *by* + agent after the verb. Encourage students to omit the agent whenever possible. In many cases, *by* + agent sounds wrong and adds no extra information to the sentence, e.g. *This invention has been used by people since 1908.*

Only verbs with an object (transitive verbs) can be made passive. Verbs without an object (intransitive verbs) normally cannot form a passive sentence (as there is no object that can become the subject of the passive sentence), e.g. *The earthquake happened in Japan.* (NOT ~~*The earthquake was happened in Japan.*~~)

1 Ask students to complete the exercise. Have them compare in pairs before you check answers in open class.

Answers

1 gave, given **2** design, designed **3** used, are used **4** was been, was **5** stole, stolen **6** with, of **7** with, by **8** have, are

2 Ask students to complete the exercise. Have them compare in pairs before you check answers in open class.

Answers

1 Many years ago, jeans were worn by factory workers.
2 Many items of clothing are sold cheaply these days.
3 Where were your new trainers made?
4 These shoes were bought with my birthday money.
5 Jeans material is known as 'denim', from the name of the French town Nimes.
6 A special dye is used to make the clothes bright pink.

3 Ask students to complete the exercise. Have them compare in pairs before you check answers in open class.

Suggested answers

1 are / have been designed by **2** are worn by **3** is based on **4** was set up, was given **5** has been given **6** was named

Mixed ability

Give less confident students the answers in a jumbled order: *has received / are worn by / was set up / was named / are designed by / is based on / was given*

Ask more confident students to write one or two comprehension questions on the text, e.g. *What clothes does she design?*, etc. They can ask their questions in open class.

Homework OWB

Assign students Grammar 1 exercises 1 and 2 on page 62 of their Workbook.

VOCABULARY

Topic vocabulary | Phrasal verbs | Word formation

→ Student's Book, page 83 SB

Lesson aims

Understand the correct usage of:

- words connected with *clothes and accessories*
- phrasal verbs
- word formation

Lead-in

Write the clothing items below on the board and check students know what they are. Ask them to associate the clothes with a decade (50s, 60s, 70s, 80s, 90s) and ask them if any of the items have come back into fashion or if there are any items on the list they like.

chains, colourful trousers / big baggy trousers, hoodies, baseball caps / multicoloured dresses, big hats / leather jackets, ponytails / long hair, miniskirts

Answers

50s: leather jackets, ponytails
60s: long hair, miniskirts
70s: multicoloured dresses, big hats
Late 70s–80s: chains, colourful trousers
90s: big baggy trousers, hoodies, baseball caps

Words connected with *clothes and accessories*

1 2.71 Ask students to complete the exercise. Play the audio for them to listen and check their answers.

Answers/Audioscript

parts of clothes: button, collar, pocket, sleeve
accessories: belt, bracelet, cap, earring, glove, handbag, jewellery, necklace, wristband
other items of clothing: jumper, sandals, shorts, socks, suit, sweatshirt, trainers

Refer students to the Vocabulary reference, page 166, for more information on topic vocabulary.

Phrasal verbs

2 2.22 Ask students to complete the exercise. Have them compare in pairs before you play the audio for them to listen and check their answers.

Answers/Audioscript

1 ✓ I went to a fashion show and all the models *had* really strange clothes *on*.
2 Why don't you *hang* your clothes *up* instead of leaving them on the floor?
3 ✓ I was in a hurry but I couldn't *do* the zip *up* on my coat!
4 ✓ Do we need to *dress up* for the party or is it just an informal event?
5 I was glad to get home and be able to *take* my shoes *off* after a long day!
6 If you're going out, make sure you *put* a coat *on* because it's going to rain.
7 Kieran *tried* about a dozen tops *on* but he didn't like any of them.
8 ✓ My trainers are starting to *wear out* so I'll need some new ones soon.

Fast finishers

Read out these definitions for students to match to the phrasal verbs in Exercise 2:
start wearing something (put on)
remove (take off)
put on a piece of clothing to see how it looks (try on)
hang a piece of clothing on something (hang up)
fasten (do (the zip) up)
put on clothes that are more formal than the clothes you usually wear (dress up)
be wearing particular clothes (have on)
use something a lot so that it can no longer be used (wear out)

3 Ask students to complete the exercise. Have them compare sentences in pairs before you elicit some sentences from different students around the class.

Suggested answers

I always hang my clothes up when I get home.
I tried a lot of shoes on the other day, but I didn't buy any.
My gym shoes have worn out so I'm going to buy some more.
It was raining so I put my coat on.

Refer students to the Vocabulary reference, page 166, for more information on phrasal verbs.

Adjectives/nouns/verbs

4 2.23 Ask students to complete the exercise. Have them compare in pairs before you play the audio for them to listen and check their answers.

Highlight that word formation tasks are very popular in official exams. Remind students to look at the word they have to change and think of words that are in the same word family. Remind them that the beginning of the word is often the same and the end of the word changes. Emphasise the importance of good spelling as this is a common way for students to lose marks in this kind of exam task.

Answers/Audioscript

1 new clothes, the clothing industry **2** celebrity designer, badly designed **3** a trendy outfit, a real trendsetter **4** to my amazement, feel amazed, an amazing experience **5** express your creativity, feel creative, the creator of a design **6** a fashionable pair of jeans, an old-fashioned shirt **7** improve your appearance, become apparent **8** a beautiful face

5 Ask students to complete the exercise. Have them compare in pairs before you check answers in open class.

Answers

1 clothing **2** designers **3** trendy **4** amazing **5** creative **6** fashionable **7** appearance **8** beautiful

Refer students to the Vocabulary reference, page 166, for more information on word formation.

Homework OWB

Assign students Vocabulary exercises 1, 2 and 3 on pages 62–63 of their Workbook.

LISTENING
Gap fill

→ Student's Book, page 84 SB

Lesson aims

- Focus on predicting missing information
- Practise a gap-fill exam task

Lead-in

Write a list of different materials on the board (e.g. *leather*, *cotton*, etc.) then put students into small groups. Ask them to write down of as many different clothing items as they can in two minutes for each of the categories. The group with the most correct answers wins.

1 In pairs or as a group, students complete the exercise. Elicit answers from different students around the class.

Answers

Students' own answers

EXAM SKILL

Predicting missing information

Ask students to read the tips.

- Point out that predicting missing information can help students identify relevant points in a listening exam and guess unknown words and phrases more easily. They will practise this skill in Exercise 2.
- If students predict the sort of things they are going to hear, they can reduce the amount they need to listen out for during the test. Students usually have 30 seconds before the first listening to think of alternative ways of saying the same thing.

2 Ask students to complete the exercise. Check answers in open class.

Answers

1 a place / a year **2** a year / a person **3** basketball/tennis/ volleyball, etc. **4** sports **5** (accept any reasonable answer, e.g. an adjective) **6** a noun

OPTIMISE YOUR **EXAM**

Gap fill

Ask students to read the tips.

- An awareness of how this type of listening test works is key for scoring high marks. Students should know that the sentences follow the order of the listening.
- They should write the exact words they hear, but point out that the words surrounding the gaps are not worded in exactly the same way. This type of exercise is not a dictation. Remind them not to change the words they hear and not to repeat words that they read.
- Remind students that most answers in this type of exercise are concrete pieces of information, e.g. places, dates, numbers, proper nouns, etc.

▼ Exam task

3 2.24 Play the track for students to listen and complete the exercise. Don't check answers yet as they will listen again in Exercise 4.

4 2.24 Play the track again for students to check their answers. Check answers in open class.

Answers

1 (the) 1870s **2** America **3** basketball **4** (young) actors **5** popular **6** technology

Cultural note

The company Keds was founded in America in 1916. They produced the first mass-market 'sneakers' in 1917. They were called sneakers because they had rubber soles which meant they were so quiet you could sneak up on someone without being heard. Americans still say *sneakers* (British English – *trainers*).

THINK | RESEARCH | CULTURE | LEARN | ME

Ask students to complete the task. Elicit answers from different students around the class.

Optional extension

Have a ***Class debate***. A class debate can be really successful if it's carefully staged. Remind students that they must be respectful of each others' views at all times.

Write the motion *Expensive trainers are worth it* on the board. Flip a coin to see which team can choose their 'side' in the argument. The other team has to take the opposite view. Divide the class into two teams – for and against – and ask students to prepare their arguments, first in pairs and then as a team. Feed in some key points if necessary (see below for ideas). At the end of the debate, take a vote and ask if the debate has changed anybody's mind.

For:

They look cool. They're status symbols.

They support and protect better. You can risk injury with cheaper trainers.

Quality is worth it. More expensive trainers are better quality and last longer.

Against:

No, trainers can be attractive at any price.

It is wasteful – some people don't even have shoes.

Many products in the market can be just as good, durable and fashionable as brand-named ones.

Homework

OWB

Assign students Listening exercises 1 and 2 on page 64 of their Workbook.

GRAMMAR 2
Question tags

→ Student's Book, page 85 SB

Lesson aims

- Focus on question tags
- Practise using question tags

Lead-in

Play ***A blackboard race*** to revise useful vocabulary from the unit. Small groups race against each other to think of and write on the board five words for each of five categories. When they have five full lists, they shout out 'Finished'. Check their answers. For each correct list, they get a point. The group with the most points wins the game.

Suggested categories: *materials, phrasal verbs, words connected to fashion, items of clothing, parts of clothes, accessories.*

Grammar in context

Ask students to complete the task. Refer them to the information in the *Remember* box if they aren't sure. Check their answers in open class.

Remind students that they can find more information in the Grammar reference, Unit 8, page 156.

Answers

1 asking us to agree **2** *Are trainers everywhere?* The person asking the question doesn't know and is asking us for information. *Trainers are everywhere, aren't they?* The person asking wants us to agree with their opinion.

Extra support

Elicit more example sentences for each of the points in the *Remember* box. If appropriate, ask students to come up and write them on the board.

Language note

Remind students that when we reply to question tags, we use the auxiliary or the modal verb, not the main verb, e.g. *You like classical music, don't you? Yes, I **do**.*

Remind students that we use rising intonation on the question tag if we are not sure and falling intonation if we are certain of the response.

1 Ask students to complete the exercise. Have them compare in pairs before you check answers in open class.

Answers

1 A **2** C **3** C **4** B **5** A **6** C

2 Ask students to complete the exercise. Have them compare in pairs before you check answers in open class.

Answers

1 aren't they **2** will you **3** isn't it **4** have they **5** wouldn't you **6** isn't it **7** won't it **8** shall we **9** aren't they **10** won't they

3 Ask students to complete the exercise. Have them compare in pairs before you check answers in open class.

Answers

1 You're from Germany, aren't you?

2 You haven't brought a coat, have you?

3 Let's try on those expensive trainers, shall we? / Let's try those expensive trainers on, shall we?

4 Mo's not / isn't going to wear his cowboy hat tonight, is he?

Optional extension

Elicit five personal questions, e.g. *When's your birthday?* and write them on the board. In pairs, students take turns to ask each other the questions, without taking notes. When they have asked the questions, they check they have remembered their partner's answers by adding question tags, e.g. *Your birthday's in February, isn't it?* Remind students to use rising intonation if they are not sure and falling intonation if they are quite certain.

SAY IT RIGHT

Intonation in question tags

TRC

For the *Say it right* pronunciation activity and instructions, go to the Teacher's Resource Centre.

Homework

OWB

Assign students Grammar 2 exercises 1 and 2 on page 63 of their Workbook.

Assign students the Flipped classroom tasks on page 86 of their Student's Book if you'd like them to prepare for the next lesson. To complete this task, students need to watch the *Talk2Me* video which can be found on the Resource Centre.

SPEAKING
Collaborative task

→ Student's Book, page 86 SB

Lesson aim

- Discussing alternatives

The *Talk2Me* video in this unit focuses on people discussing alternatives. Students answer some comprehension questions and then listen out for ways of contrasting and comparing options. The video can be used in one of two ways:

Flipped classroom

Flipped classroom option

Using this approach, students watch the video and complete the exercises for homework. This prepares students for the speaking lesson by introducing them to the topic and the key phrases to use in the exam task. Teachers who use this method will find they have more class time to spend on activating the target language and developing fluency for the final task.

***Talk2Me* worksheet**

Ask students to also complete the *Talk2Me* worksheet on the Resource Centre for more detailed comprehension exercises and more practice of the key phrases.

Classroom option

Lead-in

Divide the class into teams. Ask one student from each team to go up to the board. Describe an item of clothing. The winner is the first student to write the correct word with correct spelling. Other students can call or in most cases shout out the word! Pre-teach some of the vocabulary students will come across in the lesson, e.g. *scarf, shirt, trainers, tie, polo shirt, jumper, jacket, trousers, skirt, top, cardigan.*

1 Ask students to read the questions. Play the *Talk2Me* video for students to complete the exercise. Play the video again, if necessary, before checking their answers.

Answers

1 Jamie doesn't mind other people's birthdays. He really likes his own. **2** a scarf and a shirt **3** one

2 Play the *Talk2Me* video again, so students can underline the phrases in the *Phrase expert* box. Pause the video from time to time if necessary. Check answers in open class.

Answers

All phrases are used except *A isn't as … as B* and *A is …, whereas B is …*

Talk2Me worksheet

Ask students to also complete the *Talk2Me* worksheet on the Resource Centre for more detailed comprehension exercises and more practice of the key phrases.

Answers

The transcript and answer key for the *Talk2Me* video exercises and Worksheet can be found on the Teacher's Resource Centre.

3 In pairs or groups, students ask and answer the questions. Elicit answers from different students around the class.

Suggested answers

1 In the top photo, they are all wearing the same clothes whereas the people in the photo below are all wearing different clothes. The clothes in the top photo looks more like a uniform. They are all wearing blue jumpers and white shirts. However, in the bottom picture they're wearing different tops and colours. One boy is wearing a blue jumper and the girl next to him is wearing a stripy cardigan. One girl is wearing a T-shirt and one boy is wearing a black shirt.

2 Students' own answers

EXAM SKILL

Discussing alternatives

Ask students to read the tips.

- Students tend to overuse *but*. They will score higher marks if they use a variety of expressions to compare and contrast options.
- Highlight to students that most contrasting phrases like *On the other hand* can be replaced with *However*, but the reverse is usually not true. *But* is the only expression that can always replace *However. On the other hand* is only used when working towards a conclusion, such as choosing between two options.

4 Ask students to complete the task. Check answers in open class.

Answers

Students' own answers

5 2.25 Play the track for students to listen and complete the task. Elicit which points in their answers in Exercise 4 students ticked in open class.

Answers

Students' own answers

6 2.25 Play the track again for students to listen and complete the task. Elicit answers from different students around the class.

Answers

On the one hand … but on the other hand, might not be formal enough, I don't think they're as practical or as comfortable as, … would be too formal …, … it'd be better to wear a polo shirt, much more practical to wear and easier to wash, a jacket looks more formal than a jumper, equally uncomfortable, but some girls may prefer …, most comfortable / most popular

OPTIMISE YOUR EXAM

Collaborative task

Ask students to read the tips.

- Highlight the way one of the students in Exercise 5 shows initiative by summarising the task instruction and suggesting a place to start (*Student A: OK, so we have to select two items for the new uniform. Shall we talk about the trainers first?*).
- Point out to students that they can get marked down for hesitation and long pauses. If the conversation stops, you can ask questions and summarise your partner's ideas with phrases like *So do you mean …?* or summarise the ideas you've had so far *So what we've said is …*.

Exam task

7 In pairs, students complete the task in the two-minute time limit. Walk round, monitoring students and noting down good use of language and errors to go over in a feedback session at the end of the activity.

Optional extension

After the feedback session, ask students to repeat the activity with another partner to see if they can improve their performance.

Homework OWB

Assign students Speaking exercises 1, 2 and 3 on pages 64–65 of their Workbook.

LANGUAGE IN USE

Sentence transformation

→ Student's Book, page 87 SB

Lesson aims

- Focus on verb patterns with *-ing* form and infinitive
- Practise a sentence-transformation exam task

Lead-in

Play ***A–Z race***. In pairs, students race against each other to make a list of clothes and accessories for every letter of the alphabet (except *i, q, x* and *y*). Set a three-minute time limit and give regular updates, e.g. *Only two minutes to go …*, etc. When the time is up, ask them to count how many clothes they have in their lists. Ask the pair with the most clothes and accessories to read out their list and ask the rest of the class to say if they are correct.

Suggested answers

anorak, bracelet, coat, dress, earrings, fleece, glove, headband, jewellery, kimono, leather jacket, miniskirt, necklace, overcoat, purse, ring, socks, trainers, underwear, vest, wristband, zipper jacket

1 In pairs, students complete the exercise. Elicit answers from different students around the class. Find out if anyone has ever been to a fancy-dress party and what they wore or would wear if they went to one.

Answers
Students' own answers

Remember

Students are tested on common verb patterns in all the different sections of the main exams, especially in *Language in Use* papers. Remind them that they can look up verb patterns for individual verbs in a good monolingual dictionary, such as the *Macmillan* Dictionary (www.macmillandictionary.com). Ask students to read the information.

Refer students to the Grammar reference, Unit 8, page 156, for more information.

Language note

Elicit some verbs students know that follow the pattern verb + full infinitive (*afford, agree, attempt, choose, expect, hope, manage, offer, pretend, promise, want, wish*) and verbs + *-ing* form (*admit, deny, dislike, enjoy, fancy, imagine, involve, risk*).

Ask students if they know some verbs that take verb + full infinitive or *-ing* form, with little or no change in meaning (*begin, start, continue, hate, intend, love, prefer*).

Elicit verbs that take verb + full infinitive or *-ing* form but with a change in meaning (*try, stop, remember, forget*).

2 Ask students to complete the exercise. Have them compare in pairs before you check answers in open class.

Answers
1 shopping **2** to find **3** getting **4** to buy **5** to get **6** taking **7** to use **8** wearing

3 Ask students to complete the exercise. Check answers in open class.

Answers
1 wearing **2** to wear **3** to buy **4** buying **5** asking **6** to ask

OPTIMISE YOUR EXAM

Sentence transformation

Ask students to read the tips.

- In some exams, sentence-transformation questions are worth a lot of points and it is worthwhile spending time in class on this task. Emphasise the importance of including all the information and that not doing this is a common way to lose marks.

Exam task

4 Remind students that they have worked on sentence transformations in Units 2 and 4. Elicit the answer to the first question as an example. Ask them to complete the exercise. Check answers in open class.

Answers
1 to get **2** to hire **3** to help **4** doing **5** in making **6** seeing

Mixed ability

When checking answers to Exercise 4, divide the class into A and B pairs, mixing up higher- and lower-level students. Give Student A sentences 1–3 and Student B sentences 4–6. They challenge each other to formulate the second sentence with the words given, without looking at their answers. If the answer is correct, Student B continues. If they make a mistake, Student A has a turn with one of their sentences. The aim of the game is for both students to go through all the sentence transformations in one go without making any mistakes.

Homework OWB

Assign students Language in Use exercises 1, 2 and 3 on page 65 of their Workbook.

WRITING
A story

→ Student's Book, pages 88–89 SB

Lesson aims

- Focus on language for writing descriptions
- Plan and write a story

Lead-in

Write these sentences on the board in a jumbled order. Ask students to order the 'rags-to-riches' life events of supermodel Natalia Vodianova. Check answers in open class.

She was born in Gorky, Russia in 1982.

As a child, she helped sell fruit on the street.

She enrolled in a modelling agency when she was a teenager.

She moved to Paris and signed her first contract with Viva Models.

In the 90s, she did photo shoots and ad campaigns with the most famous photographers.

She has walked in over 400 runway shows and appeared in every major international magazine.

Today, she's one of the highest paid models in the world.

Elicit names of other supermodels students may know (e.g. *Kate Moss, Alessandra Ambrosio, Miranda Kerr, Adriana Lima, Jason Shaw, Tyson Beckford*).

1 Focus students' attention on the photo and elicit what they can see (*models walking on a runway/ catwalk at a fashion show*). Ask students to complete the exercise. Elicit answers in open class.

Answers
Students' own answers

EXAM SKILL

Writing descriptions

Ask students to read the tips.

- Remind students that examiners don't want to read about a nice day, they want to know why it was just 'nice'. Students can use adjectives to tell them, e.g. *exciting*, *fantastic* and then explain why in another sentence. Adverbs, like adjectives, give the examiners more information and keep them interested. Adverbs answer the questions *why, when, where, how* and *to what extent*.

Language note

Elicit that adjectives are words that describe or modify another person or thing in the sentence. Unlike adverbs, which can appear almost anywhere in a sentence, adjectives nearly always appear immediately before the noun or noun phrase that they modify.

Adverbs are words that modify a verb (*He walked slowly.* – How did he walk?), an adjective (*He drove a very fast car.* – How fast was his car?) or another adverb (*She moved quite slowly down the aisle.* – How slowly did she move?).

Remind students that one of the key features of adverbs is their ability to move around in a sentence, e.g. *Quickly, he ran (quickly) into the dark room (quickly).* Putting the adverb at the front of a sentence gives it more emphasis and effect.

2 Ask students to complete the exercise. Check answers in open class.

Answers
1 He/She expects to watch a school fashion show.
2 He/She becomes a model in the fashion show after one of the models gets/falls ill.
3 excited, ill, shocked, amazing, fantastic, pleased
4 suddenly, nervously, quickly

OPTIMISE YOUR EXAM

A story

Ask students to read the tips.

- Highlight that using more descriptive language will earn students higher marks in writing examinations. *Say* and *tell* are standard verbs which are used to indicate direct speech in any narrative. Choosing more colourful verbs will add life to their texts, e.g. *reply, ask, insist, warn, inform, persuade, respond, suggest, interrupt*.

For more information on writing stories, refer students to the Writing reference, page 172.

Exam task

3 Ask students to complete the exercise.

Answers
Students' own answers

Extra support

First, discuss the questions to the right of the task in Exercise 3 in open class. Then, elicit ideas and brainstorm ideas. Write them on the board for students to refer back to when they write their story.

4 Plan Ask students to complete the paragraph plan using their notes from Exercise 3. You may want to look at students' plans, if this is possible, to check them and give advice and suggestions for improvement before students write.

5 Write Students write their story in about 100 words, in an appropriate style. Depending on time, it may be a good idea to set this and the subsequent checklist exercise for homework.

6 Check Students complete the checklist before they hand in their story.

Optional extension

Students swap texts and give each other feedback using the checklist in Exercise 6 as a guide.

Homework OWB
Assign students Writing exercises 1, 2, 3 and 4 on page 66 of their Workbook and Progress check 8, page 67.

Answers PROGRESS CHECK Units 7–8

Exercise 1
1 was **2** than **3** bargain **4** on **5** be **6** up **7** are **8** to

Exercise 2
1 out **2** around **3** up **4** off **5** back **6** by **7** up **8** up

Exercise 3
1 bigger than **2** the most expensive **3** less enjoyable than **4** the worst **5** prettier than **6** the least fashionable

Exercise 4
1 do you **2** isn't it **3** didn't you **4** will he **5** shall we **6** have they

Exercise 5
1 amazement **2** director **3** creative **4** trendy **5** librarian **6** beautiful **7** lawyer **8** assistant

Exercise 6
1 taking **2** to do **3** had lost **4** to buy **5** of **6** are sold **7** been stolen **8** been chosen

Exercise 7
1 exchange **2** dye **3** voucher **4** browse **5** sleeve **6** change

9 Playing to win!

UNIT AIMS

Exam preparation in Unit 9:

- understand implication in an online article
- listen for attitude and opinion in an interview
- talk about other people in an interview
- recognise verbs with similar meanings and use them in a multiple-choice cloze exercise
- give opinions in a short message

TEACHER'S PRESENTATION KIT

- *Talk2Me* videos
- Speaking test videos
- Class and Workbook audio
- Workbook pages and answer key

UNIT OVERVIEW

Student's Book / Digital Student's Book SB		Workbook / Online Workbook OWB
LESSON / EXAM TASK	EXAM SKILLS / LANGUAGE FOCUS	CONSOLIDATION
Reading **Multiple choice**	Understanding implication An online article	Workbook, pp 68–69, Exercises 1, 2, 3 Unit 9, Reading, Exercises 1, 2, 3
Grammar 1	Conditionals (1): zero, first and second conditionals	Workbook, p 70, Exercises 1, 2, 3 Unit 9, Grammar 1, Exercises 1, 2, 3
Vocabulary	Words connected with *people in sport* Phrasal verbs Collocations with *do*, *play* and *go*	Workbook, pp 70–71, Exercises 1, 2, 3 Unit 9, Vocabulary, Exercises 1, 2, 3
Listening **Multiple choice**	Listening for attitude and opinion	Workbook, p 72, Exercises 1, 2, 3 Unit 9, Listening, Exercises 1, 2, 3
Grammar 2	Time clauses	Workbook, p 71, Exercises 1, 2 Unit 9, Grammar 2, Exercises 1, 2
Speaking **Interview**	Talking about other people	Workbook, pp 72–73, Exercises 1, 2, 3 Unit 9, Speaking, Exercises 1, 2, 3
Language in Use **Multiple-choice cloze**	Verbs with similar meanings	Workbook, p 73, Exercises 1, 2 Unit 9, Language in Use, Exercises 1, 2
Writing **A short message**	Giving opinions	Workbook, p 74, Exercises 1, 2, 3, 4 Unit 9, Writing, Exercises 1, 2, 3, 4
		Workbook, p 75, Progress check and Cumulative progress Progress check and Cumulative progress

Additional material

PRESENTATION KIT	TEACHER'S / STUDENT'S RESOURCE CENTRE RC	TEST GENERATOR
Talk2Me video *I don't think I've ever …*	**Unit 9 worksheets:** *Optimise your grammar* (Standard and Higher), *Optimise your vocabulary* (Standard and Higher), *Talk2Me* video, *Say it right* **Units 9–10 worksheets:** CLIL, Culture, Everyday English (TRC only), Grammar communication (TRC only)	Unit Test 9 (Standard and Higher)

READING

Multiple choice | An online article

→ Student's Book, pages 92–93 SB

Lesson aims

- Focus on understanding implication
- Practise a multiple-choice exam task

Lead-in

Divide the class into teams. Ask students to race to think of as many sports as they can in a three-minute time limit. When the time is up, ask students to total how many sports they have thought of. The team with the most sports wins the game. Elicit the sports and, if appropriate, ask the team to write the answers on the board to check spelling. Draw students' attention to the photo and ask them to describe what they can see (*sports trophies and medals*). Ask students to look at the unit title ***Playing to win!*** and elicit what it means (*to play in an especially competitive manner, focused on winning*). Ask them to say what they think the unit is going to be about (*sports*).

1 In pairs or as a group, students complete the exercise. Elicit answers from different students around the class.

Answers

Students' own answers

2 Ask students to complete the exercise. Set a three-minute time limit to encourage them to read quickly. Elicit answers in open class.

Answers

1 c **2** d **3** f **4** a **5** g **6** b **7** e

Extra support

Elicit the key words in each paragraph that helped them choose their answers.

EXAM SKILL

Understanding implication

Ask students to read the tips.

- Students often struggle to understand implication and extract meaning from a text. They need to develop strategies which help them read ideas, rather than words, and infer, rather than find, meaning. In reading exam tasks, students have to draw conclusions by inferring unstated meanings based on social conventions, shared knowledge, shared experience or shared values.
- Highlight that when we read or listen in our own language, we understand most information indirectly, by inference. Good writers often only hint at what they mean, and mean much more than they actually seem to say. A simple sentence can contain a lot of information and a number of assertions.

3 Ask students to complete the exercise. Check answers in open class.

Answers

1 b **2** a

OPTIMISE YOUR EXAM

Multiple choice

Ask students to read the tips.

- Remind students that they mustn't read their own ideas into the text: there must be sufficient evidence present to support their interpretations. They need to find answers by reasoning from evidence and mustn't jump to conclusions or make something up.
- Understanding implication in reading texts can help students improve their own writing. They will learn that readers often have to interpret the writer's thoughts and will realise how important it is to make their meaning as clear as possible with sufficient explanations and examples.

Exam task

4 3.01 **Note: The reading text is also available on the audio CD. You may want to have students listen and read the text before doing the exam task.**

Ask students to complete the exercise. Have them compare in pairs before you check answers in open class.

Answers

1 D **2** C **3** A **4** C

Extra support

Elicit the key sentences that helped them choose their answers:

1 *There are boys and girls in each team – a maximum of four boys or four girls.*

2 *I wouldn't want to be a chaser – we throw quite hard!*

3 *The seekers come on a minute later.*

4 John Clark specifies a position and justifies his choice.

5 Ask students to complete the exercise. Check answers in open class.

Suggested answers

defend = protect from attack
fan = someone who likes reading, listening or watching something very much
goalposts = the two posts that the ball must go between to score a goal
match = a game in which players or teams compete against each other
opposing team = the people you compete against
pitch = the ground for playing sport
position = where a particular player plays
sports kit = clothes or equipment needed for sport

Mixed ability

For less confident students, write the definitions in Suggested answers in a jumbled order on the board for them to match to the words in the box in Exercise 5. More confident students can prepare a written definition of the words in Exercise 5. When everyone has finished, they can read them out for other students to match to one of the words or phrases in the box.

THINK | RESEARCH | CULTURE | LEARN | ME

In pairs or small groups, students complete the task. Elicit answers from different students around the class and ask them to justify their choices.

Optional extension 3.01

Play the recorded reading text and ask students to underline words and phrases connected with sport. Ask them to organise the vocabulary into these categories: *verbs, nouns for people, other nouns and noun phrases*. Elicit their answers in open class.

Suggested answers

Verbs: play, score (goals), throw, kick, get points, hit, drop, hold, touch, defend, try, catch, pull, choose

Nouns for people: team, player, team captain, runner

Other nouns and noun phrases: game, volleyball, ball, hoop, on the pitch, match, goalposts, sports kit

Cultural note

The first intercollegiate quidditch match was played in 2007 (not Quidditch, as the International Quidditch Association uses a lowercase spelling to separate it from the sport depicted in the *Harry Potter* books). A squad includes 21 players in total. Seven players with brooms between their legs are on the field at any time. At the IQA World Cup in 2016 there were 25 teams from around the world. A lot of the players are students, with the majority of players in university teams.

Homework OWB

Assign students Reading exercises 1, 2 and 3 on pages 68–69 of their Workbook.

GRAMMAR 1

Conditionals (1): zero, first and second conditionals

→ Student's Book, page 94 SB

Lesson aims

- Focus on zero, first and second conditionals
- Practise using the zero, first and second conditional

Lead-in

Write these groups of words on the board and tell students that only three of the four options in each group logically belong with each other. In pairs, ask them to pick the odd one out. Check answers in open class and ask students to justify their choices.

snitch, volleyball, quaffle, bludger
pitch, hoops, runner, goalposts
throw, kick, hit, pull
captain, fan, defender, player
seeker, quaffle, beater, chaser

Answers

snitch (the other three are all balls)
runner (the others are all things you need to play quidditch)
pull (you can't pull a ball)
fan (all the others are names for people who play sport)
quaffle (all the others are positions in quidditch)

Grammar in context

Ask students to complete the task. Refer them to the information in the *Remember* box if they aren't sure. Check answers in open class.

Remind students that they can find more information in the Grammar reference, Unit 9, page 157.

Answers

1 b **2** d **3** a **4** c

Language note

Remind students that when the *if* clause comes first, a comma is usually used and clauses are interchangeable with no difference in meaning, e.g. *If you don't play sport, you get unfit. / You get unfit if you don't play sport.*

Students should also note that they can use *was/were* with *If I/he/she*, e.g. *If I* **were** *you, I'd play more sport.*

Remind students we can also use *when* instead of *if. When* means a time, often an expected time of completion, and *if* conveys conditionality.

When you play the match on Saturday, you will have to play really well. (you know you are going to play)

If you play the match on Saturday, you will have to play really well. (you don't know if you are going to play)

The future tense can have other forms besides the usual *will*, e.g. *going to* or modals, such as *might* or *could* (*We might/could play indoors if it rains.*), etc.

Extra support

Ask students to complete these sentences in a logical way with *unless*:

1 ... she is feeling better. (visit)
2 ... you want to lose weight. (go on a diet)
3 ... I meant it. (say)
4 ... you help me. (come)

Suggested answers

1 Don't visit her unless she is feeling better.
2 Don't go on a diet unless you want to lose weight.
3 I wouldn't say it unless I meant it.
4 I won't come unless you help me.

1 Ask students to complete the exercise. Have them compare in pairs before you check answers in open class.

Answers

1 hits, loses **2** goes, gets **3** doesn't return, wins
4 don't knock down, don't get

2 Focus students' attention on the photo. Elicit what the girl might be doing. (*She is running in an event called a parkrun.*) and ask if anyone has ever participated in a similar activity.

Ask students to complete the exercise. Have them compare in pairs before you check answers in open class.

Answers

1 want **2** 'll love **3** would **4** had **5** does **6** go **7** go **8** were **9** 'd **10** unless

Fast finishers

Ask students to write one or two comprehension questions based on the text in Exercise 2, e.g. *Why does Max recommend parkrun to Jan? Where does Jan live?* When everyone has finished, they can read out their questions for others to answer.

3 Ask students to complete the exercise. Have them compare their sentences in pairs. Elicit interesting and unusual sentences from different students around the class.

Suggested answers

1 … I'll play football in the park with my friends.
2 … we might go to the beach.
3 … I'd probably choose a team game.
4 … I'd ask my friend Billy to come with me.
5 I wouldn't go to a parkrun event unless my friend Billy came with me.

Optional extension

Write these prompts on the board:

If I went to live in another country …

If I were a famous sports personality …

If I could run very fast …

If I could be brilliant at any sport …

In pairs or small groups, the first student completes the sentence in a way that is both logical and grammatically correct, e.g. … *I would choose to live in France.* The next student says a follow-up sentence which must also be logically and grammatically correct, e.g. *If I lived in France, I would speak great French.* Students continue the chain until they run out of ideas. Ask students to count how many second conditional sentences they can make with each prompt. Elicit the longest chains from around the class.

THINK | RESEARCH | CULTURE | LEARN | **ME**

Ask students to complete the task. Elicit answers from different students around the class.

Homework

OWB

Assign students Grammar 1 exercises 1, 2 and 3 on page 70 of their Workbook.

VOCABULARY

Topic vocabulary | Phrasal verbs | Collocations

→ Student's Book, page 95 SB

Lesson aims

Understand the correct usage of:

- words connected with *people in sport*
- phrasal verbs
- collocations with *do, play* and *go*

Lead-in

Play ***Twenty questions***. Students have to guess the name of a famous sportsperson (*Lionel Messi, Serena Williams, Ricky Rubio,* etc.) by asking you up to 20 *Yes/No* questions. Elicit students' favourite sportspeople and what they like about them.

Words connected with *people in sport*

1 3.02 Focus students' attention on the photos in Exercise 1. Elicit the names of the sports (*gymnastics* and *athletics*). Ask students to complete the exercise. Play the audio for them to listen and check their answers.

Answers/Audioscript

1 someone in a football/basketball team: *player*
2 someone who plays computer games: *gamer*
3 someone who leads a sports team: *captain*
4 someone who judges a football/basketball match: *referee*
5 someone on a horse or sometimes a bike: *rider*
6 someone on a bike but not a horse: *cyclist*
7 someone who does athletics, or who is good at sport: *athlete*
8 someone who does gymnastics: *gymnast*
9 someone who can balance and jump well, often in a circus: *acrobat*
10 someone who goes up mountains, walls or rocks: *climber*

Refer students to the Vocabulary reference, page 167, for more information on topic vocabulary.

Phrasal verbs

2 3.03 Ask students to complete the exercise. Have them compare in pairs before you play the audio for them to listen and check their answers.

Answers/Audioscript

1 Mum, they won't let me *join in* with the game!
2 The team with the lowest points at the end of the round is *knocked out*.
3 The referee held up a red card and *sent* Garcia *off*.
4 She's had to *pull out* of the competition because of a knee injury.
5 The weather's so bad, I think we'll have to *put* the match *off* until next week.
6 Can you help me *set up* the table tennis net?
7 *Put away* all the equipment when you've finished using it, please.
8 I'm surprised that real-life quidditch *caught on* so quickly!

3 Ask students to complete the exercise. Have them compare in pairs before you check answers in open class.

Answers

1 pull out **2** set up **3** join in **4** catch on **5** put away **6** send off **7** put off **8** knock out

Refer students to the Vocabulary reference, page 167, for more information on phrasal verbs.

Collocations with *do, play* and *go*

4 3.04 Ask students to complete the exercise. Have them compare in pairs before you play the audio for students to listen and check their answers.

Answers/Audioscript

1 How often do you *play* tennis/football/basketball?
2 Have you ever *played* golf?
3 Do you *do* athletics at school in the summer?
4 How often do you *go* swimming in the winter?
5 Have you ever *been* ice skating?
6 Do you *do* gymnastics sometimes in PE?
7 Have you ever *been* windsurfing?
8 Do you know anyone who *goes* horse-riding regularly?
9 When was the last time you *went* for a bike ride?
10 Have you ever *been* water-skiing?
11 Do you know anyone who *goes* surfing regularly?
12 Do you know anyone who *does* yoga?

Language note

Do, play, go

Do is used for a recreational activity or a non-team sport that does not use a ball, e.g. *do yoga, judo, karate,* etc.

Play is used with ball sports or competitive games where we play against another person, e.g. *play basketball, badminton, football,* etc.

Go is used with activities that end in *-ing*. We go somewhere to do something, e.g. *go hiking, swimming, fishing,* etc.

Remember

Ask students to read the information.

Refer students to the Vocabulary reference, page 167, for more information on collocations.

SAY IT RIGHT

Silent letters

TRC

For the *Say it right* pronunciation activity and instructions, go to the Teacher's Resource Centre.

Homework

OWB

Assign students Vocabulary exercises 1, 2 and 3 on pages 70–71 of their Workbook.

LISTENING
Multiple choice

→ Student's Book, page 96 SB

Lesson aims

- Listen for attitude and opinion
- Practise a multiple-choice exam task

Lead-in

In pairs or small groups, ask students to brainstorm as many water sports as they can think of in a time limit of two minutes. When they have finished, ask them to add up the number of water sports in their list. The pair or group with the most wins the game. Elicit which ones they think sound the most interesting and if they have tried any of them.

Suggested answers

surfing, windsurfing, kite surfing, sailing, swimming, water-skiing, kayaking, whitewater rafting, scuba diving, snorkelling, jet skiing, yachting, wakeboarding, water polo, rowing, diving, synchronised swimming, fishing, bodyboarding, water aerobics, paddle boarding, parasailing

1 In pairs or as a group, students complete the exercise. Elicit answers from different students around the class.

Answers

Students' own answers

Cultural note

Surfing is one of the world's oldest sports and was important in ancient Polynesian culture. It was probably first described by a European around 1769 when Joseph Banks was writing about the voyages of James Cook on the *HMS Endeavour.*

EXAM SKILL

Listening for attitude and opinion

Ask students to read the tips.

- Elicit the differences between facts (*concrete observations*), opinions (*thoughts based on those observations*) and attitude (*a way of thinking or feeling reflected in your behaviour*). Elicit an example about surfing, e.g. *Surfing is an ancient sport / Surfing is great / We need to protect surfing beaches.* People often mix facts, attitudes and opinions together when they speak.
- Students have already worked on intonation (Listening, Unit 3) to indicate a speaker's attitude or opinion. A fast and enthusiastic tone expresses a positive attitude – the pitch goes up at the end of the sentence – and a falling intonation can indicate a negative attitude. Remind students to listen for tone, pitch, volume and speed, as well as the words.
- Opinions are often qualified with adjectives (e.g. *great, fantastic*), adverbs (e.g. *really, totally*) and comparatives and superlatives (e.g. *better, the best*).

2 3.05 Play the track and ask students to complete the exercise. Check answers in open class.

Answers
1 F **2** O **3** O **4** B **5** F **6** B

Extra support

Elicit the key words and numbers that helped them understand that the speaker was expressing an opinion or a fact:

1 *There were 16 of us – all from the same school – and three of our teachers came too.* (Here there are just numerical facts to describe a situation with no expressions of opinion / adjectives.)

2 *Do it! You'll really enjoy it.* (a recommendation not a fact / enthusiastic tone, slightly louder pitch and faster speed)

3 *It seems to me …* (an expression we use to signal we are going to express an opinion)

4 *The first evening, we had a welcome party* (dates and situation – facts) *which was great fun!* (adjective to express mood, attitude and emotion)

5 *Then in the evenings we did various different things, including singing round the campfire and learning bushcraft skills.* (time reference and a list of activities – facts)

6 *On the final day, we had a Beach Olympics* (time reference, naming an event – facts) *which was brilliant!* (again, an adjective tells us how the speaker feels or what they think)

OPTIMISE YOUR EXAM

Multiple choice

Ask students to read the tips.

- Phrases for expressing opinions and attitude give students verbal cues about what information is important. Point out that good listeners pick up more on these cues to help them understand the different points in a discussion. Highlight that if students know these cues, they will be able to rapidly tune in when the speaker is expressing an opinion or attitude.
- This skill is useful in listening exams, and raising students' awareness of how we indicate our opinion and attitude will also help them improve their performance in oral exams.

Exam task

3 3.06 Play the track for students to listen and complete the exercise. Don't check answers yet as they will listen again in Exercise 4.

4 3.06 Play the track again for students to check their answers. Check answers in open class. Elicit the key words and phrases that helped them decide on their answers.

Answers
1 C (*… I was a bit nervous, to be honest*)
2 C (*… they gave us a cooked dinner in the evening.*)
3 B (*… school lessons in the afternoon on the beach – things like creative writing, art, English and geography.*)
4 A (*… before long I felt I was able to surf quite well! It really built up my confidence …*)
5 B (*Do it! You'll really enjoy it.*)

Mixed ability

For less confident students, play the track again for students to compare the words in the incorrect options with the actual words in the audioscript. Alternatively, give stronger students a copy of the audioscript for them to underline the 'trick' information. Elicit whether each question asks students to listen out for opinion/attitude, facts or both.

Answers

1 Opinion/Attitude – students have to listen out for how Megan felt.

A She says, *Well, some of the friends who I went with were excited about going* – but she was a bit nervous.

B She says, *I didn't know what it would be like* – not how she felt.

2 Both – students have to listen for facts about times of meals and what Megan thought about them.

A She says, *We had a lovely big breakfast each morning*, so this option is true.

B She says, *… we prepared our own packed lunch which we had at around midday*, so this option is also true.

3 Fact – students have to deduce when Megan could have written a poem from the facts about the course timetable.

A She says, *… we had surfing lessons all morning*, so she couldn't have written anything in the morning.

C She says, *Then in the evenings we did various different things, including singing round the campfire*, so again, she couldn't have written anything then.

4 Opinion/Attitude – students have to listen out for how Megan felt.

B She says, *… so I was terrified of the idea to start with …*, so she only felt scared at the beginning.

C She says, *But the instructors were so kind and patient …* – she talks about the instructors and how they were, but not how she felt herself.

5 Opinion/Attitude – students have to listen out for her advice/opinion.

A She says, *And as soon as you've had a couple of surfing lessons, you'll feel like an expert surfer!* – she doesn't say that you should only go if you want to become an expert.

C She says, *I don't like speaking in public, but the activities we did there really helped me.* – she only mentions speaking in public as a different skill the course helped her with.

THINK | RESEARCH | CULTURE | LEARN | ME

Ask students to complete the task. Elicit answers from different students around the class.

Homework

OWB

Assign students Listening exercises 1, 2 and 3 on page 72 of their Workbook.

GRAMMAR 2
Time clauses

→ Student's Book, page 97

Lesson aims

- Focus on time clauses
- Practise using time clauses

Lead-in

Drill these questions about cycling:

Have you got a bike? If so, what type of bike is it? How often do you ride it?

Can you cycle safely where you live?

Have you ever fallen off a bike?

In pairs or small groups, students take turns to ask and answer the questions. Elicit some unusual or interesting answers from different students around the class.

Grammar in context

Ask students to complete the task. Refer them to the information in the *Remember* box if they aren't sure. Check answers in open class.

Remind students that they can find more information in the Grammar reference, Unit 9, page 157.

Answers

1 get **2** As soon as

Language note

Time clauses

Time clauses are introduced by conjunctions, such as *after, as soon as, before, till, until, when, whenever, while* or time expressions, such as *the minute, the moment*, etc.

Elicit why we use *as soon as* (*to emphasise immediacy*) and the meaning of *until/till* (*up to the point in time or the event mentioned*) and *while* (*during the time that / at the same time as*).

1 Ask students to complete the exercise. Have them compare in pairs before you check answers in open class.

Answers

1 before **2** after **3** soon **4** while/when **5** until **6** when/after

Remember

Ask students to read the information.

Highlight other synonyms for *once*, e.g. *immediately after, the instant/moment/second/minute*.

2 Ask students to complete the exercise. Have them compare in pairs before you check answers in open class.

Answers

1 get / have got **2** I will call / I'll call **3** find / have found / 've found **4** am

3 Ask students to complete the exercise. Have them compare in pairs before you check answers in open class.

Answers

1 I finish / I've finished / I have finished **2** I've practised / I have practised / practising **3** we set / we've set / we have set **4** I do / I'm doing / I am doing **5** comes back / 's come back / has come back **6** until you show / until you've shown

Mixed ability

When checking the answers to Exercise 3, divide the class into A and B pairs, mixing up higher- and lower-level students. Tell Student A to read out the first sentence and the words given as prompts. Student B tries to formulate the second sentence without looking at their answers. If the answer is correct, Student B continues. If they make a mistake, Student A has a turn, starting again from sentence 1. The aim of the game is for both students to go through all the sentence transformations in one go without making any mistakes.

Homework (OWB)

Assign students Grammar 2 exercises 1 and 2 on page 71 of their Workbook.

Assign students the Flipped classroom tasks on page 98 of their Student's Book if you'd like them to prepare for the next lesson. To complete this task, students need to watch the *Talk2Me* video which can be found on the Resource Centre.

SPEAKING
Interview

→ Student's Book, page 98

Lesson aim

- Talking about other people

The *Talk2Me* video in this unit focuses on people talking about friends and their family. Students answer some comprehension questions and then listen out for ways of talking about people they know. The video can be used in one of two ways:

Flipped classroom

Flipped classroom option

Using this approach, students watch the video and complete the exercises for homework. This prepares students for the speaking lesson by introducing them to the topic and the key phrases to use in the exam task. Teachers who use this method will find they have more class time to spend on activating the target language and developing fluency for the final task.

***Talk2Me* worksheet**

Ask students to also complete the *Talk2Me* worksheet on the Resource Centre for more detailed comprehension exercises and more practice of the key phrases.

Classroom option

Lead-in

Play ***Alphabet race***. In pairs, students race against each other to make a list of sports for every letter of the alphabet (except q and u) in a three-minute time limit. Give regular updates, e.g. *Only two minutes to go …*, etc. Stop students and ask them to count how many sports they have in their lists. Ask the pair with the most sports to read out their list to see if they are correct and if they are winners of the game.

Suggested answers

athletics, basketball, cycling, diving, equestrian, football, golf, hockey, ice-skating, jogging, kayaking, long jump, martial arts, netball, orienteering, pool, rowing, skiing, table tennis, volleyball, windsurfing, x-treme sports, yachting, zip-lining

1 Ask students to read the questions. Play the *Talk2Me* video for students to complete the exercise. Play the video again, if necessary, before checking their answers.

Answers

1 Jamie laughs at Maddy's homework because she has misunderstood the question to 'find the x'. **2** 10 **3** He is good at music. He is not good at football.

2 Play the *Talk2Me* video again, so students can underline the phrases in the *Phrase expert* box. Pause the video from time to time if necessary. Check answers in open class.

Answers

I don't think I've ever ..., but (you obviously have). Take my (cousin), for example, She … all the time, You absolutely love (maths), can't stand (sport), I'm a keen (sportswoman)

Talk2Me worksheet

Ask students to also complete the *Talk2Me* worksheet on the Resource Centre for more detailed comprehension exercises and more practice of the key phrases.

Answers

The transcript and answer key for the *Talk2Me* video exercises and Worksheet can be found on the Teacher's Resource Centre.

3 In pairs or as a group, students ask and answer the questions. Elicit answers from different students around the class.

Suggested answers

Students' own answers

EXAM SKILL

Talking about other people

Ask students to read the tips.

- Remind students to use examples from their own life; it's much easier to talk more fluently about their own experiences. Students can prepare for this section by making a list of family members and friends and noting down vocabulary they would need to talk about each one and practising the pronunciation of any new vocabulary. Mind maps are quick and useful for this kind of activity.
- Encourage students to write questions for the topics they may be asked. They can then record themselves answering the questions and listen to see how they can improve your responses.

4 3.07 Play the track for students to listen and complete the task. Elicit which key words helped students decide on their answers.

Answers

4 my dad loves watching football on TV … I think it's a bit boring … I'm not so keen on sitting in front of the TV watching football
2 cousin, dangerous
1 all the time, every day … We play … football … we often play with a ball … best friend … video games … board games like Scrabble and Monopoly.
3 competitive, win

Mixed ability

Ask students to brainstorm possible answers for each question before they listen. Write interesting ideas and useful vocabulary on the board for less confident students to refer to in Exercise 5.

5 In pairs, students take turns to ask and answer the questions. Elicit answers from different students around the class.

Answers

Students' own answers

6 Individually, ask students to complete the task.

Answers

Students' own answers

OPTIMISE YOUR EXAM

Interview

Ask students to read the tips.

- Highlight language that is useful in this section, e.g. ways of expressing likes and dislikes, linkers like *though* and *so* and tenses to talk about the past and present and your experiences, e.g. *I've been to a few of his races or I've watched a game.*
- Remind students to not worry about the time. The examiner will stop them when time is up. Tell them also not to worry if the examiner stops them before they have finished. They will not be penalised for not concluding their talk.

Exam task

7 In pairs or as a group, students complete the task. Walk round, monitoring students and noting down good use of language and errors to go over in a feedback session at the end of the activity.

Homework

OWB

Assign students Speaking exercises 1, 2 and 3 on pages 72–73 of their Workbook.

LANGUAGE IN USE

Multiple-choice cloze

→ Student's Book, page 99

SB

Lesson aims

- Focus on words with similar meanings
- Practise a multiple-choice cloze exam task

Lead-in

Play ***Snowman*** with words connected to sport. Divide the class into two teams. On the board, draw one line for each letter in a word. The teams take turns to guess letters in the word. If a letter is guessed correctly, write it into the correct space. If a letter is guessed which is not in the word, draw part of the snowman. The team which guesses the word first receives a point, and the game starts again.

Typically, the snowman should consist of nine parts: large circle (lower body), medium circle (upper body), circle (head), hat, buttons, arms, nose, eyes and mouth.

1 In pairs or as a group, students complete the exercise. Elicit answers from different students around the class.

Answers

Students' own answers

Remember

Ask students to read the information.

2 Ask students to complete the exercise. Have them compare in pairs before you check answers in open class.

Answers

1 involves **2** ✓ **3** contains/includes **4** include **5** ✓

3 In pairs or as a group, students complete the exercise. Check answers in open class.

Suggested answers

1 An activity is something a person or group does. A hobby is an activity you do in your free time for pleasure. A sport is an activity involving physical effort and skill, often involving competition.

2 When you see something, you perceive it with your eyes. When you imagine something, you form a mental image of it. When you dream of something, you have an ambition or an ideal. When you view something, you see it from a particular place.

3 When you hold something, you support it with your arms or hands. When you carry something, you hold it using your hands, arms or body and move it from one place to another. When you bring something, you take it from one place and have it with you when you arrive somewhere else. When you take something, you move it from one place to another.

4 When you catch a ball, you take it and hold it with your hand. When you kick a ball, you strike it with your foot. When you hit a ball, you bring your hand or an implement into contact with it, usually quickly and forcefully. When you throw a ball, you propel it through the air with a movement of your arm and hand.

OPTIMISE YOUR EXAM

Multiple-choice cloze

Ask students to read the tips.

- In this exam task type, students are tested on their grammatical knowledge (it may involve choosing a word that fits in with the grammar of the sentence) or meaning (it may involve choosing the right word for the context) or a combination of both. Multiple-choice cloze also tests students' knowledge of phrasal verbs, collocations and fixed phrases.

4 In pairs or as a group, students complete the exercise. Check answers in open class.

Answers

Name of sport	jollyball
Number of teams in a game	two
Number of players in each team	two or three
Other sports it has similarities with	juggling, volleyball, tennis
Object placed between the teams	a (table tennis or badminton) net
Each player has in their hands	two juggling balls
What a player has to do when they get the ball	juggle with it and the other two balls (before making it go back over the net)

Exam task

5 Ask students to complete the exercise. Check answers in open class.

Answers

1 C **2** D **3** A **4** C **5** B **6** B **7** A **8** D

Homework

OWB

Assign students Language in Use exercises 1 and 2 on page 73 of their Workbook.

WRITING
A short message

→ Student's Book, pages 100–101 SB

Lesson aims

- Focus on language for giving opinions
- Plan and write a short message

Lead-in

Divide students into two teams. Ask a volunteer from each team to come to the front with their backs to the board. Tell them you have a list of 10 words from the unit. Write a different word on the board (one word at a time) behind each volunteer. Each team defines the word without saying it or giving any clues as to its spelling. The first volunteer to say the correct word wins their team a point. Swap volunteers and continue the game until all the words have been used.

Suggested words: *team, juggle, surf, competition, hobby, referee, parkrun, quidditch, bowling, sky-diving.*

1 Focus students' attention on the photo and elicit what they can see (*teenagers bowling at a bowling alley*). Ask students to complete the exercise. Elicit answers from different students around the class.

Answers
Students' own answers

EXAM SKILL

Giving opinions

Ask students to read the tips.

- An opinion needs a good reason, so students should give their opinion and add their personal thoughts, e.g. *Personally, I think that's a fantastic idea!* (opinion) *We'll have a great time!* (reason).
- Giving students appropriate words and phrases to give their opinion can be a great way to help them get started and organise their thoughts.

2 Ask students to complete the exercise. Check answers in open class.

Answers
1 is **2** Sunday **3** information

3 Ask students to complete the exercise. Check answers in open class.

Answers
1 Personally, I think **2** For me,

4 Ask students to complete the exercise. Check answers in open class.

Answers
1 In **2** concerned **3** seems **4** mind **5** view

OPTIMISE YOUR EXAM

A short message

Ask students to read the tips.

- Remind students that they have to be clear and economical when the task is a short message. They only have 35–45 words, about six sentences in total, so they have to be well organised.
- Highlight how important it is for them to reread their work. They can read it out to themselves and pretend they are the intended audience, to make sure the message is clear and concise. Ask them to focus on the message and purpose as well as checking for errors.

For more information on writing short messages, refer students to the Writing reference, page 169.

▼ Exam task

5 Ask students to complete the exercise. Check answers in open class.

Answers
1 Give your opinion (*tell her you think that's a good idea*)
2 Make an offer (*offer to find out online about the rules*)
3 Make a suggestion (*suggest that she arranges a meeting*)

6 **Plan** Ask students to complete the paragraph plan. You may want to look at students' plans, if this is possible, to check them and give advice and suggestions for improvement before they write.

▼ Exam task

7 Ask students to complete the exercise.

Answers
1 Thank (*thank Ed for inviting you*)
2 Give a reason (*explain why you don't want to go sky-diving*)
3 Make an offer (*offer to come with him just to watch*)

8 **Plan** Ask students to complete the paragraph plan. You may want to look at students' plans, if this is possible, to check them and give advice and suggestions for improvement before they write.

9 **Write** Students write their short messages in 35–45 words, in an appropriate style. Depending on time, it may be a good idea to set this and the subsequent checklist exercise for homework.

10 **Check** Students complete the checklist before they hand in their short messages.

Homework OWB

Assign students Writing exercises 1, 2, 3 and 4 on page 74 of their Workbook and Progress check 9, page 75.

10 All in good fun!

UNIT AIMS

Exam preparation in Unit 10:

- understand linking words and phrases in a blog post
- select relevant information in a talk
- listen and respond in a discussion
- understand and form *wish* and *if only* sentences and use them in an open-cloze exercise
- describe how to do something in an article

TEACHER'S PRESENTATION KIT

- *Talk2Me* videos
- Speaking test videos
- Class and Workbook audio
- Workbook pages and answer key

UNIT OVERVIEW

Student's Book / Digital Student's Book SB		Workbook / Online Workbook OWB
LESSON / EXAM TASK	EXAM SKILLS / LANGUAGE FOCUS	CONSOLIDATION
Reading **Open questions**	Understanding linking words and phrases A blog post	Workbook, pp 76–77, Exercises 1, 2, 3, 4 Unit 10, Reading, Exercises 1, 2, 3, 4
Grammar 1	Conditionals (2): third conditional	Workbook, p 78, Exercises 1, 2 Unit 10, Grammar 1, Exercises 1, 2
Vocabulary	Words connected with *people in the media* Phrasal verbs Word patterns	Workbook, pp 78–79, Exercises 1, 2, 3 Unit 10, Vocabulary, Exercises 1, 2, 3
Listening **Gap fill**	Selecting relevant information	Workbook, p 80, Exercises 1, 2 Unit 10, Listening, Exercises 1, 2
Grammar 2	The causative	Workbook, p 79, Exercises 1, 2 Unit 10, Grammar 2, Exercises 1, 2
Speaking **Discussion**	Listening and responding	Workbook, pp 80–81, Exercises 1, 2, 3 Unit 10, Speaking, Exercises 1, 2, 3
Language in Use **Open cloze**	*wish* and *if only*	Workbook, p 81, Exercises 1, 2, 3 Unit 10, Language in Use, Exercises 1, 2, 3
Writing **An article**	Describing how to do something	Workbook, p 82, Exercises 1, 2, 3, 4 Unit 10, Writing, Exercises 1, 2, 3, 4
Progress check	Check language progress for Units 9 and 10	Workbook, p 83, Progress check and Cumulative progress Progress check and Cumulative progress

Additional material

PRESENTATION KIT	TEACHER'S / STUDENT'S RESOURCE CENTRE RC	TEST GENERATOR
Talk2Me video *That sounds like fun.*	**Unit 10 worksheets:** *Optimise your grammar* (Standard and Higher), *Optimise your vocabulary* (Standard and Higher), *Talk2Me* video, *Say it right* **Units 9–10 worksheets:** CLIL, Culture, Everyday English (TRC only), Grammar communication (TRC only)	Unit Test 10 (Standard and Higher)

READING
Open questions | A blog post

→ Student's Book, pages 102–103 SB

Lesson aims

- Focus on linking words and phrases
- Practise an open-questions exam task

Lead-in

Write these gapped sentences on the board:

1 _____ was it taken?
2 _____ are the people doing?
3 _____ else can you do there?

Ask students to complete these questions about the photo on page 102 with the correct question words. Check their answers and ask them, in pairs, to take turns to speculate what the answers might be. Elicit ideas from around the class and ask them if they have been to a similar event and encourage them to talk about films, e.g. *What kind of films do you like? Who is your favourite actor?*, etc.

Ask students to look at the unit title ***All in good fun!***, and elicit what it means (*something done for enjoyment*). Ask them to say what they think the unit is going to be about (*entertainment*).

Answers / Suggested answers

1 *When/Where* was it taken? (It could be the outskirts of a European city. It might be summertime.)

2 *What* are the people doing? (They may be watching a film at an open-air cinema.)

3 *What* else can you do there? (You can get food and drink from the surrounding stalls.)

1 In pairs or as a group, students complete the exercise. Elicit answers from different students around the class.

Answers / Suggested answers

I posted a comment on a great music video on Instagram.
I download films and music videos from YouTube and Netflix.
I click 'like' if someone recommends a good video on Facebook.
I uploaded a film trailer to my blog.

Cultural note

In 2016, there were over 2.31 billion users of social networks worldwide. In the UK, teenagers have an average of three social media accounts per user, spending an average of 100 minutes a day on social media. Facebook is the social network leader, followed by WhatsApp and QQ. These social media sites serve different types of users by targeting different needs and interests. WhatsApp, for example, offers instant messaging as well as other services like sharing pictures, videos and location, and voice messaging.

2 Ask students to complete the task. Set a three-minute time limit to encourage them to read quickly. Elicit answers in open class.

Answers

A 3 **B** 6 **C** 7 **D** 1 **E** 4 **F** 5 **G** 2

Fast finishers

Elicit the key words and ideas in each paragraph that helped them choose their answers.

Suggested answers

A The paragraph lists three characters.
B *skeleton*
C *history, today* and a date
D *real, unusual, incredible* – the character Gollum is really strange
E *makes life easier for actors, also makes life easier for animators*
F *video games … pop videos too*
G The paragraph asks questions to find out the audience's opinions.

EXAM SKILL

Understanding linking words and phrases

Ask students to read the tips.

- Highlight that linking words and phrases can be very informal and characteristic of spoken language (e.g. *By the way, Mind you, Still …*) or quite formal and characteristic of written language (e.g. *However, Nonetheless*).
- Linking phrases are the 'glue' that makes the different parts of the text stick together and show the connection between what has already been written or said and what is going to be written or said. Understanding how they might mark a shift in or continuation of ideas, rather than trying to understand each and every word, can be helpful and time-saving in an exam.

3 Ask students to complete the exercise. Check answers in open class and elicit the sentence that contains each linking word and phrase.

Answers

1 a (*In other words, they can make the actor look like a penguin, or a monster, or a chimp.*)
2 b (*Take Gollum in* The Lord of the Rings *films.*)
3 a (*Instead, she could act wearing motion capture sensors on a special suit …*)
4 a (*However, they didn't do that.*)
5 b (*Of course, if they had worn chimp suits, we wouldn't have been able to see their expressions.*)

OPTIMISE YOUR EXAM

Open questions

Ask students to read the tips.

- Point out that underlining the key words in the questions will help them identify the synonymous ideas in the text (they will practise this in the next exercise), which, in turn, will help them locate the answer.

Exam task

4 3.08 **Note: The reading text is also available on the audio CD. You may want to have students listen and read the text before doing the exam task.**

Ask students to complete the exercise. Have them compare in pairs before you check answers in open class.

Answers

1 after filming **2** Back in (1937) **3** (a) rubber suit **4** motion capture sensors **5** (real) dancers **6** it used motion capture

5 Ask students to complete the exercise. Check answers in open class.

Answers

1 cartoon **2** make-up **3** characters **4** unique **5** filmmakers

Mixed ability

Give less confident students the answers in a jumbled order for them to match to the definitions in Exercise 5. More confident students find two more words in the text and write definitions. When everyone has finished, they can read out their definitions for other students to match to one of the words in the text.

THINK | RESEARCH | CULTURE | LEARN | ME

In pairs or small groups, students complete the task. Elicit answers from different students around the class.

Homework OWB

Assign students Reading exercises 1, 2, 3 and 4 on pages 76–77 of their Workbook.

GRAMMAR 1
Conditionals (2): third conditional

→ Student's Book, page 104 SB

Lesson aims

- Identify the correct usage of the third conditional
- Practise using the third conditional

Lead-in

Divide the class into two teams, A and B. Choose a word from the text in the previous lesson and say it to team A for them to spell it, letter by letter. If they spell the word correctly, they score one point. However, if at any point they say an incorrect letter, the part-word is handed over to team B (and back again if they make an error). This continues until one team finishes the word and wins the point. The team with the most points wins the game.

Suggested words: *unusual, capture, skeleton, animator, filmmaker, character, appearance.*

Grammar in context

Ask students to complete the task. Refer them to the information in the *Remember* box if they aren't sure. Check answers in open class.

Remind students that they can find more information in the Grammar reference, Unit 10, pages 157–158.

Answers

1 No **2** Yes **3** No **4** No

Language note

Third conditional

We use the third conditional to speculate about the past and say what could have happened if things had been different. The main clause of the third conditional can contain past modal verbs, e.g. *could* or *might*, according to the meaning we wish to convey.

The third conditional is formed by an *if* clause and a main clause, namely the condition and the consequence. The order of these two elements can be inverted. In this case, we do not usually separate the clauses with a comma, e.g. *I would have got to work on time if my alarm had gone off.*

Highlight that it's common to use contractions with the third conditional, e.g. *If I'd studied harder, I would have got better marks.*

Optional extension

Ask students to write about the four situations below using the third conditional. Do the first one as an example with the class. Write their answers on the board and drill the pronunciation, paying attention to the contracted forms and the weak form of *have* /əv/. Remind them that weak forms are syllable sounds that become unstressed in connected speech and are often then pronounced as a schwa /ə/.

1 She caught a cold because she was filming in the rain.

2 I didn't have time to see the actor and now it's too late.

3 We arrived late and we missed the film.

4 The cinema was empty because the film had bad reviews.

Answers

1 She wouldn't have caught a cold if she hadn't been filming in the rain.

2 If I'd had time, I'd have seen the actor.

3 If we'd arrived on time / If we hadn't arrived late, we'd have seen the film.

4 The cinema would have been full if the film had had good reviews.

1 Ask students to complete the exercise. Have them compare in pairs before you check answers in open class.

Answers

1 Andy Serkis didn't wear a rubber suit so he looked very unusual.

2 They filmed real dancers for *Happy Feet*, so illustrators didn't draw the dancing penguins.

3 They used motion capture so we were able to see / could see their expressions.

2 Ask students to complete the exercise. Have them compare in pairs before you check answers in open class.

Answers

1 hadn't explained **2** hadn't **3** hadn't **4** had been, have found **5** hadn't, wouldn't **6** would have thought, hadn't heard

3 Elicit what is happening in the photo. (*A young person has arrived at the North Pole. It looks like she has been participating in a race.*)

Ask students to complete the exercise. Have them compare in pairs before you check answers in open class.

Answers

1 hadn't posted **2** wouldn't have taken **3** have decided **4** hadn't met **5** hadn't been **6** had/'d gone, would/'d have/'ve felt

Fast finishers

Ask students to write one or two comprehension questions based on the text in Exercise 3, e.g. *How old was Jade when she reached Everest Base Camp? Where's she planning to go next? Why did she decide to go there?* When everyone has finished, students can read out their questions for others to answer.

Optional extension

Ask students to think about two things in their lives that could have been different and write three true sentences and one false one using the third conditional. In pairs, they read out their sentences, while their partner asks questions in order to guess which sentence is false.

Homework OWB

Assign students Grammar 1 exercises 1 and 2 on page 78 of their Workbook.

VOCABULARY

Topic vocabulary | Phrasal verbs | Word patterns

→ Student's Book, page 105 SB

Lesson aims

Understand the correct usage of:

- words connected with *people in the media*
- phrasal verbs
- word patterns

Lead-in

Write these prompts on the board: *Got a speeding fine – Missed the bus – Missed the interview – Couldn't find her shoes – Went to a party – Put on high-heeled party shoes – Took the car – Didn't hear the alarm.*

In pairs or small groups, ask students to put the events of 'Jane's Terrible Day' in order. Check their answers and ask them to make as many third conditional sentences in a three-minute time limit as they can. Elicit an example in open class first. The pair/group with the most sentences wins the game.

Suggested answers

Went to a party – Didn't hear the alarm – Couldn't find her shoes – Put on high-heeled party shoes – Missed the bus – Took the car – Got a speeding fine – Missed the interview

If she hadn't gone to the party, she wouldn't have missed her alarm.

If she had prepared the night before, she would have been able to find her shoes.

Words connected with *people in the media*

1 3.09 Elicit what *stage door* means in the photo in Exercise 1 (*the door that is used by the actors and theatre workers when entering and leaving the theatre*).

Ask students to complete the exercise. Play the audio for them to listen and check their answers.

Answers/Audioscript

1 I play the violin and piano, and I really want to be a professional *musician* when I'm older. **2** The editor of the magazine sent a *journalist* to interview David Guetta, the famous French *DJ* and record producer. **3** What's the name of the *presenter* of the quiz show *The Chase*? **4** Eddie Redmayne is a great *actor* – he was amazing in *Fantastic Beasts*! (also accept: performer) **5** Who is the *author* of the *Divergent* books? **6** She's a really talented *performer* – she can act, sing and dance. **7** When you're a *celebrity*, photographers follow you everywhere. (also accept: actor, author, musician, performer, presenter) **8** Two of my aunt's paintings are in our local *art gallery*. **9** They hold an outdoor *music festival* near here every summer. **10** As I walked out onto the *stage*, all my nerves disappeared! **11** The band are making their next album in a *recording studio* in New York. **12** The film starts at eight, so let's meet inside the *cinema* at quarter to. **13** We're going to the *theatre* tonight to see a play. **14** When we visit the *science museum* next week, you'll see a dinosaur skeleton! **15** The Grafton Centre is a great *venue* for concerts, shows and parties.

Extra support

Give less confident students the first or last letter of each word.

Refer students to the Vocabulary reference, page 167, for more information on topic vocabulary.

Phrasal verbs

2 3.10 Ask students to complete the exercise. Have them compare in pairs before you play the audio for them to listen and check their answers.

Answers/Audioscript

1 Enter your username and password to *log onto/into* the site. **2** We're going to *put on* a school play at the end of term! **3** When I wrote a fan letter to J.K. Rowling, I didn't expect her to *write back*, but she did! **4** If you don't *log out of* Facebook on a public computer, someone might post a joke comment or status update pretending to be you! **5** Can you *turn down* the volume? It's too loud! **6** Can you *turn up* the volume? I can't hear it! **7** I hate it when people talk in the cinema. Why can't they just *shut up* and watch the film? **8** The two comics I buy every week *come out* on a Friday.

Refer students to the Vocabulary reference, page 167, for more information on phrasal verbs.

Word patterns

3 3.11 Ask students to complete the exercise. Have them compare in pairs before you play the audio for them to check their answes. Check answers in open class.

Answers/Audioscript

1 How did you manage *to get* tickets to the opening night of the show?
2 Are you able *to come* with us to the cinema on Friday?
3 Ella's definitely capable *of winning* the talent show.
4 The school play is a great chance *to show off* your acting skills.
5 What are my chances *of getting* a main part in the play?
6 I don't think my parents will let me *go* to the music festival next weekend.
7 I don't think my parents will allow me *to go* to the music festival next weekend.
8 I don't think I'll be *allowed* to go to the music festival next weekend.

Language note

Highlight that *allow* and *let* have a similar meaning, i.e. give permission or make it possible for somebody to do or have something. In the passive, *let* is not possible. We must use *allow*: *I **was allowed** to film the demonstration.*

Fast finishers

Elicit the word patterns for the different verbs and expressions in Exercise 3 and ask students to think of more examples including negative and question forms.

Optional extension

Write these sentence prompts on the board and ask students to make full sentences. Walk round, monitoring students and helping with vocabulary if necessary. Ask students to compare with their partner and share the most interesting or unusual sentences in open class.

1 I managed …
2 I was able …
3 I am capable …
4 I have a great chance to …
5 What are my chances of …
6 I don't think my parents will let …
7 I don't think my parents will allow …
8 I don't think I'll be allowed …

Refer students to the Vocabulary reference, page 167, for more information on word patterns.

SAY IT RIGHT

/j/ before vowels

TRC

For the *Say it right* pronunciation activity and instructions, go to the Teacher's Resource Centre.

Homework

OWB

Assign students Vocabulary exercises 1, 2 and 3 on pages 78–79 of their Workbook.

LISTENING
Gap fill

→ Student's Book, page 106 SB

Lesson aims

- Listen to decide what is relevant information
- Practise a gap-fill exam task

Lead-in

Play ***Noughts and crosses*** to recycle phrasal verbs from the previous lesson. Divide the class into two teams: X and O. Draw two three-by-three grids on the board. Write these phrasal verbs in each square of one of the grids, in random order: *log onto, put on, write back, log out of, turn down, turn up, shut up, come out, show off.* Each team must think of a grammatically correct sentence using a third conditional and a phrasal verb in the square they choose to win, e.g. *If I had written back to her, she'd have known I won the competition.* If they win a square, write X or O in the same square of the second grid. The first team to get a line in a row, wins the game.

1 Focus students' attention on the photo and elicit what the teenagers might be doing. (*They might be rehearsing a play in school.*) In pairs or as a group, students complete the exercise.

Elicit answers from different students around the class and ask students to share their experiences if they have performed in a school musical.

Suggested answers

1 They need to hold auditions and choose a cast. A team needs to be in charge of backstage, lighting, costumes and set designs. They need to have a good director for the rehearsals. Somebody needs to design the programme and tickets and be responsible for selling them beforehand and on the night.
2 Students' own answers

EXAM SKILL

Selecting relevant information

Ask students to read the tips.

- Remind students they will need to write down the actual words they hear in the recording. Here 'word-spotting' is an important skill: they need to listen out for a word, or words, used in the listening to help them identify the gap area. They then need to listen carefully to what is said around this area.
- Remind them that key words are usually stressed (very) strongly.

2 3.12 Play the track for students to complete the exercise. Don't check their answers yet.

3 In pairs, students discuss their answers. If necessary, play the track again for them to listen and check.

Answers

1 nervous **2** director **3** bedroom **4** the school **5** neighbour

Extra support

Point out that single-word answers are more common in this type of exam task. Go through each answer and elicit why the other option was incorrect.

Answers

1 *too, of course* is unnecessary information

2 *was lovely* is irrelevant and doesn't fit with the following colon and name

3 we only need the place

4 *didn't have any* doesn't fit grammatically

5 *my* doesn't fit grammatically

OPTIMISE YOUR EXAM

Gap fill

Ask students to read the tips.

- Remind students that they have brainstormed vocabulary for a school play in Exercise 1. This should help them predict what type of information they are going to listen to.
- On the first listening, remind students to keep the first two or three gaps in mind so that they are focused and ready. They should then note anything they hear which might be relevant to the gaps as there will be time to work out which of those things are relevant in the second listening.
- Highlight that the information that is filled in already is there to help them situate themselves in a longer monologue. Point out that the gaps are always in the same order as the recording.

Optional extension

Turning statements into questions will help your students to see what kind of information is missing. To help them do this, train them to highlight some content words in the notes. These are often nouns that carry meaning. They can expect to hear some of these words in the recording and this will help them know which question they are up to.

Suggested answers

1 What type of school production is it going to be this year?

2 Who is Mr Farah?

3 Where are the auditions? (Highlight the preposition *in* indicates they should be listening for a place here.)

4 When are the rehearsal days?

5 What is happening on the 4th of June? Who is coming?

6 When are tickets available?

▼ Exam task

4 3.13 Play the track for students to listen and complete the exercise. Don't check answers yet as they will listen again in Exercise 5.

5 3.13 Play the track again for students to check their answers. Elicit the key words and phrases that helped them decide on their answers.

Answers

1 (a) musical (*This year we're going to do a musical.*) **2** costumes (*Mr Farah will be responsible for the costumes.*) **3** (the) school hall (*We're going to hold auditions next Wednesday and Thursday after school, here in the school hall.*) **4** Thursday and Friday (*… we'll have lots of rehearsals between now and then, usually on Thursday and Friday evenings.*) **5** (a) (professional) photographer (*Actors will have their photo taken for the programme by a professional photographer on the 4th of June.*) **6** next week (*Tickets will be on sale from the start of next week.*)

THINK | RESEARCH | CULTURE | LEARN | ME

Ask students to complete the task. Elicit answers from different students around the class.

Homework

Assign students Listening exercises 1 and 2 on page 80 of their Workbook. OWB

GRAMMAR 2
The causative

→ Student's Book, page 107 SB

Lesson aims

- Understand the correct usage of the causative
- Practise using the causative with *have/get*

Lead-in

In pairs, students race to write as many sentences as they can to describe the differences between the photos on page 107. Elicit the character and the name of the actor (*Ralph Fiennes played Lord Voldemort in the* Harry Potter *series.*) and ask students what they know about the film or the actor. Set a three-minute time limit. Give regular updates: *Only two minutes to go …*, etc. Stop students and ask them to count how many sentences they have. Ask the pair with the most sentences to read out their list to see if they are correct and if they are the winners of the game.

Cultural note

Ralph Fiennes (pronounced *Rafe Fines*) is the actor who plays Lord Voldemort in the *Harry Potter* films. Fiennes trained at the Royal Academy of Dramatic Art and joined the Royal Shakespeare Company in 1988. In 2001, Fiennes received the William Shakespeare Award from the Shakespeare Theatre in Washington, DC.

Grammar in context

Ask students to complete the task. Refer them to the information in the *Remember* box if they aren't sure. Check answers in open class.

Remind students that they can find more information in the Grammar reference, Unit 10, page 158.

Answers

1 had **2** printed **3** their photo taken

Language note

***Have/get* something done**

Highlight that in all the example sentences the person who does the action is not the subject at the start of the sentence – it is somebody else (*by* introduces this agent in sentences 1 and 3). The object of the sentence (i.e. the noun) goes in the middle of this construction, e.g. *We have our hair cut by a top hairdresser.*

1 Ask students to complete the exercise. Have them compare in pairs before you check answers in open class.

Answers
1 b **2** c **3** a **4** f **5** e **6** d

2 Ask students to complete the exercise. Have them compare in pairs before you check answers in open class.

Answers
1 He had his appearance completely changed by make-up artists.
2 He didn't have his eyebrows shaved.
3 Instead, he had his eyebrows and forehead covered with gelatine.

3 Ask students to complete the exercise. Have them compare in pairs before you check answers in open class.

Answers
1 had the shape of his nose changed **2** have false teeth put in
3 have his skin lightened **4** had false fingernails put

THINK | RESEARCH | CULTURE | **LEARN** | ME

Ask students to read the information in the *Remember* box again and think about their own language and if they have any similar structures to the causative. Then ask them to complete the task. Elicit answers from different students around the class.

Homework

OWB

Assign students Grammar 2 exercises 1 and 2 on page 79 of their Workbook.

Assign students the Flipped classroom tasks on page 108 of their Student's Book if you'd like them to prepare for the next lesson. To complete this task, students need to watch the *Talk2Me* video which can be found on the Resource Centre.

SPEAKING
Discussion

→ Student's Book, page 108 SB

Lesson aim

- Listening and responding

The *Talk2Me* video in this unit focuses on people listening and responding when someone speaks. Students answer some comprehension questions and then listen out for ways to show they have understood. The video can be used in one of two ways:

Flipped classroom

Flipped classroom option

Using this approach, students watch the video and complete the exercises for homework. This prepares students for the speaking lesson by introducing them to the topic and the key phrases to use in the exam task. Teachers who use this method will find they have more class time to spend on activating the target language and developing fluency for the final task.

***Talk2Me* worksheet**

Ask students to also complete the *Talk2Me* worksheet on the Resource Centre for more detailed comprehension exercises and more practice of the key phrases.

Classroom option

Lead-in

Play ***Twenty questions***. Ask a student to come to the front of the class and choose a famous TV personality or actor (the character can be living or deceased or fictitious, e.g. a cartoon or movie character). After the student has chosen a person, the other students take turns to ask *Yes/No* questions in order to guess what the chosen answer is. Keep track of the number of guesses that are used until it reaches the limit of 20. If a player correctly guesses the famous person before then, they become 'it' for the next game and choose the next person. Otherwise, the answer is revealed.

1 Ask students to read the questions. Play the *Talk2Me* video for students to complete the exercise. Play the video again, if necessary, before checking their answers.

Answers
1 She accused him of cheating during a card game by looking at her cards.
2 They promise to play nicely / not to argue.
3 Justin Timberlake
4 So that they won't be able to argue.

2 Play the *Talk2Me* video again, so students can underline the phrases in the *Phrase expert* box. Pause the video from time to time if necessary. Check answers in open class.

Answers
Really? That sounds like fun. Same here. I completely agree.
That isn't quite how I see it.

***Talk2Me* worksheet**

Ask students to also complete the *Talk2Me* worksheet on the Resource Centre for more detailed comprehension exercises and more practice of the key phrases.

Answers
The transcript and answer key for the *Talk2Me* video and Worksheet can be found on the Teacher's Resource Centre.

3 In pairs or as a group, students ask and answer the questions. Elicit answers from different students around the class.

Answers
Students' own answers

EXAM SKILL

Listening and responding

Ask students to read the tips.

- In this part of the exam, students need to show the examiner that they can have a conversation with a partner by asking questions, listening to their partner's ideas and responding appropriately. Students can react, nod their head, or say something to show how they feel about their partner's ideas.
- Point out that it is important to look at their partner when they are having their discussion. Remind them they are not talking to the examiner.
- Remind students that if they disagree with their partner, they must be polite. They can say something like *Really? I'm not sure about that, Good idea but I prefer ....*

4 3.14 Play the track for students to listen and complete the task. Elicit which key words helped students decide on their answers.

Answers
1 a (*I love reading crime novels ... I enjoy trying to guess who did it. ... I'm a big fan of Sherlock too.*)
2 a (*... love memes ... they're short ... find out about the original source and then end up reading a news article ... I love creative writing ... upload short stories. We read them and then add comments.*)
3 a (*... I don't think it's a problem. You shouldn't have to read if you don't want to. It's important to only read things you enjoy .... It's very important for teenagers to read regularly.*)

Cultural note

A meme is an activity, concept, catchphrase or piece of media that becomes a social phenomenon travelling from person to person quickly through social media. The majority of modern memes are captioned photos that are intended to be funny, often as a way to publicly ridicule human behaviour. Other memes can be videos and verbal expressions.

5 3.14 Play the track again for students to listen and complete the task. Elicit answers from different students around the class.

Answers
Really? I never thought of that. That's interesting! That sounds like fun. I'm not sure I agree.

OPTIMISE YOUR EXAM

Discussion

Ask students to read the tips.

- Recommend that students initiate the discussion by putting a question to their partner first. This sounds better than starting to talk about themselves or pausing because they are unsure who should speak first.
- Remind students that the conversation should be 50% them speaking and 50% their partner speaking. They don't get extra points for speaking more. Their opinions on each idea should not be very long: one or two sentences and then ask a question. This shows that they are communicating with their partner and that they are having a natural conversation.
- Encourage students to get a feeling for how long you need to speak (about two or three minutes). Remind them not to answer the question too quickly.

Exam task

6 In pairs, students complete the task. Walk round, monitoring students and noting down good use of language and errors to go over in a feedback session at the end of the activity.

Homework OWB
Assign students Speaking exercises 1, 2 and 3 on pages 80–81 of their Workbook.

LANGUAGE IN USE
Open cloze

→ Student's Book, page 109 SB

Lesson aims

- Focus on *wish* and *if only*
- Practise an open-cloze exam task

Lead-in

Focus students' attention on the photo on page 109 at the top of the page and elicit what they can see (*a teenager holding a smartphone with a cracked screen*), what might have happened (*she dropped it*) and how she feels (*sad*). Introduce the target structure by saying *She regrets dropping her phone.* and highlight that the verb *regret* means to feel sad, repentant or disappointed over something that one has done or failed to do.

1 In pairs or as a group, students complete the exercise. Elicit answers from different students around the class.

Answers
Students' own answers

Remember

Ask students to read the information.

Refer students to the Grammar reference, Unit 10, page 158, for more information.

Language note

Wish* and *if only

In this lesson, students study two types of *wish / if only* sentences:

1 with the past perfect to talk about things we would like to change in the past, e.g. *If only / I wish I had joined the school team, I would have had more friends.*

2 with the past simple to talk about things we would like to change in the present, e.g. *If only / I wish I had more time, I would do so much.*

Remind students that when we use the verb *to be*, we often use *were* in the first and third person, e.g. *I wish I were a millionaire. He wishes he were richer!*

If only is used as a means of stressing the importance of the wish or hypothetical situation. This form is often used with an exclamation mark.

Point out that it is common to use contractions, particularly when we speak, e.g. *If only I'd studied harder!*

2 Ask students to complete the exercise. Have them compare in pairs before you check answers in open class.

Answers

1 had **2** had seen / 'd seen **3** hadn't lied / had not lied **4** had allowed **5** could / was able to

OPTIMISE YOUR EXAM

Open cloze

Ask students to read the tips.

- Remind students to read the whole sentence. Sometimes the answer required for the space is dependent on a word or reference many words before or after it.
- Point out that in the exam they should not leave the answer sheet blank for any question. If they don't know the correct answer, they should always make a guess. They will not lose marks for incorrect answers.

Exam task

3 In pairs or as a group, students complete the exercise. Check answers in open class.

Answers

1 to **2** If **3** wish **4** only **5** to **6** to **7** had **8** had

Homework

OWB

Assign students Language in Use exercises 1, 2 and 3 on page 81 of their Workbook.

WRITING
An article

→ Student's Book, pages 110–111 SB

Lesson aims

- Focus on language for describing how to do something
- Plan and write an article

Lead-in

Ask students to create a mind map with vocabulary related to the unit theme. In pairs or small groups, students write *Entertainment* in the centre of a blank page and draw branches from the centre with these subheadings: *People / Places / Words connected with theatre, TV and film / Words connected with promoting events*. Set a time limit of five minutes for students to race to find words and phrases for each category from the previous lessons. After five minutes, draw the mind map on the board and ask for volunteers to come and write their words, if appropriate.

Suggested words:

People: *make-up artist, photographer, celebrity, fan, animator, dancer, filmmaker, actor, band, journalist, DJ, musician, performer, presenter, author, editor*

Places: *museum, cinema, theatre, studio, gallery, venue*

Words connected with theatre, TV and film: *stage door, stage, lighting, costumes, make-up, cast, rehearsals, (hold) auditions, lighting, set design, red carpet, play, musical, festival, special effects, cartoon, motion capture, character*

Words connected with promoting events: *tickets, programme, posters, blog post, comment, download, upload, print*

1 Focus students' attention on the photos and elicit what they can see. (*The boys might be watching a film and the girl looks like she's listening to music.*)

Ask students to complete the exercise. Elicit answers in open class. Elicit which two words make up the word *podcast* (*iPod* and *broadcast*). Ask students to share their experience of podcasts they have listened to or if they have recorded or produced their own podcasts in open class.

Answers

Students' own answers

Cultural note

Podcasting is the name given to the publishing of audio (usually MP3 files) via the internet that is commonly downloaded onto an iPod or other MP3 hardware for mobile listening. Podcasts can also be played directly from your computer. They can be anything from a pre-recorded song to a radio programme. Students can listen to podcasts graded at their level or authentic, and more difficult, podcasts that can be very motivating. They can also record and produce their own podcasts.

EXAM SKILL

Describing how to do something

Ask students to read the tips.

- Remind them of important factors when giving instructions:
  - Break things down – if the activity has several parts, give the instructions part by part.
  - Give an overview of the purpose behind the activity.
  - Create a step-by-step outline.
  - Give examples so the reader can 'see' what the activity looks like.
  - Think about how to prevent any misunderstandings.
- When giving instructions or explaining things, it is useful to use sequence markers, words which guide the listener or reader through the instructions, e.g. *You begin by …, before that …, the last step is …* It is also important to keep the instructions or explanations short and simple.
- Remind students that we also use the imperative to give instructions, e.g. *Begin by … Don't take …*

2 Ask students to complete the exercise. Check answers in open class.

Suggested answers

1 a smartphone or computer that can record audio **2** with others (friends) **3** an interesting topic to discuss **4** speak clearly, make it interesting and entertaining, be enthusiastic **5** give it an interesting title, share it using social media or a podcast app, make one regularly

3 Ask students to complete the exercise. Check answers in open class.

Answers

1 Make **2** Don't talk **3** should **4** Remember **5** delete **6** to ask

OPTIMISE YOUR EXAM

An article

Ask students to read the tips.

- Elicit what will impress an examiner apart from good spelling, grammar and punctuation, e.g. *a great introduction, strong opening sentences that tell the reader what the paragraph is going to be about, clear and logical progression of ideas, interesting language and a variety of structures, good pronoun referencing (not repeating the same noun again and again), an interesting idea!*
- Rhetorical devices (questions where you don't really expect an answer) such as *Do you listen to podcasts?* are effective because they address the reader directly – you have to read on to find out what the writer is talking about. By using some simple writing techniques, students can earn high marks in writing exams at this level.

For more information on writing articles, refer students to the Writing reference, page 170.

Exam task

4 Ask students to complete the exercise. Check answers in open class.

Answers

1 b **2** e **3** d (also accept: e) **4** a **5** c

5 Ask students to complete the exercise individually.

Extra support

First, discuss the task in Exercise 5 in open class. Elicit advice and encourage students to use some of the phrases in Exercise 3. Write some key words and expressions on the board that less confident students can refer back to when they write their essay.

6 Plan Ask students to complete the paragraph plan. You may want to look at students' plans, if this is possible, to check them and give advice and suggestions for improvement before students write.

7 Write Students write their article in about 100 words, in an appropriate style. Depending on time, it may be a good idea to set this and the subsequent checklist exercise for homework.

8 Check Students complete the checklist before they hand in their articles.

Homework OWB

Assign students Writing exercises 1, 2, 3 and 4 on page 82 of the Workbook and Progress check 10, page 83.

Answers PROGRESS CHECK Units 9–10

Exercise 1
1 score/will score **2** practised **3** would **4** ✓ **5** ✓/will **6** will/'ll listen

Exercise 2
1 catch **2** log **3** send **4** put **5** turn **6** put **7** knock **8** come

Exercise 3
1 had **2** were **3** had brought **4** had/'d gone **5** had/'d been **6** hadn't agreed

Exercise 4
1 go **2** manage **3** doing **4** allow **5** able **6** do

Exercise 5
1 have/get, cut **2** had/got, painted **3** had/got, pierced **4** have/get, taken **5** have/get, delivered **6** had/got, tested

Exercise 6
1 get, will/'ll call **2** will/'ll keep, learn (also accept: kept, learnt) **3** arrive, will/'ll buy **4** will/'ll continue, stops (also accept: continued, had stopped) **5** will/'ll look after, shop **6** won't start, is (also accept: didn't start, was)

Exercise 7
1 d **2** f **3** a **4** b **5** c **6** e

Exercise 8
1 hadn't scored **2** would have helped **3** had been **4** have done **5** had been **6** have become

11 Curious minds

UNIT AIMS

Exam preparation in Unit 11:

- make deductions in an online guide
- understand implication in short extracts
- express uncertainty in a photo task
- understand spelling of irregular forms and use them in a word-formation exercise
- use given information in a short message

TEACHER'S PRESENTATION KIT

- *Talk2Me* videos
- Speaking test videos
- Class and Workbook audio
- Workbook pages and answer key

UNIT OVERVIEW

Student's Book / Digital Student's Book SB		Workbook / Online Workbook OWB
LESSON / EXAM TASK	EXAM SKILLS / LANGUAGE FOCUS	CONSOLIDATION
Reading **Multiple matching**	Making deductions An online guide	Workbook, pp 84–85, Exercises 1, 2, 3, 4 Unit 11, Reading, Exercises 1, 2, 3, 4
Grammar 1	Reported speech	Workbook, p 86, Exercises 1, 2, 3 Unit 11, Grammar 1, Exercises 1, 2, 3
Vocabulary	Words connected with *studying* Phrasal verbs Idioms for *education and learning*	Workbook, pp 86–87, Exercises 1, 2, 3 Unit 11, Vocabulary, Exercises 1, 2, 3
Listening **Multiple choice (extracts)**	Understanding implication	Workbook, p 88, Exercises 1, 2 Unit 11, Listening, Exercises 1, 2
Grammar 2	Reported questions	Workbook, p 87, Exercises 1, 2 Unit 11, Grammar 2, Exercises 1, 2
Speaking **Photo task**	Expressing uncertainty	Workbook, pp 88–89, Exercises 1, 2, 3 Unit 11, Speaking, Exercises 1, 2, 3
Language in Use **Word formation**	Spelling of irregular forms	Workbook, p 89, Exercises 1, 2, 3 Unit 11, Language in Use, Exercises 1, 2, 3
Writing **A short message**	Using given information	Workbook, p 90, Exercises 1, 2, 3, 4 Unit 11, Writing, Exercises 1, 2, 3, 4
		Workbook, p 91, Progress check and Cumulative progress Progress check and Cumulative progress

Additional material

PRESENTATION KIT	TEACHER'S/STUDENT'S RESOURCE CENTRE RC	TEST GENERATOR
Talk2Me video *I'm not sure, but …*	**Unit 11 worksheets:** *Optimise your grammar* (Standard and Higher), *Optimise your vocabulary* (Standard and Higher), *Talk2Me* video, *Say it right* **Units 11–12 worksheets:** CLIL, Culture, Everyday English (TRC only), Grammar communication (TRC only)	Unit Test 11 (Standard and Higher)

READING

Multiple matching | An online guide

→ Student's Book, pages 114–115

Lesson aims

- Focus on making deductions
- Practise a multiple-matching exam task

Lead-in

Ask students to look at the unit title ***Curious minds*** and elicit what it means. (*Someone who has a curious mind likes to learn new things and is open to new experiences and exploring ideas.*) Elicit why being curious is important in life (*People who are curious have an adventurous life.*) and some tips to help develop curiosity (*learn new things, read*, etc.). Ask them to say what they think the unit is going to be about (*education*).

Focus students' attention on the photo on page 114 and elicit what the girls are doing (making a bicycle), where they are and what they are wearing. Elicit what is different about the bicycle. Ask students if they have worked on similar projects at school.

1 In pairs or as a group, students complete the exercise. Elicit answers from different students around the class.

Suggested answers

1 Students' own answers

2 a certificate is a piece of paper you get that shows you have passed an exam; a degree is what you get when you finish a course at university; a diploma is a kind of professional qualification, e.g. a diploma in nursing; a qualification is a general term for anything you get at the end of completing a course, such as a degree, etc.

EXAM SKILL

Making deductions

Ask students to read the tips.

- Point out the difference between *inference* and *deduction*. A *deduction* is an understanding based on the evidence given in the text (a detective uses deduction to solve a crime). *Inference* is an interpretation that goes beyond the literal information given.
- Readers often have to guess things in a text and frequently need to find small clues that lead them to make deductions and understand things that the author doesn't explicitly state. They need to use information in the text – facts, contextual clues – and their prior knowledge to guess other things about the text.
- By asking the reader to make deductions, the writer makes us think and use our imagination. We have to work to figure out what the facts and clues mean and make logical conclusions.
- In the next exercise, students will practise making deductions based on information in the text.

2 Ask students to complete the exercise. Set a three-minute time limit to encourage them to read quickly. Elicit answers in open class.

Answers

1, 2, 3 D, E, H (in any order) **4** E **5** H **6** D

OPTIMISE YOUR EXAM

Multiple matching

Ask students to read the tips.

- Point out that it is a good idea to read the questions first and underline the key words, then look for that information in the text. Remind them to always start by reading the introduction to the task and the title of the text and then read the text first to get an overall impression and understanding of it.

▼ Exam task

3 3.15 **Note: The reading text is also available on the audio CD. You may want to have students listen and read the text before doing the exam task.**

Ask students to complete the exercise. Check answers in open class and elicit the key words that helped them decide on their answers. Elicit why the other three camps aren't suitable.

Answers

1 D (*put up a tent, climb trees … isn't for you / turn you into a confident performer / write material … practise your show … audience*)

2 F (*a break from our smartphones / no electricity / get away from the pressures of their online lives / make friendships / growing and preparing your own food* – We make deductions here that teenagers will be offline and that the camp revolves around meeting new people and food. At Kids' Culinary Academy (C), young people learn about cuisine and make friends, but it doesn't offer the opportunity to take a break from their online lives.)

3 G (*learn water sports / Students select different activities each day to develop their own individual skills / may get a certificate in important skills* – We make deductions here that this is an active course where Marcus may get certified in water sports. We also deduce that there is no set programme.)

4 E (*From songwriting to playing as a band / You'll perform live and make recordings / we'll also teach you all you need to know about … surviving in the music industry* – We make deductions that Maria will find out how to begin her career as a music performer.)

5 B (*we'll give you all kinds of tips about starting and running your own business / You'll graduate from camp with your own business plan ready to go!* – We deduce from the information that this camp is probably indoors and there's a high component of online activities. At Robotics Camp (A), Dylan could program a robot and learn about software, but he wouldn't get any tips on how to sell his apps.)

Extra support

Ask students to underline each teenager's key interest and other important information in options 2–5 before they do the exam task. Elicit their answers in open class.

2 Natasha – cooking (*she spends a little too much time on social media / meet new people and experience something completely different*)

3 Marcus – active (*doesn't like following a programme / would also like to get a qualification at the end of the camp*)

4 Maria – to be on stage in front of an audience (*doesn't know where to begin / meet people who share her love of music*)

5 Dylan – indoor activities / online (*He has lots of ideas for apps and games and would like to sell some of them*)

4 Ask students to complete the exercise. Have them compare in pairs before you check answers in open class.

Answers

1 professionals **2** experts **3** educational **4** basics **5** experience **6** enrol **7** guide **8** graduate

Mixed ability

Give less confident students the answers in a jumbled order for them to match to the definitions in Exercise 4. More confident students find two more words in the text and write definitions. When everyone has finished, they can read out their definitions for other students to match to one of the words in the text.

THINK | RESEARCH | CULTURE | LEARN | **ME**

In pairs or small groups, ask students to complete the task. Elicit answers from different students around the class.

Optional extension 3.15

In pairs or small groups, ask students to use their imaginations and write a short description of a camp they'd like to attend. Students could present their camps in open class for others to say which one sounds the most fun.

Play the recorded reading text and ask students to underline words and phrases they find useful for writing their short descriptions. Elicit answers in open class.

Homework OWB

Assign students Reading exercises 1, 2, 3 and 4 on pages 84–85 of their Workbook.

GRAMMAR 1
Reported speech

→ Student's Book, page 116 SB

Lesson aims

- Focus on reported speech
- Practise using reported speech

Lead-in

Write these famous quotes about curiosity on the board:

'The cure for boredom is curiosity. There is no cure for curiosity.' (Dorothy Parker – writer and poet)

'People die when curiosity goes.' (Graham Swift – English writer)

Discuss the meaning of the quotes in open class first. Then ask students to change them into reported speech, e.g. *Dorothy Parker said …* Point out the difference between direct speech (where we keep the exact words and use quotation marks) and reported speech (where we keep the idea and change the tense, pronouns, etc.).

Answers

Dorothy Parker said (*that) the cure for boredom was curiosity and that there was no cure for curiosity.*

Graham Swift said (that) people died when curiosity went.

Grammar in context

Ask students to complete the task. Refer them to the information in the *Remember* box if they aren't sure. Check the answer in open class.

Remind students that they can find more information in the Grammar reference, Unit 11, page 159.

Answer

Sentence a

Language note

Reported speech

Remind students that although the tense of the verbs usually changes in reported speech, there are some exceptions:

- when the information is immediately reported (e.g. *A: **I'm going** to the shops. B: What did Peter just say? C: He said he**'s going** to the shops.*)
- for general statements about things which are still true (e.g. *A: I **always watch*** Game of Thrones. *B: He said he **always watches*** Game of Thrones.)
- if the reported words refer to an unreal situation (e.g. *Mike: I wish I **was** a vet; then I could spend my life working with animals. Mike wished he **was** a vet, so he could spend his life working with animals.* [he is not older])

Remind students that the past simple and continuous don't always need to be changed if there is a time context which makes everything clear, e.g. *I **was born** in 1980 – He said he **was born** in 1980.*

When we use *say*, we don't need a personal object to say who we are saying something to. However, when we use *tell* in reported speech, it is always followed by a pronoun or a noun indicating the person spoken to, e.g. *Jane told **us** (that) she was learning a lot on the camp.*

Fast finishers

Say some simple sentences for students to report back to you, e.g. *We like English.* → *They said they liked English.* / *He's going to the camp.* → *He said he was going to the camp.*, etc.

1 Ask students to complete the exercise. Have them compare in pairs before you check answers in open class.

Answers

1 was enjoying **2** was **3** had stayed **4** had been thinking **5** would **6** had been, before **7** had taught him **8** they had had, before

2 Ask students to complete the exercise. Have them compare in pairs before you check answers in open class.

Answers

1 Priya said (that) it was the best summer camp ever.
2 Zoe said (that) they were having a great time there.
3 Nadia said (that) Jack had given her a few camping tips.
4 Sam said (that) they had been there for over a week.
5 Joshua said (that) he could cook really well after a few lessons.
6 Fatima said (that) I would love it there.

3 Ask students to complete the exercise. Have them compare their sentences in pairs before you check answers in open class.

Answers

1 'I've / I have never been to a summer camp before,' Ryan said. (If Ryan was talking about the past, then 'I'd never been to a summer camp before that summer.' is also possible.)
2 'I'm / I am feeling better now I've made a few friends,' Luke said.
3 'I went to the same camp this year as last year,' Alina said. (If Alina was talking about the past, then 'I had gone to the same camp that year as the year before.' is also possible.)
4 'I've / I have been having canoe lessons since last summer,' Leah said. (If Leah was talking about the past, then 'I'd / I had been having canoe lessons since the summer before.' is also possible.)

THINK | **RESEARCH** | CULTURE | LEARN | ME

Ask students to complete the task. If you don't have internet access in class, set this for homework. Students can present their research at the beginning of the next class. You could ask them to read out their quotes for others to change to reported speech.

Homework

Assign students Grammar 1 exercises 1, 2 and 3 on page 86 of their Workbook. OWB

VOCABULARY

Topic vocabulary | Phrasal verbs | Idioms

→ Student's Book, page 117 SB

Lesson aims

Understand the correct usage of:

- words connected with *studying*
- phrasal verbs
- idioms for *education and learning*

Lead-in

Focus students' attention on the illustrations on page 117. Elicit what the students are doing in each illustration (*revising, learning something (off by heart), celebrating the passing of an exam*). In pairs or small groups, students brainstorm three top tips for passing exams. Elicit ideas in open class and make a list of the top five tips.

Words connected with *studying*

1 3.16 Ask students to complete the exercise. Play the audio for them to listen and check their answers.

Answers/Audioscript

1 A school *lesson* is a period of time when you are in the classroom.
2 A school *subject* is an area of study, like maths, English or history.
3 When you *study*, you try to learn something.
4 When you *read*, you look at letters on a page to see what they mean.
5 In the UK, you go to *primary* school between the ages of 5 and 11.
6 In the UK, you go to *secondary* school between the ages of 11 and 18.
7 You *take* or sit an exam when you try to answer the questions on an exam paper.
8 You *pass* an exam when your mark is high enough. (elicit the antonym – *fail*)
9 A *pupil* is someone at primary or secondary school, but not university.
10 A *student* is someone at school, at college or at university.

Cultural note

All British children and teenagers aged five to 16 are entitled to a free-of-charge place at a state school. The National Curriculum is constructed in five Key Stages:

Key Stage 1 – Years 1 to 2 – for pupils aged between 5 and 7 years old

Key Stage 2 – Years 3 to 6 – for pupils aged between 7 and 11 years old

Key Stage 3 – Years 7 to 9 – for pupils aged between 11 and 14 years old

Key Stage 4 – Years 10 to 11 – for pupils aged between 14 and 16 years old

At the age of 16 (the end of Key Stage 4 and Year 11), most pupils take a series of exams called the General Certificate of Secondary Education (GCSE), usually in about eight to 10 subjects, which must include English and mathematics.

Refer students to the Vocabulary reference, page 168, for more information on topic vocabulary.

Phrasal verbs

2 3.17 Ask students to complete the exercise. Have them compare in pairs before you play the audio for them to listen and check their answers.

Answers/Audioscript

1 (d) Our teacher asked us to *copy out* the vocabulary from the textbook.
2 (a) Our school *breaks up* for the holidays on Friday!
3 (c) We have to *hand* our homework *in* on Monday morning.
4 (f) We asked the teacher to *go over* the explanation one more time.
5 (b) My brother was at college but he *dropped out* because he didn't like it.
6 (e) Make sure you study or you'll *fall behind* the other students.

Fast finishers

Write these definitions on the board:

1 to repeat a series of things in order to understand them completely (go over)

2 to leave school or an activity before you have finished what you intended to do (drop out)

3 to write something again exactly as it has been written (copy out)

4 to make less progress than other people who are doing a similar activity (fall behind)

5 when students and teachers stop working at the end of term (break up)

6 to give something to a person in authority (hand in)

Ask students to match the phrasal verbs in Exercise 2 to the definitions.

Refer students to the Vocabulary reference, page 168, for more information on phrasal verbs.

Idioms for *education and learning*

3 3.18 Ask students to complete the exercise. Have them compare in pairs before you play the audio for them to listen and check their answers.

Answers/Audioscript

1 (a) 'You always *have your nose in a book*! You should go outside for some fresh air.' – read

2 (a) 'We have to *learn* these words *by heart*. And we've only got two days to do it!' – study and remember

3 (b) 'Congratulations. You've *passed* the test *with flying colours*!' – with a high mark

4 (b) 'How are we going to solve the problem? We'll have to *put our thinking caps on*.' – consider something carefully

5 (a) 'When I started my new job, it didn't take long to *learn the ropes*.' – know what to do

6 (b) 'Ben's always playing tricks on me. I'm going to *teach* him *a lesson*!' – punish someone so they behave better

4 In pairs, students complete the exercise. They then perform their dialogue in groups or in open class.

Refer students to the Vocabulary reference, page 168, for more information on idioms.

Answers

Students' own answers

THINK | RESEARCH | CULTURE | **LEARN** | ME

Ask students to complete the task in pairs or in small groups. Ask them to vote on the best dialogue.

Homework OWB

Assign students Vocabulary exercises 1, 2 and 3 on pages 86–87 of their Workbook.

LISTENING
Multiple choice (extracts)

→ Student's Book, page 118 SB

Lesson aims

- Focus on understanding implication
- Practise a multiple-choice (extracts) exam task

Lead-in

Phrasal verb review. Write the following prompts on the board for students to write sentences:

go over / last week's lesson; drop out / university; fall behind / rest of class; break up / tomorrow

Ask students to write sentences using the prompts. Elicit answers in open class.

1 Focus students' attention on the photo and elicit what is happening. (*A teacher is helping pupils with their work.*) In pairs or as a group, students complete the exercise. Elicit answers from different students around the class.

Suggested answers

1 Best things: feeling you're making a difference, good holidays, shorter working day, reasonable pay and benefits in state school positions, prestige, sense of belonging, ongoing training, variety of tasks, etc.
Worst things: marking and administration, difficult students, tiring, demanding, stressful, dealing with difficult parents, hard work, etc.

2 Students' own answers

EXAM SKILL

Understanding implication

Ask students to read the tips.

- Exam questions usually involve 'paraphrasing' – using a sentence with the same meaning but not using the same words. Using synonyms is one of the main methods of paraphrasing. It is a very important skill that will help students in all areas of an exam.
- Often the actual words in the options are not mentioned but referred to in some way. Remind students that by reading the questions first, they can identify key words, predict answers and clarify exactly what information they are listening for.

2 Ask students to complete the exercise. Check answers in open class.

Answers

1 PE / Physical education. The teacher refers to equipment and getting into teams.

2 History. The teacher refers to a soldier's diary from 1940.

3 Geography. The teacher refers to the climate and what grows in a particular place.

OPTIMISE YOUR EXAM

Multiple choice (extracts)

Ask students to read the tips.

- Students should listen for gist initially, choosing the best option or eliminating an incorrect option as they do so. They should then check carefully on the second listening to ensure they have the correct answer. Students will need to understand the key information in the text in order to arrive at the correct answer.

Extra support

Elicit key vocabulary for each option in the questions in Exercise 3. Write it on the board for students to refer to:

1 A – a calculator and a set of compasses; B – a scientific flask; C – a globe

2 A – a boy sitting at a school desk; B – a boy sitting at a school dining table, eating lunch; C – a boy sitting on a chair by a door

3 A – a girl on a climbing wall; B – a girl playing the piano; C – a girl playing chess

4 A – a car; B – a bus; C – a bicycle

Exam task

3 3.19 Play the track for students to listen and complete the exercise. Don't check answers yet as they will listen again in Exercise 4.

4 3.19 Play the track again for students to check their answers. Check answers in open class. Elicit the key words and phrases that helped them decide on their answers.

Answers

1 A (*... what the area of this shape is.*)

2 C (*... I've got to see the headteacher.* The girl says *I'm surprised to see you here.* This should indicate to students that the boy is not in a usual place in the school.)

3 C (*... I know it'll take a lot of practice to learn all the right moves, but I don't mind losing if I learn something!*)

4 A (*Anyway, my dad finally got the car going and dropped me off.* Highlight the distractor at the beginning of the extract: *The problem was that my dad's car wouldn't start* and the adverb *Anyway* which means 'despite what has been stated before'.)

Mixed ability

For stronger students, play the track again for them to note down the distractors for each question. Alternatively, give less confident students a copy of the audioscript for them to underline the information. Students need a wide range of vocabulary to be able to deal with the answers in this type of task. It is important to spend time analysing which key words and phrases helped them decide on their answers and why they got things wrong.

Answers

1 B – *you might need to experiment a little* (a double meaning of *experiment* – here meaning try different things, rather than do an experiment in a glass container)
C – *It's a hemisphere, which is half of a circle.* (The picture of the globe might make students think of northern and southern hemispheres.)

2 A – *Mrs Robinson caught me copying off the boy next to me in class during the test* (but this isn't where he is now)
B – *I should be having lunch now, really. And I'm starving!* (but this isn't what he's doing now)

3 A – *I'd like to advance to the next level to see how high I can go* (Students need to listen to the next part of the dialogue to understand the girl isn't talking about climbing.)
B – *I know the basics of how to play* (Again, students need to listen to the rest of the dialogue to realise she isn't talking about playing the piano.)

4 B – *when I got to the bus stop it had already gone* (so he couldn't have got to school on the bus)
C – Teacher: *Why not cycle?* Boy: *I used to do that, but I got wet all the time* (so he didn't go to school by bike)

THINK | RESEARCH | CULTURE | LEARN | **ME**

Ask students to complete the task. Elicit answers from different students around the class.

Homework OWB

Assign students Listening exercises 1 and 2 on page 88 of their Workbook.

GRAMMAR 2
Reported questions

→ Student's Book, page 119 SB

Lesson aims

- Focus on reported questions
- Practise using reported questions

Lead-in

Write these question words and prompts on the board: *How long, When, Where, Who, What time, How many, What kind of, How old, certificate, new skills.* In pairs, students race to write 10 questions to ask for information about a course. When a pair has thought of 10 questions, stop and ask them to read them out to see if they are correct. Write them on the board to refer to later on in the lesson (*Extra support*).

Suggested answers

1 How long is the course? **2** When does it start? **3** Where does the course take place? **4** Who is teaching the course? **5** What time does the course start? **6** How many people are there in the class? **7** What kind of course material do I need to buy? **8** How old are the participants? **9** Do I get a certificate at the end of the course? **10** Am I going to learn new skills?

Grammar in context

Ask students to complete the task. Refer them to the information in the *Remember* box if they aren't sure. Check answers in open class.

Remind students that they can find more information in the Grammar reference, Unit 11, page 159.

Answers

1 b **2** a

Language note

Reported questions

Point out that in reported questions, the subject goes before the verb (i.e. normal word order).

Highlight that reported questions are not real questions and therefore do not need question marks, e.g. *He asked him what he was doing here.*

Questions that do not begin with a question word (e.g. *Yes/No* questions) are reported using *ask + if/whether*. We don't use auxiliary *do* in these questions.

The intonation in reported questions usually falls at the end.

The most common reporting question verb is *ask*. Other common reporting question verbs are: *want to know, enquire*, etc.

Extra support

Ask students to change the questions they came up with in the *Lead-in* activity to reported questions. Monitor carefully, helping students if necessary. Elicit answers in open class.

1 Ask students to complete the exercise. Have them compare in pairs before you check answers in open class.

Answers

1 had gone, went/go **2** ✓ **3** have forgotten your, had forgotten my **4** did put, had put **5** did I spend, I had spent / I spent **6** ✓

2 Ask students to complete the exercise. Have them compare in pairs before you check answers in open class.

Answers

1 what, was **2** asked me, I had been **3** asked me if/whether, had ever passed **4** asked me if/whether, could help her **5** asked, had

3 Ask students to complete the exercise. Have them compare in pairs before you check answers in open class.

Remind them that sometimes we don't need to change the present tense into the past if the information in direct speech is still true (e.g. things which are general facts). This is the case in numbers 1, 3, 4, 5, 6 and 7.

Answers

1 (me) what school I go/went to **2** (me) when I had started there
3 (me) if/whether my school has/had a school uniform
4 what it is/was like **5** (me) if/whether everyone has/had to wear it
6 (me) if/whether students can/could wear their own clothes
7 (me) if/whether I think/thought a school uniform is/was a good idea

SAY IT RIGHT

/s/ and /ʃ/ TRC

For the *Say it right* pronunciation activity and instructions, go to the Teacher's Resource Centre.

Homework

OWB

Assign students Grammar 2 exercises 1 and 2 on page 87 of their Workbook.

Assign students the Flipped classroom tasks on page 120 of their Student's Book if you'd like them to prepare for the next lesson. To complete this task, students need to watch the *Talk2Me* video which can be found on the Resource Centre.

SPEAKING
Photo task

→ Student's Book, page 120 SB

Lesson aim

- Expressing uncertainty

The *Talk2Me* video in this unit focuses on people guessing information about people and situations. Students answer some comprehension questions and then listen out for words, phrases and modal verbs to express uncertainty. The video can be used in one of two ways:

Flipped classroom

Flipped classroom option

Using this approach, students watch the video and complete the exercises for homework. This prepares students for the speaking lesson by introducing them to the topic and the key phrases to use in the exam task. Teachers who use this method will find they have more class time to spend on activating the target language and developing fluency for the final task.

***Talk2Me* worksheet**

Ask students to also complete the *Talk2Me* worksheet on the Resource Centre for more detailed comprehension exercises and more practice of the key phrases.

Classroom option

Lead-in

Ask students to imagine they are going on a school trip. In pairs, ask students to think of questions they have about the trip. In a less confident class, brainstorm a few examples together in open class, e.g. *Where are we going? How much does it cost? What do I need to take?* Elicit questions from students and write them on the board. In open class, ask students to change the questions to reported questions using a variety of verbs. Monitor carefully, helping students if necessary. Elicit answers in open class.

Suggested answers

We asked where we were going.
We enquired how much it cost.
We wanted to know what we needed to take.

1 Ask students to read the questions. Play the *Talk2Me* video for students to complete the exercise. Play the video again, if necessary, before checking their answers.

Answers
1 Angus: history; Maddy: English; Jamie: food tech
2 False. Byron said 'Now I shall go to sleep. Goodnight.'
3 bananas

2 Play the *Talk2Me* video again, so students can underline the phrases in the *Phrase expert* box. Pause the video from time to time if necessary. Check answers in open class.

Answers
It looks as if …, (It) could be …, (He) may be …, (It's) possible that …, It could be that …, It isn't clear whether (he's) … or …

***Talk2Me* worksheet**

Ask students to also complete the *Talk2Me* worksheet on the Resource Centre for more detailed comprehension exercises and more practice of the key phrases.

Answers
The transcript and answer key for the *Talk2Me* video exercises and Worksheet can be found on the Teacher's Resource Centre.

3 In pairs or as a group, students ask and answer the questions. Elicit answers from different students around the class.

Answers
Students' own answers

EXAM SKILL

Expressing uncertainty

Ask students to read the tips.

- Highlight to students that in this lesson they are looking at the language of guessing. They will need this language if it is difficult to say what is happening in the photo. Remind them that they can use their imagination and it is not important that their ideas are correct.
- Point out to students that we often use expressions with *look* when we are making guesses and deductions based on visual evidence. Revise three key structures:
  look like + noun (when it means *be similar to*, e.g. *It looks like a museum.*)
  look + adjective (when it means *seem*, e.g. *He seems interested.*)
  look as if / as though + verb phrase (this also means *be similar to*, but attention must be paid to the grammatical construction, e.g. *He looks as if he is having fun.*)
- Remind students that using *I think* before a modal usually shows that the speaker is more certain about something, e.g. *I think it might be a castle or a museum.* However, a sentence like this with extra stress on the modal indicates slightly less certainty, e.g. *I think it **might** be a castle.*

4 3.20 Play the track for students to listen and complete the task. In pairs, ask students to reconstruct the points that the student made. Elicit answers from students around the class.

Suggested answer
She describes the photo (who the people are, the location and where the people are in the photo). She speculates about what they are doing and gives some impressions and opinions.

5 3.20 Play the track again for students to listen and complete the task. Elicit answers from different students around the class.

Answers
1 as **2** suppose **3** guess **4** seems **5** imagine

Optional extension

Do a ***Dictogloss***. In small groups, students reconstruct the text. Ask them to note down the key words they remember as a base for reconstruction. Then play the track again for students to take notes and reconstruct the text. Compare their versions in open class before playing the track for students to compare their reconstructed text to the original.

OPTIMISE YOUR EXAM

Photo task

Ask students to read the tips.

- Remind students that they will get top marks if they show they can speak for an extended period of time on their own and if they use a variety of structures and vocabulary.
- Candidates should be encouraged to describe the people and activities in the photographs as fully as possible. Give students a useful framework, for example:
  describe – They should imagine that they are describing the photograph to someone who can't see it, naming all the objects, where they are and including illustrative detail, such as colour, people's clothes, time of day, weather, etc.
  speculate – make guesses about what you don't know
  react – give your impressions and opinion
  recapitulate – give extra information about the scene to add further details to your description.

Exam task

6 In pairs, students complete the task. Ask students to time each other for at least a minute. Walk round, monitoring students and noting down good use of language and errors to go over in a feedback session at the end of the activity.

Homework
Assign students Speaking exercises 1, 2 and 3 on pages 88–89 of their Workbook. OWB

LANGUAGE IN USE
Word formation

→ Student's Book, page 121 SB

Lesson aims

- Focus on irregular word forms
- Practise a word-formation exam task

Lead-in

Play ***First to five*** to revise useful vocabulary from the unit. Pairs or small groups race against each other to think of five words for each of five categories. When they have five full lists, they shout out 'First to five'. Check their answers. For each correct list, they get a point. The pair or group with the most points wins the game.

Suggested categories: *types of summer camps, people connected with learning, words connected with studying, phrasal verbs connected with learning, idioms connected with learning.*

1 In pairs or as a group, students complete the exercise. Elicit answers from different students around the class and ask who has the longest journey.

Answers

1 A row of parked yellow school buses
2 Students' own answers

Optional extension

Small group analysis: In open class, decide on some parameters for the average journey time to school, e.g. *less than 15 minutes / 16–30 minutes / 31–50 minutes / more than 51 minutes*. Divide the class into groups and appoint a secretary in each group. In small groups, students ask and answer number 2 in Exercise 1 and prepare a short report. Secretaries report back to the whole class. Write the results on the board and some prompts, e.g. *all / most / some / (quite) a few / none of us*. Elicit conclusions in open class, e.g. *Most of us take 15 minutes to get to school*, etc.

Remember

Ask students to read the information.

Refer students to the Vocabulary reference, page 168, for more information on word formation.

Language note

Irregular verbs

The English language has a large number of irregular verbs; and many are the most common verbs. In most cases, only the simple or the past participle are irregular.

The verb *be* has irregular forms throughout the present tense, and the verbs *have*, *do* and *say* have irregular forms.

2 Ask students to complete the exercise. Provide them with dictionaries if necessary. Have them compare in pairs before you check answers in open class.

Answers

1 belief **2** choice **3** daily **4** depth **5** length **6** loss **7** proof **8** solution **9** speech **10** success **11** thought **12** width

OPTIMISE YOUR EXAM

Word formation

Ask students to read the tips.

- In the word formation task in Language in Use exams, students will often need to add a prefix or a suffix or make other changes to the word in capitals. Sometimes students can only gain a sense of whether words are positive or negative by understanding the meaning of the whole text, not just the line including the gap. Remind them that the beginning of the word is often the same and the end of the word changes.
- Emphasise the importance of good spelling as this is a common way for students to lose marks in this kind of exam task.

3 Focus students' attention on the image and the title and ask them to predict what the text is about. Ask students to complete the exercise. Check answers in open class.

Answers

1 Because some young people live far from their nearest school.
2 They either went away to school or did lessons by post.
3 It takes a long time to get the answer to any questions.
4 Teachers and students communicate using two-way radio.

Exam task

4 In pairs or as a group, students complete the exercise. Check answers in open class.

Answers

1 children **2** solution **3** choice **4** length **5** success **6** daily **7** secondary **8** proof

THINK | RESEARCH | CULTURE | LEARN | ME

Ask students to complete the task. Elicit answers from different students around the class.

Suggested answers

Advantages: students don't have to get up early, they live in the middle of nature, they don't have to carry heavy rucksacks, they have a flexible timetable and can organise themselves as they want

Disadvantages: new technology isn't always reliable, optional subjects are limited, students don't have access to laboratories, may be difficult to find virtual teachers, they can cheat!

Homework

OWB

Assign students Language in Use exercises 1, 2 and 3 on page 89 of their Workbook.

WRITING
A short message

→ Student's Book, pages 122–123 SB

Lesson aims

- Focus on using given information in your work
- Plan and write a short message

Lead-in

Ask students to create a mind map with vocabulary related to the unit theme. In pairs or small groups, students write *Education* in the centre of a blank page and draw branches from the centre with these subheadings: *Verbs / Nouns / Expressions / Phrasal verbs*. Students race to find words and phrases for each category from the previous lessons.

Suggested words:

Verbs: *join a course, pass, fail, study, take an exam, punish*

Nouns: *knowledge, certificate, award, degree, diploma, qualifications, secondary, primary, lesson, session, skill, subject*

Expressions: *learn by heart, have your nose in a book, pass with flying colours, put your thinking cap on, learn the ropes*

Phrasal verbs: *go over, drop out, copy out, fall behind, break up*

1 Ask students to complete the exercise. Elicit answers in open class.

Suggested answers

1 You might write a short note to a friend to give them information about homework, to ask them to do something for you, to arrange to meet them, etc. You might write a postcard to tell someone about your holiday. You might write an email to invite a friend from another country to visit you. You might write a text to arrange to meet a friend.
2 Students' own answers

EXAM SKILL

Using given information

Ask students to read the tips.

- Students can lose marks in this task if their information is in the wrong order. It is important for them to follow the task prompts in order.
- They can use the same words as the prompts, but they will gain extra marks if they paraphrase the words as much as possible. Remind them that they can be creative with verbs and adjectives, but they must be careful not to change the key words (usually nouns).

2 Ask students to complete the exercise. Check answers in open class.

Answers

1 in the first two sentences (Highlight how Abigail explains why she missed lessons in her own words … *because I was ill. I had a really bad cold.*)
2 in the next two sentences (*What work did I miss? Was it interesting?*)
3 in the last two sentences (Elicit another way students could ask to borrow something [*lend*, e.g. *Can you lend me your lesson notes …?*].)

OPTIMISE YOUR EXAM

A short message

Ask students to read the tips.

- Students lose marks in this type of exam task because their message is too long or too short or they have included irrelevant information. When they edit their work, they should always keep in mind the three points for inclusion. They must edit out any irrelevant information, but make sure not to cut their text in any way that affects coherence.

For more information on writing short messages, refer students to the Writing reference, page 169.

▾ Exam task

3 Ask students to complete the exercise. Check answers in open class.

Answers

1 I'm thinking of going to … ✓ I'm considering going to … ✓ I've decided to go to … ✓
2 What about you? ✓ Do you have any plans for …? ✓ Are you thinking of going …? ✓
3 Why don't you come …? ✓ You could come … ✓ You should think about coming … ✓

4 Plan Ask students to complete the paragraph plan. You may want to look at students' plans, if this is possible, to check them and give advice and suggestions for improvement before they write.

▾ Exam task

5 Ask students to complete the exercise. Check answers in open class.

Answers

Students' own answers

6 Plan Ask students to complete the paragraph plan using their notes from Exercise 5. You may want to look at students' plans, if this is possible, to check them and give advice and suggestions for improvement before they write.

7 Write Students write the short messages in exercises 3 and 5. Remind them to write 35–45 words, in an appropriate style. Depending on time, it may be a good idea to set this and the subsequent checklist exercise for homework.

8 Check Students complete the checklist before they hand in their short messages.

Homework OWB

Assign students Writing exercises 1, 2, 3 and 4 on page 90 of the Workbook and Progress check 11, page 91.

12 Our wonderful world

UNIT AIMS

Exam preparation in Unit 12:

- understand instructions in short messages
- think logically when answering true/false/not stated options when listening to a conversation
- reach a decision in a collaborative task
- understand the form and function of auxilary verbs and apply them in an open-close exercise
- give reasons in an essay

TEACHER'S PRESENTATION KIT

- *Talk2Me* videos
- Speaking test videos
- Class and Workbook audio
- Workbook pages and answer key

UNIT OVERVIEW

Student's Book / Digital Student's Book SB		Workbook / Online Workbook OWB
LESSON / EXAM TASK	EXAM SKILLS / LANGUAGE FOCUS	CONSOLIDATION
Reading **Multiple choice**	Understanding instructions Short messages	Workbook, pp 92–93, Exercises 1, 2, 3, 4 Unit 12, Reading, Exercises 1, 2, 3, 4
Grammar 1	Future perfect	Workbook, p 94, Exercises 1, 2, 3 Unit 12, Grammar 1, Exercises 1, 2, 3
Vocabulary	Words connected with *natural habitats* Phrasal verbs Adjectives and nouns	Workbook, pp 94–95, Exercises 1, 2, 3 Unit 12, Vocabulary, Exercises 1, 2, 3
Listening **True/false/not stated**	Thinking logically	Workbook, p 96, Exercises 1, 2, 3 Unit 12, Listening, Exercises 1, 2, 3
Grammar 2	Modal perfect	Workbook, p 95, Exercises 1, 2, 3 Unit 12, Grammar 2, Exercises 1, 2, 3
Speaking **Collaborative task**	Reaching a decision	Workbook, pp 96–97, Exercises 1, 2, 3 Unit 12, Speaking, Exercises 1, 2, 3
Language in Use **Open cloze**	Auxilary verbs	Workbook, p 97, Exercises 1, 2, 3 Unit 12, Language in Use, Exercises 1, 2, 3
Writing **An essay**	Giving reasons	Workbook, p 98, Exercises 1, 2, 3, 4, 5 Unit 12, Writing, Exercises 1, 2, 3, 4, 5
Progress check	Check language progress for Units 11 and 12	Workbook, p 99, Progress check and Cumulative progress Progress check and Cumulative progress

Additional material

PRESENTATION KIT	TEACHER'S / STUDENT'S RESOURCE CENTRE RC	TEST GENERATOR
Talk2Me video *Shall we make a final decision?*	**Unit 12 worksheets:** *Optimise your grammar* (Standard and Higher), *Optimise your vocabulary* (Standard and Higher), *Talk2Me* video, *Say it right* **Units 11–12 worksheets:** CLIL, Culture, Everyday English (TRC only), Grammar communication (TRC only)	Unit Test 12 (Standard and Higher) End-of-year Test (Standard and Higher)

READING
Multiple choice | Short messages

→ Student's Book, pages 124–125 SB

Lesson aims

- Understand instructions
- Practise a multiple-choice exam task

Lead-in

Ask students to look at the unit title ***Our wonderful world*** and elicit what they think the unit is going to be about (*the natural world*). Write these words on the board: *Oceans and rivers, Forests, Deserts, Animals, Weather.* Brainstorm in open class what's going wrong in these interrelated ecosystems and how we can reverse it.

Cultural note

We are causing unprecedented damage to our planet. Deforestation, pollution, the death of coral reefs, species extinction, climate change and overpopulation are putting many of our most important ecosystems at risk. According to a United Nations report called the Global Biodiversity Outlook (GBO), we are losing biodiversity at a rate never before seen in history.

1 In pairs or as a group, students complete the exercise. Elicit answers from different students around the class. Elicit other actions students take to protect the world around us.

Suggested answers

1 giraffe, volcano, an atoll/lagoon, hummingbird, anteater, lightning

2 Students' own answers

EXAM SKILL

Understanding instructions

Ask students to read the tips.

- Short written messages are common in the workplace and in everyday life. In messages, verbs tell us what the action the person giving the message wants us or someone else to take. There are often signal words that let us know important information is coming, e.g. sequence words (*first, then, next, after that, also, finally,* etc.) and requests (*Could you …?, Will you …?, Would you …?, Would you mind …?, Don't forget to …, I need you to …, You should …, Please, …, Remember …*).
- We often use the imperative in messages for giving orders and instructions, warning, making invitations and giving advice. Imperatives are direct, we are telling someone what to do, and it's important for students to note that the imperative can often sound quite strong, even when meant as advice.

Language note

The imperative

Elicit examples of the imperative that students may have seen on signs and public notices, e.g. *Reduce speed, Fasten seat belts, Do not lean out of the window (on a train)*, etc. Point out that there is an additional imperative form we sometimes use for general prohibitions, consisting of the word *No* + gerund, e.g. *No smoking.*

We also see the imperative in instructions (*Bake for 20 minutes*), commands (*Wake up!*), reminders (*Don't forget the milk*) and friendly expressions, such as invitations, making a wish, making an apology, etc. (*Come in and sit down!, Have a nice trip!, Pardon me!*). Elicit an example of all these different uses of the imperative and write them on the board.

Highlight that the basic structure of the imperative is just the infinitive, e.g. *Sit*, or an infinitive followed by additional information, e.g. *Sit there.* Negative imperatives add *do* + *not* before the base form of the verb, e.g. *Don't sit there.*

When we use the imperative, we leave out the subject of the sentence, e.g. *You must sit there* = *Sit there.*

2 Ask students to complete the exercise. Elicit answers in open class.

Answers

1 a **2** b **3** a **4** a **5** a

3 Ask students to complete the exercise. Set a time limit of two minutes to stop students from focusing on the text in detail at this stage. Have them compare in pairs before you check answers in open class.

Answers

1 a project to clean up a river **2** start a club

OPTIMISE YOUR EXAM

Multiple choice

Ask students to read the tips.

- Point out that the questions always follow the order of the text and a good exam technique is to stop after the first question and look at the options and to continue like this until they have answered all the questions.
- Remind students that all the responses are usually plausible in multiple-choice options, however only one is 100% correct. It's important that they read the question and each option very carefully indeed. A single missed word can make the difference between right and wrong, so they mustn't rush into the task thinking they know the right answer. The key is to go carefully and read all the options.
- A strategy some students use is to cover the options and just read the question to see if they know the answer already. When they look at the options, if they see their own answer, it's probably correct. However, they should check through all the options before choosing their answer.

Exam task

4 3.21 **Note: The reading text is also available on the audio CD. You may want to have students listen and read the text before doing the exam task.**

Ask students to complete the exercise. Check answers in open class and elicit the key words that helped students decide on their answers.

Answers

1 C (*For transport, contact tim@riverways.org.*)
2 A (*Ring or text me before 6 tonight to go with me and Mum.*)
3 C (*Mum asks if you'll take us there tomorrow morning at the same time as she's busy!*)
4 C (*They said you should call before 5 to arrange your interview for tomorrow's show.*)
5 B (*Get in touch for details of the first meeting … holly@postbox.com*)

5 Ask students to complete the exercise. Have them compare in pairs before you check answers in open class.

Answers

1 litter **2** environment **3** rubbish **4** pollution **5** wildlife
The secret word is 'nature'.

Mixed ability

Give less confident students the answers in a jumbled order for them to match to the definitions in Exercise 5. More confident students find two more words in the text and write definitions. When everyone has finished, they can read out their definitions for others to match to one of the words in the text.

Homework OWB
Assign students Reading exercises 1, 2, 3 and 4 on pages 92–93 of their Workbook.

GRAMMAR 1
Future perfect

→ Student's Book, page 126 SB

Lesson aims

- Understand the correct usage of the future perfect
- Practise using the future perfect

Lead-in

Write these sentences on the board or dictate them to students:

1 By the year 2040, all of the snow on the peak of Mount Kilimanjaro will have melted.

2 Global temperatures will have risen by 3° by 2040.

3 Global sea levels will have risen by 0.88 to 0.9 metres by 2040.

Ask students if they think these predictions will come true and, if so, what steps we can take to solve these environmental issues. Highlight the future perfect in the sentences and elicit the form (*will* + *have* + past participle). Ask students to make similar predictions using the future perfect about coral reefs, fossil fuels and glaciers for the year 2040. Walk round, monitoring students for use of the future perfect, listening for errors to pick up on in the lesson.

Suggested answers

By 2040, most of the world's coral reefs will have become extinct.
By 2040, most of the world's fossil fuels will have run out.
By 2040, most of the world's glaciers will have melted.

Grammar in context

Ask students to complete the task. Refer them to the information in the *Remember* box if they aren't sure. Check answer in open class.

Remind students that they can find more information in the Grammar reference, Unit 12, page 159.

Answer

The correct meaning is b.

Language note

Future perfect

We often use the future perfect with *by* or *in*: *I think we will have landed on Mars by the year 2030. / I'll have finished in a while, then you can use the computer.*

By means 'not later than a particular time' and *in* means 'within a period of time'. We don't know exactly when something will finish, but it will finish before the stated time.

Point out that *will* and *going to* can be used interchangeably in the future perfect, e.g. *By 2050, all the world's fossil fuels are going to have been used up.*

Extra support

Ask students to rephrase the future perfect sentences in *Grammar in context* in the negative and interrogative forms.

1 Ask students to complete the exercise. Have them compare in pairs before you check answers in open class.

Answers

1 finish, finished **2** had, have had **3** ✓ **4** has, have **5** ✓ **6** eat, eaten **7** clean, cleaned **8** ✓

SAY IT RIGHT

Pronunciation of *have* in the future perfect TRC
For the *Say it right* pronunciation activity and instructions, go to the Teacher's Resource Centre.

2 Ask students to complete the exercise. Have them compare in pairs before you check answers in open class.

Answers

A *bioblitz* is a record of all the plants and creatures in an area done in a short time, such as one day.
1 have **2** recorded **3** will **4** have **5** taken **6** learnt

3 Ask students to complete the exercise. Have them compare in pairs before you check answers in open class.

Answers

1 will have taken **2** will have learnt **3** will have happened **4** won't have found / might not have found **5** will have done **6** will have helped

Fast finishers

Ask students to write a couple of comprehension questions on the text using the future perfect to ask the class when everyone has finished, e.g. *What will Ed have done by the end of the week?* (his second bioblitz, he will have helped clean a river) *How many bioblitzes will have happened in his area by the end of the year?* (over a dozen – highlight this means more than 12).

THINK | **RESEARCH** | CULTURE | LEARN | ME

Ask students to complete the task. Students can present their research at the beginning of the next class.

Homework OWB

Assign students Grammar 1 exercises 1, 2 and 3 on page 94 of their Workbook.

VOCABULARY

Topic vocabulary | Phrasal verbs | Word formation

→ Student's Book, page 127 SB

Lesson aims

Understand the correct usage of:

- words connected with *natural habitats*
- phrasal verbs
- adjectives and nouns

Lead-in

Write the word *Environmental* on the board. In pairs, students race to make as many words with three letters or more in three minutes from this word. Ask them to add up the number of words they have thought of and ask the pair with the most words to read them out in open class.

Suggested answers

environment, revelation, elevation, elevator, elevate, interval, inventor, invent, innovate, oriental, violent, trainee, retail, mental, meant, mortal, viral, mean, lean, lent, more, iron, near, train, main, vain, rain, lane, tore, rent, name, tame, male, tale

Words connected with *natural habitats*

1 3.22 Ask students to complete the exercise. Play the audio for students to listen and check their answers.

Answers/Audioscript

rainforest: gorilla, monkey, snake, tiger (Suggested answers: frog, parrot)

desert: camel, lizard, snake (Suggested answers: mountain lion, coyote)

ocean: dolphin, shark, whale (Suggested answers: octopus, fish)

grassland: elephant, giraffe, lion, monkey, zebra (Suggested answers: cheetah, hyena)

Refer students to the Vocabulary reference, page 168, for more information on topic vocabulary.

Phrasal verbs

2 3.23 Ask students to complete the exercise. Have them compare in pairs before you play the audio for them to listen and check their answers.

Answers/Audioscript

1 Nocturnal animals *wake up* at night and sleep during the day.

2 Camels can live without water for up to eight days before they need to *fill up* again.

3 Male penguins can *bring up* a baby penguin until the mother returns.

4 Salmon are born in rivers, then swim downstream and *end up* in the ocean.

5 Beavers and wolves mate for life but other animals *split up* after mating.

6 We should support the WWF so they can *keep up* their good work with animals.

7 This bear has *grown up* in a zoo and so can't live in the wild.

8 Rabbits have sharp teeth and can *cut up* most plants and trees.

Extra support

Write the definitions of each phrasal verb on the board to help students with the exercise:

1 *to wake up* – to wake from sleep and start to feel lively

2 *to fill up* – to eat enough food so they are no longer hungry

3 *to bring up* – to look after an offspring until it becomes an adult

4 *to end up* – to eventually arrive somewhere

5 *to split up* – to separate / end a relationship

6 *to keep up* – to continue to do something

7 *to grow up* – to change from being a baby to being an adult

8 *to cut up* – to cut something into several pieces

3 Ask students to complete the exercise. Have them compare in pairs before you check answers in open class.

Answers

1 brought up **2** cut up **3** grow up **4** end up

Refer students to the Vocabulary reference, page 168, for more information on phrasal verbs.

Adjectives and nouns

4 3.24 Ask students to complete the exercise. Have them compare in pairs before you play the audio for them to listen and check their answers.

Answers/Audioscript

1 I find bugs and worms absolutely *disgusting*!
2 What's the *explanation* for the peacock's amazing tail feathers?
3 The *natural* world is amazing and I love learning about animals.
4 Some of the frogs in the rainforest are *poisonous*.
5 The *scenery* and the views on safari in Africa are incredible.
6 A bioblitz is much simpler than a proper *scientific* study.
7 Almost all plants need *sunshine* to grow.
8 Many *tropical* birds and fish are very colourful.

Refer students to the Vocabulary reference, page 168, for more information on word formation.

THINK | RESEARCH | CULTURE | LEARN | ME

Ask students to complete the task. Elicit answers in open class.

Optional extension

Play ***Twenty questions***. Working in groups, not pairs, students each choose an animal, then take turns to guess the name of each animal by asking up to 20 *Yes/No* type questions. A 'yes' answer earns the questioner another chance to ask, a 'no' means the next player can ask a question.

Homework

OWB

Assign students Vocabulary exercises 1, 2 and 3 on pages 94–95 of their Workbook.

LISTENING
True/false/not stated

→ Student's Book, page 128 SB

Lesson aims

- Learn about making logical conclusions
- Practise a true/false/not stated exam task

Lead-in

Divide the class into teams. Call out one half of the phrasal verbs from the previous lesson (e.g. *split*). Students work in teams to write the other half on the board (e.g. *up*) and a definition as quickly as possible. The team with most points wins the game.

1 In pairs or as a group, students complete the exercise. Elicit answers from different students around the class.

Suggested answers

1 Vets are treating a rabbit in a surgery.
2 Best things: lots of work, treating sick animals and feeling you're making a difference, good pay, prestige, ongoing training, variety of tasks, etc.
Worst things: long degree course, giving bad news, witnessing animal cruelty, writing medical records, difficult customers, tiring, demanding, stressful, hard work, etc.

EXAM SKILL

Thinking logically

Ask students to read the tips.

- Remind students that they are matching meaning, not words. They might have to listen and make sense of a chunk of text and figure out what the facts mean in order to make logical conclusions.
- Point out that many words will be paraphrased so they should watch out for this.

2 Ask students to complete the exercise. Check answers in open class.

Answers

Students should tick: 1, 3, 4

OPTIMISE YOUR EXAM

True/false/not stated

Ask students to read the tips.

- Point out that it's a good idea to read the questions first and underline the key words, then listen for that information in the text. A single missed word can make the difference between right and wrong as this type of task may have two very similar options.
- Remind students not to jump to conclusions if they hear the exact words in the text to match the question. A speaker may go on to qualify the statement slightly so that it is more similar to another option.
- *Not stated* means that the whole meaning of the statement is not in the passage. The key words might be found but not the full meaning of the statement. Students can learn this 'mantra' to help them decide: *Does the text definitely and clearly say …*
- There will be at least one of all three answers. If you don't have at least one 'true', 'false' or 'not stated', you have at least one answer wrong.

Exam task

3 3.25 Play the track for students to listen and complete the exercise. Don't check answers yet as they will listen again in Exercise 4.

4 3.25 Play the track again for students to listen and check their answers. Check answers in open class. Elicit the key words and phrases that helped them decide on their answers.

Answers

1 a (*... but the vet said he needs to get more exercise.*)

2 b (*The show's all about how he and his assistants find unusual solutions to the animals' problems.*)

3 a (*When animals are hit by cars or hurt in some other way,* ***he*** *helps them recover. That's what he's best known for.* – Highlight how pronoun referencing helps students connect the ideas in the text together.)

4 b (*Oscar's owners must have been really pleased.* – Students draw a logical conclusion that Noel is not Oscar's owner from this statement.)

5 c (*He grew up on a farm in Ireland. He was bullied when he was young because he had problems reading and writing. He says that because of that he developed friendships with animals. I guess he might have decided to become a vet because of that.* – Here students are asked to understand a large chunk of text which give facts about his early life, but we are not told specifically that he was unhappy on the farm.)

6 b (*Then he went to Ireland to work on farm animals before he moved to England.* – Point out that students have to draw a logical conclusion that farm animals are not small animals and therefore this is false.)

7 b (Erin says *'And I'd love to be a vet, just like him.'* but not a famous one *'No, I hate being the centre of attention,'* – Point out that this is a clear example of how a speaker says the exact words in one of the options, but then goes on to qualify the statement so that it is no longer a match.)

Optional extension

Have a ***Class debate***. Write the motion *Cats or dogs* on the board. Flip a coin to see which team can choose their 'side' in the argument. The other team has to take the opposite view. Divide the class into two teams – for and against – and ask students to prepare their arguments, first in pairs and then as a team. Write some prompt words on the board and remind students to anticipate the other team's arguments, e.g. *clean, friendly, intelligent, dangerous, birds, mice, trust, bite, scratch, expensive, loving, noisy, playful, exercise, lazy, fur, active.*

At the end of the debate, take a vote and ask if the debate has changed anybody's mind.

Homework OWB

Assign students Listening exercises 1, 2 and 3 on page 96 of their Workbook.

GRAMMAR 2
Modal perfect

→ Student's Book, page 129 SB

Lesson aims

- Understand the correct usage of the modal perfect
- Practise using the modal perfect

Lead-in

Draw students' attention to the photo of the Northern Lights. Write some facts about Iceland on the board in word clouds. Ask students to think of the questions that correspond with the answers in each cloud. Elicit what else they know about Iceland, if they have visited it or they would like to go there.

Words for the word clouds: *hot springs, oysters, volcanoes, the Northern Lights; approximately 332,000; Reykjavik; 103,000; Icelandic króna; Icelandic.*

Answers

(given in same order as words above)

What's Iceland famous for? What's the population of the Republic of Iceland? What's the name of the capital and largest city? How many square kilometres is the island? What's the name of Iceland's currency? What language do they speak?

Grammar in context

Ask students to complete the task. Refer them to the information in the *Remember* box if they aren't sure. Check answers in open class.

Remind students that they can find more information in the Grammar reference, Unit 12, page 160.

Answers

1 yes **2** very **3** the past **4** He didn't realise that his pet needed more exercise.

Language note

Modal perfect

Modal verbs for speculation and deduction are used to express a degree of certainty about a past action or a situation. Remind students that we use *may have, might have, could have* when there is 50% possibility that something is true. Elicit the negative forms: *may not have, might not have.*

We use *must have* when we are 90% certain something is true.

We use *can't have* when we are 90% certain that something isn't true.

Ought not to have can be used in the same way as *shouldn't have* but sounds more formal and isn't as common.

1 Ask students to complete the exercise. Have them compare in pairs before you check answers in open class.

Answers

1 b **2** a **3** b **4** b **5** b **6** a

Extra support

Elicit the following information:

- how certain the speaker is in 1 and 2 (1 – very certain it is on the bus; 2 – very certain the dog isn't far)
- which sentence criticises an ongoing situation (3) and which criticises a past action (4)
- which two sentences describe a hypothetical past (which didn't happen) (5 – the speaker passed the test; 6 – the speaker didn't buy a present because he/she didn't have any money).

2 Ask students to complete the exercise. Have them compare in pairs before you check answers in open class.

Suggested answers

1 must have gone out **2** may/might/could have forgotten to call me **3** should / ought to have arrived home (by now) **4** should / ought to have studied (for the test) **5** shouldn't / ought not to have invited Tom (to the party)

3 Ask students to complete the exercise. Have them compare in pairs before you check answers in open class.

Answers

1 can't have been **2** must have been **3** must have lasted **4** would/should have videoed **5** could have been **6** should have come

Homework OWB

Assign students Grammar 2 exercises 1, 2 and 3 on page 95 of their Workbook.

Assign students the Flipped classroom tasks on page 130 of their Student's Book if you'd like them to prepare for the next lesson. To complete this task, students need to watch the *Talk2Me* video which can be found on the Resource Centre.

SPEAKING
Collaborative task

→ Student's Book, page 130 SB

Lesson aim

- Reaching a decision

The *Talk2Me* video in this unit focuses on people discussing options and reaching a decision. Students answer some comprehension questions and then listen out for words, phrases to say whether they agree or not. The video can be used in one of two ways:

Flipped classroom

Flipped classroom option

Using this approach, students watch the video and complete the exercises for homework. This prepares students for the speaking lesson by introducing them to the topic and the key phrases to use in the exam task. Teachers who use this method will find they have more class time to spend on activating the target language and developing fluency for the final task.

***Talk2Me* worksheet**

Ask students to also complete the *Talk2Me* worksheet on the Resource Centre for more detailed comprehension exercises and more practice of the key phrases.

Classroom option

Lead-in

Play ***Noughts and crosses*** to recycle phrasal verbs from previous lessons. Divide the class into two teams: X and O. Draw two three-by-three grids on the board. Write these phrasal verbs in each square of one of the grids, in random order: *break up, go over, drop out, wake up, fill up, end up, split up, keep up, grow up*. Each team must think of a grammatically correct sentence with a phrasal verb in the square they choose to win, e.g. *I grew up in Greece, but I was born in England*. If they win a square, write X or O in the same square of the second grid. The first team to get a line in a row, wins the game.

1 Ask students to read the questions. Play the *Talk2Me* video for students to complete the exercise. Play the video again, if necessary, before checking their answers.

Answers

1 The USA: Disneyland, New York and California (surfing)
2 Maddy: sports, Angus: pop music and fashion, Jamie: history
3 a walking holiday

2 Play the *Talk2Me* video again, so students can underline the phrases in the *Phrase expert* box. Pause the video from time to time if necessary. Check answers in open class.

Answers

So which one do you think we should choose? Shall (we) make (a) final decision? I'd choose …, My first choice would be …, Of all the options, I think … is the best. That's sounds like a good decision.

***Talk2Me* worksheet**

Ask students to also complete the *Talk2Me* worksheet on the Resource Centre for more detailed comprehension exercises and more practice of the key phrases.

Answers

The transcript and answer key for the *Talk2Me* video and Worksheet can be found on the Teacher's Resource Centre.

3 In pairs or as a group, students ask and answer the questions. Elicit answers from different students around the class.

Suggested answers

1 In the first photo, a girl is feeding some deer at a farm or zoo. In the second photo a family are in a forest together – it looks like they are hiking or exploring.
2 Students' own answers

EXAM SKILL

Reaching a decision

Ask students to read the tips.

- Beginning with a question to their partner is a good way to start this section. It shows that the student has understood the topic and is trying to communicate with their partner. It also gives the student time to think about what he or she can say next.
- Remind students that it is important to respond to what their partner is saying, give their opinion, explain their choice and ask another question to move the conversation along and change the topic, e.g. if their partner says *Do you like farms?* they should say something like *I like farms, because I love animals, but I prefer zoos. Do you enjoy going to zoos?* Remind students that they don't want to get stuck on one topic for a long time.
- Students can make their answers more interesting and detailed by giving real opinions and talk about their experience. It will help them talk for the full three minutes and attain a higher score.

4 Ask students to complete the task. Elicit answers from different students around the class.

5 3.26 Play the track for students to listen and complete the task. Elicit if students made the same points in Exercise 4 that the students also mention.

6 3.26 Play the track again for students to listen and complete the task. Elicit answers from different students around the class.

Answers

1 doing **2** choice **3** about **4** what **5** going **6** agree

OPTIMISE YOUR EXAM

Collaborative task

Ask students to read the tips.

- In order to play for time, to give yourself time to think, students can use hesitation words or sounds (*Er …, Let me see …, Mmm …, Then …, I mean …, You know what I mean*). Remind them not to use sounds from their own language; they may sound strange to the examiner.
- Highlight to students that they shouldn't be afraid to ask their partner to repeat or clarify a question if they don't understand, e.g. *I don't (really) understand … Do you think you could say/explain that again? Would you mind repeating it, please?*
- The examiner asks students to speak about two things together for three minutes. Point out that many students forget to talk about both points.

Exam task

7 In pairs, students complete the task. Walk round, monitoring students and noting down good use of language and errors to go over in a feedback session at the end of the activity.

Homework

OWB

Assign students Speaking exercises 1, 2 and 3 on pages 96–97 of their Workbook.

LANGUAGE IN USE

Open cloze

→ Student's Book, page 131 SB

Lesson aims

- Focus on auxiliary verbs
- Practise an open-cloze exam task

Lead-in

Play a ***blackboard race*** to revise useful vocabulary from the unit. Small groups race against each other to think of five words for each of five categories and write them on the board. When they have five full lists, they shout out 'Finished'. The pair or group with the most points wins the game.

Suggested categories: *environmental problems, words connected with natural habitats, ways to save the environment, different examples of the modal perfect, names of animals.*

1 In pairs or as a group, students complete the exercise. Elicit answers from different students around the class.

Suggested answers

1 When ships transporting oil/fuel crash or are damaged, the oil leaks into the surrounding water and onto beaches.

2 Oil is poisonous to many types of plants and animals. If it gets on a bird's feathers it can make them stick together and stop them from being able to fly. It can also cause chemical burns on their skin. The area has to be properly cleaned by people before things can live there again.

Remember

Ask students to read the information.

Refer students to Grammar reference, Unit 12, page 160 for more information.

Language note

Auxiliaries

Auxiliary verbs are also known as 'helping verbs'. The three most common auxiliary verbs are *be*, *do* and *have*, but students will often be tested on their knowledge of auxiliary verbs like *will*, *must*, etc. in open-cloze tasks.

2 Ask students to complete the exercise. Have them compare in pairs before you check answers in open class.

Answers

1 had swimming, had been swimming **2** people been leaving, people have been leaving **3** When they, When are they **4** What you think, What do you think **5** bottles being used, bottles are being used **6** council done, council has/have done

3 Ask students to complete the exercise. In pairs, they take turns to ask and answer the questions. Elicit some answers from around the class to close the activity.

Answers
1 Have **2** do **3** don't **4** do

OPTIMISE YOUR EXAM

Open cloze

Ask students to read the tip.

- Remind students that it is important to read the text for general understanding first.
- Point out that they can expect to be tested on many different things in gapped texts, but most of the gaps are usually grammatical words not topic vocabulary. Students should look out for fixed expressions, dependent prepositions after certain words and linking words and phrases.

Exam task

4 Ask students to complete the exercise. Check answers in open class.

Answers
1 do **2** was **3** have **4** is **5** is/gets **6** does **7** be **8** being

Mixed ability

Give less confident students the answers in a jumbled order. Ask more confident students to think of one or two comprehension questions based on the text in Exercise 4. When everyone has finished, ask them to read out their questions for other students to answer.

Cultural note

Although scientists had predicted that plastic would be accumulating in the North Pacific, nobody had actually seen the GPGP (Great Pacific Garbage Patch) until sailor and oceanographer, Charles Moore, was returning to California after the Los Angeles to Hawaii sailing race. He took an unusual short cut across the North Pacific Subtropical Gyre and noticed millions of pieces of plastic in the ocean – up to 10 metres deep and just below the water surface, composed mainly of non-degradable plastics. One type of plastic pollution comes from *nurdles*, small plastic pellets used to make most of the world's plastic products. These often end up in rivers or oceans, and as they are tiny (often under 5 mm across) fish and other marine life eat them, and then choke on them. Pesticides and other industrial products are readily absorbed into the nurdles from the ocean water making them even more harmful.

Homework OWB

Assign students Language in Use exercises 1, 2 and 3 on page 97 of their Workbook.

WRITING
An essay

→ Student's Book, pages 132–133 SB

Lesson aims

- Focus on language for giving reasons
- Plan and write an essay

Lead-in

Play ***Snowman*** with the word *dolphin*. Divide the class into two teams. On the board, draw one line for each letter of the word. The players take turns to guess letters in the word. If a letter is guessed correctly, write it into the correct space. If a letter is guessed which is not in the word, draw part of the snowman. The team which guesses the word first receives a point, and the game starts again with a new word.

1 Ask students to complete the exercise. Elicit answers in open class.

Suggested answers
1 dolphins performing in a show / dog-mushing – huskies pulling a sled
2 Students' own answers

EXAM SKILL

Giving reasons

Ask students to read the tips.

- Remind students that reasons illustrate and drive an argument and should offer detail and evidence. In the following exercises, they will work on a wide variety of linking words and phrases for giving reasons. This will help them show clear and logical relationships between their arguments and reasons in their writing.
- Elicit alternatives students can use instead of *because* for giving reasons, e.g. *as, as a result of, due to, thanks to, since,* etc.

2 Ask students to complete the exercise. Check answers in open class.

Answers
1 c **2** They disagree with the statement. **3** a, b, d

3 Ask students to complete the exercise. Check answers in open class.

Answers
1 reason **2** because **3** Another

4 Ask students to complete the exercise. Check answers in open class.

Answers
1 Because of this **2** For this reason **3** as

OPTIMISE YOUR EXAM

An essay

Ask students to read the tips.

- Effective organisation and cohesion are important features of a successful essay and will help students score higher marks. Remind them that every paragraph of their essay should have a main idea, point or goal that they're trying to get across.
- Highlight the importance of the topic sentence, which usually comes at the beginning of a paragraph and lets the reader know what to expect from each paragraph. To write good topic sentences, students need to know what their paragraphs are going to be about.
- Remind them that they should not worry about counting exact words in the exam. Most people write about 10–12 words per line so if they are going to write a total of 100 words, they should write about 10 lines in total. Students shouldn't worry if they run slightly over the word limit by about 10 words.

For more information on writing essays, refer students to the Writing reference, page 174.

Exam task

5 Ask students to complete the exercise. Check answers in open class.

Answers

Students' own answers

Extra support

In open class, elicit students' opinions about the statement and write the arguments for and against the use of animals in the tourist entertainment industry on the board. Add some key words and expressions that less confident students can refer back to when they write their essay.

Suggestions:

For: *cultural heritage, at risk of extinction, well cared for, entertaining, conservation, protection*

Against: *malnourished, distressed, sick, exploited, in need of veterinary care, illegal trafficking, cause irreparable harm, drugged*

6 Plan Ask students to complete the paragraph plan. You may want to look at students' plans, if this is possible, to check them and give advice and suggestions for improvement before they write.

7 Write Students write their essays in about 100 words, in an appropriate style. Depending on time, it may be a good idea to set this and the subsequent checklist exercise for homework.

8 Check Students complete the checklist before they hand in their essays.

Optional extension

Students swap essays and give marks from 1–5 for four different areas typically used for marking writing exams:

1 Content / task achievement – meaning properly answering the question.

2 Communicative achievement – successfully communicating ideas at the right level of formality.

3 Organisation – overall organisation and linking together sentences and paragraphs.

4 Language – level and accuracy of grammar and vocabulary.

Homework

OWB

Assign students Writing exercises 1, 2, 3, 4 and 5 on page 98 of the Workbook and Progress check 12, page 99.

Answers PROGRESS CHECK Units 11–12

Exercise 1
1 heart **2** colours **3** caps **4** nose **5** learn **6** lesson

Exercise 2
1 out **2** in **3** down **4** around **5** out **6** on **7** out **8** over **9** out **10** behind

Exercise 3
1 b **2** a **3** c **4** c **5** a **6** b

Exercise 4
1 explanation **2** belief **3** scientific **4** loss **5** natural **6** thoughts **7** disgusting **8** success

Exercise 5
1 ✓ **2** shouldn't have bought **3** must have been **4** should have finished **5** will have sat **6** ✓

Exercise 6
1 secondary **2** whale **3** litter **4** pupil **5** giraffe **6** professional **7** subject **8** graduate

Exercise 7
1 haven't, were **2** do, are **3** don't, are **4** has, been **5** had, been, was **6** have, haven't

OPTIMISE YOUR EXAMS

The *Optimise your exams* pages are designed to give your students extra training in exam tasks. Each task includes OPTIMISE boxes, which contain tips for students. Remind students to read these boxes before they start each of the exam tasks. Students can work on the tasks in class or for homework, and the tasks can be done at whatever stage you feel is most appropriate for your class.

Your students should complete these pages before they move on to the Practice test in the Workbook.

READING AND WRITING

SB pages 136–141

1

Students' own answers

2

Suggested answers

Text 1:

1 It's a note. **2** It's from one friend to another. **3** To suggest that look at a room together.

Text 2:

1 It's an invitation. **2** It's from two friends to their party guests. **3** To invite people to a house-warming party.

3

place to live = accommodation/rooms

food and drink = refreshments

room = space

4

1 B, 2 C

Question 1

A Adriana mentions the noticeboard because she saw an advert there – not because she was looking for a place to put up a notice.

C The text doesn't mention hobbies.

Question 2

A The invitation says that refreshments are provided.

B The party starts at 7.30 but the invitation doesn't say that guests must arrive at that time.

5

1 Carlos **2** Rebecca **3** Maya **4** Rebecca **5** Carlos **6** Maya

6

1 B **2** E **3** D

7

Suggested answers

Maya

She'd like to set up a company and be her own boss → we'll give you all kinds of tips about starting and running your own business

When she leaves the camp, she hopes to have some ideas for her company → You'll graduate from camp with your own business plan ready to go.

Carlos

He wants to learn how to become popular with bigger audiences and manage in a competitive business → we'll also teach you all you need to know about getting more fans and surviving in the music industry.

Rebecca

She knows exactly what she wants → if you're full of opinions

She gets nervous before she performs and wants to feel more relaxed. → We'll take you and turn you into a confident performer.

Her dream is to perform on stage, entertaining people and telling jokes. → You'll soon have the audience laughing!

8

It's an article about a teenage chef and media star.

9

Question 3

10

2 C

By the age of seven, Remmi was a real foodie who could cook complete meals for her family.

3 B

She believes that when young people make their own food, they care more about what they eat.

11

Students' own answers

12

B

13

2 five; one to three, the same **3** note; 35–45 **4** two; story, 100 **5** one; 15

14

1 to go (The maximum number of words you can write is three.)
2 took (We can use the verb' take' with 'journey'.)
3 the best (You need a superlative form here.)

15

A 2 **B** 3 **C** 1

16

1 a note **2** your friend Alex **3** three

17

1 C **2** B **3** D, A

18

Students' own answers

19

1 an English friend **2** films **3** two **4** informal **5** 100

20

1 B **2** C **3** A **4** D

21

Students' own answers

22

Students' own answers

LISTENING SB pages 142–143

1
1 30 **2** one mark **3** should **4** twice **5** will

2
Suggested answers

B A tennis racket in a wardrobe. **C** A tennis racket on the floor.

3
1 A girl and her father. **2** Her tennis racket, which she can't find.
3 At home. **4** Yes.

4
B

5
became interested in helping with = was keen to get involved
information = advert/ information
encouraged him to take part = suggested that I help organise it
do something for others = doing charity work or helping people
difficult = challenge
manage people = organising everyone
calm = relaxed
have original ideas = creative; thinking of fun activities

6
1 A

B he became interested in helping with the event before the teacher encouraged him

C he says he'd never thought about doing charity work before

2 B

A He says he doesn't usually get stressed

C He says he's a creative person and finds it easy to think of fun activities

7
1 a type of celebration **2** a number (an amount of money)
3 a name or word **4** a phone number

8
1 weddings **2** 600 **3** RANMERE **4** 7946 0874

9
Maths – the amount of homework they get, their teacher and their classes at school.

10
Suggested answers:

1 Carl and Jenny agree that their maths teacher gives them too much homework.

2 In Jenny's opinion, the teacher doesn't explain things well.

3 They both think group work is useful.

1 B
2 A
3 A

SPEAKING SB pages 144–147

1
A, B, D. E, F

2
1 D **2** B **3** F **4** E **5** A

3
1 do a bath = go for a swim **2** add suggested answer?

4
Students' own answers

5
1 students **2** camp **3** mountains **4** together **5** could **6** exciting

6
Students' own answers

7
Students' own answers

8
Students' own answers

9
1 D **2** B **3** A **4** E **5** C

10
Students' own answers

11
Students' own answers

12
Sabin:
1 homework **2** writing **3** next **4** because **5** background **6** fruit **7** case **8** dark

Federico:
1 having **2** drinking **3** kitchen **4** are **5** enjoying **6** lot **7** wooden **8** happy

13
Sabin:

~~which it~~ looks like she's doing her homework ⟶ **who** looks like she's doing her homework

there ~~is~~ some frying pans ⟶ there **are** some frying pans

there ~~have~~ a lot of files ⟶ there **are** a lot of files

she needs help ~~at~~ her homework ⟶ she needs help **with** her homework

Federico:

it doesn't ~~seem as~~ a kitchen ⟶ it doesn't **look like** a kitchen

It's in the ~~atrium~~ ⟶ it's in the **hall**.

They're enjoying. ⟶ They're enjoying **themselves**.

14
Students' own answers

15
1 S **2** F **3** S **4** S

16
1 E **2** C, D **3** B, D **4** A, C

17
Students' own answers

Workbook Answer Key

UNIT 1

Pages 4–5

Reading

Exercise 1

c

Exercise 2

1 A **2** B **3** D **4** B

Exercise 3

1 g **2** h **3** d **4** f **5** b **6** c **7** a **8** e

Page 6

Grammar 1

Exercise 1

1 c **2** a **3** b **4** c **5** a **6** b

Exercise 2

1 don't know **2** is becoming **3** performs **4** isn't dancing **5** is trying **6** is appearing **7** is writing **8** are looking **9** Do you think **10** is doing **11** isn't acting **12** writing **13** is posing **14** loves **15** is designing **16** doesn't want

Pages 6–7

Vocabulary

Exercise 1

1 generous, generosity **2** polite, politeness **3** unreliable, reliability **4** creative, creativity **5** shy, shyness **6** curious, curiosity **7** dependable, dependability **8** serious, seriousness

Exercise 2

1 d **2** f **3** a **4** c **5** b **6** e

Page 7

Grammar 2

Exercise 1

1 b **2** c **3** a **4** b **5** a **6** c **7** a **8** b **9** b **10** c **11** c **12** a

Exercise 2

1 Many **2** every **3** Both of **4** students **5** all of **6** Most of **7** enough **8** others

Exercise 3

1 All of **2** much money/lots of money **3** every teenager **4** enough time **5** all of

Page 8

Listening

Exercise 1

1 a tour guide **2** Barcelona **3** a cinema **4** at a radio station

Exercise 2

1 b **2** d **3** c **4** a

Exercise 3

1 A **2** B **3** C **4** B

Pages 8–9

Speaking

Exercise 1

1 a **2** b **3** b **4** a **5** b

Exercise 2

1, 3, 6, 7

Exercise 3

1 g **2** c **3** e **4** a **5** l **6** i **7** k **8** h **9** d **10** f

Page 9

Language in Use

Exercise 1

1 c **2** b **3** a **4** b **5** a **6** c **7** b **8** c

Exercise 2

c

Exercise 3

2, 3, 7

Exercise 4

1 D **2** B **3** A **4** C **5** B **6** A **7** C **8** D

Page 10

Writing

Exercise 1

1 friendly and conversational **2** is

Exercise 2

Yes, she did.

Exercise 3

Suggested answers

Paragraph 1

Purpose: thank the person for their letter/email and refer to a piece of news they wrote about

My notes: It was great to hear from you! Congratulations on passing your Spanish exam!

Paragraph 2

Purpose: refer to their project, say which festival you celebrate

My notes: Your project sounds fun. You asked me about a festival I celebrate with my family. We always celebrate Name Days – similar to birthdays, give/get presents.

Paragraph 3

Purpose: talk about some activities you do with your friends

My notes: With my friends, I go to sports events and we also hang out together and watch films.

Paragraph 4

Purpose: say you hope it helps and mention something you're going to do or something about your life

My notes: Hope that helps! Wish me luck because I'm playing in an important basketball match!

Exercise 4

1 glad (O) **2** Congratulations (O) **3** Write (C) **4** write (C) **5** Anyway (C) **6** Best (C) **7** so (O) **8** It (O)

Page 11

Progress check

Exercise 1

1 is looking, think, is walking **2** hate, agree, is getting **3** don't like, I do like, talks **4** each, some of the **5** All, lots **6** Both of, much

Exercise 2

1 reliable **2** awake **3** shy **4** deep **5** serious **6** personal **7** big **8** creative

Cumulative progress

Exercise 3

1 long **2** of **3** fast **4** little **5** more/some **6** are **7** personality **8** look

UNIT 2

Pages 12–13

Reading

Exercise 1

1 c **2** e **3** f **4** a **5** g

Exercise 2

1 At Ruth's house **2** Sara

Exercise 3

1 B **2** C **3** B **4** A **5** C

Exercise 4

1 g **2** e **3** c **4** a **5** f **6** h **7** d **8** b

Page 14

Grammar 1

Exercise 1

1 was raining **2** was hurrying **3** was holding **4** blew **5** stepped **6** was shaking **7** drove **8** splashed **9** had **10** arrived **11** was waiting **12** Did he forget **13** walked

Exercise 2

1 did you do **2** ✓ **3** wasn't sleeping **4** ✓ **5** was blowing **6** were you going

Exercise 3

1 Was he cleaning, slipped, fell
2 was working, stopped
3 sent, didn't reply, was helping, didn't hear

4 was looking, learnt, didn't have
5 weren't watching, arrived, were
6 went, had
7 was shopping, were painting
8 shared, bought

Pages 14–15

Vocabulary

Exercise 1
1 hedge **2** dining room **3** balcony **4** chimney **5** garage **6** attic **7** basement **8** study **9** fence

Exercise 2
1 b **2** f **3** d **4** h **5** c **6** a **7** e **8** g

Exercise 3
1 a **2** c **3** c **4** a **5** b **6** b

Page 15

Grammar 2

Exercise 1
1 c **2** b **3** a **4** c **5** b **6** a

Exercise 2
1 never used to read books
2 would often fall asleep on the sofa
3 used to wash the windows every week
4 didn't use to be a lot of cafés here
5 Did he use to visit his cousins
6 wouldn't go to the park near her home

Page 16

Listening

Exercise 1
1 buildings and objects **2** mountain **3** explodes **4** an open space **5** is full of people **6** all

Exercise 2
1 T **2** T **3** F **4** F **5** T

Exercise 3
1 C **2** A **3** B **4** B **5** A

Pages 16–17

Speaking

Exercise 1
1 In **2** To **3** below **4** behind **5** At **6** On **7** near **8** background

Exercise 2
Photograph A

Exercise 3
1 In the foreground, on the right
2 in the middle of the photo, in front of the sofa
3 on top of the table
4 in the background, to the right, in front of a small bookshelf
5 on top of the bookshelf, next to the vase with bright flowers
6 on the wall behind the chair

Page 17

Language in Use

Exercise 1
1 b **2** d **3** f **4** h **5** a **6** c **7** g **8** e

Exercise 2
1 c **2** a **3** b **4** a **5** c **6** b

Exercise 3
1 big/large enough **2** such a difficult / a really difficult **3** so many **4** is enough space **5** too far

Page 18

Writing

Exercise 1
1 ask, information **2** politely, mind, help, think

Exercise 2
Note B is better because it gives more information for point 2 and Sam makes a polite request (Could you …?) rather than being more direct (Come and paint …) which is actually a command.

Exercise 3
1 a, b **2** a, c **3** b, c

Suggested answer
Dear Grace,
Thanks so much for a wonderful weekend. It was fantastic! I'll never forget the concert, it was the best part of the weekend! Why don't you come and stay one weekend? How about next weekend? Let me know.
Bye!
Mark

Page 19

Progress check

Exercise 1
1 used to **2** had **3** would **4** got **5** found **6** was sitting **7** never **8** would always have **9** didn't **10** was doing **11** called **12** have

Exercise 2
1 from, stay **2** move out, pull down **3** garage, basement **4** on, worth **5** move in, do it up **6** roof, to stay **7** rent out, attic **8** balcony, on

Cumulative progress

Exercise 3
1 B **2** C **3** A **4** D **5** A **6** D **7** B **8** C **9** C **10** D

UNIT 3

Pages 20–21

Reading

Exercise 1
1 The age range for The Den at Camp Bestival Festival.
2 The number of places the YHA has where you can stay in England and Wales.
3 The number of young people under 18 who stayed in youth hostels last year.
4 The number of days Carla and her friends went youth hostelling for.
5 The cost of annual membership for the YH if you're under 26.
6 The approximate cost of a One Country InterRail Pass.

Exercise 2
1 (incorrect) 'Trying new things like these …' means these are suggestions Carla is making, not that she has done them all.
2 (correct) 'If you're looking for' means 'if you want to do' and the writer says 'try' which means she is suggesting this.
3 (incorrect) 'has been travelling' means she started doing it at some point in the past and is still doing it.

Exercise 3
1 B **2** A **3** B **4** A **5** B **6** A **7** B **8** B **9** A **10** B

Exercise 4
1 e **2** a **3** h **4** b **5** g **6** d **7** f **8** c

Page 22

Grammar 1

Exercise 1
1 a has been going **1** b went **1** c has gone
2 a Has she been driving **2** b Has she driven **2** c Did she drive
3 a haven't been working **3** b didn't work **3** c haven't worked
4 a have been having **4** b have had **4** c had

Exercise 2
1 yet **2** never **3** since **4** for **5** already **6** still

Exercise 3
1 have been trying **2** have you been **3** have been swimming
4 Have you been doing **5** haven't seen **6** has happened
7 have been waiting **8** have you heard **9** have been looking
10 Have you had

Pages 22–23

Vocabulary

Exercise 1
1 guided **2** voyage **3** school **4** cruise **5** package **6** journey

Exercise 2
1 hostel **2** resort **3** tourists **4** backpackers **5** luggage **6** guidebook

Exercise 3
1 to sitting, uncomfortable **2** disabled, from travelling
3 walking, impatient **4** in going, irresponsible **5** on renting, illegal
6 unpopular, impossible

Page 23

Grammar 2

Exercise 1
1 is, luggage, It's, much, little, is
2 is, is, amount, information, a little, a few

Exercise 2
1 ✓ **2** much **3** ✓ **4** lot **5** amount **6** few

Exercise 3
1 many, much **2** fewer, a few **3** a little, less
4 weren't, wasn't

Page 24

Listening

Exercise 1

1 disappointed
When I saw the dirty swimming pool, I realised I had made a terrible mistake.
2 surprised
I honestly never expected to win a holiday to a luxury resort in the Caribbean!
3 impatient
Nothing could stop me from jumping into the blue water of the Aegean.
4 uncertain
When I quit my job to travel, I wasn't sure that it was the right decision.
5 worried
They said it was a safe place, but they were wrong, and I didn't sleep during the holiday.
6 annoyed
The service was terrible, so we didn't leave a tip for the waiter.
7 interested
I asked the tour guide a lot of questions about the history of the area.
8 angry
When the taxi broke down on the way to the airport, I just wanted to scream!

Exercise 2

1 interested **2** impatient **3** surprised **4** angry/annoyed
5 disappointed **6** uncertain **7** worried/uncertain

Exercise 3

1 F **2** T **3** T **4** F **5** T **6** T

Pages 24–25

Speaking

Exercise 1

They use all the phrases.

Exercise 2

1 like **2** take **3** hit **4** protect **5** see **6** keep

Exercise 3

Students' own answers

Page 25

Language in Use

Exercise 1

1 c/d **2** b **3** b/d **4** b **5** d **6** a

Exercise 2

1 c **2** f **3** a **4** e **5** b **6** d

Exercise 3

1 many **2** fewer **3** time **4** set **5** on **6** in **7** guided **8** yet

Page 26

Writing

Exercise 1

1 shouldn't, informal **2** is, can **3** should, can, fine **4** before

Exercise 2

Suggested answers

1 Are you on holiday … / Do you like art … / If so, then you'll love … / The trail guides you … / You need to speak English …
2 Are you on holiday in London? / Do you like art and enjoy exploring on foot?
3 you'll love… / It's a fun … / it's quite reasonable… / the art isn't … / I wouldn't recommend …
4 The trail is ideal for teenagers and adults who want a fascinating way to explore London, but I wouldn't recommend it for younger children.

Exercise 3

1 fun **2** reasonable **3** disappointing **4** fascinating

Exercise 4

Suggested answers

1 visiting Manchester; love sport
2 try a class at the Free running Academy
3 learn how to do free running, overcoming obstacles in a safe environment
4 fun
5 very reasonable
6 book in advance, classes are often full
7 for people of all ages, children
8 challenging yourself physically, recommend it

Page 27

Progress check

Exercise 1

1 c **2** b **3** a **4** b **5** a **6** c **7** a **8** b **9** a **10** c

Exercise 2

1 spend **2** currency **3** sightseers **4** business **5** keen **6** campsite
7 luggage **8** have **9** resort **10** prevent **11** guidebook **12** journey

Cumulative progress

Exercise 3

1 helpful **2** untidy **3** impossible **4** uncomfortable **5** impatient
6 irresponsible **7** uncertain **8** popularity

UNIT 4

Pages 28–29

Reading

Exercise 1

1 F **2** C, E, G **3** B **4** A **5** H **6** D

Exercise 2

1 B **2** F **3** E **4** D **5** C

Exercise 3

1 energetic **2** judge **3** rapids **4** participates **5** recreates **6** graduate
7 reveal **8** operate

Page 30

Grammar 1

Exercise 1

1 d **2** c **3** e **4** b **5** a

Exercise 2

1 is going to **2** are going to **3** Shall **4** will **5** won't
6 Is your sister going to

Exercise 3

1 will be **2** am going to celebrate **3** will come **4** Shall I bring
5 isn't going to be **6** are going to go **7** Will it be **8** will have
9 won't be **10** will ask

Pages 30–31

Vocabulary

Exercise 1

1 sailing **2** sky-diving **3** rock climbing **4** snowboarding
5 horse-riding

Exercise 2

1 sleep in **2** works out **3** eat out **4** take up **5** call off **6** went out
7 staying up **8** get together

Exercise 3

1 c **2** a **3** f **4** b **5** d **6** e

Page 31

Grammar 2

Exercise 1

1 I'm making **2** leaves **3** are you taking **4** I'm going **5** starts
6 Are you doing **7** doesn't open **8** I'm going **9** does it finish
10 We aren't going

Exercise 2

1 are filming **2** am not sleeping in **3** leaves **4** arrive **5** start
6 am practising **7** Are you doing **8** gets

Page 32

Listening

Exercise 1

1 ✗ **2** A **3** ✗ **4** B **5** ✗ **6** C

Exercise 2

1 B **2** C **3** A **4** B **5** C **6** C

Pages 32–33

Speaking

Exercise 1

1 don't mind, because **2** feel strongly about, as
3 preference, That's because **4** a big fan of
5 not keen on, The reason is that **6** prefer, for the reason that
7 don't really like, since

Exercise 2

Students' own answers

Exercise 3

1 OK then. Shall I start?
2 Please do.

3 Well, I'm a big fan of video games. I spend hours playing with my friends.
4 Is that because you don't like being outside?
5 No, I don't mind playing football, but it rains a lot where I live. What about you? Do you play a sport?
6 The truth is, I'm not very keen on sport. The reason is that I've never been good at it.
7 So what do you do in your free time?
8 Actually, I go to a dance school. I think dancing is the best activity of all!
9 Why do you think that?
10 Because it's fun and it keeps me fit too. You should try it!
11 Um, no thanks. I'm sure I would be terrible at it.
12 Why do you feel that way? You won't know until you have a go!
13 No, I definitely wouldn't be a good dancer. But I would like to try something exciting like sky-diving when I'm older.
14 I don't think I would be brave enough to try sky-diving, but I would like to go horse-riding in the future.

Page 33

Language in Use

Exercise 1
1 in spite **2** Even though **3** even though **4** despite **5** in spite of **6** Although

Exercise 2
1 thin, Nate is very strong
2 he is thin, Nate is very strong/Nate is thin, he is very strong
3 Nate is very strong, even
4 spite of the fact that he
5 the fact that he

Exercise 3
1 he wasn't **2** not having **3** despite the fact **4** Despite eating **5** even **6** the view was

Page 34

Writing

Exercise 1
1 information **2** point **3** experience

Exercise 2
1 T **2** F **3** T **4** F

Exercise 3
Phrases to include: 1, 4, 5, 6, 7, 9
Order: 7 – 9 – 5 – 1 – 4 – 6

Exercise 4

Suggested answers

Opening
Purpose: say hello
My notes: Hey Sam!

First point
Purpose: explain what you are doing and how your skateboard got broken
My notes: I'm in a skateboarding show but my skateboard is broken. I crashed into a wall when I was using it yesterday.

Second point
Purpose: ask to borrow Sam's skateboard
My notes: Do you think I could borrow your skateboard?

Third point
Purpose: say when you will need it
My notes: The skateboarding show is on Sunday at 10 am

Closing
Purpose: say goodbye
My notes: Let me know. Bye for now!

Page 35

Progress check

Exercise 1
1 b **2** a **3** b **4** c **5** c **6** c

Exercise 2
1 taken up, horse-riding, take, make
2 sailing, call off, enjoy
3 get together, hiking, have, spend

Cumulative progress

Exercise 3
1 C **2** B **3** A **4** B **5** B **6** D **7** A **8** C **9** D **10** C

UNIT 5

Pages 36–37

Reading

Exercise 1
1 B **2** C **3** A

Exercise 2
1 When MSF began, international medical teams were common.
Médecins Sans Frontières (MSF) … founded in France in 1971… At that time, the idea of international medical teams travelling to wherever they were needed was completely new … (lines 1–5)
2 MSF was the first international humanitarian organisation to win the Nobel Peace Prize.
In 1999, MSF won the Nobel Peace Prize for its work. (lines 10–11)
3 Emma Hammett was a nurse before she began First Aid for Life.
She worked as a nurse for many years before starting First Aid for Life … (lines 14–15)
4 First Aid for Teenagers is the most popular course run by FAFL.
They run a huge variety of courses, including First Aid for Teenagers. It's very popular with teens … (lines 18–19)
5 UK ISAR teams are only sent to disasters and emergencies in Europe.
The team can be sent … to an accident or disaster anywhere in the world … (lines 23–25)
6 UK ISAR use animals to help them in their rescue operations.
ISAR has about 260 members, most are firefighters, but they also include doctors, paramedics and nurses, a team of search dogs and vets … (lines 26–28)

Exercise 3
1 F **2** NS **3** T **4** NS **5** F **6** T

Exercise 4
1 f **2** a **3** h **4** b **5** d **6** c **7** g **8** e

Page 38

Grammar 1

Exercise 1
1 didn't have to **2** can **3** could **4** should **5** mustn't **6** I don't need to

Exercise 2
1 should **2** mustn't **3** could **4** can **5** didn't have to **6** don't need to

Exercise 3
1 Can **2** able/allowed **3** to **4** have/need **5** let **6** allowed **7** can/may **8** must **9** should **10** can

Pages 38–39

Vocabulary

Exercise 1
1 cut, chin, blood, hurt, infection, prescription
2 cough, ached, cold, flu, medicine
3 injured, ankle, bones, bandage, skin

Exercise 2
1 f **2** c **3** a **4** h **5** d **6** g **7** e **8** b

Exercise 3
1 take, make **2** took, have **3** do, had **4** made, doing **5** made, did **6** Make, have **7** have, take

Page 39

Grammar 2

Exercise 1
1 certainty **2** possibility **3** probability **4** certainty **5** probability **6** possibility **7** possibility

Exercise 2
1 may/might **2** should/ought to **3** can't/must **4** could **5** can't **6** ought to

Exercise 3
1 must be **2** may/might/could **3** should/ought to **4** can't be

Page 40

Listening

Exercise 1
1 D **2** A **3** D **4** D **5** D **6** A

Exercise 2
1 c **2** b **3** a **4** b

Exercise 3
1 F **2** F **3** T **4** F **5** T **6** T

Pages 40–41
Speaking
Exercise 1
1 often **2** a **3** at **4** on **5** on **6** in **7** rarely **8** all **9** often **10** twice
Exercise 2
1 I always make my bed before I go to school.
2 ✓
3 This Saturday I'm not going to the match because I'm not well.
4 ✓
5 ✓
6 When I feel up to it, I go hiking at the weekend.
7 I usually take a shower in the morning before breakfast.
8 ✓
Exercise 3
1 b **2** f **3** d **4** c **5** a **6** e

Page 41
Language in Use
Exercise 1
1 accommodation **2** ✓ **3** amazement **4** ✓ **5** decision
6 enjoyment **7** entertainment **8** ✓ **9** excitement **10** illness
11 improvement **12** ✓ **13** operation **14** organisation
15 prescription **16** protection **17** ✓
Exercise 2
1 accommodation **2** entertainment **3** organisation **4** equipment
5 protection **6** decision
Exercise 3
1 prescription **2** treatment **3** infection **4** operation **5** improvement
6 communication **7** enjoyment **8** agreement

Page 42
Writing
Exercise 1
1 simple **2** continuous, when **3** tenses
Exercise 2
3 Students' own answers
Exercise 3
1 B **2** D **3** A **4** C
Exercise 4
Possible answer:
Title
Possible Plan: an interesting title to engage the reader
My notes: A birthday surprise
First paragraph
Possible plan: Set the scene: Who is Esme? Who else is there? What are they doing? How does Esme feel?
My notes: Esme had always secretly been scared of horses. 'Why did Mum give me a riding trip for my birthday?' she thought.
Middle paragraph
Possible plan: What happens? Is Esme finding it easy or difficult? Does she have an accident?
My notes: Esme had always secretly been scared of horses. 'Why did Mum give me a riding trip for my birthday?' she thought.
Last paragraph
Possible plan: describe what happened at the end, finish with the ending they've given you
My notes: Esme's heart was beating wildly, but she held on and managed to stop the horse. 'I did it!' thought Esme proudly.

Page 43
Progress check
Exercise 1
1 c **2** a **3** b **4** b **5** c **6** a **7** b **8** c
Exercise 2
1 hurts **2** skin **3** an operation **4** injured **5** shoulders **6** get over
7 cheered up **8** come down with **9** get **10** have **11** make **12** taking
13 doing **14** take
Cumulative progress
Exercise 3
1 up **2** get **3** have **4** able **5** less **6** that **7** out **8** must

UNIT 6
Pages 44–45
Reading
Exercise 1
1 changed **2** set up **3** home baking **4** young people **5** tips
6 elderly **7** worldwide
Exercise 2
1 B **2** C **3** D **4** A **5** B
Exercise 3
1 d **2** b **3** h **4** g **5** a **6** e **7** c **8** f

Page 46
Grammar 1
Exercise 1
1 that/which **2** who/that **3** where **4** which **5** whose **6** who
7 when **8** whose
Exercise 2
1 – **2** (that) **3** (which) **4** – **5** (who) **6** –
Exercise 3
1 I can remember the year/time when our local food festival started.
2 The food festival, which was really good, was on last weekend. / The food festival, which was on last weekend, was really good.
3 I watched a celebrity chef who made a delicious curry.
4 There were lots of stalls which sold different kinds of food.
5 There was a pop-up restaurant where you could eat Italian food.
6 The organisers, who worked very hard, say it's been the most successful year ever.

Pages 46–47
Vocabulary
Exercise 1
1 juicy **2** sweet **3** salty **4** sour **5** bitter **6** spicy
Exercise 2
1 c **2** a **3** c **4** b **5** b **6** a **7** b **8** c
Exercise 3
1 tasteless **2** mixture **3** fried **4** frying **5** spicy **6** creamy **7** boiled
8 satisfied

Page 47
Grammar 2
Exercise 1
1 – **2** the **3** the **4** the **5** an **6** a **7** the **8** the **9** – **10** a
Exercise 2
1 an **2** the **3** The **4** – **5** – **6** the **7** the **8** the **9** a

Page 48
Listening
Exercise 1
1 a 3 b 1 c 2 **2** Students' own answers
Exercise 2
1 food **2** wear **3** lasts **4** sports **5** demonstrations **6** run by
Exercise 3
1 4,000 kilos **2** Young people **3** four/4 days **4** skiing and skating
5 famous chefs **6** volunteers

Pages 48–49
Speaking
Exercise 1
Students should tick:
Places: kitchen, home
People: family, father and son
Action: chopping, preparing food
Exercise 2
1 shows **2** are wearing **3** look **4** 's/is watching **5** are **6** has got
7 's/is chopping **8** 's/is made **9** 's/is talking **10** is
Exercise 3
Students' own answers

Page 49
Language in Use
Exercise 1
1 f **2** h **3** b **4** e **5** a **6** g **7** d **8** c
Exercise 2
1 B **2** C **3** D **4** B **5** C **6** C **7** C **8** A

Page 50

Writing

Exercise 1
1 is **2** all **3** before

Exercise 2
1 What about making a Spanish omelette?
2 … you could also add vegetables like peppers for variety.
3 Why not serve it with some olives and salad?

Exercise 3

Suggested answers
1 Why don't you try some nasi goreng? It's fried rice with chicken or seafood.
2 You could buy some tortilla chips and guacamole.
3 What about going for a set lunch menu called table d'hôte?
4 Don't forget to try mezze – it's a collection of hot and cold dishes, salads and dips that are shared at the table.
5 One thing you could do is go to a local market and buy some fresh fish.

Exercise 4
Students' own answers

Page 51

Progress check

Exercise 1
1 who **2** a **3** when **4** whose **5** – **6** – **7** the **8** –/that/which

Exercise 2
1 crisps **2** mixing **3** sour **4** satisfied **5** frying **6** Creamed **7** tasteless **8** wide **9** fell **10** make **11** up **12** cut **13** chop up **14** off

Cumulative progress

Exercise 3
1 C **2** B **3** D **4** A **5** A **6** C **7** B **8** D

UNIT 7

Pages 52–53

Reading

Exercise 1
1 D **2** B **3** E **4** A **5** F **6** C

Exercise 2
1 a **2** b **3** b

Exercise 3
1 F **2** T **3** F **4** F **5** T **6** F **7** F **8** T

Exercise 4
1 barcode **2** bargains **3** worth it **4** change your mind **5** price tags **6** budget **7** sticking to **8** reduces

Page 54

Grammar 1

Exercise 1
1 saw, had bought **2** spilt/spilled, had given **3** had worked, decided
4 hadn't thought, suggested **5** bought, had always borrowed
6 Had you never shopped, took

Exercise 2
1 had seen **2** had been shopping **3** hadn't tried **4** had sold
5 hadn't been waiting **6** been paying

Exercise 3
1 needed **2** wanted **3** had seen **4** had been saving up
5 didn't want **6** discovered **7** hadn't noticed **8** told
9 had been making **10** hadn't sold

Pages 54–55

Vocabulary

Exercise 1
1 cost, bargain, special offer, cash card, half price, order
2 second-hand, brand-new, rent

Exercise 2
1 b **2** a **3** d **4** c **5** f **6** e

Exercise 3
1 window shopping **2** it's on me **3** Go on a shopping spree
4 like a bull in a china shop

Page 55

Grammar 2

Exercise 1
1 b **2** a **3** c **4** a **5** b **6** c **7** b **8** c

Exercise 2
1 less **2** the most famous **3** not as important **4** least expensive
5 the best **6** less popular **7** the ugliest **8** more comfortable than

Page 56

Listening

Exercise 1
1 d **2** c **3** a **4** b

Exercise 2
1 Tom **2** Beth **3** the boy's mum **4** the boy **5** Jane **6** Luke
7 Michael's mum

Exercise 3
1 C **2** B **3** A **4** A

Pages 56–57

Speaking

Exercise 1
1 Have **2** Would **3** Do **4** Who **5** How **6** Do you prefer

Exercise 2
1 How about you, Personally **2** What do you think, I agree with you
3 Do you agree that, That's a good question **4** Why do you think that
5 I'm not sure

Exercise 3
Students' own answers

Page 57

Language in Use

Exercise 1
1 assistant **2** buyer **3** customer **4** electrician **5** lawyer **6** librarian
7 managing director **8** mechanic **9** optician **10** owner
11 receptionist **12** shopper **13** supervisor **14** visitor

Exercise 2
1 librarian **2** receptionist **3** supervisor **4** assistant **5** shoppers
6 customers **7** director **8** buyer

Page 58

Writing

Exercise 1
1 title, read **2** direct **3** sets the scene, main events, happened

Exercise 2
2

Exercise 3
1 'This necklace is beautiful,' he said. **2** ✓ **3** 'Can I help you?' said the assistant. 'Yes, I'm looking for a present,' Sarah answered. **4** ✓
5 'I'll take it,' Sarah said. 'Thanks!'

Exercise 4

Suggested answers

Possible Plan:
1 Start with the sentence they've given you. Who is Sarah (a teenager? an adult?) Who is her friend? (male or female? age?) Why does she want to buy a special present for her friend? (a special occasion? a birthday? a surprise? to say thank you?)

My notes:
Sarah is 15 years old.
It's her friend Jamie's 16th birthday.
He's in her class at school.

Possible Plan:
2 Where does she go to buy it? (a shop? a market? somewhere else?) Is anyone with her? Who?

My notes:
An antique shop – Jamie loves old things.
No, she's alone.

Possible Plan:
3 What present does she find?

My notes:
An old watch

Possible Plan:
4 What happens in the end? What is special about the present?

My notes:
Sarah buys the watch and finds it has the initials 'J.M.T' on the back – exactly the same as Jamie's! She's found the perfect present.

Exercise 5

Suggested answer
Sarah wanted the perfect present for her friend – but what? It was her friend Jamie's 16th birthday and she'd been looking for something brilliant for ages.

One Saturday as she was walking into town she passed a shop she'd never noticed before. The sign in the window said 'Antiques'. She went in and started looking at the dusty shelves.
Suddenly, she saw a beautiful old watch. 'How much is this?' she asked the shop assistant.
'Fifteen pounds,' he replied.
'I'll take it!' Sarah said happily.
Later, when she was wrapping the watch, Sarah noticed it had the initials J.M.T on the back – Jamie's initials! She really had found the perfect present!

Page 59

Progress check

Exercise 1
1 hadn't been working **2** had bought **3** had been waiting **4** Had you been looking **5** hadn't been **6** had been dancing

Exercise 2
1 the nicest **2** expensive than **3** carefully than **4** the fastest **5** the most interesting **6** less popular **7** as high **8** the worst

Exercise 3
1 shop around **2** save up **3** take **4** run out of **5** cash card **6** offer **7** second-hand **8** price **9** return **10** order **11** shopping **12** on

Cumulative progress

Exercise 4
1 C **2** B **3** A **4** D **5** C **6** A **7** B **8** D

UNIT 8

Pages 60–61

Reading

Exercise 1
1 T **2** F **3** T **4** F **5** T

Exercise 2
A 2 **B** 1 **C** 3 **D** 6 **E** 5

Exercise 3
1 a **2** a **3** a **4** b **5** b **6** b **7** a **8** a

Page 62

Grammar 1

Exercise 1
1 create, is used **2** meet, are shown **3** is decided **4** cut, are made **5** aren't kept **6** pick, are ordered **7** have, is **8** choose, takes, arrive

Exercise 2
1 are often started by **2** they are seen **3** were copied **4** hair was burnt **5** were set by **6** were admired by **7** White powder was used **8** Their hair wasn't dyed **9** was discovered **10** were coloured **11** white of an egg was spread **12** were hidden

Pages 62–63

Vocabulary

Exercise 1
1 handbag, gloves **2** earring, jumper **3** jewellery, bracelet **4** sandals, socks **5** sweatshirt, trainers **6** cap, collar **7** suit, sleeves **8** button, pocket **9** necklace, wristband **10** shorts, belt

Exercise 2
1 take … off **2** worn out **3** do up **4** hanging up **5** try … on **6** put on **7** dress up

Exercise 3
1 creative **2** fashionable **3** clothing **4** designed **5** beauty **6** amazement **7** trend **8** appearance

Page 63

Grammar 2

Exercise 1
1 isn't it **2** will you **3** has he **4** didn't she **5** should I **6** isn't it **7** will you **8** shall we **9** do they **10** did you **11** haven't they **12** could I

Exercise 2
1 aren't you, shall we **2** did they, didn't they **3** shouldn't I, are you **4** has it, would they **5** can't he, isn't he

Page 64

Listening

Exercise 1
1 a place, a year **2** an adjective **3** a noun **4** a place, a year **5** Possible answer: singers **6** Suggested answers big/huge/large/wide

Exercise 2
1 France **2** famous **3** 1873 **4** California **5** singers **6** huge

Pages 64–65

Speaking

Exercise 1
Students' own answers

Exercise 2
1 but it isn't as practical as **2** more formal than, whereas **3** However **4** On the one hand, On the other hand **5** equally uncomfortable

Exercise 3
Students' own answers

Page 65

Language in Use

Exercise 1
1 visiting, to wear **2** to get, spending **3** looking, to find

Exercise 2
1 to spend **2** replacing **3** to buy **4** looking for **5** going **6** to find **7** to get **8** losing

Exercise 3
1 to buy **2** getting **3** spending too **4** to fit **5** to like **6** to try

Page 66

Writing

Exercise 1
1 description, feelings **2** adverbs **3** simple

Exercise 2
1 C **2** A **3** D **4** B

Exercise 3
1 suggested **2** boring, excited **3** Luckily **4** fantastic, perfect **5** nervous **6** amazing

Exercise 4
Suggested answers
1 I usually feel bored.
2 Today I felt excited because I was looking forward to the school dance.
3 I had to buy an outfit for the school dance.
4 I chose an amazing outfit, it was perfect for the dance. I was really pleased.
5 Everyone loved my outfit. I had a wonderful time.
6 I felt really happy – I'll never forget that amazing evening.

Possible answer:

Title
Purpose: make the reader want to read your story
My notes: The perfect outfit?

Paragraph 1:
Purpose: use the sentence you are given;
describe the situation and your first thoughts/feelings
My notes: Usually, I hate shopping for clothes, but this time was different. Today I felt excited because I was looking forward to the school dance – I had to buy an outfit for it.

Paragraphs 2&3:
Purpose: describe what happened and how you felt
My notes: I looked and looked and was about to give up when I saw an amazing outfit! It was perfect for the dance. I was really pleased!

Paragraph 4:
Purpose: describe what happened and how you felt in the end
My notes: Everyone loved my outfit and I had a wonderful time. I felt really happy – I'll never forget that amazing evening.

Page 67

Progress check

Exercise 1
1 were taken by **2** are produced **3** were made of **4** was given **5** wasn't cancelled **6** Is … filmed

Exercise 2
1 shall we **2** have you **3** couldn't she **4** will you **5** isn't it **6** don't they **7** had it **8** won't we

Exercise 3
1 bracelet, beautiful, try **2** trendy, gloves, dress **3** clothes, hang them up, suits **4** do up, shorts, apparent **5** cap, has on, old-fashioned

Cumulative progress

Exercise 4
1 can **2** used **3** have **4** away **5** despite **6** than **7** is **8** by

UNIT 9

Pages 68–69

Reading

Exercise 1
1 b **2** a

Exercise 2
1 D **2** C **3** C **4** D

Exercise 3
1 e **2** a **3** g **4** b **5** f **6** h **7** c **8** d

Page 70

Grammar 1

Exercise 1
1 a **2** b **3** a **4** c **5** c **6** a **7** c **8** b

Exercise 2
1 when I see **2** What would they do **3** I'll go **4** ✓ **5** ✓
6 unless there is / if there isn't

Exercise 3
1 went to another team, the fans would be **2** won't let you go
3 Call me if you need **4** would go to the final if the tickets weren't
5 my team loses, I get **6** unless I'm ill

Pages 70–71

Vocabulary

Exercise 1
1 gamer **2** referee **3** athlete **4** acrobat **5** cyclist **6** gymnast

Exercise 2
1 pull out **2** sent … off **3** join in **4** put … off **5** caught on **6** Set up

Exercise 3
1 goes **2** go **3** been **4** went **5** going **6** plays **7** does **8** does **9** play
10 went

Page 71

Grammar 2

Exercise 1
1 when **2** While **3** After **4** before **5** as soon as **6** Once

Exercise 2
1 until **2** I've been / I go **3** I'm doing **4** we put away
5 fixes / has fixed **6** have set up / set up

Page 72

Listening

Exercise 1
1 F **2** O **3** B – The winner gets a gold medal (factual) / and I think that's pretty cool (opinion) **4** B – An instructor will teach you (factual) / so there's no reason to worry (opinion) **5** F **6** O

Exercise 2
1 F **2** B **3** F **4** O **5** F **6** O

Exercise 3
1 B **2** C **3** A **4** B **5** A

Pages 72–73

Speaking

Exercise 1
1 does **2** have **3** Take **4** quite **5** can't **6** keen

Exercise 2
1 Are you a member of any sports team?
2 Do any of your friends do a sport or activity that you would like to try?
3 Do you prefer watching sports at the stadium, at home on TV, or at a café on a big screen?
4 Have you ever been injured while you were playing a sport?

Exercise 3
Students' own answers

Page 73

Language in Use

Exercise 1
1 includes **2** consists **3** contains **4** involves **5** hobbies **6** sports **7** activities **8** see **9** dreamt of **10** view **11** Imagine **12** threw
13 catch **14** kick **15** hit

Exercise 2
1 B **2** C **3** D **4** A **5** B **6** C **7** A **8** D

Page 74

Writing

Exercise 1
1 points, paragraph, sentence **2** opinion, offers

Exercise 2
3

Exercise 3

Giving opinions	Making suggestions	Making offers
As far as I'm concerned … In my view … Personally, I think …	How about …? Why don't you …?	I'll …, if you like. Would you like me to …?

Exercise 4
Suggested answers
1 In my view, that's a fantastic idea!
2 Why don't you speak to the head teacher about it?
3 I'll make posters for the team, if you like.

Page 75

Progress check

Exercise 1
1 soon, will/'ll **2** could/would, have **3** go, were, wouldn't **4** while, have
5 until, were **6** after, unless **7** when, don't **8** before, weren't

Exercise 2
1 c **2** b **3** a **4** b **5** a **6** c **7** c **8** b **9** a **10** b

Cumulative progress

Exercise 3
1 athletes **2** appearance **3** protection **4** illnesses **5** prescription
6 happiness **7** amazement **8** decision

UNIT 10

Pages 76–77

Reading

Exercise 1
1 C **2** – **3** A **4** E **5** D **6** B

Exercise 2
2

Exercise 3
1 The actors' appearance **2** The actors **3** The 1930s **4** He won an Oscar **5** To create realistic injuries **6** Make adjustments or repairs

Exercise 4
1 essential **2** took off **3** take them for granted **4** masks **5** scale
6 under pressure **7** injuries **8** film crews **9** adjustments

Page 78

Grammar 1

Exercise 1
1 b **2** b **3** a **4** a **5** a **6** b

Exercise 2
1 hadn't gone, wouldn't have seen **2** hadn't got, wouldn't have been
3 not have heard, had become **4** hadn't done, wouldn't have got
5 had decided, not have become **6** wouldn't have won, hadn't acted

Pages 78–79

Vocabulary

Exercise 1
1 festival, stage, performers **2** journalist, musician, studio
3 presenter, celebrity **4** gallery, museum

Exercise 2
1 e **2** a **3** c **4** f **5** b **6** d

Exercise 3
1 go **2** to show off **3** of directing **4** to practise **5** to meet
6 of winning

Page 79

Grammar 2

Exercise 1
1 b **2** c **3** a **4** c **5** b **6** a

Exercise 2
1 will have/get her life story filmed **2** had her violin broken
3 was having/getting her nails done **4** has/gets his dogs walked
5 have had the contract checked **6** won't have the studio painted

Page 80

Listening

Exercise 1
1 famous **2** 7.30 **3** record **4** wrote herself **5** drama teacher

Exercise 2
1 film **2** posters **3** library **4** hair **5** town centre **6** 10 July

Pages 80–81

Speaking

Exercise 1

Suggested answers

1 I completely agree. You can learn so much at a museum.
2 Really? Can you recommend a few that I might like?
3 That sounds like fun. I haven't been to one yet, but I'd like to go.
4 Same here. I love the theatre because it's so exciting.
5 I'm not sure I agree. Not everyone is interested in it.
6 I think you're right. They just want to be famous and have lots of money.
7 That's interesting! What's the name of your band?
8 I never thought of that. Maybe I should read more!

Exercise 2

1 a **2** a **3** b

Exercise 3

1 I completely agree; Really?
2 Same here; That's interesting!
3 that sounds like fun; I see what you mean, but; I'm not sure I agree

Page 81

Language in Use

Exercise 1

1 could find **2** hadn't broken **3** would perform **4** knew **5** had been **6** had had **7** wouldn't talk **8** hadn't bought

Exercise 2

1 I wish I hadn't left my phone at home this morning.
2 If only I knew where my favourite singer lived.
3 If only he had been able to go backstage at last night's concert.
4 I wish I didn't have to study tonight.
5 If only the music festival wasn't/weren't so far away.
6 I wish you wouldn't watch TV all the time.

Exercise 3

1 wish **2** of **3** to **4** would **5** allowed **6** let **7** only **8** able

Page 82

Writing

Exercise 1

1 asking a question **2** give instructions

Exercise 2

1 T **2** F **3** F **4** T

Exercise 3

Suggested answers
2 Decide on the location – outside is best, e.g. in a park
3 Use a variety of shots – close-up, zoom, moving, from a distance
4 Edit the video, matching the shots to the music and upload using social media

Exercise 4

Possible answer:
Title
Purpose: explain what the article is about
My notes: Make a music video!
Paragraph 1
Purpose: introduce the subject and explain why it's fun to make a music video
My notes: Have you ever wanted to make a music video? It's not difficult and it's great fun!
Paragraphs 2–4
Purpose: give advice and suggestions, using your notes from Exercise 3
My notes: Choose a song or record your own. Then you should decide on the location for the filming. It's best to do it outside. When you film it, don't forget to use a variety of shots (close-up, from a distance, moving). Edit the video, trying to match the shots to the music. Upload it using social media. Good luck!

Page 83

Progress check

Exercise 1

1 had had **2** have gone **3** organised **4** it made **5** I'm getting **6** knew **7** hadn't rained **8** fixed

Exercise 2

1 c **2** a **3** c **4** b **5** b **6** c **7** c **8** a

Cumulative progress

Exercise 3

1 are **2** them **3** like **4** worst **5** an **6** For **7** few **8** who

UNIT 11

Pages 84–85

Reading

Exercise 1

1 E **2** G **3** H **4** C **5** A **6** B **7** D **8** F

Exercise 2

1 T **2** F **3** T **4** F **5** F **6** T **7** F **8** T

Exercise 3

1 B **2** G **3** C **4** E **5** H

Exercise 4

1 tools **2** developing your online brand **3** shots **4** coding **5** grow **6** concentration **7** survival skills **8** energetic

Page 86

Grammar 1

Exercise 1

1 was going **2** at that moment **3** had **4** the day before **5** could **6** the following day **7** that **8** had gone **9** before **10** would

Exercise 2

1 (that) she couldn't come to the school dance
2 (that) his best friend didn't like writing essays
3 (that) they/we were going to visit the science museum the next/following day
4 (that) Lucy and Helen would help him with his art project
5 (that) they had to finish their maths homework that night
6 (that) he was watching an interesting documentary then
7 (that) Andy could explain it to me
8 (that) her cousins might come to the school production

Exercise 3

1 I went to a great camp last summer
2 I've already read half of your book
3 I'll never understand physics
4 My class has/have been working hard all term
5 I can help you to revise tomorrow
6 We're going to go snowboarding later today

Pages 86–87

Vocabulary

Exercise 1

1 taking, pass **2** reading, studying **3** primary, secondary **4** subject, lesson **5** student, pupil

Exercise 2

1 over **2** out **3** behind **4** up **5** out **6** in

Exercise 3

1 b **2** e **3** a **4** f **5** d **6** c

Page 87

Grammar 2

Exercise 1

1 b **2** a **3** b **4** c **5** c **6** a

Exercise 2

1 me if/whether I had felt nervous
2 me what I had talked about
3 me if/whether I had been able to answer confidently
4 me how long the interview had gone on for
5 me if/whether I thought I had passed
6 me when I would get my results
7 me if/whether I could give her some advice

Page 88

Listening

Exercise 1

1 science **2** history **3** art **4** maths

Exercise 2

1 B **2** C **3** A **4** B

Pages 88–89

Speaking

Exercise 1

1 C **2** B **3** A **4** C **5** A/B **6** A **7** B **8** C **9** A/B

Exercise 2

1 clear **2** guess **3** as **4** Perhaps **5** seems **6** sure **7** could **8** might **9** possible

Exercise 3

Students' own answers

Page 89

Language in Use

Exercise 1
1 depth **2** strength **3** truth **4** warmth **5** belief **6** relief **7** thief
8 success **9** excess **10** solution **11** evolution **12** children **13** lives
14 people **15** terrible

Exercise 2
1 daily **2** loss **3** proof **4** speech **5** choice **6** thought **7** secondary
8 depth

Exercise 3
1 terrible **2** electricity **3** lives **4** Children **5** solution **6** daily
7 depth **8** success

Page 90

Writing

Exercise 1
1 words **2** idea **3** points **4** add

Exercise 2
1 a **2** b **3** a

Exercise 3
Suggested answers
1 I'm thinking of ... / I'm considering ...
2 I want to ... because ... / A talent contest is a good way of ...
3 Would you like to ... / Could you ...

Exercise 4
Suggested answers

Opening
Purpose: say hello
My notes: Hi Alex,

First point
Purpose: explain what you want to do
My notes: I'm considering organising a talent contest at school.

Second point
Purpose: say why you want to do it
My notes: I think it would be a great idea because it's a good way to raise money for the school.

Third point
Purpose: ask your friend to help
My notes: Would you like to help me?

Closing
Purpose: say goodbye
My notes: See you!

Page 91

Progress check

Exercise 1
1 his **2** loved **3** school was **4** whether I had found **5** the time was
6 that **7** had to **8** if I would

Exercise 2
1 break, read, have **2** took, study, go, pass **3** lesson, hand, taught, copy
4 primary, learning, pupils

Cumulative progress

Exercise 3
1 B **2** D **3** C **4** A **5** B **6** D **7** C **8** D

UNIT 12

Pages 92–93

Reading

Exercise 1
1 c **2** g **3** f **4** a **5** b

Exercise 2
1 TreesForAll **2** On Saturday **3** Amelie and Jake

Exercise 3
1 C **2** A **3** B **4** B **5** A

Exercise 4
1 press **2** sign up **3** picking (us) up **4** give away **5** hole **6** experts
7 remove **8** equipment

Page 94

Grammar 1

Exercise 1
1 have sat **2** have finished **3** have **4** been **5** won't have completed
6 get **7** Will you have **8** will have cleaned

Exercise 2
1 finish / have finished **2** will have planted **3** will have grown
4 will have arrived **5** won't have wasted **6** will have contributed
7 start **8** will have helped

Exercise 3
1 I will have read the book before the next lesson.
2 How many countries will you have visited by 2020?
3 They won't have built the house by the time she arrives.
4 I'm sure they won't have left yet.
5 Will she have finished her exams when we go on holiday?
6 We will have returned by the time it gets dark.

Pages 94–95

Vocabulary

Exercise 1
1 rainforest, snakes, gorillas, monkeys, tigers
2 deserts, camel, lizards
4 oceans, Dolphins, whales, sharks

Exercise 2
1 wake **2** grow **3** bringing **4** end

Exercise 3
1 sunlight, natural **2** disgusting, poisonous **3** explanation, scientific
4 tropical, scenery

Page 95

Grammar 2

Exercise 1
1 c **2** a **3** d **4** b **5** e

Exercise 2
1 must **2** should **3** might **4** couldn't **5** can't **6** shouldn't **7** could
8 should

Exercise 3
1 should/ought to have come **2** would have joined **3** couldn't have had
4 can't have seen **5** could/might have been **6** must have been

Page 96

Listening

Exercise 1
Statements 1 and 4 must be logically true.

Exercise 2
5

Exercise 3
1 c **2** a **3** b **4** b **5** c **6** a **7** c

Pages 96–97

Speaking

Exercise 1
Students' own answers

Exercise 2
1 So shall we make a final decision? **2** Yes, let's do that. **3** Of all the options, I think the tiger is the best. **4** I agree. I'd also choose the tiger.
5 Great! We agree, then. **6** That sounds like a good decision.

Exercise 3
1 which one **2** I'd **3** first choice **4** we should choose **5** with each other

Page 97

Language in Use

Exercise 1
1 Did **2** is being **3** can't **4** were **5** should **6** have **7** Is **8** don't
9 hasn't been **10** is having

Exercise 2
1 Where does **2** I had been **3** is often **4** Was it **5** must have been
6 were/are recorded **7** How are they **8** Has the beach **9** did you feed
10 We had

Exercise 3
1 is **2** does **3** are **4** has **5** was **6** have **7** been **8** be **9** being **10** is

Page 98

Writing

Exercise 1
1 formal, should, shouldn't **2** should **3** reasons

Exercise 2
Agree

Exercise 3
a The main reason **b** Another reason **c** Because of this/So
d Because of this/So

Exercise 4
1 A **2** D **3** D **4** A **5** A **6** D

Exercise 5
Possible answer:
Paragraph 1
Purpose: introduce the subject and give your opinion in general
My notes: Zoos a good thing – they protect endangered species
I believe that ... The main reason for this is that ...
Paragraph 2
Purpose: give one key point and explain the reason
My notes: Zoos allow people to see and learn about animals – they are more likely to want to protect their habitat
Another reason is that ... Because of this ...
Paragraph 3
Purpose: give another key point and explain the reason
My notes: Zoos provide good facilities for animals. The animals have a safe environment and don't die
So ...
Paragraph 4
Purpose: conclude with a summary and your opinion
My notes: It is acceptable if zoos are good quality and the animals are well looked after.
I believe ... To conclude, ...
Possible answer:
Paragraph 2: Another reason is that zoos allow people to see and learn about animals. Because of this, they are more likely to want to protect the animals' natural habitat.

Paragraph 3: Finally, good zoos provide great facilities for animals. So, they have a safe environment with plenty of space and are well-cared for, whereas in the wild they might die young.

Page 99
Progress check
Exercise 1
1 won't have arrived **2** Will you have handed in **3** will we have done **4** will have had **5** will you have known **6** Will it have got
Exercise 2
1 could **2** shouldn't **3** must **4** might **5** couldn't **6** can't
Exercise 3
1 natural, brought up **2** Whales, elephants **3** lions, grasslands, tigers, rainforests **4** poisonous, end up **5** deserts, camel **6** scientist, keep up **7** grew up, disgusting

Cumulative progress
Exercise 4
1 natural **2** scenery **3** protection **4** tropical **5** treatment **6** survival **7** Scientific **8** loss

OPTIMISE PRACTICE TEST
Pages 100–108
Reading
Part 1
1 A **2** B **3** C **4** B **5** A
Part 2
6 G **7** D **8** C **9** F **10** A
Part 3
11 A **12** B **13** A **14** A **15** B **16** B **17** B **18** A **19** A **20** B
Part 4
21 C **22** B **23** A **24** D **25** A
Part 5
26 C **27** D **28** B **29** A **30** C **31** A **32** B **33** D **34** C **35** A

Pages 109–111
Writing
Part 1
1 since **2** reading **3** used to **4** too expensive / too much money **5** until
Part 2
6 Example Answer
Hi Katy
How are you? I'm on holiday. I'm staying in a great hotel. My room is huge! The best thing is the beach. It's fantastic and I spend most of the day swimming. Where are you going for your holiday?
Write soon,
John
Part 3
7 Example Answer
Hi Tom,
We have a lot of traditions in Greece. My favourite are the May Day traditions. I love it because it means spring is coming. People make decorations with flowers. They put it on the front door of their house until it becomes dry.
Fire jumping is another May Day tradition. Women dance around a fire in a large circle and they sing songs about May and spring. The young children wet their hair and clothes and jump over the fire. It's really exciting!
Would you like to see it? Come and visit me in May!
Write soon,
Anna

8 Example Answer
Kelly looked down and saw a wallet. She picked it up from the road. It was a man's wallet and it looked very old. Kelly wondered what to do with it. She was sure the person who lost it was worrying about it. If there was an address inside, she could find the owner and give it to him. Kelly opened the wallet and looked for the information she needed. Unfortunately, there wasn't an address or a name, but there was a lot of money inside. Kelly decided to go to the police. Hopefully, someone would look for it there.

Pages 112–115
Listening
Part 1
1 B **2** C **3** A **4** B **5** C **6** B **7** A
Part 2
8 A **9** C **10** C **11** C **12** B **13** A
Part 3
14 knowledge **15** 6/six **16** sports **17** August **18** future **19** newspaper
Part 4
20 A **21** B **22** A **23** A **24** B **25** B

Pages 116–119
Speaking
Part 1
Students' own answers
Part 2
Students' own answers
Part 3
Students' own answers
Part 4
Students' own answers

Audioscripts

UNIT 1 | STUDENT'S BOOK

1.05 | Listening, page 8, Exercise 2

1

Teacher: Welcome back everyone. This term we've got someone new joining us. Everyone, this is Jared. Say hello to Jared!

Children: Hello/Hi Jared!

2

Boy: It's great, isn't it?

Girl: It's OK. I don't know most people here, so …

Boy: I'm Mike. You know me now!

Girl: Hi Mike. Nice to meet you. I'm Samantha. I'm new in the area.

3

Presenter: Welcome back to 'Question The Answers', the show where you can win a lot of money on every question – if you're clever! Our next contestant is Robert.

4

Presenter: I'm joined in the studio now by Josephine Harper. Josephine, welcome.

Josephine: It's lovely to be here.

1.06 | Listening, page 8, Exercises 3 and 4.

1 What job does Jared want to do when he's older?

Teacher: Welcome back everyone. This term we've got someone new joining us. Everyone, this is Jared. Say hello to Jared!

Children: Hello/Hi Jared!

Teacher: Jared, can you introduce yourself to the class?

Jared: Hi everyone – my name's Jared. I'm fourteen years old, and I live in the middle of town with my mum and dad and my sister Ellie. Both my parents work. My mum's a computer programmer and my dad's a nurse. They're both great jobs, but I want to be a dancer when I'm older. My sister Ellie wants to be a teacher, I think.

2 What does Samantha agree to?

Boy: It's great, isn't it?

Girl: It's OK. I don't know most people here, so …

Boy: I'm Mike. You know me now!

Girl: Hi Mike. Nice to meet you. I'm Samantha. I'm new in the area.

Boy: Can I get you something to eat? There's some great pizza in the kitchen.

Girl: I'm fine. I'm not hungry, thanks.

Boy: Do you fancy dancing?

Girl: I don't think so, thanks. I'll just stay here.

Boy: A drink of something? Maybe some lemonade?

Girl: That sounds nice, thanks.

Boy: I'll be right back!

3 What does Robert have at the moment?

Presenter: Welcome back to 'Question The Answers', the show where you can win a lot of money on every question – if you're clever! Our next contestant is Robert.

Now, Robert's twenty-two years old, works as a builder – that's right, isn't it, Robert?

Robert: That's right, yes.

Presenter: And you're an animal lover.

Robert: Yes. My dream is to have a farm one day with lots of horses in the fields, and I love cats and rabbits, of course – my brother's got several – but right now I've got a couple of mice at home called Charlie and Benny and they keep me company.

4 What is Josephine studying?

Presenter: I'm joined in the studio now by Josephine Harper. Josephine, welcome.

Josephine: It's lovely to be here.

Presenter: Now, not all of you will know who Josephine is, so let me explain. In some ways, Josephine's just a normal university student studying – what is it? Maths?

Josephine: Geography, actually.

Presenter: Right. But she's written a science book for children, a physics book about space and time and the wonders of the universe, and it's extremely popular. Josephine, tell us – how did you come up with the idea for the book?

Josephine: Well, it's quite interesting actually. I've got …

1.07 | Speaking, page 10, Exercise 4

Interviewer: Hello. What's your surname, Nisha?

Nisha: Gupta

Interviewer: How do you spell that?

Nisha: G_u_p_t_a

Interviewer: And what's your surname, Alfie?

Alfie: Dugmore

Interviewer: How do you spell that?

Alfie: D_u_g_m_o_r_e

Interviewer: Where do you live, Nisha?

Nisha: I live in a small house in a village called Tiltbury. It's near Manchester.

Interviewer: And Alfie. Where do you live?

Alfie: I live in Manchester.

Interviewer: And do you study English at school, Alfie?

Alfie: Yes, I've studied English for nearly six years now. I really enjoy it.

Interviewer: Do you study English at school, Nisha?

Nisha: Yes, I do.

Interviewer: Do you like it?

Nisha: Yes, I do.

Interviewer: What's your favourite school subject, Alfie?

Alfie: My favourite school subject is probably History, but I really like languages too.

Interviewer: Nisha, what's your favourite school subject?

Nisha: Maths, I think.

Interviewer: And what do you enjoy doing in your free time, Nisha?

Nisha: Well, I don't have a lot of free time, but when I do, I enjoy chatting online with my friends and listening to music in my room.

Interviewer: And what about you Alfie?

Alfie: I don't have a lot of free time during the week either, but at weekends I play a lot of sports. In the winter I play football and in the summer I play cricket.

Interviewer: Alfie, please tell me about your best friend.

Alfie: He's called Ben.

Interview: And Nisha, please tell me about your best friend.

Nisha: I don't have a best friend exactly, as I have many friends. But Charlotte is a very close friend. I'd say she's one of the friendliest and kindest people I know. She's good fun to be with too.

Interviewer: Thanks Alfie and Nisha.

UNIT 2 | STUDENT'S BOOK

1.12 | Listening, page 18, exercises 3 and 4

Interviewer: Hello. Leyla Murphy is an expert on the different ways people around the world live. Leyla, could you tell us about that?

Leyla: It's something that I've been interested in since I was around sixteen. I used to want to be an architect. I would often watch programmes about unusual buildings on television. My interest in houses, though, was really started by my dad getting a new job in China. It was a big change to our way of life, but we all went with him.

Interviewer: Did you get the opportunity to visit any unusual homes?

Leyla: Oh, yes. I went to Mongolia and met people living in yurts. A yurt is like a large tent. The family lives in one big room, with a fire in the middle. They stay in one place for a while with their animals and then move on after a few weeks.

Interviewer: So, they never stay in one place for very long?

Leyla: That's right. They put their yurt up where they find water and grass for the animals. After a while, the animals have eaten the grass in the area and it's time to find the next place. One family invited me to spend the night with them in their yurt. I thought it was going to be smoky, and a bit frightening, but it wasn't at all. It was really peaceful and I actually slept very well.

Interviewer: Are there other examples of unusual houses?

Leyla: One of my favourite examples is the underground houses in Tunisia. They dig a large hole in the ground and then dig rooms around the hole. It's perfectly safe, although it's very hot work digging out the rooms. It's worth it, though, when you can step into the cool air and get away from the sun.

Interviewer: Is it mostly the weather that affects the houses people build?

Leyla: Yes, generally. For example, in the Philippines some people live in stilt houses, houses on wooden legs. That can be useful for keeping rats out of the house. It also creates a space under the house for animals like sheep. The real reason, though, is that there are often floods in the area.

Interviewer: Finally, what are your plans for the future?

Leyla: I've just finished a tour visiting houses in countries all around the world, and I've written a book. I think I'm going to rest and then go back to Ireland and design a house using some of the things I learnt.

Interviewer: Thank you for talking to us today.

1.13 | Speaking, page 20, Exercise 4

This is a photo of two blonde girls in a living room. They're sitting on a sofa and both of them are using their laptops. In the background, on the left, there's a small picture on the wall. In the background behind the sofa, there are two red lamps. Between the lamps there's a big picture on the wall. On the left, next to the sofa, there are two small tables. On one of the tables, there's a plant and on the other one, there's a small lamp and some candles. On the sofa, to the left of the girls there are two green cushions and on the sofa to the right of the girls there are two more cushions. In the foreground, on the floor in front of the sofa, there's a bright orange rug. In the foreground on the right, you can see part of another sofa.

UNIT 3 | STUDENT'S BOOK

1.19 | Listening, page 30, exercises 3 and 4

Daniel: Hi, Gemma!

Gemma: Hi, Daniel!

Daniel: Great to see you! How was your summer?

Gemma: Oh, it was brilliant, thanks. I had a fantastic time with my cousins in Canada!

Daniel: Wow! How was the flight over? I know you don't like flying.

Gemma: Well, I got to the airport OK, but when I checked in, they said there was a long delay.

Daniel: Oh, that's not good.

Gemma: No, it wasn't! They told me to keep listening for information about the flight. Well, I didn't mind at first – I wanted to do some shopping, and I had a good book to read – but there weren't any announcements about my flight. I kept looking at the departures board, but all it said was 'Delayed – wait for further information'. Time went so slowly that day!

Daniel: I can imagine!

Gemma: In the end, I spent about three hours going round the shops – I'm sure I went in each shop at least four times! – before they said we could board the plane. After that, the journey was fine.

Daniel: I'm glad! You must show me your photos sometime.

Gemma: I will! So, how was your summer?

Daniel: I went to stay with my cousins too, in Germany. I took two huge suitcases with me – one with all my clothes, and another filled with presents from my family. I've never carried so much luggage on holiday before! Anyway, when I went to check in, they said they had bad news and good news for me.

Gemma: Hmm, interesting! What was the bad news?

Daniel: There was a mistake with my booking.

Gemma: Oh no! That's annoying. So, what was the good news?

Daniel: Well, because of the mistake, they decided to upgrade me to first class – for free! I couldn't believe my luck! In first class, as you may have heard, you get delicious food – the meals we had were fantastic – more comfortable seats, and more leg-room. It was the best flight I've ever been on!

Gemma: Lucky you!

1.20 | Speaking, page 32, Exercises 4 and 5

A boy is leaving his school because his family is moving to another town. The students in his class want to buy him a present. They know he likes skateboarding, cycling and football. Talk together about the different presents they could give him and then decide which one is best.

Girl: So, we know he likes skateboarding, cycling and football. I think they should get him a skateboard.

Boy: Well, he's probably got one already, hasn't he?

Girl: Yes, true.

Boy: A pair of knee pads would be useful.

Girl: Yes, it would. Good idea. Let's just think about the other ideas too. What do you think about the cycling helmet?

Boy: They're quite expensive, aren't they? And maybe he's got one already.

Girl: Yes. How about a pair of gloves?

Boy: Can you say that again, please?

Girl: They could buy some gloves ... you know, to protect his hands when he's skateboarding.

Boy: Well it's the same problem that he may have some already, but people often lose gloves or they get holes in them, so it may be a good suggestion.

Girl: Yes, or the thing for tools might be a good idea.

Boy: What's that? This thing here – you use it when you need to repair something, like a bike wheel or something. Yes, that might be really useful though not the most exciting present to receive.

Girl: Well, we know he's really keen on football. So perhaps they could buy him a ticket to a football match.

Boy: Do you mean a ticket to see his favourite team?

Girl: Yes, that's right.

Boy: I'm sure he'd love that, but do you know how much they cost? I don't think they'd have enough money.

Girl: Oh, I see. That's a shame. Well, how about a football scarf in the colours of his favourite team, then?

Boy: That's a great idea. I think he'll love it!

UNIT 4 | STUDENT'S BOOK

1.25 | Listening, page 40, Exercises 3 and 4

Max: Jenny has been finding out about the world of cinema and she's here to tell us all about it.

Jenny: Hi, Max. First of all, I went to a new type of drive-in cinema. Drive-in cinemas were popular in the 1950s. You drove into the parking area and stayed in your car to watch the movie on the big screen. The latest idea is a new kind of drive-in cinema. The cars are already there, so you don't need to be able to drive. Servers come to the cars and you can buy popcorn and drinks to have while you watch. A new drive-in cinema opens in London next month, so look out for that.

Max: I love that idea. What else?

Jenny: I've also been to a 4D cinema. You probably know about 3D movies, where you wear special glasses and things look very real. In a 4D cinema, your seat moves, you feel air and water on your face and you smell scents connected to what you can see on the screen. For example, during a car chase you might feel all the crashes in your seat. They're great fun for a group. In fact, I'm going back with some friends this weekend!

Max: And I believe you've been to a secret cinema event?

Jenny: Secret cinema is another great idea. You buy your ticket for the film you want to see and go along to the venue, without knowing what to expect. The organisers create a world that is connected to the film you are going to watch. Then you watch the film.

Max: Did you find any more interesting types of cinema?

Jenny: Yes – silent cinema. It's great to have an outdoor cinema in a busy neighbourhood. One thing that stops people having open-air cinemas is the noise. However, with wireless headsets, silent cinema solves that problem. You can sit with your friends and everyone hears the dialogue and the music through headphones.

Max: Finally, what did you find out about traditional cinemas?

Jenny: Well, Max, some cinemas are thinking about allowing you to use your phone during the film. Some young people might find this a very interesting idea, but some others find it annoying when people use their phones in the cinema. That's partly because phones are bright in a dark cinema, and make noises. So we might only see that in some screens at some cinemas. Another cool idea is 'bullet screens'. They have these in some cinemas in China. You can send messages during the film and your messages appear on the screen, next to the film.

Max: Fascinating stuff! Thanks, Jenny.

1.26 | Speaking, page 42, Exercises 4 and 5

Layla: Well, I don't have a lot of free time, but most of the things I enjoy are indoors. I love watching films, so I go to the cinema whenever I can. I'm a big fan of fantasy films. The reason is that you can relax and forget about the real world. What about you Rory?

Rory: Personally, I like doing sport in my free time. I play basketball a lot.

Layla: Me too. I also like swimming. It's really good exercise, so I go to the pool two or three times a week. Do you like swimming?

Rory: A little, but I prefer outdoor activities like rock climbing.

Layla: That's interesting. I've never been rock climbing. It must be exciting. Where do you go to do it?

Rory: During the week, I go to the sports centre where there's a climbing wall.

Layla: That sounds fun. Perhaps I'll try it sometime. Do you go rock climbing anywhere else?

Rory: Yes, I sometimes go rock climbing in the countryside with my dad. Not very often though.

Layla: I suppose that's because it's quite a long journey. You could go camping and stay the whole weekend though.

Rory: That's a great idea. Do you do any outdoor sports?

Layla: Not really. I'm not very keen on being cold. Oh ... except skiing. I did it once and I loved it. I'm going again this winter. Do you enjoy skiing, Rory?

Rory: Not really. I'm not a big fan of winter sports.

Layla: I see. So why do you like basketball and rock climbing so much?

Rory: I'm not sure really.

UNIT 5 | STUDENT'S BOOK

2.05 | Listening, page 52, Exercises 3 and 4

Adam: So, let's see it! Where's your First-Aid Certificate?

Kate: Oh, they haven't given them to us yet. We should get them in a couple of weeks.

Adam: But you did pass, didn't you?

Kate: Well, it wasn't a test. Everyone who attends the course gets a certificate.

Adam: Four hours, though. I don't know how you did it. That must be quite boring.

Kate: The opposite actually! The time flew by. I wanted it to be longer! And I learnt so many different skills.

Adam: I'm surprised. What kind of skills?

Kate: Well, we covered a whole range of things. We started by looking at what to put in a first-aid kit, and how to use it. Then, how to deal with major and minor bleeding, things that have got in your eyes, ears and nose, nose bleeds …

Adam: That must be scary. All that blood!

Kate: We didn't actually see any real blood!

Adam: That's good! I know what you're like when someone cuts their finger.

Kate: Not anymore! Not after this course! Anyway, then we talked about what to do if you find someone who's unconscious – how to put them into the recovery position, how to give them CPR.

Adam: CPR? What's that?

Kate: You know, you've seen it in TV programmes. It's when they push on someone's chest and blow in their mouth.

Adam: Oh yeah. That can't be very useful in real life though.

Kate: You'd be surprised how many thousands of people have survived because of CPR. You never know when you might need to use it – at the swimming pool, in the playground, in the street. If you know how to give CPR, you can save someone's life.

Adam: I guess you're right. So, was that it?

Kate: No way! We did loads of other things too: what to do if someone gets burnt, dealing with allergies and allergic reactions, head injuries, broken arms and legs. It was brilliant!

Adam: Well, you never know, I may do it soon too. It does sound interesting!

Kate: You should. I think you'd enjoy it.

Adam: Cool!

2.06 | Speaking, page 54, Exercises 4 and 5

Student 1: Oh, not bad. On schooldays, it's not too early as I live near school. At the weekend, I can stay in bed longer.

Student 2: Yes, I go to the gym. I try to go once or twice a week – usually at the weekend, when I have time.

Student 3: Oh, I rarely have a bath – maybe once a month. I have a shower every day, though.

Student 4: Well, I have a check-up every six months, and actually at the moment I've got a brace on my teeth to make them straighter, so I have to see my orthodontist once every three or four weeks.

UNIT 6 | STUDENT'S BOOK

2.11 | Listening, page 62, Exercises 3 and 4

Woman: Today, we're looking at world records connected to food. Many of us love to eat a hamburger once in a while, but the world's biggest cheeseburger was enough to feed hundreds of people! It weighed 913.54 kilos and was prepared at the Black Bear Resort in Minnesota, USA. It was over three metres across and had about 24 kilos of tomatoes, more than 18 kilos of American cheese and 8 kilos of pickles on it!

The burger took four hours to cook, and they had to use a crane to flip it over! Even the bread took seven hours to cook. In order to claim the world record, you have to be able to eat the burger, and everyone at the event had a taste. I wouldn't want to do the washing-up! Takeru Kobayashi obviously likes hamburgers because he holds the record. He got through a dozen of them on a TV show! Competitors had three minutes to eat as many as they could. In competitions like this, most people have a special way of eating them. They make each one wet by dipping it in water. That makes it less difficult to get down. Of course, it's important that the hamburgers are all the same size. Before being grilled and then added to the bun, which weighs 50 grams, the burgers all have the same weight: 110 grams.

Kobayashi holds a number of other world records, such as eating 62 slices of pizza in 12 minutes! Before each competition, he gets ready just like an athlete does. His preparation involves eating 6,000 calories a day and then exercising to avoid putting on weight.

And remember – food world records can be dangerous, so don't try any of this at home!

2.12 | Speaking, page 64, Exercise 4

1 The family is having dinner at home together.
2 It looks like it's somebody's birthday. There are balloons and a cake.
3 The cake looks delicious.
4 I think the girl is opening a present.
5 Everyone seems to be having a good time.

UNIT 7 | STUDENT'S BOOK

2.17 | Listening, page 74, Exercise 2

1

Dan: What are you doing, Mum?

Mum: I'm looking at this website and trying to choose a present for your cousin Tim. It's his birthday soon.

2

Mark: This is boring, Aisha. What are we doing here, anyway? You haven't got any money, so you're not going to buy anything.

Aisha: I like looking. I won't be long, Mark.

3

Dad: There you are, Karen. I've been looking for you!

Karen: Sorry, Dad. I can't believe how many stalls there are.

Dad: I know – you should think of having a stall.

Mum: All of these shoes are on special offer. And these are half price.

2.13 | Listening, page 74, Exercises 3 and 5

1 What do they decide to get Tim?

Dan: What are you doing, Mum?

Mum: I'm looking at this website and trying to choose a present for your cousin Tim. It's his birthday soon.

Dan: Get him a gift voucher. Then he can choose something he likes. That's what I always want!

Mum: I know that Dan, but he's two years younger than you. When you're younger, it's nice to actually get a present. I was thinking of this video game.

Dan: Mum! He's eleven, not six! He wouldn't like that.

Mum: I knew you'd be better at this than me! Any ideas, then?

Dan: Why don't you get him a book?

Mum: I don't know what he's already got. Actually, I think you were right. If we get him a gift card, he can choose his own book.

Dan: I told you!

2 **What does Aisha decide to try on?**

Mark: This is boring, Aisha. What are we doing here, anyway? You haven't got any money, so you're not going to buy anything.

Aisha: I like looking. I won't be long, Mark. This jumper's nice, though. It would suit you.

Mark: It is nice! But I won't try it on because I'm not buying anything today.

Aisha: I know! Neither am I! Oh – look at this T-shirt. Lovely colour! It goes well with these shorts here.

Mark: You need some new shorts, don't you?

Aisha: Yeah, but my mum's going to order some online for me.

Mark: Right, shall we go? Put the T-shirt back.

Aisha: Hold on – I'm just going to see what I look like in it. I'll only be a second …

Mark: *[sighs]*

3 **What did Karen like the most?**

Dad: There you are, Karen. I've been looking for you!

Karen: Sorry, Dad. I can't believe how many stalls there are.

Dad: I know – you should think of having a stall.

Karen: Good idea! But they seem to have everything here already. Did you see the handmade soap and candles? Some of them were lovely.

Dad: Yes, they were. My favourite was the cake stall! I've bought several to take home with us.

Karen: Mmmm, great! Do you know what I saw? A fantastic painting of a skyline. It was one of the best paintings I've ever seen. I talked to the artist – he's only thirteen! Dad, can I have one of those cakes now? I'm starving!

4 **How does Jack's mum pay for his shoes?**

Mum: All of these shoes are on special offer. And these are half price. Do you like any of them, Jack?

Jack: I like these, Mum. They'd be good for school.

Mum: Yes, they would. Do you want to try them on?

Jack: OK – hold on. *[short pause]* Yes, they fit really well. They're more comfortable than the shoes I'm wearing now.

Mum: Great! Let's get them. I think I've got a voucher for this shop here somewhere.

Jack: Oh look – it says here because it's a sale you can't use vouchers or gift cards.

Mum: Oh well. It's not important. I'm sure I can use my credit card. I hope so because I haven't got any cash on me.

Jack: Yes, of course you can. Let's find an assistant.

2.19 | Speaking, page 76, Exercise 4

Boy: Right, so, last year, I saved up to buy a really nice birthday present for my mum. It took me about three months!

Girl: Personally, I think that's a great idea. What did you get her?

Boy: I got her a necklace. She loved it! How about you? Have you saved up for anything?

Girl: Yes, I really wanted a new bike, so I saved up for that. People gave me money for my birthday, and I saved some of my pocket money each week.

Boy: How much did it cost?

Girl: It was about 150 euros. It's a great bike! You can see it in this photo – look! What do you think?

Boy: It's amazing.

Girl: So, are you saving up for anything at the moment?

Boy: Yes, I actually want a new bike too. I'm trying to save 10 euros a month.

Girl: When do you think you'll have enough money?

Boy: I'm not sure! Maybe in five or six months. Are you saving up for anything?

Girl: No, not at the moment. I need a new phone, but it's my birthday soon and I'm hoping I'll get one then.

Boy: Who do you think will give it to you?

Girl: That's a good question. My mum and dad, I hope!

UNIT 8 | STUDENT'S BOOK

2.24 | Listening, page 84, Exercises 3 and 4

Trainers are everywhere, aren't they? Do you own a pair? If you do, then you are just like millions of other people around the world. In America, where these shoes are called sneakers, the industry is worth a billion dollars a year! But where did trainers come from?

The first shoes with rubber soles were produced in the 1870s. During that decade, more people became involved in sport. Ordinary shoes with leather soles weren't very good for sports such as tennis. People needed something softer.

In 1916, simple trainers called Keds were made in America. They became popular with children, who wore the shoes for running and playing. Keds are still made today, over a hundred years later.

Another well-known trainer that is still made today is Converse All-Stars. They were first worn in the 1920s by basketball players. The classic design allows a player to move quickly around the court and also supports the ankle.

In the 1950s, young actors, like James Dean and Marlon Brando, wore jeans and trainers to show they were different from older people, and many young people copied this style to look like them.

However, it was in the 1980s that trainers really took off. In 1984, the Air Jordans became popular when they were worn by the basketball star Michael Jordan. They cost $65, which was a lot of money back then.

Today, there are many different kinds of trainer in the shops in a wide variety of colours and styles. Some of them are created with the help of technology. These designs help people run faster, jump higher and, of course, look cool while they do it!

2.25 | Speaking, page 86, Exercises 5 and 6

Your school is going to have a new school uniform and the headteacher is thinking about including some of the items of clothing in the pictures below. In pairs, talk together for two minutes about which items the new uniform should include.

Student A: OK, so we have to select two items for the new uniform. Shall we talk about the trainers first?

Student B: Yes, I really like the idea of wearing trainers to school.

Student A: Yes, me too to a certain extent. On the one hand, they're comfortable and practical, but on the other hand, some trainers can be very expensive.

Student B: Yes, and they might not be formal enough.

Student A: So, do you think we should choose formal shoes?

Student B: No, I don't. Even though they may look smart, I don't think they're as practical or as comfortable as the trainers.

Student A: I agree. What about the clothes? A shirt and tie would be too formal, wouldn't it?

Student B: Yes, it'd be better to wear a polo shirt. They're much more practical to wear and easier to wash.

Student A: What do you think about having a jumper?

Student B: Well, it's very warm in winter, isn't it? However, it's too hot in the summer.

Student A: Yes, you're right. So, what about a jacket instead?

Student B: Well, a jacket looks more formal than a jumper, so the teachers may like it.

Student A: And it has a lot of pockets which can be useful.

Student B: But the jacket and the jumper are equally uncomfortable though.

Student A: I definitely agree with that. What about trousers?

Student B: Well, they look smart, but some girls may prefer to wear a skirt.

Student A: Yes, you're right.

Student B: So shall we choose the trainers and the polo shirt?

Student A: Yes, I think so. They're the most comfortable and the most popular with students. We want them to be happy at school, don't we?

UNIT 9 | STUDENT'S BOOK

3.05 | Listening, page 96, Exercise 2

1 There were 16 of us – all from the same school – and three of our teachers came too.

2 Do it! You'll really enjoy it.

3 It seems to me it can really help you in other ways too.

4 The first evening, we had a welcome party, which was great fun!

5 Then in the evenings we did various different things, including singing round the campfire and learning bushcraft skills.

6 On the final day, we had a Beach Olympics, which was brilliant!

3.06 | Listening, page 96, Exercises 3 and 4

Interviewer: Today I'm joined by 13-year-old Megan Hooper.

Megan: Hi!

Interviewer: Megan's just been to Cornwall to take part in a five-day summer school camp organised by The Wave Project. It combines surfing with school lessons and other activities. Megan will tell us all about it in a moment, but first, Megan, when you found out about this, how did you feel?

Megan: Well, some of the friends who I went with were excited about going, but I was a bit nervous, to be honest. I didn't know what it would be like, and I don't like that feeling. I'm not very confident sometimes – but actually, I'm a lot more confident now I've been to the camp!

Interviewer: That's great! So, tell me about some of the practical things. Where is it? Where do you stay? What about food?

Megan: We actually stayed in tents near the beach. There were 16 of us – all from the same school – and three of our teachers came too. Of course, The Wave Project also has its own teachers and instructors. We had a lovely big breakfast each morning, we prepared our own packed lunch which we had at around midday, and then they gave us a cooked dinner in the evening.

Interviewer: Camping near the beach. It sounds lovely! What did you do each day?

Megan: As you said, the course is a mixture of surfing lessons and school lessons. The first evening, we had a welcome party, which was great fun! It was a really good chance to meet the instructors. Then for three days, we had surfing lessons all morning, and then school lessons in the afternoon on the beach – things like creative writing, art, English and Geography. Then in the evenings we did various different things, including singing round the campfire. On the final day, we had a Beach Olympics, which was brilliant!

Interviewer: Tell me about the surfing lessons.

Megan: I'm not a good swimmer, so I was terrified of the idea to start with. But the instructors were so kind and patient, taught us all the basic skills, and before long I felt I was able to surf quite well! It really built up my confidence, as I said.

Interviewer: It sounds like you enjoyed it and benefited from it. What advice would you give to someone thinking of going?

Megan: Do it! You'll really enjoy it. Before you go, you might feel nervous, but when you get there, they'll welcome you and make you feel really comfortable. And as soon as you've had a couple of surfing lessons, you'll feel like an expert surfer! It seems to me it can really help you in other ways too. I don't like speaking in public, but the activities we did there really helped me. I'd say go – you'll have a fantastic time, and learn lots too.

Interviewer: Megan, thanks for talking to me today.

3.07 | Speaking, page 98, Exercise 4

1

Oh, all the time! Probably every day! We play things like football in the playground at school, and we often play with a ball in the park after school. My best friend absolutely loves video games – though I'm not so keen on them, and board games like Scrabble and Monopoly.

2

Take my cousin Alex, for example, he competes in motorcycle races. That can be quite dangerous! I've been to a few of his races. They're great fun to watch!

3

I'm a keen athlete and I'm actually very competitive – I really like to win! – so I wouldn't say any of my friends are more competitive than me. That isn't possible! But a couple of them are very competitive like me, and others are not so competitive.

4

Well, my dad loves watching football on TV and, to be honest, I think it's a bit boring. I don't think I've ever sat and watched a whole game. I like playing football, but I'm not so keen on sitting in front of the TV watching football for an hour and a half. I'd rather do something more active!

UNIT 10 | STUDENT'S BOOK

3.12 | Listening, page 106, Exercise 2

I'm really keen on drama, and always audition for the school play! In the past, I've always been given a small part, but this year I got a main part! I was so excited – and nervous too, of course. Mrs Nowak the director was lovely – really kind and helpful. She taught me a lot. The most difficult thing was learning all the lines. I locked myself in my bedroom for hours and hours, saying them over and over again until I'd remembered them. The one problem I had was my costume. We all had to get our own costumes as the school didn't have any. I wasn't sure what to do – I needed to look like a woman from hundreds of years ago. In the end, I had my dress made by my neighbour, Mrs Davis. She's really good at sewing. She did an amazing job, and I looked fantastic. I'm so grateful to her.

3.13 | Listening, page 106, Exercises 4 and 5

Hi everyone! Now, I've got something exciting to tell you. As you know, we usually put on a school play or concert at the end of the summer term. This year, we're going to do a musical. It's called Disco Inferno, and it's lots of fun! You're going to love it! Mr Taylor, the head of the drama department, is going to be the director, Mrs Patel will be musical director, Miss Watson will do the set design, and Mr Farah will be responsible for the costumes.

Now, there are lots of different roles, and we need people who can sing and dance. We're going to hold auditions next Wednesday and Thursday after school here in the school hall. Please come along, however old you are. There are parts for people of all ages. If you can't make it on those days but want to be in it, please get in touch with Mr Taylor. We also need people to help backstage, so let Mr Taylor know if you're interested in helping with lighting or things like that.

Usually when we do a show we do it for one night only, but this year – because we think it's going to be really popular – we're going to do it three nights in a row, on July the 12th, 13th and 14th, so if you get a part, make sure you're free on those dates. And of course we'll have lots of rehearsals between now and then, usually on Thursday and Friday evenings.

We're going to get programmes printed, of course, and these will have photos of the cast. Actors will have their photo taken for the programme by a professional photographer on the 4th of June.

It's quite expensive to put on a big musical like this, so it won't be free this year. Tickets will be on sale from the start of next week. They'll cost £5 each, and I think they'll sell out quickly, so please remind your parents to buy them as soon as they can.

3.14 | Speaking, page 108, Exercises 4 and 5

1

Student A: I love reading crime novels like the Robin Stevens novels and of course, Sherlock Holmes. I enjoy trying to guess who did it.

Student B: Really? That's interesting. I'm a big fan of Sherlock too. It's so clever how he solves the crimes.

2

Student C: Well I use Instagram a lot. Me and my friends love memes. Even though they're short, I like them because they're funny. Sometimes I want to find out about the original source and then end up reading a news article about the original story or event.

Student D: That sounds like fun. Well, I love creative writing, so I'm often on a site where teenagers upload short stories. We read them and then add comments. As well as getting people to read your work, the feedback can help you improve your writing.

Student C: That's interesting. I never thought of that.

3

Student E: I don't read very often, but I don't think it's a problem. You shouldn't have to read if you don't want to. It's important to only read things you enjoy.

Student F: I'm not sure I agree, to be honest. It's very important for teenagers to read regularly. It's good for the imagination, and for learning about the world. If people don't read when they're children and teenagers, they won't read when they're adults.

UNIT 11 | STUDENT'S BOOK

3.19 | Listening, page 118, Exercises 3 and 4

1 What subject is the teacher teaching?

Teacher: OK, now you'll have to put your thinking caps on to answer the next question. I'd like you to work in groups to decide what the area of this shape is. It's a hemisphere, which is half of a circle. So, you might need to experiment a little but you should be able to work it out. I'll give you five minutes to think about it and then we'll see who's got the right answer.

2 Where is Callum now?

Girl: Hi, Callum. I'm surprised to see you here.

Boy: Yes, I know. I should be having lunch now, really. And I'm starving! But I've got to see the headteacher.

Girl: Why's that?

Boy: Mrs Robinson caught me copying off the boy next to me in class during the test.

Girl: Oh, no! Perhaps you'll know not to do that next time! See you!

3 What does the girl want to learn?

Girl: Hello, I'm ringing about the course that's starting next week ... That's right, yes ... I know the basics of how to play, but I'd like to advance to the next level to see how high I can go. ... I know it'll take a lot of practice to learn all the right moves, but I don't mind losing if I learn something! ... My mum asked how much the course was. And she asked if I needed to buy anything. Hold on. I'll just get a pen.

4 How did Mike get to school today?

Teacher: I'm afraid you're late, Mike.

Boy: I know, Miss. Sorry, Miss. The problem was that my dad's car wouldn't start and then when I got to the bus stop it had already gone so I went home again!

Teacher: It's not far from school to your house. Why not cycle?

Boy: I used to do that, but I got wet all the time. Anyway, my dad finally got the car going and dropped me off. I won't let it happen again, Miss.

3.20 | Speaking, page 120, Exercises 4 and 5

This is a photo of a group of girls and their teacher. It looks as if they're at school because there are posters on the windows in the background. Perhaps they're doing a dance lesson or a theatre lesson. All the girls are in a line and the teacher is standing on the left. The girls in the foreground are lying on the floor and the teacher is pointing at the girls in the background. I suppose she wants them to lie on the floor too. I'm not sure why they're doing that, but it seems to me that they're pretending to fall over. I guess they could be practising part of a play or a dance performance. I can't see their faces very well, so it isn't clear whether they're all having fun, but I imagine they're all enjoying themselves.

UNIT 12 | STUDENT'S BOOK

3.25 | Listening, page 128, Exercises 3 and 4

Erin: Hi, Reece. Did you find out what the problem was with Harry?

Reece: Oh, hi, Erin. He was fine. I thought he might have a problem with his legs, but the vet said he needs to get more exercise. I should have realised hamsters need more exercise when he started putting on weight.

Erin: That's good. Talking of vets, I saw a famous vet on TV last night. He's called Noel Fitzpatrick and he has a show called Supervet. He treats animals with difficult problems that other vets can't cure. The show's all about how he and his assistants find unusual solutions to the animals' problems. It's a great programme. Have you seen it?

Reece: No, but I've heard of it. Why is he so famous?

Erin: When animals are hit by cars or hurt in some other way, he helps them recover. That's what he's best known for. He even helps animals that have lost feet or legs. I read about it online. He helped a cat called Oscar and made new legs for him. It was amazing! Oscar's owners must have been really pleased.

Reece: Wow! New legs! Imagine doing that! I'd love to be a vet. I wonder how he started.

Erin: He grew up on a farm in Ireland. He was bullied when he was young because he had problems reading and writing. He says that because of that he developed friendships with animals. I guess he might have decided to become a vet because of that.

Reece: Yes, possibly. I imagine it takes a long time to train and get so good.

Erin: He trained for four years and then worked and studied in America. Then he went to Ireland to work on farm animals before he moved to England. Now he sees animals every morning and operates on them every afternoon.

Reece: You know a lot about him! You must be a real fan.

Erin: I am! He obviously loves animals. He thinks we need to use the same ideas in animal medicine as in human medicine. And I agree with that. And I'd love to be a vet, just like him.

Reece: You could be Supervet 2!

Erin: No, I hate being the centre of attention. But it would be great to help animals and their owners in the same way he does.

Reece: Why don't you start by helping me take my dog for a walk?

Erin: Good idea! Let's go!

3.26 | Speaking, page 130, Exercises 5 and 6

You both love nature. You are thinking of going on a weekend trip together. Look at the pictures below and talk together about the different places you could visit and then decide which two would be best.

Niko: So, we have to choose two activities to do at the weekend. What do you enjoy doing, Adela?

Adela: Well, we have to decide together, so let's discuss them all. Shall we start with going to the beach? I love going to the beach, especially when it's hot.

Niko: Mmm ... it might get too hot, but we could swim in the sea.

Adela: Yes, or if you like swimming, we could go to the lake.

Niko: True. We could go fishing there too. I love fishing.

Adela: Yes, but there's often lots of insects in the summer.

Niko: Well, we could go to the mountains. I love rock climbing.

Adela: That sounds dangerous. I suppose in the winter we could go skiing.

Niko: Mmmm ... or what about going to the forest. That could be fun. We may see wild animals.

Adela: Well, I do like animals, but some wild animals are dangerous.

Niko: True. So how about the zoo? We could see lots of animals there. We can watch them being fed.

Adela: Yes, it can be lovely to watch the animals in the zoo. But I sometimes think they're sad. We could go to a farm though. Although, you've probably seen those animals before, you can interact with the animals in farms and learn a lot about them.

Niko: That sounds like fun. So what do you think we should choose?

Adela: Well, we haven't mentioned the river yet. I think we agree with each other that we both like animals – there's lots of wildlife and birds by the river. You could go fishing and I can do a bit of sunbathing. So my first choice would be the river. What would your first choice be?

Niko: I think the river too.

Adela: What else do you think we should choose?

Niko: My second choice is the farm.

Adela: That's funny. I was going to say that too. I think we agree, then. So we're choosing the farm and the river. Great choices.

Niko: Yes, I think so too.

OPTIMISE YOUR EXAMS STUDENT'S BOOK

3.27 | Optimise your exams, page 142, Listening, exercises 3 and 4

Girl: Dad, have you seen my tennis racket? I've got a match this afternoon.

Father: Did you leave it in the car when Mum picked you up from school?

Girl: I've already looked and it isn't there!

Father: Let's go and check your bedroom. It's probably there. *[pause]* Why are all these things on the floor? When are you going to tidy your room?

Girl: Sorry, Dad! Oh, look! It's here in my wardrobe, next to my jacket.

3.28 | Optimise your exams, page 142, Listening, exercises 5 and 6

Phillip: Hi everyone! I'm here to talk about our school charity sports day. I was keen to get involved after I saw an advert for it on the school website. The website didn't give a lot of details, so I went to see Ms Mathers, the teacher in charge of the event. She told me it was a great opportunity and suggested that I help organise it. I'd never really thought about doing charity work or helping people before, but now I'm really glad I did it. It was a fantastic experience. I worked with the activities team and as I'm pretty creative, thinking of fun activities was easy for me. The challenge was organising everyone. Luckily, I'm quite a relaxed person, so I don't usually get stressed in these kinds of situations – and you couldn't say that about all the members of the team, that's for sure!

3.29 | Optimise your exams, page 143, Listening, exercise 8

Are you celebrating something special? At the Ranmere Hotel, we have over 25 years' experience in organising weddings and parties. With space for up to 80 guests, our beautiful Stanlow Room is available for just 400 pounds from Sunday to Thursday evenings, and 500 pounds on Fridays and 600 pounds on Saturdays. For an extra fee, we will also provide drinks, light refreshments and full meals. We can also organise the music for your event, whether you want a DJ, a live band or classical musicians. If you have any questions about your big day, our celebrations team will be happy to advise you.

To make an enquiry, just visit our website at www.ranmere.co.uk. That's R-A-N-M-E-R-E. Or you can call us on 7946 0874. We look forward to helping you organise an event to remember.

3.30 | Optimise your exams, page 143, Listening, exercises 9 and 10

Carl: Hi Jenny. How's your maths homework going?

Jenny: Oh, Carl. *[sigh]* I haven't finished it yet and I've got four more subjects to do before Friday. I hate maths!

Carl: I thought you loved maths. You did last term!

Jenny: I know, but I think we get too much maths homework. Sometimes it feels as if there's no time to do anything else!

Carl: I suppose that's true. Mr Jarvis likes to give us a lot of extra work. But maybe we need it – I mean, to pass the final exams. I'd say it's the right amount of homework.

Jenny: Well, I don't feel that he gives us much help. I mean, he doesn't show us different ways to solve problems.

Carl: That's difficult when there are 30 of us in the class. What about the project we're doing in the IT room? I think working in groups is better because you can help each other.

Jenny: I suppose so. I didn't like the people in my group much at first, but actually, you're right. Group work is definitely a good way to learn.

UNIT 1 | WORKBOOK

01 | Listening, page 8, exercise 1

1

Guide: Hi and welcome to London. My name's Lexi. I'm going to show you the sights of the city and explain some of its history. And this is Dan – he's our driver today.

Man: Morning all.

2

Pilot: Good afternoon, passengers. This is your captain speaking. First I'd like to welcome everyone on flight nine-four-seven from Manchester to Barcelona.

3

Boy 1: Excuse me. Is anyone sitting here?

Boy 2: No, that space is free.

Boy 1: Do you mind if I sit next to you?

Boy 2: Not at all. I'll just move my shopping bags.

4

Radio DJ: Our next caller is Simon. Hi there, Simon. Are you ready to win some concert tickets?

Man: Absolutely!

02 | Listening, page 8, exercises 2 and 3

Narrator: 1 Where are they at the moment?

Guide: Hi and welcome to London. My name's Lexi. I'm going to show you the sights of the city and explain some of its history. And this is Dan – he's our driver today.

Man: Morning all.

Guide: Right, well, is everybody here? There's no-one still at the hotel? No? Excellent. Let's go then. Our first stop today – if we can get through all of this traffic – is Buckingham Palace. You can take photos of the palace, but please don't speak to the guards.

Narrator: 2 What is the time?

Pilot: Good afternoon, passengers. This is your captain speaking. First I'd like to welcome everyone on flight nine-four-seven from Manchester to Barcelona. It is now 1:15. Our flight to Barcelona will take two hours and 20 minutes. Barcelona is clear and sunny, with a high of 25 degrees for this afternoon. In about ten minutes, you will be able to buy drinks and snacks. I'll talk to you again before we reach our destination. Until then, relax and enjoy the flight.

Narrator: 3 Where are the boys?

Boy 1: Excuse me. Is anyone sitting here?

Boy 2: No, that space is free.

Boy 1: Do you mind if I sit next to you?

Boy 2: Not at all. I'll just move my shopping bags.

Boy 1: Thanks. I'm Tim.

Boy 2: Hi, Tim. I'm Andy.

Boy 1: Pleased to meet you, Andy. I like this new cinema.

Boy 2: Yes, it's great. It's really comfortable and the snacks are delicious. I just hope it doesn't rain.

Boy 1: Me too, but I suppose that's the risk you take when you go to an outdoor movie.

Narrator: 4 What does the man win?

Radio DJ: Our next caller is Simon. Hi there, Simon. Are you ready to win some concert tickets?

Simon: Absolutely!

Radio DJ: OK! Here's your question. What is singer Bruno Mars' real name?

Simon: Well ... er ... um ... I'm sure I read it in a book somewhere. Er ... Is it Peter? It's Peter something, yeah.

Radio DJ: I'm afraid that's only part of the answer, Simon. His real name is Peter Gene Hernandez. No tickets for you, but I tell you what – we'll send you a voucher to download his latest song.

UNIT 2 | WORKBOOK

03 | Listening, page 16, exercises 3 and 4

Interviewer: Hello, listeners. Georgia Holt is an archeologist and an expert on ancient Roman houses. Could you tell us about that, Georgia?

Georgia: Yes. I've been interested in ancient history since I was a child. I would always borrow books from the library about ancient Greece and Rome. My interest in houses, though, started when I was 15 during a visit to Pompeii, in Italy, the city that was buried when the volcano Mount Vesuvius erupted.

Interviewer: What interested you about the things you saw there?

Georgia: They told a story of how the people lived – their homes and shops, the places where they met, the theatres they went to for entertainment. It felt like they were still there. Famous sights like the Colosseum and the Parthenon are very impressive, but to me, the daily lives of the people are more important. Seeing where and how they lived tells us so much more about the past.

Interviewer: And what were their homes like?

Georgia: People are surprised when I tell them that there were different kinds of houses, just like in our cities. Wealthy Romans had holiday villas with gardens in the countryside around Pompeii. Other houses were detached and semi-detached, like ours, but that's where any similarity ends. They had a courtyard with no roof and there were bedrooms, a dining room, a bathroom and a kitchen around it. At the front there was a central hall which had a hole in its roof and a pool underneath. They used it to collect the rain water. It was very open and there was a lot of light. They were actually quite nice homes and the people lived well.

Interviewer: So where did the poor people live?

Georgia: In apartments. Now, when I say 'apartments', don't imagine anything like what we have today with living rooms and nice balconies. These were crowded, uncomfortable spaces, and usually just one small room for the whole family. There was nothing to make life easier. They cooked and washed outside with their neighbours, who lived in the same building. They didn't have bathrooms – they used public toilets. So, although they died horribly when the nearby volcano erupted, in many ways what is sadder is how they lived.

Interviewer: Finally, what do you think archeologists of the future will learn about us when they study our cities and homes?

Georgia: Probably some of the same things that we learnt about the Romans. Times change, of course, but we can't say the same about people. Wealthy people will always have big, luxurious houses. And there will always be people living in poor conditions, trying to improve their lives. I think when archeologists study us, they will realise that some things, such as society, tend to stay the same.

Interviewer: Thanks for talking to us today.

04 | Speaking, page 16, exercise 2

Boy: This is a photo of a girl in a kitchen. She's got long, fair hair and she's wearing an apron. The girl is in the middle of the photo. In the foreground to the right, there's a big pan and to the left there's a big white bowl. In the background on the left there's a large white clock on the wall and a picture. I think it's a calendar or maybe some holiday photos. In the background there are also lots of bowls and bottles. To the right of the girl and in the background there are two big windows. I think there's a garden outside because you can see trees. The girl is cooking something in a big black frying pan. Perhaps she's preparing dinner for her family.

05 | Speaking, page 17, exercise 2

Girl: This is a photo of a boy in his living room, he's playing a game on his tablet and he's wearing headphones. In the foreground and on the right of the photo, I can see a big blue sofa which the boy is sitting on. There are two orange cushions on the sofa, one cushion is to the left of the boy, in the foreground. The other cushion is in the background. In the middle of the photo, in front of the sofa, there is a table. There are mugs and bowls on top of the table and the boy has his feet on it! In the background, to the right there is a blue chair with a white cushion on it. The chair is in front of a small bookshelf. On top of the bookshelf there is vase with some bright flowers in it. They are next to a small basket. On the wall behind the chair there is a painting. On the left of the photo there are some big windows.

UNIT 3 | WORKBOOK

06 | Listening, page 24, exercise 3

Matt: Hi, Laura!

Laura: Hi there, Matt! It's great to see you again. Did you have a good holiday?

Matt: Yes, thanks, it was fantastic. I went to Edinburgh to see my cousins and I travelled there by bus.

Laura: Really?! That's a long journey, isn't it? What did you do to pass the time?

Matt: Yes, it's 10 hours from London to Edinburgh. At first, I watched a film on my tablet and listened to music. Then after a while I just wanted to sleep, but I couldn't.

Laura: Why not? Were you uncomfortable?

Matt: Actually no, it wasn't that. There was a boy sitting behind me and he kept kicking my seat. He probably thought it was funny but I certainly didn't! Anyway, I complained to his parents, and they did absolutely nothing about it!

Laura: Oh, no! I bet you were happy to finally arrive in Edinburgh.

Matt: I was! I couldn't wait to see my cousins. They're really fun to be with. But what about you? What did you do during the break?

Laura: Well, it was really unexpected. You see, my mum won a holiday for the whole family to New York!

Matt: Oh, wow! That's incredible! I've never been to New York, or anywhere in the USA. What was it like?

Laura: I wasn't sure what to expect. But when I got there, it was just like in the films! People were selling hot dogs on the street, there was noise and traffic! New York was buzzing. Of course, we saw all the famous sights like the Statue of Liberty and the Empire State Building. And we went on a guided tour too. Did you know it hasn't always been called New York? It was called New Amsterdam at first because people from Holland went to live there. I had no idea!

Matt: That's really interesting!

Laura: See, that's what I love about travelling – all the unexpected things you can discover!

Matt: I agree!

07 | Speaking, page 24, exercise 1

Girl: OK, so we have to decide what they should take on holiday.

Boy: How about a guidebook? They'll definitely need one.

Girl: Yes, I agree. I think it would be useful to have a guidebook because there's lots of important information in it.

Boy: Yes, especially if they haven't been to the place before.

Girl: What do you think about a backpack? They're easy to carry.

Boy: Well, if they don't want to take a lot of things with them, a backpack might be a good idea.

Girl: OK. I think they should also take some local currency with them. I mean, what if they arrive and they can't find a cash machine? They'll need some money.

Boy: Yes, of course. Perhaps they could get enough for a few days, just in case they can't find a cash machine straight away.

Girl: So, we agree on what they should take?

Boy: Yes.

UNIT 4 | WORKBOOK

08 | Listening, page 32, exercise 2

Helen: Since the first film was shown in Paris in 1895, a lot has changed in cinema. Here to tell us about a new development is Will.

Will: Hi, Helen. Yes, lots has changed. The French Lumière brothers made that first film and it's called 'Workers Leaving The Lumière Factory in Lyon' – you can look it up on YouTube, actually. Unlike today's films, it was less than two minutes long, and it showed lots of people leaving a factory after work. For us, it's unusual because it doesn't tell a story.

Helen: Is that all? Just people leaving somewhere?

Will: Mainly, yes. They're rushing to get home, there's a dog running around, a man on a bike and a horse and carriage leaving the factory. It's in old-fashioned black and white, of course – colour came later – and there's no sound, not even music. But that was a huge technological development at the time – the idea of moving images on a screen. Now, imagine all of that in a virtual reality film.

Helen: I've never heard of virtual reality cinema. What exactly is it?

Will: When we watch a film at the cinema, we have sound and picture. Some films have amazing special effects too, especially those created with computers. But we're still just an audience watching something – we don't experience the action. But with virtual reality cinema, it's like you are in the film because the action happens all around you.

Helen: And how is that possible?

Will: You wear a headset that covers your eyes and you experience the action with that. It's as if the screen in the cinema was all around you. So, if the Lumière film was in virtual reality and you were watching it, you would be surrounded by a crowd of workers, a man approaching you on a bike, a dog that maybe wanted to bite you and a horse coming towards you very fast – all happening at the same time!

Helen: It sounds exciting! But I'm not sure everyone would enjoy it. When can we expect to see virtual reality films at the cinema?

Will: That's the big question. Two things need to happen – film-makers have to make films in virtual reality and cinemas have to spend the money for the new technology, like the headsets I mentioned, maybe special gloves too, for the sensation of touching and feeling. But even if that happens, how popular will the films be? Remember, we've had 3D films too, but people were annoyed with the special glasses they had to wear. Will the same thing happen with virtual reality? Who knows? But virtual reality games are very popular, especially in the horror category, so maybe virtual reality horror films will find their audience too.

Helen: I can't wait! Thanks, Will.

09 | Speaking, page 32, exercise 1

1

Student 1: I don't mind staying at home at the weekend because I can play video games then!

2

Student 2: I feel strongly about high-tech gadgets like smartphones and tablets as I think they are taking over our lives.

3

Student 3: I like spending time with my friends. I don't have a strong preference about what we do. That's because we always have fun.

4

Student 4: Football is my favourite sport. I'm a big fan of Liverpool and I always try to go to their matches when they play.

5

Student 5: Even though I like the snow, I'm not keen on snowboarding. The reason is that every time I've tried it, I've fallen over!

6

Student 6: I prefer playing sport to watching it for the reason that I enjoy being outside in the fresh air.

7

Student 7: I don't really like hiking since it can be very tiring if you're out all day, and sometimes it rains too!

10 | Speaking, page 33, exercise 3

Boy: OK then. Shall I start?

Girl: Please do.

Boy: Well, I'm a big fan of video games. I spend hours playing with my friends.

Girl: Is that because you don't like being outside?

Boy: No, I don't mind playing football, but it rains a lot where I live. What about you? Do you play a sport?

Girl: The truth is, I'm not very keen on sport. The reason is that I've never been good at it.

Boy: So what do you do in your free time?

Girl: Actually, I go to a dance school. I think dancing is the best activity of all!

Boy: Why do you think that?

Girl: Because it's fun and it keeps me fit, too. You should try it!

Boy: Um, no thanks. I'm sure I would be terrible at it.

Girl: Why do you feel that way? You won't know until you have a go!

Boy: No, I definitely wouldn't be a good dancer. But I would like to try something exciting like sky-diving when I'm older.

Girl: I don't think I would be brave enough to try sky-diving, but I would like to go horse-riding in the future.

UNIT 5 | WORKBOOK

11 | Listening, page 40, exercise 3

Gina: So, what's it like being a dad? Is your foster puppy cute?

Tony: Oh, they haven't given me one to foster yet. I've got to be prepared, you know. There are some things I need to do before I can look after a dog. I've done one so far – a pet first aid course.

Gina: They have first aid courses for pets? Wow, I had no idea. But what if you don't pass the course? Does that mean you can't foster?

Tony: No, it's not like that. You don't 'pass' or 'fail'. The purpose of the course is to teach you some valuable skills. You never know when you might need to use them.

Gina: It must be difficult to help them, though. I mean, animals can't tell you what's wrong with them.

Tony: You'd be surprised how much animals can communicate with us – you just need to understand the signs. That's something we learnt on the course, by the way.

Gina: What kind of signs?

Tony: Well, animals don't act like we do when we're ill. We tend to make a lot of noise – you know, like crying. But a cat that is in pain might sit quietly under a bed and avoid attention.

Gina: Yes, that's true. OK, so how do you treat a sick pet? Did you learn that?

Tony: No way! That's for a vet to do. We learnt how to make a pet more comfortable before taking it to the vet and how to prevent a health emergency from getting worse.

Gina: Even broken bones?

Tony: Especially broken bones! That's a really dangerous situation because the animal is in pain and could be losing a lot of blood.

Gina: I would pass out if I saw something like that! How do you stop the bleeding?

Tony: You gently press a clean cloth on the injured part of the body and then wrap a bandage around it. Sometimes, the animal might not be breathing.

Gina: I'm sure you can't do CPR on an animal!

Tony: The opposite, actually. It is possible. It's not just for people.

Gina: Really? How?

Tony: Why don't you do the course and find out? It only takes about six hours.

Gina: Erm ... yes ... we'll see ...

12 | Speaking, page 41, exercise 3

Narrator: 1

Student 1: I think so, yes. I always keep my room tidy and I do the dishes after dinner most nights. At the weekend I often wash the car and help with the shopping too.

Narrator: 2

Student 2: I try to do as much as I can at the library because it's fairly noisy at my house. I've got two brothers and a sister, so it's rarely quiet.

Narrator: 3

Student 3: I took up volleyball about six months ago because I wanted to get fit. I train twice a week and my team takes part in competitions most weekends.

Narrator: 4

Student 4: I never take the bus as my school isn't far from my home, so I usually walk. But if the weather is bad, my mum drives me.

Narrator: 5

Student 5: All the time! We're at the same school, in the same class actually, so it's every day. Then at the weekend, we often meet up and go out.

Narrator: 6

Student 6: On schooldays, it's always in the evening, after dinner, and my dad does it in the morning. At the weekend, I take him out twice a day because he's a big dog.

UNIT 6 | WORKBOOK

13 | Listening, page 48, exercise 3

Woman: Today we're looking at unusual food festivals around the world. You've probably been to a food festival where you can try different foods, but these are ... well, a bit different!

In the north of Thailand, the Monkey Buffet is held at the end of November each year. More than 3,000 local monkeys are given a delicious lunch at a monastery – they are fed 4,000 kilos of fruit, vegetables and cakes! The festival was started in 1989 by a local businessman to attract tourists and now thousands come every year. Young people dress up in monkey costumes and there are music and dancing performances.

If you like watermelons, then you should definitely go to the Chinchilla Melon Festival in Australia. It takes place every two years and is on for four days in the town of Chinchilla, which is famous for producing nearly 25% of all Australian watermelons. There are lots of fun sports events involving watermelons, such as melon skiing, melon skating, melon bungee jumping and melon tossing! There's also a parade, a free concert and lots of arts and crafts you can do, as well as markets where you can do your food shopping.

The Gilroy Garlic Festival is one of the largest food festivals in the USA, held in July every year. There are cooking demonstrations by famous chefs, cooking competitions and arts and crafts for all the family. There is also live music entertainment on three stages. You can eat food such as pasta pesto, sausage sandwiches and of course the very famous garlic ice cream! It is run by over 4,000 volunteers from 150 different groups and last year over 100,000 people came. The festival, which was started in 1979, raises money for local charities. So far, it has raised over 9 million dollars.

UNIT 7 | WORKBOOK

14 | Listening, page 56, exercise 1

1

Tom: Do you want to come to the shops with me, Beth? This T-shirt is too small and I have to get a bigger size.

Beth: Sure, Tom. I need to get a few things too.

2

Kyle: What are you doing, Dad?

Dad: I want to get something special for your mum. What do you think of this ring? Do you think she'll like it?

3

Mum: Luke, they haven't got the bag now, but they can get one in a week or two.

Luke: Hmmm, I don't know. What if they can't deliver it before Jane's birthday?

4

Mum: Why aren't you wearing the sports watch I bought you, Michael?

Michael: I took it back to the shop, Mum. It had stopped working.

15 | Listening, page 56, exercises 2 and 4

Narrator Situation 1
Tom: Do you want to come to the shops with me, Beth? This T-shirt is too small and I have to get a bigger size.
Beth: Sure, Tom. I need to get a few things too.
Tom: Great, let's go.
Beth: Was the T-shirt a present for your birthday?
Tom: Sort of. My grandparents gave me money and I used it to buy some clothes.
Beth: Didn't you try the T-shirt on before you bought it?
Tom: Well, I was in a hurry and the shop was closing. I usually wear a medium, but the T-shirt wasn't big enough.
Beth: Yeah, I've done that before. Hopefully, you'll find another one in the right size. It's a really cool T-shirt!
Narrator Situation 2
Kyle: What are you doing, Dad?
Dad: I want to get something special for your mum. What do you think of this ring? Do you think she'll like it?
Kyle: It's lovely. Oh … is that the price? Dad, are you sure?
Dad: Yes, I know … but it's a special occasion. Our 20-year wedding anniversary.
Kyle: Still … Why don't you get a less expensive piece of jewellery and go on a holiday too? You haven't been away in ages.
Dad: You know, that sounds great. Somewhere warm would be just the thing. Maybe the Bahamas or Greece. Why didn't I think of that?
Kyle: I'll help you look for a different ring if you like.
Narrator Situation 3
Mum: Luke, they haven't got the bag now, but they can get one in a week or two.
Luke: Hmmm, I don't know. What if they can't deliver it before Jane's birthday?
Mum: Well, that's what I need to find out. There's no point in buying it if it arrives after her birthday.
Luke: Let's see, she'll be 16 on the 21st and it's the 7th today. That's in exactly two weeks.
Mum: If they can deliver it by the 20th, I'll be able to wrap it nicely.
Luke: OK, let's email them and find out.
Mum: No, I'll call them instead. There's a phone number on the website. We need to find out straightaway. And if they can deliver it in time, I'll order it today.
Narrator Situation 4
Mum: Why aren't you wearing the sports watch I bought you, Michael?
Michael: I took it back to the shop, Mum. It had stopped working.
Mum: After just a few weeks? What a pity. But they can fix it, can't they?
Michael: Apparently, but I don't want it now. What if they fixed it and it happened again?
Mum: Well, wasn't there anything else you liked in the shop?
Michael: There were some cool trainers, but they cost more than the watch.
Mum: You don't need another pair of trainers, Michael. Anything else?
Michael: Yes, a skateboard. But if I told you how much it cost, you would probably faint! Don't worry, I didn't buy it – it was even more expensive than the trainers!

16 | Speaking, page 57, exercise 3

1
Examiner: What's the most expensive thing you have ever bought? How much did it cost?
2
Examiner: Do you prefer going to a big indoor shopping centre or buying from small shops in your area? Why?
3
Examiner: What would you buy now if you won a lot of money?
4
Examiner: Why is it a good idea to shop around before you buy?
5
Examiner: Have you ever lost money? How did it happen?

UNIT 8 | WORKBOOK

17 | Listening, page 64, exercise 2

Man: Denim. It's what is used to make jeans, and we all wear jeans, don't we?
Historians believe that the word 'denim' came from the name of the city in France where the cloth was made. The word 'jeans' came from the sailors of Genoa in Italy. The French called the sailors 'Genes', spelt G-E-N-E-S because they were from Genoa. They wore denim, and in this way, the words 'denim' and 'jeans' became connected.
Now, when we think of denim and jeans, we connect them with America. And that's because of a man named Loeb Strauss, who changed his name to Levi Strauss. Does that name sound familiar? It should, because he invented the most famous jeans in the world, Levis.
Although denim had already existed for about 300 years, it didn't become popular until 1873 when Strauss made the first Levis jeans. He chose the denim cloth to make tough, inexpensive clothing for the men who were looking for gold in California.
Jeans became fashionable in the 1950s, in America, when teenagers started wearing them. They wanted to look like the famous actors who wore them in their films, and singers they heard on the radio. Jeans became a symbol of youth, but by the 1970s, people of all ages around the world had started wearing denim.
Now, in the 21st century, we can buy denim in a huge variety of colours, from white and blue to brown and black. It is worn by fashion models, movie stars and ordinary people. Jeans have become the favourite choice of clothing for millions of people around the world. Jeans will always be cool!

18 | Speaking, page 65, exercise 2

Narrator: 1
Girl: A handbag is OK when you go out, but it isn't as practical as a backpack for every day.
Narrator: 2
Boy: Shoes are more formal than trainers. You would wear trainers at home, whereas you'd wear a pair of shoes to a wedding or an interview.
Narrator: 3
Girl: Jeans are good to wear in winter. However, they're very warm in summer, aren't they?
Narrator: 4
Girl: On the one hand, a leather jacket will keep you warm. On the other hand, it's quite expensive to buy.
Narrator: 5
Boy: A shirt with a collar and a tie are equally uncomfortable in my opinion!

UNIT 9 | WORKBOOK

19 | Listening, page 72, exercise 2

1 My dad was working in the States, in Hawaii actually.
2 Everyone surfs there, I mean, they're crazy about it.
3 And it was through surfing that I met people my age.
4 I don't think he wanted to be left alone.
5 I took him to the beach with me and he kept jumping onto my board.
6 But the best thing is, he's more confident now.

20 | Listening, page 72, exercise 3

Interviewer: Today in the studio I'm joined by 14-year-old Kyle Stevens.
Kyle: Hi everyone.
Interviewer: Kyle has just returned from an extraordinary surfing competition in the United States. What makes it so unusual? Well, it's not the surf boards that are used or where the competition takes place. No, there's nothing unique about those. What will surprise you are the surfers. Can you tell us about that, Kyle?
Kyle: Sure, well as you say, the surfers are not who you would expect. They're dogs actually and it's called dog surfing. Some surf with their owners, and others do it alone. It really is a surfing competition with a difference and it attracts a huge crowd. What's really cool – well, apart from surfing dogs, of course – is that the event raises money for animal charities, and not just those that help dogs.
Interviewer: Fantastic! And how did you get involved in dog surfing?
Kyle: My dad was working in the States, in Hawaii actually. Everyone surfs there, I mean, they're crazy about it. Being the new kid at school, it was hard to make friends. Yeah, I was a bit lonely at first. Anyway, I was really excited to try surfing, even though I was a bit scared because, you know, you hear stories about sharks. And it was through surfing that I met people my age.
Interviewer: I see, and what about your dog?
Kyle: I found Buddy at an animal shelter. Someone had left him on the side of the road, so he hadn't had a great life. Because of that experience, I don't think he wanted to be left alone. So I took him to the beach with me and he kept jumping onto my board – he was worried that I would leave him, I think.
Interviewer: And how did you teach Buddy to surf? I can't imagine it was easy!
Kyle: At first, I taught him to stay on the board – that was after he'd fallen in the water loads of times. And now he even knows how to move the board in different directions. But the best thing is, he's more confident now. He's no longer afraid of being left alone.
Interviewer: That's wonderful. So what happened at the competition? And what's next for you and Buddy?
Kyle: We came third and we got a medal too! I'd love to take him to the World Dog Surfing Championship, but that's in the

USA and we're back in Britain now, so forget about that. I don't know ... maybe I'll start a competition here. There are some good waves for surfing in Cornwall.

Interviewer: Kyle, thanks for being on the show today ...

21 | Speaking, page 72, exercise 2

Narrator: 1

Student: No, not at the moment because I'm really busy with school, but I used to be. I was on the swimming team at my local club and I took part in competitions.

Narrator: 2

Student: Well, one of them recently took up horse-riding, and I think it would be really interesting to do that, so I might have a go at that.

Narrator: 3

Student: If I'm with a group of friends, I don't really mind where I watch because it's fun being together. But I have to say, being there is the most exciting of all.

Narrator: 4

Student: I haven't, but my best friend has. Luckily, it wasn't serious. She was doing gymnastics at school and hurt her foot. She couldn't walk on it for a few days because it was painful.

UNIT 10 | WORKBOOK

22 | Listening, page 80, exercise 1

Jess: I think I'm going to be a star! I've always wanted to be successful and famous just like Beyoncé, and now, I've got my chance. You see, I'm going to audition for Pop Icon this Saturday. I'm sure you know which talent show I mean – it's on every Monday night at 7:30 in the evening and it's great. The winner records a song in a studio with a professional record producer and musicians. I've been practising my song at home for weeks. I wrote it myself and it's called 'Heartbreak City'. Yeah, it's a sad love song about a summer romance. The thing is, you have to put on a performance, you can't just stand on the stage and open your mouth – you've got to move around, put some feeling into the lyrics, look sad, you know? My drama teacher at school helped with that. If I win, it will be because of her.

23 | Listening, page 80, exercise 2

Good morning everyone! Now, I've got some exciting news for you. As you know, we usually put on a school play at the end of the year. This year, we're going to do something very different. We're going to make a film! We've never done that before! Our new drama teacher, Mrs Safar, is going to be the director, Mr Jones will be the cameraman, Mrs Smith will organise the costumes and the head of the art department – Mr Roberts – will design the posters.

Now, there is so much for you to do. First of all, we need a script. If you'd like to be involved in writing it, see Mr Brown from the English department. It will be his job to help the scriptwriters. So, have a think about it and come up with your own ideas for a story. The first meeting to discuss the script will be next Thursday after school in the library. Then you'll have a month to write and edit the script. Once it is ready, we'll hold auditions. We won't only need actors, of course. If you're good with hair and make-up, please see Mrs Bitar to let her know you're interested and available. Usually when we do a show we do it for one night only, but this year our film will be shown for a week at the Capital Theatre in the town centre. We're going to have a premiere too, on the 10th July. It'll be very exciting with photographers and reporters! However, before any of that can happen, we'll need to have plenty of rehearsals. Well, I think I've covered everything, but if you need any more information, please see Mrs Safar.

24 | Speaking, pages 80–81, exercises 2 and 3

Narrator: 1

Girl: I don't think I have a preference. I mean, if it's a good story, I can watch anything. Oh, and I absolutely love documentaries. What about you?

Boy: I completely agree with you about a good story. That really is the most important thing, isn't it? But generally, I enjoy adventure films more.

Girl: Really? Why?

Boy: Well, I like lots of action.

Narrator: 2

Boy: I'm not sure how to answer that because I've only seen one play, but I did enjoy it. It was a modern drama, but I think I'd like to see a play by Shakespeare next.

Girl: Same here. I haven't got much experience of the theatre, but the performance I saw was great. I'm going to see a musical next.

Boy: That's interesting!

Narrator: 3

Girl: I've been to a number of museums with my school. Personally, I think the Science Museum is the best because it's got lots of famous inventions. Have you been there?

Boy: Not yet, but that sounds like fun. When I visited London, I went to the British Museum. It's fantastic. It's full of great things from other countries.

Girl: I see what you mean, but isn't it just full of ancient artefacts? There's nothing modern there, is there?

Boy: I'm not sure I agree.

UNIT 11 | WORKBOOK

25 | Listening, page 88, exercise 2

1 What subject is the teacher teaching?

Teacher: I know it looks like a lot to learn by heart, but you've got two months before the production. Just a little every day and you'll soon know it all. I find it's easier to do if you practise the lines with a friend – they can help you along if you get stuck. Now, Mark, in the last scene you'll be alone on the stage with some soft music playing in the background, and you have to speak to the audience.

2 Where does Lucy need to go?

Boy: Hi, Lucy. Are you going home? We can walk together if you like.

Girl: Sorry, no. I've got to find a book and it's not at the library.

Boy: You always have your nose in a book! So what are you looking for?

Girl: It's a novel by one of my favourite writers. I think I'll have to buy it.

Boy: You'd better hurry then. The mall closes in half an hour.

3 Which course will the man do?

Man: Hello, I'd like some information about your French courses ... Yes, but not very well ... it was ages ago at school. I mean, I can remember the basics, sort of, but I want to reach an advanced level ... I don't know, I might have a bit of trouble with the intermediate class. It wasn't my best subject, to be honest ... Yes, that's what I'll do, and if I find it's too easy, I'll change levels.

4 Where is Abby's homework?

Girl: I haven't got my essay with me, Sir.

Teacher: That's not like you, Abby. What happened?

Girl: Well, after I'd printed it out, it must have slipped under my desk, and my dog ate it.

Teacher: Oh, Abby ...

Girl: No, no. When I realised, I tried to get another copy, but the printer had stopped working. So I've put it on this USB stick. Would you mind printing it in your office, Sir?

26 | Speaking, pages 88–89, exercises 1 and 2

Narrator: 1

Girl: It isn't clear whether she's studying or just reading.

Narrator: 2

Girl: I guess the person in the middle is the coach.

Narrator: 3

Girl: It looks as if they're training to become chefs.

Narrator: 4

Girl: Perhaps she's at university.

Narrator: 5

Girl: She seems to be showing them the correct way to do something.

Narrator: 6

Girl: I'm not sure, but I think the one in the middle is the teacher.

Narrator: 7

Girl: It could be that they want to join a team.

Narrator: 8

Girl: She might be doing her homework.

Narrator: 9

Girl: It's possible that the students are doing this for the first time.

UNIT 12 | WORKBOOK

27 | Listening, page 96, exercise 3

Amy: Hey, Marcus. You've been reading that book for hours. Why don't we go out?

Marcus: I can't put it down, Amy. The author must believe it but I think she might be imagining it. Apparently, though, it's been really successful – thousands of copies have been sold!

Amy: *How To Talk To Animals: A Guide For Beginners* by Susan Howell. No way!

Marcus: Listen to this. She says a hamster named Willy told her that he liked rock music!

Amy: Oh, come on! That can't be true!

Marcus: It says here the owner played it loudly in the living room all the time and Willy developed a taste for it! But he wasn't so keen on rap or hip-hop.

Amy: How does she do it? I mean, how does she <u>say</u> she does it? Because I don't believe it.

Marcus: She says you have to listen with your heart, not your mind. You must ask questions with love. And you need to tune in to the animal's energy field.

Amy: It's not exactly clear, is it? Does she mean to ask nicely? Does she mean to ask in a soft voice? And how do animals reply? They can't talk. Are we supposed to read their minds?

Marcus: To be honest, I don't understand that either. But she says everyone can communicate with animals and the only reason we don't is because we've been told we can't.

Amy: Well, I'm pretty sure I can't.

Marcus: Imagine if we could communicate with animals, though – have a real conversation. That would be amazing! What would you ask Fred?

Amy: Hmmm … I think I'd ask him where he put my iPod. I can't find it anywhere!

Marcus: I'd ask him what he thinks of me. I mean, I just assume that he loves me, but what if he doesn't? What if he thinks I'm boring or something?

Amy: Let's ask him!

Marcus: Yeah, let's try it! You never know … he might surprise us and …

28 | Speaking, page 97, exercise 2

Boy: So shall we make a final decision?

Girl: Yes, let's do that.

Boy: Of all the options, I think the tiger is the best.

Girl: I agree. I'd also choose the tiger.

Boy: Great! We agree, then.

Girl: That sounds like a good decision.

29 | Speaking, page 97, exercise 3

Girl: So which one do you think we should choose?

Boy: I'd choose the gorilla. What about you?

Girl: My first choice would be the dolphin.

Boy: Why do you think we should choose the dolphin?

Girl: Because I think they are intelligent and we know that they communicate with each other.

Boy: Hmm, yes, it would be interesting to find out more about them. So let's choose the dolphin.

Girl: Good! I think we agree with each other. We choose the dolphin.

The *Optimise Practice test* audioscript can be found on the Teacher's Resource Centre.

Macmillan Education
4 Crinan Street
London N1 9XW
A division of Macmillan Publishers Limited

Companies and representatives throughout the world

ISBN 978-0-230-48849-6

Written by Anna Cole

First published 2017

Text designed by Designers Collective
Typeset by J & D Glover Ltd
Cover design by Designers Collective

The authors and publishers would like to thank the following for permission to reproduce their photographs:
plainpictures/Johner/Susanne Kronholm p49

Commissioned photographs by
Creative Listening p16(tr); **MTJ Media** pp 8(tl, tr), 16(tl, b).

Full acknowledgements for photographs in the facsimile pages can be found in the Student's Book and the Workbook.

Printed and bound in the UK

2021 2020 2019 2018 2017
10 9 8 7 6 5 4 3 2